An Indian Odyssey

By the same author

Grains of Sand
Absolute Altitude

An Indian Odyssey

Martin Buckley

Hutchinson
London

Published by Hutchinson 2008

2 4 6 8 10 9 7 5 3 1

Copyright © Martin Buckley 2008

First published in Great Britain in 2008 by
Hutchinson
Random House, 20 Vauxhall Bridge Road,
London SW1V 2SA

www.rbooks.co.uk

Addresses for companies within The Random House Group Limited can be found at:
www.randomhouse.co.uk/offices.htm

The Random House Group Limited Reg. No. 954009

A CIP catalogue record for this book
is available from the British Library

ISBN 9780091925765 (Hardback)
ISBN 9780091795252 (Trade paperback)

The Random House Group Limited supports The Forest Stewardship
Council (FSC), the leading international forest certification organisation. All our
titles that are printed on Greenpeace approved FSC certified paper carry the FSC logo.
Our paper procurement policy can be found at www.rbooks.co.uk/environment

Mixed Sources
Product group from well-managed
forests and other controlled sources
www.fsc.org Cert no. TT-COC-2139
© 1996 Forest Stewardship Council
FSC

Typeset by SX Composing DTP, Rayleigh, Essex
Printed and bound in the UK by CPI Mackays, Chatham ME5 8TD

To my Son, Leo

And to Paul Sidey—

Per tutto . . .

CONTENTS

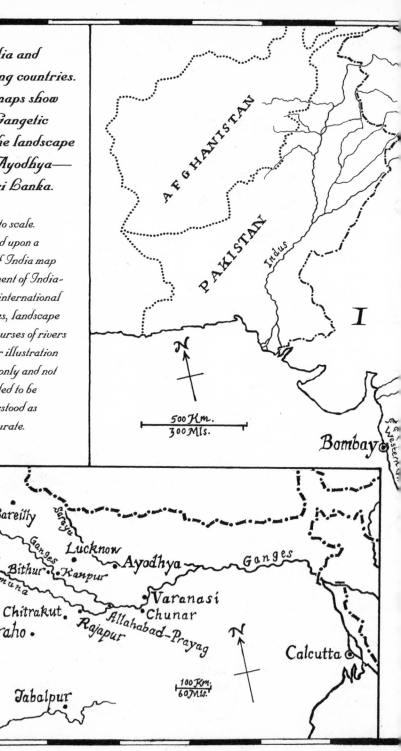

India and surrounding countries. Inset maps show the Gangetic plain—the landscape around Ayodhya—and Sri Lanka.

Not to scale. Based upon a Survey of India map © Government of India—however, international boundaries, landscape features, courses of rivers etc. are for illustration purposes only and not intended to be understood as accurate.

AFGHANISTAN

PAKISTAN

Indus

I

N

500 Km.
300 Mls.

Bombay

Western Gh

Delhi

Bareilly

Sarayu

Ganges

Agra

Bithur

Kanpur

Lucknow

Ayodhya

Ganges

Yamuna

Varanasi

Chitrakut

Allahabad-Prayag

Chunar

Khajuraho

Rajapur

N

Calcutta

Jabalpur

100 Km.
60 Mls.

Bhopal

Preface

RECENT YEARS HAVE seen a striking resurgence in ancient Greek nationalism. In 1992, hardliners destroyed a Macedonian mosque built on the site where, according to tradition, Odysseus, the hero of Homer's celebrated epic, was born. Still recited daily in millions of Greek homes, the *Odyssey* has lost little of its power or relevance. Now, protestors are taking to the streets over the government's plan to dredge the Hellespont for a shipping canal, which would, according to traditionalists, destroy the remnants of Xerxes's legendary bridge. The intensity of the passions raised could lose the government the next election. All in all, violent clashes and protests related to Odysseus and Xerxes have, since 1992, cost the lives of 13,000 Greeks.

Well, no. Such events are inconceivable in modern Europe. But as this book goes to press, a prehistoric epic poem threatens to overshadow the next national election in India. The poem is Valmiki's *Ramayana*, The Wanderings of Rama, which dates from approximately the same time—circa 500–700 BC—as the *Odyssey*. During the 1990s a bitter conflict over the birthplace of Rama, at Ayodhya in north India, was the crucible of the birth of the BJP, the right-wing, pro-Hindu party that went on to become India's main opposition party and completed a five-year term in government in 2004. In the numerous Hindu–Muslim clashes that followed the Ayodhya conflict, approximately 13,000 people have died, most recently the 2,000 Muslims murdered in Gujurat in 2002.

Now, the source of controversy is the "bridge" supposedly built by Lord Rama from India to Sri Lanka. The government wants to cut a hole out of the structure for a shipping canal. Pro-Rama

Hindus nationwide are screaming once again that their religious sensibilities are under assault.

But this book is not about politics. It is an attempt to bring to Western readers one of the oldest stories ever told, a literary masterwork little known in the West, but loved by a billion Hindus throughout south-east Asia. So I have woven into this travelogue my own version of the tale, condensed and very tentatively updated. The *Ramayana* is an epic story of love and loss. Its characters are, in some ways, heroic ideals—but the story also tries to show us how we should respond to crises that destabilize us and bring out the worst in us. Even the evil characters in the *Ramayana* are touched by redemptive qualities. Even the good characters make mistakes— sometimes tragic ones that bring heartbreaking consequences in their wake.

I first encountered the *Ramayana* in Sri Lanka twenty-five years ago, as the country tipped into war between Hindus and Buddhists. Then, as I travelled through India, I began to realize that the *Ramayana* played a central role in the lives of Hindus, and that its representation of the enemy, "the Other", shaped the way con- flicting groups on the Indian subcontinent saw each other and had done for a thousand years. A quarter-century on, I undertook a new journey, in the footsteps of Rama, to try to understand the extraordinary enduring power of the epic. Today, as I write, a new TV adaptation of the *Ramayana* is captivating viewers and catapulting the channel broadcasting it to success in the ratings. Like that other Indian epic, the *Mahabharata*, the *Ramayana* cannot be viewed as some kind of literal history lesson. It does take us, however, into the heart and the soul of India, ancient and modern.

An Indian Odyssey is directed chiefly at Western readers, but it will be published in India. I would plead with readers there to be indul- gent towards my inevitable simplifications and misunderstandings. Any factual errors brought to my attention will be corrected in the next edition. I have tried to be sympathetic, factual where possible, and (mostly) inoffensive. But controversies relating to the *Ramayana* provoke violent reactions in India on a regular basis. Devout Hindus should take note before reading any further that they *may* find aspects of this book disagreeable.

I have spent more than five years of my life in India; I love the country, its culture and its people. In recent years Westerners have developed greatly more understanding of that ancient Indian religion, Buddhism, aided by the work of its globe-trotting ambassador the Dalai Lama, and some influential Hollywood voices. A far more ancient and mysterious religion has lacked such starry advocacy of late. If *An Indian Odyssey* persuades a few of its Western readers to peer more deeply into the profound riches of Hinduism— then I will not have failed completely.

A NOTE ON PRONUNCIATION

(For phonetic spellings here and in most of this book I have rejected the conventional systems, which present difficulties to beginners, and have opted for a simpler system of my own. It should enable English-speaking readers to approximate Indian pronunciations, but I apologise to Indians readers, to whom they will seem—at best— rather odd.)

Rama	= R*ah*ma
Ramayana	= Rahm-*eye*-un-a
Lakshman	= *Lahk*-shmun
Ravan	= *Rah*-vun
Sita	= *See*-tah
Bharat	= B'*ha*-r't
Ayodhya	= Eye-*odd*-hyah
Manthara	= Munt-*hah*-ra
Hanuman	= *Ha*-noo-*mahn*

The "R" in *Ramayana*, Rama and Ravan is slightly rolled with the tongue at the front of the palate, in the Italian or Scottish style, rather than the French.

The majority of Indians know Rama as Ram and his story as the *Ramayan*, not, as it's invariably rendered into English, as the *Ramayana*. The final "a"s in English translations are added for scholarly Sanskritist reasons I won't go into here. As English readers are now familiar with Rama and the *Ramayana*, I have retained those spellings, but most Indians say Ram (pronounced with a long "a", R*ah*m) and *Ramayan* (pronounced R*ah*m-*eye*-un, with the first two syllables stressed almost equally). Otherwise, I have tended to follow contemporary Hindi pronunciation.

Rama's brother is Lakshman (pronounced *Lahk*-shmun). Rama's faithful lieutenant is Hanuman (*Ha*-noo-*mahn*). Their enemy is Ravan (*Rah*-vun).

PART I

CHAPTER 1

Overture

I LOOKED FOR my reflection in the river, but it was too dark. The water was thick with that super-saturated sunset light that makes flower blossoms throb. Five girls were waist-deep in the shallows, sarongs knotted above their breasts, dipping and splashing and kneading water from ropes of black hair. They looked in their teens; I was twenty-two. Chatter and laughter tinkled prettily, and it was tempting to believe that they were teasing me. No, they were too innocent.

Now a column of teenage monks, saffron Buddhist platoon, advanced across the bridge with a long, sandalled lope. They seemed, like me, to be uneasily ignoring the figures in the water—eyes, *front!*—but I was probably wrong about that, too. There *was* an innocence about Sri Lanka. Or could it be reticence? Anyway, what price sexual innocence in the aftermath of a massacre? Later, when I reached the north, one of the first things I'd notice would be the brash Bollywood hoardings, all pneumatic tits and murderous blood-streaked faces. I wondered if there was a difference between Buddhist southern and Hindu northern Sri Lanka. Were the southerners more reticent, the country cousins? Did they fear that the bolder, brasher Hindus were taking control? Buddhism and Hinduism, the two great religions of the Indian subcontinent—I knew next to nothing about either of them. Only that here, in gorgeous green Sri Lanka, they seemed to be at war.

The sirens, or *apsaras*, completed their toilette and disappeared among the palms along the river bank. Their tinkling voices drifted away. The trapdoor of tropical sunset snapped shut, turning the river black. The sun had gone, but the air was still torrid. I turned and walked back into town, through a chiaroscuro of ash and ink, trying to avoid the patches of sewage.

7

A cinema was showing a James Bond movie. Spelled out unevenly over the entrance it said, *"For Your Rice Only"*. I wondered when the cinema manager would realize someone had misheard him. A power cut had plunged the market place into darkness. Hurricane lamps swung in shop doorways, turning them into sinister caves. Stalls were illuminated by flickering oil lamps and even the wandering peanut vendors bore candles. The constellation of flames created an air of mystery, as though some sacred procession were about to begin.

I stopped a passing peanut man. He twisted a cone from a strip of paper torn from a schoolbook—numerals etched in neat fountain pen—and funnelled the nuts through slender fingers. I needed a razor, and found a stall heaped with cheap mirrors and those plastic jugs used for carrying water to the latrine. If toilet paper was rare in Sri Lanka, that other Western decadence, the disposable razor, had yet to arrive. The vendor handed me a safety razor made of yellow plastic, brittle and trashy, made in China; the blades, in a tiny golden packet (and virtually blunt), were Indian. Two moribund socialist economies; this was 1982.

I was staying at a budget lodge, the one in *Lonely Planet*, with a dorm room to myself. But when I got back, I had company. Another backpacker was unbackpacking gauzy tie-dye sarongs, like a magician comically pulling out an endless handkerchief. Birgitte, she said she was. From Germany. And comic, she was not.

She was very different from the dusky *apsaras* of the bridge: north-Europeanly long and angular, straw-blonde, ungiggling, untinkling. My bed was by the far window, and I noticed she'd chosen one close to it. I'd have selected the most distant, pretended, as on a crowded tube train, that I was alone.

I sat down and grinned at her. "Two's company, they say."

"Please?"

"Sorry, it's, er . . . Hey, have you had dinner?"

Next to the lodge was a travellers' café whose hip young owner spoke English with a would-be American twang. His multilingual menu provided the blandest possible pancakes and omelettes to soothe the traumatized foreign palate. We decided to go for something more authentic. Down a side street we found a crumbling restaurant with no sign on the outside, but a low window let you peer in at twenty tightly-packed men. We found seats at a table where two labourers with grimy faces flashed us shy grins and kept eating. A sort of mattress of cigarette smoke hung from the ceiling. There were no menus, no one spoke English. I pointed to a lurid red dish, which seemed to contain lumps of khaki-coloured fish. Birgitte, by contrast, was able to display some knowledge of Sinhalese, though she still asked for "Rice, *ja*?"

"For your rice only," I quipped.

"Please?"

I told her about the cinema. She smiled without enthusiasm. "James Bond movies are bourgeois shit, they are obscene," she said.

"I thought it was funny—"

She frowned. "Reactionary British world of men in these black suits what are they called, like with the black tie—"

"DJs—no, tuxedos."

"Tucks heat toss? *Ja*, maybe. And sexism. Violence it's like a cartoon. Fascist. You don't sink?"

"Well, actually, I've always wanted to be James Bond." Birgitte's eyes widened. "No, but I did until I was about fifteen. He probably is a role model for English boys. Boys everywhere. If 'For Your Rice Only' can find audiences in rural Sri Lanka, Bond must represent a fairly universal set of values."

"*Ja*. This is how capitalism transmits its fascist ideology."

Her meal arrived, an archipelago of wholesome green. My curry, by contrast, was the colour of a warning, and soon I knew why. Birgitte began to describe Unawatuna, an international socialist beach Utopia where she'd spent the summer. I listened, weeping. Sweat dripped from my nose to beat a tattoo on the aluminium plate.

She looked concerned. "Pay attention! Are you quite well?"

"I—I'm fine. We English are used to eating curry. It's our national dish." I quenched my mouth with plain rice.

Birgitte was making her beach sound like a kibbutz. I'd heard it was a hippie joint where accommodation and dope were cheap. In the midst of plotting the overthrow of global capitalism, Birgitte had managed to acquire an admirably deep, hazelnut-brown tan. Her shapely shoulders gleamed in the dim-lit room of men in shabby working gear. She told me her comrades had flown back to their other lives, and she wasn't enjoying her sudden solitude. She had decided, a little sheepishly, that after two months on the beach she should grab some Sri Lankan culture before returning home. "But I should have left with my friends." A look of distaste pinched her lips. "It is now the rains."

"It never rains in Germany?" I asked.

After a moment, Birgitte gave an exaggerated grin. She had acknowledged a joke.

We talked about the journeys we intended, up to the centre of the island where the great Buddhist monuments were. We were heading for the same places—it could make sense for us to team up. Neither of us said so, the idea merely hovered in the air. Birgitte pulled her chair a little closer as we pored over my *Lonely Planet*, dotting its pages with the red sauce of my fish curry.

We returned to the dormitory with its eight empty beds. Birgitte and I had just met and had little in common. And so, in the manner of the times, we made love, without guilt or emotion or tangible contraception.

FAST FORWARD TWENTY-FIVE years.

An hour before dawn, I kick-start the Bullet, nod at the night-watchman and pull out of the hotel forecourt. I circle Connaught Circus almost gingerly, the early hours emptiness of New Delhi's hub somehow emphasizing the uncertainties of the journey ahead. I twist the throttle more briskly and speed past the darkened colonial façades and sleepy khaki-clad guards, down Vivekanand Marg and Jawaharlal Nehru Marg. The boulevards are unnaturally empty and cool. In the spooky silence I hear the Bullet's four-stroke thumping steadily.

When I reach Old Delhi and the Red Fort, there's a hint of pink in the sky. The great hunched citadel is three centuries old, built to express the ineluctable power of Shah Jehah. But Mughal power was challenged, and defeated, by the wily British. The former embodiment of Islamic might is now a tourist attraction. At the age of twenty-two I had lain on its quiet lawns, watching a white bullock tow a lawnmower in circles around me, grass clippings sparkling in the sunlight like spray. A quarter-century on I experience the shock of the new: hovering in the dawn grey beyond the Red Fort, paralleling the banks of the Yamuna, is a multi-lane highway. I'd anticipated creeping through crowded Old Delhi lanes—but India is changing. Mughals and memsahibs, highways, superhighways.

I climb the access ramp and speed along carriageways as deserted as those of some sci-fi apocalypse. By the time I cross the Yamuna, the Great Trunk Road is coming to life. Buses are crammed with sleeping commuters, their faces squashed against the windows. They jolt over roadworks, another highway under construction. India is trying to keep up with the Chinese.

As I enter the flat farmland of the great Gangetic plain, the sun segues from blood-orange to the pale yellow of an unappetising egg yolk. That cold morning sun gets me every time, I'm always shocked by the heat it unleashes as it pales. I have a five-hundred mile drive ahead of me to Ayodhya. For most of it the highway—the Trunk Road—will be a winding country road overhung by immense trees, bisecting villages and towns, without traffic-calming measures or bypasses, an overloaded lane designed three centuries ago for horse traffic. How long will this first stage of my journey take me? Three days? I hope, two.

I pull into a service station and a woman steps out. She wears a starched scarlet boiler suit and her long hair is coiled under a Shell baseball cap. She's dark, pretty, with a smile out of a toothpaste ad. Low caste, no doubt, to be pumping fuel—but a symbol of a changing India. Beyond New Delhi's determined modernity, I was going to find fuel pumps served by barefoot boys in oily rags, absolute poverty—but India *is* changing. Growth, consumerism and optimism are arousing the sleepy subcontinent I first met fresh from university. Prime Minister Rajiv Gandhi, before he was atomized by a Tamil Tiger bomb, prodded India out of four decades of isolation. My Enfield motorbike is a fifties design still in production, a symbol of that sleepy India which endured almost until the 1990s—but every other bike around me is a Hero-Honda or a Bajaj-Yamaha. Westerners have so often, so complacently, described India as "unchanging". That is now a romantic untruth.

This country, often described as a subcontinent, is in the grip of an industrial revolution. In the 1980s India produced one model of portable typewriter. It now produces more computer software than the USA. But I'm searching for an older India, one perhaps literally as old as the hills—could a story of mountains swallowed by seas be a folk memory of the waters' rise at the end of the Ice Age? Is 6,000 years such a long time in the story-memory of mankind? I plan to follow a thread of narrative and culture. It will lead me to mysteries I have never heard of. Just as some great cathedral might have secrets hidden in its very stonework, the *Ramayana* is a repository of ancient clues. They might provide a key to pull this India of infinite contrasts—this cacophony of cultures, races, religions, languages, costumes, cuisines—into a single palpitating focus. On the other hand they might cloud the past, deepen the uncertainty, even create a misleading and dangerous sense of certainty, of mystical national destiny. The poem is prehistoric, emerging from a time scholars know little of—which doesn't stop them brawling about it in print. For cynical politicians it's a political football. Endlessly manipulated, it reveals again and again its capacity to unleash violent emotions. This must be a candidate for literature's wildest statistic: that since 1992, more than 13,000 people have died because of the *Ramayana*.

As I WRITE this book, a small paragraph in the Foreign News Round-up of a newspaper folded on my desk suddenly catches my eye:

> Three people were killed yesterday in the north Indian town of Ayodhya . . .

For Hindus, Ayodhya is one of the holiest places on earth. Once glorious, its praises sung by visitors from as far away as China, it's now a neglected little town deep in the broad green plains around the River Ganges, several hours from any major city, well off the main drag of Hindu tourism. Many of its ancient temples are in ruins. Other Indian pilgrimage sites attract large crowds, and donations. But the millions of faithful who visit Ayodhya are mostly poor, illiterate peasants who arrive on foot. They join queues that snake towards a dusty mound where, tradition has it, the God-King Rama was born a hundred million years ago. When I first visited Ayodhya there was a riot during which a policeman was killed and militiamen fired over the crowd's heads. A week or so later, six terrorists got themselves shot as they tried to let off suicide bombs at this Holy of Holies.

No ordinary shrine, then.

The *Ramayana*, The Wanderings of Rama, is one of the great books of the ancient world, though little known in the West. It's a sort of spiritual epic, as familiar to Hindus as the nativity is to Christians—though much more red-blooded. The *Ramayana* is also erotic, depicts jealousy and hatred, has the twists and turns and domestic details of a soap opera, and contains battles of hair-raising savagery. (It also contains literature's first flying machine, leading some to claim that Rama was an alien . . .) Good triumphs over Evil, but only just. I have read that the *Ramayana* was one of the books admired by the twentieth century's best myth-maker, J. R. R. Tolkien. Its Sanskrit verse is said to be exquisite, something hard to judge as the available translations are often disappointingly dull (I've attempted my own, not-dull, abridgement).

The *Ramayana* is said to have been dictated to its author, Valmiki, by God, making it holy writ as auspicious and potent as the Bible or the Koran. According to tradition,

> A reading of this sacred poem
> Absolves the reader's every sin
> And grants eternity . . .

The *Ramayana* could be described, with apologies to a certain best-seller, as *The India Code*—a puzzle that, if unravelled, might lay out the whole tangled story of life in India since Aryan invaders came to India from central Europe and seized control of this vast subcontinent. (Or did they? I didn't know, until I began this journey, how deep that question lies in the psyche of India.)

Rama's wanderings begin in impossibly holy Ayodhya, that Indian Bethlehem, a backwater that would be forgotten if it weren't for its staggering burden of history, its hundreds of decaying temples, many now serving as houses, barbershops—even stables. But the *Ramayana* reaches its climax where this story, my story, begins, a quarter-century ago: in the swollen teardrop that trembles on the south-eastern cheek of India.

I mean, of course, Sri Lanka.

CHAPTER 2

Serendipities

JULY 1982. I'd timed my visit badly: Sri Lanka was picking up the pieces after race riots had killed 5,000. And the monsoon was starting.

The Antonov descended into an incandescent afternoon. I was hung-over. After two complimentary vodkas I'd asked, humorously, for a third. The Aeroflot stewardess had the musculature of an Olympic shot-putter—I wondered if the Party's reward for a medal was a glamorous job on the airlines. She slammed a litre bottle in front of me and snarled, "Drink!" I'd tried to rise to the challenge. Now, she or one of her Amazonian colleagues heaved at a handle and the doorway became a blinding white rectangle. I stepped into it. Sweat tingled in my armpits before I even set a foot on the tarmac.

The air in the terminal was humid and heavy with disinfectant. Outside, even the palm trees were drooping. I climbed into a bus whose open windows were fan heaters. It was my first time in the tropics and I wondered where all this heat was coming from. Surely it was being *wasted*?

The bus clanged over an iron bridge resembling something left by the sappers of an advancing army. The river was hot chocolate. Palm groves lined the road. Colombo approached slowly, low-rise, dotted with colonial villas. I found a guest house in a lane leading down to the sea, a crumbling bungalow that had once belonged to some sola-topeed servant of Empire. My room had several sticks of hardwood furniture and the mushroom cloud of a mosquito net, the first I'd ever seen. This exotic textile was full of holes, therefore useless—but I didn't find that out until my first long and very disturbed tropical night. It turned out that I was sharing the room with one other occupant, who lived on the ceiling: an immense monitor lizard, as long as my arm. The monster's breath rasped like a big dog dying of dehydration, but I found his presence reassuring—he was on my team, his long tongue whipping round in the dark, destroying my new enemy, the mosquitoes.

The tropics evidently were places of excess—excessive heat, colour, noise. I loved it all. Colombo's colonial heart of miniature Selfridges and Buckingham Palaces was surrounded by vivid markets the Empire's aloof architecture had tried and failed to negate. These markets were antically alive—yet gorgeously draped women cleaved the chaos with the composure of figureheads. What was this calm? Was it Buddhism? Or snobbery? The Sri Lankans struck me as good-looking people, their quick smiles expressing an un-English air of happiness. In particular, they seemed happy about God, and were forever bobbing in front of ubiquitous statues of the Buddha. These heavy-lidded, implacable deities—were they Sri Lanka's symbol of order, an oriental equivalence of the Empire's plate-glass department stores and traffic lights? I peeked past temple doorways framed by demons or demonic gods, but I was too shy to go in and join the milling crowds. At home, I wouldn't have hesitated to enter a church, but here I was intimidated by the fervour. The force, the tangibility of faith persuaded me that this was *real* religion, to be treated with awe. I wasn't yet ready to be exposed to it.

Day began early in Sri Lanka, before the sun got up. By 6 a.m. columns of children were en route to school, neat in the white school uniforms inherited from the British, crisp shorts or skirts over brisk brown legs. In contrast to this cool colonial formality were those saris, tongue-pink or bud-burst-green to resist the bleaching midday light. The sea was peacock-blue. The ubiquitous monks wore saffron, though their sun umbrellas were black. Somebody told me a monk was allowed just five possessions: two robes, a food bowl, a wristwatch and an umbrella against the sun. Heat was the principal fact of tropical life.

I've always been too restless to enjoy holidays, and the idea of a whole year without purpose was already making me jittery. Many travellers recognize that moment, soon after the start of a long journey through far-off places, when the elation of preparation and arrival begins to wear off, and suddenly you wonder what the hell you're doing in a place where you know no one, the climate seems crazy and everyone you meet wants to sell you something. That's when loneliness can get a grip.

The monsoon air grew impossibly thick, my summer clothes clung like candlewax. For a few pounds I had new clothes made from gossamer cotton. The clouds broke and fat raindrops slapped into the dust like copper coins. The gutters were quickly overwhelmed, streets became canals. I sat on the veranda outside my room watching the solid volley of water from a broken drainpipe, put out my hand and found with astonishment that the water was warm. I stepped into it and took a shower. Back in my room, the BBC World Service was serializing *Lady Chatterley's Lover*, a scene where the sated couple crouch by the fireplace of their woodland cottage. The sound effect of a crackling fire was, for me, a sound of home, wood burned to banish cold. I was in a place where they had hot rain.

But luckily, rescue from nostalgia was at hand. The next day at the beach I met Kishore, a law student at the university. He pointed at a building behind us. "That's the Colombo Swimming Club. I come down here to swim every day, round about 6.30. Why don't you join me?"

For a week it was a daily rendezvous. We'd change in pistachio-painted plywood cabins and enter the water just as the sun broke over the horizon. The disturbed monsoon ocean was dark and murmurous, and we'd discover strange creatures churned from its depths onto the rain-curdled sand. Kishore swam further out than I did, powerfully, then straight back, as he had done daily for years. Conditioned by grey 1970s England, I struggled to imagine the sensuality of a life lived beside this soupy ocean. Kishore had a body like a porpoise, sleek, rounded, yet muscular—especially his thick shoulders. I took a surreptitious delight in seeing sunlit drops of water on his oily, brown-black skin.

After our swim, we'd go to some café or other and drink coffee and eat some pastries. Kishore was a good companion, intelligent, generous, with a quick smile and warm, liquid eyes. He told me he was a Tamil—a member of the minority Hindu community originally from south India. He introduced me to his extended family, a smart bunch of barristers and journalists and artists who lived in leafy streets in airy colonial bungalows, where servants padded barefoot, flicking damp dusters at Victorian sideboards. They ate well and talked well, and were extraordinarily welcoming. They introduced me to the war.

Days before I arrived, thousands of Tamils had been massacred in a co-ordinated attack by elements of the majority, Buddhist, community. Tamils had been driven out of their homes, robbed, raped, murdered. I knew this when I arrived, and the grey gashes of burned-out Tamil businesses and homes scarred the streets. But it was hard to reconcile that hatred with a city that seemed so cheerfully alive. Kishore brought it home to me.

"Do you remember the river you cross on the way in from the airport?"

"The old metal bridge?"

"A cousin of mine was found there. The bodies of dozens of other Tamil boys were found in that river—it was swollen with bodies. You know how one of my uncles survived? His house was attacked by a mob, but he had a shotgun—he emptied it several times into the crowd. A lot of other houses were burned down. First they were looted. Others have been occupied, you know? They've been taken over by thugs, crooks, elements associated with Buddhist politics. No one knows where the owners have gone. Of course, we do know— they're dead."

Kishore's grandfather was a dapper old man, a former barrister with spiky white hair and a face, once very handsome, still attractive and wonderfully alert. He'd been British-educated in the early years of the century and sounded like a cylinder recording of Lloyd-George. He spoke in long, elegant sentences, as though dictating op-eds. I'd been invited to Sunday lunch, during which the recent violence was touched on only with a few anxious phrases. After the meal the old man invited me to his book-lined study. I asked him why the Hindus and Buddhists were at war.

"Hindus and Buddhists? No. This is nothing to do with religion per se. The two communities have lived together all my lifetime, we attend the same schools, we celebrate each other's festivals. Of course, there have always been tensions, but the root of the problem is historic. Regretfully, it has its roots in the time of British rule. Please don't misunderstand me. I tell you very frankly, since the British left this country it has gone to the dogs! I do not say this to flatter you. The moral case for the end of colonialization was unarguable. But we Sri Lankans have brought little glory upon ourselves in the way we have run our own affairs since 1948. We have been led by donkeys!"

I smiled. "If you say so."

"I do. Now. What is Ceylon most famous for the world over?"

"Tea?"

"Tea. In Ceylon, as you know, the British found ideal conditions for the cultivation of tea. Naturally, tea pluckers were required."

"'Tea *pluckers*?'"

"To pluck the tea leaves! With their fingertips! They are sharp, the leaves! Go to one of the gardens, you will find these girls—examine their fingertips. Calloused, blackened. Well; the Ceylonese were not interested in such labour. This island is a paradise, the earth yields two crops a year with very little effort. Why toil under the sun, tugging sharp leaves from the tips of tea bushes? The British looked instead to south India, where there were impoverished Tamils eager for work. In time, the brightest Tamils were sent to colonial schools. We became the pen pushers of Imperial Ceylon. Ultimately, we dominated the professional classes of the country.

"Now, did you know that India is closer to Ceylon than Calais is to Dover?" The old man's eyes twinkled. "But the Tamils were ethnically and culturally quite different from the Ceylonese. Tamils belonged to the Dravidian race, with thicker hair, dark skin. Like Kishore, no? He is black."

I laughed. "I suppose he's *dark*, yes—"

"The Ceylonese had paler skins, you see," the old man hurried on, "inherited from a mix of bloods—Aryan, Malaysian and what-not. We Tamils observed the old religion of Hinduism, derived from a time of daemons and wood spirits. *The Faerie Queen*, no? Midsummer Night's Dream? You Europeans have done away with your Thors and fairies and wood spirits, but not the Hindus! Buddhism is an upstart, like Christianity! A new religion! It arrived in southern India only fifteen centuries ago!" The old man gave an almost girlish giggle. "But the key difference is socio-economic. After Independence, the Tamils' influence in the professional classes, in government, bred resentment among the Sinhalese. There were many moves to suppress the Tamils. This in turn led Tamils to demand autonomy. Relations worsened. Now, in the north, where we are in a majority, people are demanding independence! They're hotheads, it's excessive. But rabble-rousing politicians are depicting this as the final straw—we are aliens, we should be thrown back into the sea!"

Extremity was in the air. The Tamil Tigers, as they called themselves, would become the world's most fanatical guerrilla movement. The Tigers' cult of violence would result in the deaths of hundreds of thousands of people, the recruitment of children as soldiers, even a suicide bomber being sent in a dynamite girdle to assassinate the prime minister of India. An island routinely claimed as the original Garden of Eden was about to turn into hell.

But when I decided to go north and to see Tamil Sri Lanka for myself, all that was still in the future.

As for Kishore, he'd seen the writing on the wall and would soon emigrate to the unextreme climes of Toronto. He wrinkled his nose at the prospect of the Canadian winter, but gave a stoical shrug. "I have one uncle who has been there for some time, he will help me complete my studies. Then . . . I will be married." He unleashed an astonishingly warm, slightly shy smile. It would be a marriage arranged by his parents. I realized with a shock the scale of the chasm separating us: for Kishore, marriage, with all that it implied—the loss of his virginity and access to the sexual world, entry into adulthood, parenthood, responsibility—was in the gift of his parents.

It would be nice to know how Kishore coped, but I never saw him again.

AT COLOMBO BUS station, people were fighting—literally—for seats. The idea seemed to be to rush a bus as it approached, hook an arm through a window and hang on as it slowed, shove in your bag to secure a seat, then fight your way on board to claim it. I watched this procedure for some time before deciding to have a go myself. No quarter was given and experienced bus catchers shouldered me aside effortlessly. At last I managed to get my bag onto a good seat— a front one, just behind the driver. I scrambled aboard and sat, breathless, as people piled into the bus. When it was ready to leave, a young saffron-wrapped monk climbed aboard and stood over me. With my blood still up, I made a dismissive gesture. He didn't budge. Then I saw the glowering faces around me. Thus, I learned the hard way that the front seats on Sri Lankan buses were reserved for monks and that monks are not to be monkeyed with. I caught the next bus and spent the morning as part of the humid human mush in the aisle. Around lunchtime I claimed a seat of spiky nylon, sodden with sweat. Great vistas were appearing outside the bus as it toiled, farting black clouds of unburned diesel, into the uplands. Monsoonal Sri Lanka was in violent bloom, the roads under attack from giant pink and heliotrope flowers with leaves the size of overcoats. I was headed for Kandy, the capital of ancient Ceylon, in the heart of the hill country.

IT WAS KISHORE, a Hindu, who'd told me not to miss Sri Lanka's greatest Buddhist festival. Esala Perahera took place in Kandy during the July–August full moon. Elephants were brought in from hundreds of miles around and a relic of the Buddha—His Tooth—was paraded through the streets.

The capital of the ancient Ceylonese kingdoms was a solemn little town in a deep groove of forested hills, with a pea-green lake at its heart. Elephants were tethered everywhere I looked, like boulders set on four columns, their trunks craning blade-edged palm fronds into soft-seeming mouths.

The festival was still a few days off. Kishore had warned me that if I didn't get to Kandy early, every hotel would be full, but he'd underestimated the effects of a well-publicized massacre. I found myself alone in a dorm room. Until Birgitte arrived.

The kings of Serendib had raised great monuments in Kandy, marking its importance as a capital and repository of the True Tooth. This numinous relic was apparently kept in a jewelled casket, inside several further gold caskets, within the high walls of the Temple of the Tooth. I queued with Birgitte to visit this lofty and elegant building with its whitewashed walls and a double-hipped, steep-pitched roof. We passed through a narrow door into the dark, hushed, candlelit chamber where the Tooth resides, but it had already been removed in preparation for its process through the Kandy streets. We emerged into a long, open-sided wooden structure like a mediæval fish market.

"Ha—look how you colonial British crowded in," said Birgitte.

I looked. Next door, close enough to throw a stone at, was a long neoclassical building with the words "High Court" carved in enormous letters under the eaves.

"This temple was maybe the most important focus for the Ceylonese people, no?" she continued. "For Ceylon nationalism. So you built your courts, the symbol of your power, next door—almost on top! And look!" I looked. She fingered at a far corner of the temple compound, where there rose, behind a white, mammary Buddhist dome, the pink prick of a brick spire. "Your church, dominating the temple, no? It is caught tight between these two symbols of colonialism. They want to squeeze it. To negate it!"

Back outside, I bought a pre-war, oft-reprinted Architectural Survey pamphlet on the history of the Tooth. It contained, sacrilegiously, an essay challenging the historicity of the relic and a grainy photo by a Victorian orientalist. Snapped alongside a twelve-inch wooden ruler, the Tooth looked elephantine: it resembled the tip of a tusk. Who would give an interloping Westerner and his lens such access today? And who cares what the Tooth looks like? The festival of Esala, celebrating the Buddha's conception, had itself been superimposed on some older fertility rite, like Christmas on a Druid rite. And so it goes.

Birgitte cared. She was a rationalist, a scientific socialist. Religion was anathema to her, repulsive in all its forms. She was for bombing, Baader-Meinhofing, the bourgeoisie.

But she did enjoy a knees-up. The following night the festival began. At dusk, there was a sense of immanence in the streets. We went for dinner and emerged into drum-banging, flame-lit ecstasy. Ranks of men in scarlet and gilt costumes streamed through the streets, dancing and stomping splayed-legged and squat-kneed. Acrobats cavorted. Drummers bashed out rhythms, men cracked bull-whips over the heads of the crowd. (This display of almost violent intensity, I had to remind myself, was dedicated to the Buddha, the founder of a religion I knew rather vaguely was supposed to be about calm and non-violence.) Every face was varnished with sweat. The air was hot and oily. Light came from flaming torches fuelled by coconut husks which, when they burned low, were replenished by teams of scurrying, bright-eyed schoolboys, delighted by their essential role in the drama. More than a hundred elephants navigated the human torrent. The last was a freakishly large bull who bore in a swaying cage, illuminated by strings of miniature bulbs, the Tooth itself.

CHAPTER 3

The Pleasure Garden

THE GUTTERS GUSHED chocolate-brown water. I didn't mind the rain, I was an Englishman amused by a Victorian spa town planted on a tropical mountain. But Birgitte wasn't so much uncharmed as infuriated. Hair wet, dirt between her toes, *God*, how she hated rain!

A day's journey south of Kandy we had reached Nuwara Eliya, still known as "Little England" after the British colonialists who came here to escape the triste tropic heat. They established, as they did in all their hot colonies, a Hill Station. The naked hills, deforested to be planted with tea bushes, echoed the bare bosoms of Britain's moors and glens (though in truth, the Ceylonese mountains were far more dramatic); so the colonists dotted the hills with half-timbered cottages, which they called Glen View or The Haven or *Bien Venue* (sic). They capped them with corrugated tin, painted lincoln-green. Not for these colonists humidity, malaria and early death. Up in the clouds, Nuwara Eliya was beautiful and healthful, a demi-paradise. It was said to have been the location of royal pleasure gardens for centuries. The climax of the Hindu myth, the *Ramayana*, was supposed to have taken place in these emerald hills. The British built their church and golf course and racecourse, turning the Kandyan kings' pleasure gardens into a botanical garden. And they successfully supplied the Empire with quantities of its sacred herb—with the help of thousands of Tamil workers imported from India.

We found a gingerbread cottage with a gable and a bay window and a sign saying "Bed and Breakfast". The owner was a small man, completely hairless, with pebble-glass spectacles—Mr Seneveratne. A rigid moralist who nevertheless did not want to have an unoccupied room, he announced, turning the question into an order, "You are sleeping in separate beds?!" The twin beds in question, in the bay-windowed front room, were barely long enough for children.

Mr Seneveratne lorded it over a meek wife, who rarely left the kitchen, and three joyless children, whom we glimpsed staring solemnly at school books. They set off in the morning in their starched uniforms, white socks pulled tight over brown calves. We would be sitting in the bay window to a breakfast brought on a tray by Mr Seneveratne, who was unable to resist sniffing the air as he entered the room.

The first night, arriving late, we ate with the family. After the plates were cleared the master of the B&B had removed the dust cover from an immense radio and ceremoniously flicked the "On" switch. The rumty-tum of "Lili Bolero" had preceded the solemn intonation of the words, "This is the BBC World Service. The news, read by . . ." Mr Seneveratne worshipped for ten minutes in silence, then decisively switched off the radio and replaced its dust cover, signalling that it was time for everyone—including Birgitte and me—to retire.

Mr Seneveratne was well informed about world affairs, as well as those of his own country. He was also a bigot. He was horrified by the communalism that was scarring his country and naturally, like every Buddhist, he abhorred violence. The sad fact was, you see—the Tamils were to blame. Too rich, too complacent, too arrogant for their own good. His voice, always high-pitched, became a hectoring shriek. "All these years they had taken plum jobs in the administration, yet complained of discrimination! And these northern Tamils are demanding independence—it is *treason*! They want to tear the country apart! If army will not stop them, who will be surprised if people take up arms to remind them of their place?"

It rained some more. We sheltered in a colonial hotel. Rare for Sri Lanka, there were fitted carpets: they smelt of mildew. Tea—local, high-grown, exquisite—was served in chipped English china, by scarlet-clad waiters whose gold braid nearly dangled in the cups.

I had more time for Nuwara Eliya than Birgitte, but its kitsch charm soon palled for me, too. There's only so much pleasure to be extracted from transplanted seaside bungalows with worn tiger skins, chintz, and bulb-browned lampshades depicting fox hunts. These relics, so faithfully preserved, raised more questions than they answered. The ghosts of the colonialists, caricatured by their soft furnishings, did not materialize and tell us *how it was*, how they thought, how they felt.

As we sipped our tea under an elephant head whose tusks threw shadows across the room, Birgitte archly informed me that the British in India in the High Victorian era had been ignorant, indeed racist, occupiers. I knew that, I replied. How many of them would have cared that their predecessors had for centuries viewed Nuwara Eliya as an earthly paradise, a kingly pleasure garden; that it had been the setting for the *Ramayana*? No, Birgitte wasn't going there— religion was irrational, despicable. If colonialism did any good, she retorted, it had helped dispel the black clouds of superstition. (Whatever Birgitte's faults were, I see with hindsight that she could not be accused of Political Correctness.)

I couldn't explain to her—I hadn't tried to explain to anyone, I couldn't even explain to *myself*—why I felt different. That flash of— what?—I'd experienced three years earlier. Fleeting, inexplicable, a giddy sense of something beyond. It had prepared me to believe that there *was* something in religion, some irrational but deeply human truth. Or was I mad, along with the Blakes and Hildegards and the other mystics, the authors of ancient myths? I was to spend four more years in India, struggling with the sense that some metaphysical vision was just beyond my reach.

I found a copy of the *Ramayana* that very evening on a backstreet bookstall that did a roaring trade in bootleg paperbacks. It sold thrillers with bikinied blondes gripping sub-machine guns, and the classics of self-improvement and pop psychology—*How To Make Friends and Influence People, Better Sight Without Glasses, Games People Play*. There were buried treasures, Penguins that had lain unpurchased since the sixties. R. D. Laing and D. H. Lawrence between psychedelic covers, priced at five and sixpence. And there were heaps of religious tracts, printed on recycled paper so cheap it was studded with chunks of pulp like multicoloured cornflakes. Print and typefaces were crazily uneven. I loved these pamphlets—because their publishers couldn't afford good paper and the printers used ancient hand-set presses and the typesetters probably spoke no English. And yet, for all their weaknesses, they were books, they existed, they *spoke*. Mostly they spoke of Buddhism, but there were a number of

Hindu titles, too. One of them was a tubbier volume, battered, monsoon-splattered, sun-bleached: the *Ramayana*.

Its cover was, or had been, saffron, like the robes of the Sri Lankan Buddhists and, as I'd later discover, of Hindu monks too—saffron, the subcontinental colour of spiritual aspiration. The book had a few colour plates with scenes from the epic. One showed the young Lord Rama with an enormous bow that only he had been able to lift, a scene that put me in mind of young King Arthur, who alone had been able to draw Excalibur from the stone. Then there was the kidnap of Sita and the war to obtain her release, which seemed to echo the Greek tale of captured Helen and the siege of Troy. I'd just finished a literature degree and my mind was full of this stuff— literary-critical notions, narrative forms, the quest, kidnap, rescue, the duel, revenge, the death of the hubristic villain: bits of that lot could be found in the majority of the world's myths, from King Arthur to the *Odyssey*, not to mention *Star Wars* and *The Lord of the Rings*.

Brittle sunshine flashed off the puddles. Birgitte and I climbed into a bus that descended in zigzags out of Nuwara Eliya, through steeply terraced hills of market gardens. I'd persuaded Birgitte that, having come all this way, we should visit Nuwara Eliya's cultural spots. They generally aren't temples, or buildings of any kind. Their significance comes from the memories, or traditions, they enshrine. The *Ramayana*, I had gathered, was a holy writ cast in the form of an adventure story. It told how Sita, wife of Prince Rama, was kid-napped from north India by a many-headed demon named Ravan, who imprisoned her here, in Sri Lanka. Rama was the human incarnation of a god, but Ravan had powers that made him invincible even to a god. Rama raised a vast and magical army, and crossed the sea to Lanka. As Rama's army approached, Ravan moved Sita into the mountains near Nuwara Eliya, to his vast pleasure garden.

We climbed out at Hakgala, the fine botanical garden landscaped by the British during the 1800s. In these hills, dreaming of rescue, terrified of rape or murder, Sita spent her days. On a vertical bluff 1,500 feet overhead, sheets of exposed honey-coloured rock showed where the weapons of Rama and Ravan had struck the mountains as they fought.

We climbed into another bus. Half an hour below Hakgala was

Sita Falls, a seventy-foot waterfall. The queen would bathe in the plunge pool, unknowingly observed by her kidnapper. Ravan drew the line at rape, believing he'd woo the princess in the end, but he couldn't resist having a peep, taking the form of animals to remain undetected. The bus set us down on a bridge across a cleft in the hills. The waterfall was already gushing impressively, so soon after the first monsoon rains. Cultivation hadn't reached these hills and the slopes were lush and wild. The sun was bright now, the air hotter and stickier than it had been in Nuwara Eliya. The plunge pool was on the hillside above the bus stop; a handful of bathers, presumably pilgrims, respectable and fat, opened and closed sarongs like immense newspapers to wrap and unwrap themselves as they stepped in or out of the auspicious pool. I wondered how they might feel about the obvious eroticism of the tale, so different from the morality—indeed, the sexual loathing—of Christianity. Perhaps the Hindu gods had something in common with those of ancient Greece—beings stricken with the same weaknesses that beset us humans.

Some men were peddling postcards and gemstones at the bus stop. As we began to climb, a couple of teenage boys scrambled alongside us and from their glances at Birgitte it was clear why. I'd already understood the prudishness of Sri Lanka and I wondered how Birgitte, feminist, would respond. Angrily, slipping quickly into the black water? Would she refuse to undress? I now felt strangely uneasy at the prospect of Birgitte doing something so un-Sri Lankan as to expose herself in public.

Birgitte quickly pulled off her clothes, then sat on a rounded rock with her back straight and her knees up. She was trying to balance herself, but the result was a sort of cheesecake starlet pose. Her black bikini was briefer than usual, for stripes of white were exposed around her breasts and across her hips. Somehow, those white stripes were almost more private than if she'd been completely naked. When she eased herself into the water, she opened her legs. Pubic hair was visible against white flesh. I looked at the boys. Unselfconsciously, they were leering.

But it wasn't so different from the scene on the bridge. I had been captivated by those girls, dipping and splashing. They had seemed innocent; Birgitte very evidently was not. But there the difference ended.

CHAPTER 4

Valmiki's Ramayana

THE STORY CAME to Valmiki in a rush—a great, mysterious, elegant, witty, erotic, ironic, spiritual adventure. All human life was there. The Wanderings of Rama, he called it: *Ramayana*. In it, he would tell the true story of a man who became, in Valmiki's own lifetime, a great but tragic king, believed ultimately to have been a god. It all began with the story of Rama's father, King Dasharatha, a man whose own greatness was undermined by all too-human weakness. It began like this:

IT WAS ONE of those ironies that sometimes torment the rich and powerful: despite having several wives, and a healthy appetite for sex, King Dasharatha had never been a father. As he entered middle age, the lack of an heir became a torment to him. So he assembled his advisers and told them he'd found a solution: he was going to perform the Horse Sacrifice.
No one argued with the King's dangerous decision. A Horse Sacrifice could shape destiny, influence the gods. On the other hand it was a fantastically complex ritual, almost never performed, for the simple reason that if it wasn't done exactly right it backfired: the instigator was destroyed.
Such a high-risk strategy on the part of the King obviously couldn't be allowed to fail. So the great and the good of Ayodhya began to sweat. Ministers are experts at passing the buck, but sometimes even they get cornered. Ayodhya's ministers had a superb network of diplomats and spies throughout the world, but this time they were being asked to exercise influence in that most inaccessible of areas—the Queen's vagina.
To succeed, the Horse Sacrifice needed a holy man of the first rank. The Cabinet cast around for months before fixing their sights on

Rishyashringa, the son of one of the most powerful sages in the world, Veebandaka. Young Rishya had been raised in a hermitage, deep in the jungle, far from temptation. The only people he'd ever met were visiting monks, who brought back reports of a young man marked by spiritual genius: piety, intellect, discipline, selflessness and kindness. But how on earth to persuade him to help?

The King's advisers enlisted the help of their neighbour King Rompada, in whose kingdom Veebandaka had his hermitage. It was decided that the next time the old sage went away, his son would be contacted by ambassadors of the court—a bevy of its finest courtesans. A few weeks later, the courtesans duly set up camp close to the hermitage.

It wasn't long before young Rishya came wandering by—and was staggered by what he saw. The only humans he'd ever clapped eyes on were bearded old men, though he knew the beauty of flowers and birds, the grace of cats and deer. He had never been tempted by sweets, let alone sex. Now, Rishya encountered for the first time in his life young adults like himself—but dressed in gorgeous silks and jewels, fresh jasmine blossoms in their hair, artful arcs of rouge and kohl on their smooth, plump skin.

The girls were experts at flirtation (not to mention the other arts of love). They clustered around Rishya, simpering and cooing. They showered him with questions, and shyly he responded, telling them about his father, the great sage, and their lonely life together in the forest. He had been raised well and knew the importance of hospitality; so he invited the women to the hermitage, where he received them as he'd learned to receive elderly monks, washing their feet and offering them berries and roots. Silently amused, the girls took plump, juicy sweetmeats known as *ladhoos* and put them with their fingers straight into his mouth. Naive Rishya took them to be some extraordinary new type of fruit. Slowly the girls began to drape their arms round him, inviting him to unwrap certain other soft and rounded presents, breathing, "Oh, Brahmin, please try these sweets of ours, oh, they really *do* need tasting right away!"

The courtesans knew the boy's father could return at any minute. If they were found in flagrante, he would inflict a terrible punishment— in all probability, death. As soon as they could, they hightailed it back to their tents. But the plan had worked. Rishya spent a night of torment.

Early the next day he went to find his new friends. This time, the girls implored him to come home with them, promising him a royal welcome.

And that is what he received. The innocent Brahmin soon found himself betrothed to Shanta, the ravishing daughter of King Rompada. This made Rishya one of the most envied men in the northern kingdoms, for Shanta's bow-shaped lips and enormous heavy-lidded eyes had haunted the dreams of a long list of princely suitors. Thus was the saintly hermit turned from a life of denial to one of physical fulfilment. In fact, he would turn out to be an unusually sincere and holy priest. But more to the point, his presence would allow the Horse Sacrifice to go ahead.

For months, Ayodhyan craftsmen laboured on buildings and marquees to house the thousands of citizens and foreign luminaries who would attend. Herdsmen fattened animals and chefs procured rices and spices for a million meals. A central pavilion was built, open to the heavens so that the vapours from oblations of ghee, sandalwood and other precious substances should ascend to the Gods.

When the week of the Sacrifice arrived, Ayodhya was decked with flowers and flags. Its population swelled many times over and the grounds were crammed with milling people as far as the eye could see. The complex rituals began: Vedic hymns were sung, prayers chanted, offerings made. Dasharatha himself squeezed the *soma* creeper to obtain the intoxicating juice used by the holy men. The King passed among the crowds, ordering food to be piled onto the plates of the sick, the elderly, the young and the poor.

Posts were staked out and three hundred sacrificial animals were moved into place. In honour of the God Vishnu, a vast solid-gold altar in the form of an eagle was prepared. And at last, Dasharatha's flawless and magnificent stallion was tethered to the altar.

With one blow the horse was killed. Queen Kaushalya approached with three slender golden knives, to be seen symbolically making the kill. (That night she would sleep beside the body of the horse, a ritual copulation she dutifully endured.) The high priest took fat from the horse's body and dripped it into the holy flames, the rising scents intended to honour and command the gods. Gifts of land and gold coin were distributed, and it was seen by all that Dasharatha was cleansed of his sins. His path to heaven was clear.

But what of the ritual's principal purpose? The horse's entrails were examined for an answer. Young Rishya supplied it: "Your Majesty, there will be four sons to ennoble your dynasty." The King fell into an ecstatic trance.

The sacrifice was reaching its climax. The scene shifts heavenwards.

Almost all the Gods were assembled, with all the angels and saints. Then, He arrived: the creator of worlds, Lord Brahma. All bowed their heads before him.

They had been summoned by the ineluctable power of the ritual. But the Gods also had an urgent matter to discuss. An evil, powerful creature named Ravan had been on the rampage, wreaking havoc throughout the universe. Even the Gods themselves couldn't stop him.

Ravan had been born a demon, but staggering feats of self-discipline had transformed him into the most extraordinary holy man the Gods had ever seen. A delighted Brahma awarded Ravan a blessing—a boon—that amounted to eternal life. In Ravan's words, "No creature from heaven or hell should be able to destroy me."

Had Ravan's years in the wilderness been merely a performance to secure immortality from Brahma? Or had they driven him insane? Either way, when he re-emerged from isolation he went amok. Capricious and cruel, supported by an army of demons, he ranged the three worlds, leaving in his wake rape, murder, even cannibalism. No one was safe.

Brahma's generosity had caused the whole fabric of creation to be torn apart. Brahma saw no ill in His creation—He loved everything equally. This created huge problems for those Gods who were not so well blessed in the infinite-love department. These lesser Gods venerated Brahma; but they needed Ravan dead. Brahma's blessing was irreversible. What was to be done?

Then, the last God arrived: Vishnu, mounted on his eagle, Garuda. He wore yellow-ochre robes and gold bracelets; the conch shell, disc and mace he held in three of his four hands glittered against a black cloak. He resembled the sun trailing a black cloud—and sure enough, a shower of rain fell like a blessing on the hot and excited humans far below.

Vishnu was the Preserver to Brahma's Creator. A God of Action, He asked bluntly, "What do you want me to do? How can Ravan be killed?"

Trembling, the foreman of the assembly spoke up. "There may be one hope, My Lord—we think we've identified a chink in Ravan's armour. He asked Brahma for protection from the inhabitants of Heaven and Hell, but he ignored the inhabitants of the middle world—humans—he thinks they're too pathetic to be a threat. In theory . . ."

"In theory he could be killed by a man?"

"Yes, My Lord. No mortal would stand a chance, of course. But perhaps . . . If You were to incarnate Yourself . . ."

"Is that the considered view of this assembly? That I should incarnate myself as a human and fight him?"

The universe was governed by rigid laws which no one—even supreme Gods—could override. The evil Ravan had managed to warp these laws, and restoring order was going to be almost impossible. The consequences of failure were too terrible to contemplate. It was going to need a strategy of extreme subtlety to outwit Ravan and finally destroy him.

Far below Vishnu's feet, men were gathered in an extravagant ceremony of propitiation. One of the most powerful humans in that middle world, a king—one of the better ones—was demanding a son to succeed him. Four boys were about to be born. And one of them must be set the task of killing Ravan.

WITH THIS OVERTURE, erotic, amoral, pragmatic, supportive of the divine right of kings, but ultimately about the need for good to prevail, the *Ramayana* begins. It provides a metaphysical framework for the adventure that follows, but most of the story doesn't require the reader to believe that Rama is an incarnation of God. Many historians believe, in fact, that Rama's deity was added retro-spectively to later versions of the epic and didn't come from Valmiki's hand. It doesn't matter (there are many devout Hindus who are able at once to venerate Rama as a God and at the same time appreciate the text as a slice of literary history; that's one of the mysteries of faith). I've chosen fragments of the epic that contain, I believe, its essence—Rama's Initiation, Exile, the Kidnap of Sita, the Meeting with Hanuman, War and Death, and finally the tragic coda, the Return to Ayodhya.

My *Ramayana* differs from the original, but so do most of the versions that have travelled throughout Asia, becoming absorbed into the mythologies of many nations—and even into another religion:

Buddhism. According to Hindu tradition, Rama has incarnated thousands of times, and every incarnation has produced a new version. Mine isn't directed at the Hindu millions, but at contemporary Western (or Westernized) readers. It's one of the shortest and probably the most modern. In the nineteenth century, commentators were anxious that a work that, in the view of many, equalled or excelled the literary achievements of the ancient Greeks, was almost completely unknown in the West. It seems nothing short of bizarre that a century and a half later the *Ramayana* should still be languishing in obscurity.

The *Ramayana* is a Sanskrit poem, and most translations make this Indian *Odyssey* seem criminally dull. If the original had been, would it have lasted two and a half thousand years? Would it have spread throughout Asia, dominating entire artistic traditions, seducing and even obsessing masses and élites alike? The devotional versions of the *Ramayana* that came after Valmiki's original were undoubtedly chaster than he had been. And in the twentieth century Valmiki was let down by many mediocre translators. Modern versions that play down the sex and the violence have conformed in part to a nineteenth-century Brahminical view of what is appropriate—the Brahmins, the Hindu priestly caste, were heavily under the influence of Victorian prudery. But the aspiration of many translations was to produce dull, scholarly or safe schoolroom editions. Valmiki enjoyed delineating the form of a woman's breasts, could describe with accuracy the sexual arousal of a bull elephant, knew what it looked like to be beside a man as he coughed the bright blood of his lungs into the dust and died. All this he achieved in elegant verse (I have heard the original read aloud: Sanskrit is a beautiful, flowing, mellifluous language). I cannot equal the Sanskrit beauty of India's first epic poem. But I do feel it's time to restore to Valmiki's *Ramayana* something of its robustness, its rawness, its raunch.

AT DINNER that night I babbled about mythology, rattling out my received theories of literature long after I should have noticed Birgitte's eyes glazing over. Finally she said, "Look, who cares about kings any more?"

I stopped in mid-mouthful of rice.

Birgitte gave an irritable shrug and flicked her hair back across her nut-brown shoulders. "Who cares about kings and all that shit any more? Why are you British so obsessed with royalty? It is incredible! I mean, life is, you know, evolving, and you are so sort of stuck. In Unawatuna . . ."

She told me how her præsidium of beach bums had been briefly infected by a tiresome Brit. Loathed by the Germans and the Italians and the French, he had committed the unforgivable sin: he had defended the royal family.

I grinned across the curry platters. "What's the British royal family got to do with mythology—with an epic poem written thousands of years ago?"

Birgitte was exasperated. "It is reactionary shit, that's what! The worship of kings! Prehistoric shit! Kings control religions and religions have held people in chains for thousands of years! What does religion tell us? *Lies*! What are priests? The instruments of a huge system of *oppression*! How does religion treat women? As *possessions* to be *bought* and *sold*! So don't try to give me this ancient religious shit, Martin, I have had enough!"

She pushed her chair back from the table slightly, then jabbed at her bag for her cigarettes and lighter.

I felt my own temper rising.

"Look, here we are, in an exotic place that just might be connected with the birth of one of the world's great myths. Even if it wasn't, the power, the longevity of the *Ramayana* as something in people's imaginations give this place a kind of resonance. That's the power of myth, the whole point of literature. We tell stories to explain the world to ourselves."

The lighter spat. Birgitte held the cigarette in the V of her fingers. "It's not a story, a myth, it's religion, it's a fucking *lie!*"

"It's a fantasy, hardly the same thing! And it means something to people. That's what stories do. Something that dialectical materialism has not in fact overlooked. Myths may not be literally true but they play an important role in human beings' imaginations—like the myth of Communism or the myth that Mao Tse Tung was a saviour and not a psychopathic dictator as bad as Hitler. *Ja?*"

Birgitte eyed me scornfully. "*Ach, ja, ja.* Somehow you British

cannot have a conversation with a German without mentioning
Hitler—your friend in Unawatuna did so too. We are all Nazis, huh?
Yet this is one case—and there are many—where a German is
speaking with clarity of the injustice of the world and having a
determination to make changes, and a British man is . . . is . . .
swimming in this mysticism of royalty and religion shit. *That* sounds
like Hitler. You are afraid to open your eyes and look clearly at the
world. So you will transmit these lies to another generation. So you
will not fight, but continue the exploitation of others . . ."

The following morning I said goodbye to my own, short-lived
Sita. She couldn't get out of soggy Nuwara Eliya quickly enough—
she wanted to get back to Hamburg with her suntan intact. We'd
planned to visit the great Buddhist sites together, but this was the
parting of the ways. Irreconcilable differences. Birgitte headed west,
to the capital and the international airport, and the West. I travelled
north.

Three days later, the bus I was sitting in passed through a small
town which, in the sea of tropical green, was an atoll of grey. Fire
had turned buildings, cars, everything, to ash. This was a Hindu
town, and Buddhists had incinerated it and many of its inhabitants.
Sri Lanka was on the verge of civil war, a war that would become
notorious as one of the most deranged and surreally cruel conflicts of
the twentieth century. But I couldn't yet see the chilly parallels with
that age-old tale of Hindus and their Lankan enemies, the *Ramayana*.

CHAPTER 5

Falling Coconuts

THE NORTH OF Sri Lanka was sunburned, the vegetation sparse. The bus rattled over a long causeway between two lunar salt pan expanses. It seemed a stark declaration that Jaffna, the capital of Tamil and Hindu Sri Lanka, lay apart from the superabundance of the south. In a land of plenty, it seemed to say, the Tamils had to eat salt.

As we pulled into the main bus stand I saw cinema hoardings with plump cleavages and blood-soaked heroes bent on revenge. Otherwise, the town was asleep, the shops shuttered but for an occasional stall selling cigarettes. A general strike was in progress, a protest against the severity of the army clampdown. Security forces were stationed on every corner, impassive men in mirror-lensed shades who sat in jeeps and scrutinized passers-by. The town had a stifled atmosphere, as though the population were holding its breath.

I found a room in an old wooden villa overlooking the sea. The afternoon was overcast, a grey sky lowering over the shoreline's grey harvest of dried seawrack and urban refuse—broken flip-flops and a curious profusion of rusting thermos flasks. Crows strutted and picked at scraps of discarded rice. Nearby loomed the most celebrated example of military architecture in Sri Lanka, Jaffna's fort, built by the Dutch in the 1600s and now a museum. I saw no other visitors as I passed through a tunnel carved into the massive pentagonal walls. There was silence within, only broken by the creeks of the crows. A tall tree draped feathery limbs over a threadbare lawn where some goats ripped up grass by the roots, enviously watched by two starving dogs.

A wiry man with a thatch of greying hair leapt off a string bed and hastened towards me, introducing himself as the official guide. I followed him into a suite of rooms that could just have been vacated by the colonial masters. On whitewashed walls were framed maps and photographs of various British administrators and kings, and one Empress. There was much dark, highly polished mahogany furniture. I stared at a planter's chair—a great, deep armchair with paddles that swung out for you to put your feet up—and the guide invited me to try it out. It tipped you back at an angle so absurdly comfortable, so insolent that it was easy to imagine reclining under a fan, presenting the soles of one's boots to the servant who leant forward with one's pink gin.

We proceeded into a bedroom containing a large four-poster, complete with mosquito net.

"This", my guide told me, "is where pyem sleep."

"Pyem?"

"Pyem! Prime Minister!"

"Oh, *PM*! Sleeps? Still?"

"Yes, yes, PM was here two weeks ago only." He pointed out of the window. "Helicopter land here on grass, no? Bodyguards, they are sleeping in next room—look, Sair." He led me to a room off with a row of iron bedsteads and gave a lupine grin. "I am making tea for bodyguards."

"But—I don't understand, why does the Prime Minister stay in a museum?"

"No no, this is museum also and Prime Minister's official residence also! It is safe, no? Safest place in city—high walls, no one can enter. Sair, this is very bad time, unrest is there, no? PM had come here for to meet military chiefs and assess situation, then return straight Colombo. Never leaving fort—only this place is safe one hundred per cent in city Jaffna."

By the next day, the artificial deadness of the strike had evaporated, replaced by an atmosphere of tireless bustle. Jaffna was the major trading centre of the north, the heart of Hindu Sri Lanka, bursting with shops and stalls selling everything from broomsticks to welding equipment. Bicycles careered down the narrow lanes, often with students on them, piles of school books tied precariously with string to the racks behind. They confirmed Jaffna's other status. Its *raison d'être* was learning, providing doctors, lawyers, the country's educational élite. Every other building seemed to be a university college or a school of some kind—trees and lamp posts were plastered with flyers advertising private tuition and cramming courses. But at the heart of this learning was a shocking sight: the ruin of the huge city library. It had burned to the ground a year earlier. Already, creepers and vines were reclaiming the scorched shell.

I had discovered a place called the Palm Tree Teahouse, a cool and airy establishment where they served good, if expensive, tea. The prices guaranteed privacy, respite from the clamour of the streets.

A boy at the next table leant towards me. "You are from Germany?"

He was a Dostoevskyan student type, spectacled and intense, with a romantic lock of thick hair.

"England," I said.

"England. You have heard what had happened here in Jaffna, no? The army is destroying us. They had burned down the library. Will you tell the people of England this when you return home?"

I tried not to smile. He made the common Indian mistake of inserting the word "had" into sentences in the simple past tense. But it was the naïvety of his question, not his grammar, that made me want to smile. "The library," I said. "How did it happen?"

He glanced around him, leant closer to me and whispered, "Army! Police! They only had burned!"

It was somehow hard to take him seriously. Here we were, sitting in a café. Whom was he afraid of being overheard by?

"Is that true?" I asked. "I mean, was it a riot, did things get out of hand—I d'know—a spark, the fire brigade couldn't get there—"

His eyes flashed. "This was *deliberate*! There were so many witnesses. Uniformed officers were there, they protected the culprits!" He looked over his shoulder again. "It is not wise to talk openly. Even here, this place. It is dangerous to speak."

We finished our tea. I paid for him and we stepped outside. His name, he said, was Manmohan. We walked along the main street, past the taxi stand with its row of Morris Minors parked in the shade of the trees.

"Come," said Manmohan decisively. "You want to know what is happening in Jaffna? I will take you to my home."

He lived with his mother and sister. It took us ten minutes to walk to their small house facing the seafront. The only person home was a girl of about sixteen, whom he introduced as Lakshmi, his sister. She smiled warmly, as much with her eyes as her mouth. Lakshmi had that quality I had already detected in other Sri Lankan girls, a stillness, a steadiness, but at the same time an old-fashioned shyness—Sri Lankan girls were taught modesty, not to meet a man's gaze.

"You will take tea?" she asked.

"No thanks, we actually met at the Palm Tree."

She smiled and dropped her eyes and disappeared, to appear a few moments later with a plate of sweetmeats.

The three of us sat down on the floor, where cushions were spread on a rug. "I will show you something," said Manmohan.

With a familiar gesture, he tugged towards him a foolscap filing box and removed the lid. It held photographs. He took one off the top and passed it to me, a small, black-and-white print. As I examined it a chill passed over me. The photograph showed the dead body of a young man. His jaw and teeth were smashed, he was lying in a pool of shiny black blood.

Lakshmi's eyes were already full of tears.

"Durugan—my elder brother," said Manmohan. "He was twenty-six. They beat him to death! Close to this place—the road outside."

"They?"

"Army, police . . ."

"But, why?"

"Why! We never knew! He was a medical student, he had no involvement in politics! There are no reasons why they do these things! Maybe they stopped him to check his ID and he said something they didn't like, they beat him, he fought them. Maybe mistaken identity, they eliminated the wrong fellow. Or someone reported him—there are so many spies. Hundreds of boys have died in Jaffna like this!"

"What are you going to do?" I asked feebly.

"I am going to fight them! You have heard of the Tigers?"

I'D BEEN SITTING in the shade of a tree in the courtyard of a temple close to the lodge. From a distance I'd watched the evening *aarthi*, a ceremony of bells and drum-banging attended by a couple of hundred people, who'd left with their foreheads smeared with paste. The Hindu priest crouched beside me and grinned. He had a brilliant, toothy smile. This was his temple, he told me, in excellent English. Lean and white-haired, he wore a white loincloth, or *lunghi*, and carried another folded cloth over one shoulder. Around his neck and passing under one arm was a white thread. His forehead was almost completely covered by a streak of orange paste. I asked him some questions about Hinduism. Before we'd exchanged five sentences, he had invited me to stay in his home—free of charge, he stressed, with his glittering grin. Today, I wouldn't trust a smile like that, but then I was young and naive, and eager to think well of the world.

His house was close to the temple, small but set in a walled grove of coconut palms. He shared it with his much younger sister, a woman of about thirty who was extraordinarily beautiful—slender, bright-eyed, possessed of smooth golden skin. She was mentally handicapped; her mental age couldn't have been more than four or five.

"She is a great burden to me," the priest told me bitterly, "—but we must accept what the God gives, *na*? This is *karma* . . ."

His sister had been trained to clean the house. He scolded her constantly. When he wasn't talking, his face would slip into an anxious frown. Later, I was sitting on the veranda and the girl was kneeling among the coconut trees, washing dishes by scraping them with ash from the kitchen fire. A coconut fell seventy feet from the treetops above and exploded next to her. She looked at me with merry eyes, took in my shocked expression and shook with laughter. Falling coconuts, the priest assured me, with a peculiar smile, often hurt people, sometimes fatally. I got used to the sound of coconuts detonating in the garden—there was sometimes a *shish* from the released elasticity of a bough and only if it seemed overhead did one look up in alarm. But it needed real fatalism, it seemed to me, to live in the midst of this deadly bombardment.

The simple-minded girl took delight in defying the strictures and prohibitions of her scowling brother. I played childish games with her. She squealed with delight. The priest always made sure I left the house when he did and was never alone with his sister.

Back at the Palm Tree the following day I heard the life story of another young man. He was the son of the wealthy owner of a cinema chain, many of whose cinemas around the country had been torched during the recent riots. His father had lost a fortune, he told me. But here in the predominantly Tamil north, their cinemas still stood. Suddenly, he asked me brightly if I wanted to see a movie. "We have one starting in a few minutes. I invite you."

A car and chauffeur were waiting. They whisked us to a pink concrete box on the edge of town where exactly four men were waiting for the box office to open. The six of us filed into a giant auditorium with eight vast fans ranged along the walls—it was like a WWII aircraft hangar. The propellers began loudly pounding the torpid air. It was another ancient Bond movie, *You Only Live Twice*. Its aerial vistas of verdant volcanic islands in northern Japan are bizarrely interwoven with my memories of Sri Lanka.

When I told the priest where I'd spent the afternoon, his mouth twisted in displeasure. He had heard of the cinema owner. "He is rich," he said. He talked about money every time we spoke, a litany of grumbles about the poverty of the priesthood, the declining donations as prosperous families left Jaffna to escape the unrest. It was clear now why I'd been invited to stay—I was expected to make a contribution to household expenses. I didn't mind that, but I felt manipulated.

The following morning I was waiting for the priest's sister to vacate the shower. As she came out she defiantly showed me her naked body. I was shoved aside by the priest as he bundled her back into the bathroom, shrouding her in a towel. He began to yell. I told him I intended to move back to the lodge. I needed to be able to receive guests, I said.

"You can receive any guests *here*," he said, with a kind of desperation.

"Not really," I said. "I'm sorry."

I packed my bags. The priest stationed himself near the front door, as if preparing to block my exit. His chastened sister was peeking out from behind the kitchen door.

"I'd like to make you a gift," I said stiffly, "to thank you for your hospitality. And . . . to help a bit . . ." In return for the three nights I'd stayed with him, I was giving him the equivalent of one night in the lodge. It was roughly what I'd been planning to offer anyway.

I'd managed to find an old envelope to put the money in. He

ripped it open in front of me and counted. His face fell. "Three nights you have stayed here," he said. "Three breakfasts, two dinners. This money is very less."

"You *invited* me to stay here!" I said. "You said it was your religious duty, your pleasure, to offer hospitality to a guest. So if it's not enough, you can give it back."

Sullenly he folded the notes and tucked them into the folds of his *lunghi*. Then he stood aside from the door. His sister, eyeing me miserably as a toddler would, began to bawl. She was losing a friend, and she knew I was leaving because she'd committed the crime of showing me her naked body.

MANMOHAN LED ME furtively through back alleys, over piles of stinking refuse, into the back room of a small shop. The only illumination came through a grey net curtain over a tiny barred window. I sat at a small circular table, beside sacks of rice. After a few minutes we heard someone entering the shop from the street.

"I will wait outside," said Manmohan, going back into the tiny courtyard.

The spokesman of the Tamil Tigers he'd brought me to meet was a tubby man in his late thirties. The Tiger wore an orange safari suit with sleeves too long for his thick, stubby fingers, and spectacles with immensely thick black frames. He reminded me of my former maths teacher—and in fact he *was* a teacher, he told me, of history (the Marxist variety). With archivalist thoroughness, he proceeded to lay out the list of hurts to the Tamils, dating back to Independence and beyond. This took half an hour. When he reached the 1980s the catalogue of wrongs turned increasingly into a list of atrocities. I realized how deep the chasm now was between the Sri Lankan government and the Tamil minority.

"What do you think will happen now?" I asked him when he had come to the end of his list.

"We will fight."

"Can you fight a national army?"

"US had been defeated in Vietnam, no? We have no fear of Sri Lankan army, they will be fighting in *our* homeland. Tamil Tigers have earned the support of the Tamil masses—that is the secret of war. The people are supporting us. We are training cadres, amassing weapons. So many people are ready to help us. But we need funds. Dollars. You must go to your country, tell people what is happening to the Tamils. They will help us."

"But surely no one in this country wants war, do they? I've met plenty of Tamils in the south, educated people, who're horrified at the prospect of more violence. I mean—are you saying you're ready to use force to bring the government to the negotiating table? Is that the plan?"

"There is only one plan. We will bring about *Eelam*—Tamil homeland. Tamil-dominated areas in north and east of country will become an independent state. This is now the only path for us. You saw the library, no?"

"Yes."

"This was the biggest library in south-east Asia. Just imagine! This vast repository of our Tamil culture, ancient books, irreplaceable manuscripts. Nothing remains! This is *genocide*! The message for the Tamils is that our culture means nothing in Sri Lanka. 'We burn your books, we burn your culture, next, we will burn you!' Government itself was implicated—it has done nothing to track down those responsible. We Tamils must back down, give in, accept secondary citizen status in Sri Lanka. Suffer massacres by nationalist *gundas* and not raise a finger in self-defence!"

He fanned out his stubby fingers and jabbed them at me. "There is war in Sri Lanka—this is a fact! We will kill every soldier the Sri Lankan government sends into our territory. Thousands will die on both sides maybe, but we are ready to lay down our lives! Sinhalese troops will soon tire of coming to the north to be killed, Sinhalese mothers will tire of sending their sons to die. And we will fight until we have brought about *Eelam*!"

I still don't know the name of that Tamil ideologue. I've tried looking through photographs of the Tiger leadership in the early days, but there are few such photographs, and in any case many activists were rounded up and killed by the authorities—or, in some cases, murdered by other Tigers, in the days before one fanatical and brutal faction established its supremacy. I have sometimes wondered, would he have been so determined on the course of war if he could have seen ahead twenty-five years, to the fanaticism, the children forced against their will to take up weapons, the female suicide bombers, the savagery—and stalemate?

RAMA WAS A delightful child, bright, curious and affectionate. All four of the King's sons were raised as future leaders, but Rama's strength of character marked him out. He seemed to grasp the concepts of *dharma* instinctively. He was calm and thoughtful, he always tried to see every side of a problem. He was self-assured and able to express dissent with a degree of grace and intellectual force that never failed to charm his elders. He had an instinctive grasp of the necessary balance between a sovereign's *droit de seigneur* and the need for absolute fairness in the application of the law. Physically self-disciplined and well-built, he was an excellent horseman and perhaps the best archer in Ayodhya. He was popular in the court and adored by the populace. All in all, Dasharatha was quietly confident that his son had the makings of a superb ruler.

It was during Rama's sixteenth year that his father was startled by an unexpected visit from the spiritual master, Vishvamitra. He wasn't the kind of man who hung around court. A seer of legendary power, known to be in contact with the Gods themselves, Vishvamitra was the sort of man even kings had to make pilgrimages to meet. Surprised but delighted by this visit, King Dasharatha showed such reverence as he himself might expect from the humblest of his subjects. Kneeling to touch the sage's feet, he asked, "Whatever brings you to my door, if it is a favour you need from me, only ask it—there is nothing I could deny your holiness."

"Sire," Vishvamitra began, "I have two enemies in the forest close to my ashram. Evil men. I could deal with them, but I have sworn not to take life. I have come, My Lord, because I want you to lend me your son—young Rama, the gifted archer. I need him for ten days."

Dasharatha felt his stomach turn. He attempted a smile. "Vishvamitra! My Rama's a child, he's not yet sixteen! He has no experience of actual combat, he doesn't know how to gauge the strength or weakness of a real opponent. For goodness's sake, let me bring my army into the jungle, we'll flush out these—"

"My Lord, Ravan's behind this. He's pushing his incursions further north, attacking jungle hermits. And I've been told that it's Rama who must respond."

"*Told*? By whom? Vishvamitra, what hope would a boy of fifteen . . . No, I'm sorry, I refuse. I'll send soldiers to help you—"

Vishvamitra's face grew dark. "Sweet words you spoke a moment ago, My Lord. I've always wondered what the word of our great King might mean in practice. Now I know: nothing."

The hermit turned his back on the King and began to wrap his shawl about his shoulders. A paralyzed silence had fallen over the court. Dasharatha felt sweat running down his face. He was experiencing a kind of fear he hadn't known since, at the age of twenty-six, he'd led his father's army into battle, desperately hoping that his courage wouldn't fail him in front of a thousand charioteers. Now, terrified for his son's life, he stared at this grubby guru who, alone perhaps in all the world, had the power to take his son from him.

"Vishvamitra, I'll face the demons in single combat. But not Rama—"

"Good afternoon, My Lord."

The wisest and most patient of the King's ministers stepped forward and whispered into his ear. "Respectfully, Sire, I must remind you that you are bound by *dharma*; the King must keep his word."

Dasharatha pulled himself together. He called for both Rama and his brother Lakshman. Putting his arms around their shoulders he drew the beloved boys towards him and held their heads to his face, inhaling the familiar smell of their hair, which he'd known since their infancy, and which he feared he might never know again. Then he told them to take care of each other. And he bade them farewell.

THE PRINCES SPENT that night on a bed of grass. At dawn they prayed, then followed Vishvamitra to the bank of the Ganges. The far bank of the river was a sheer wall of forest. Inside the canopy it was dark even now, in mid morning, and intensely humid. The air was alive with insects. There were the cries and screeches of birds and monkeys and, occasionally, further off, the harsh roar of larger animals. Rama picked his way through the undergrowth, hands firmly but lightly on his weapons. This wilderness beyond the Ganges was wilder than anything he could have imagined.

"I'll tell you the story of this place," said Vishvamitra, keeping his voice low. "There were two cities here, both prosperous. Now, there's nothing. What's left of their populations live as scavengers."

"What happened?" breathed Lakshman, gazing wide-eyed into the jungle.

"Two warlords—Maricha and Subahu. Their militias patrol the jungle, raping and murdering. They eat the flesh of their victims, they believe it gives them power. That's why you are here, you two. You are going to kill them. But first you have to kill the mother of one. Her name's Tataka."

"Kill a woman, sir?" asked Rama.

"That's her you can hear, my boy—she's at least twelve miles away, but bellowing like a speared elephant. She's strong as a rogue elephant, too. And as mad. She was a *yaksha*, a semi-divine. Her son, Maricha, was a vicious bully even from his early childhood. One day her husband, Sunda, was out with Maricha and things got out of hand. The two of them uprooted trees, destroyed houses, crushed the inhabitants—these were demi-Gods, remember. And supposed to know better. Well, Sunda was condemned to death by the Gods. Tataka and her son went mad. She has become a monster now. Killing a woman seems repugnant to you, Rama, you've been taught that killing is something men do to other men, according to the rules of warfare. Yes, killing is always wrong—unless it is unavoidable, to prevent a greater evil."

THEY ENCOUNTERED TATAKA in a clearing by some ruins. She was physically larger than any woman Rama had ever seen, dressed in armour draped over with rags, and smeared with dirt. Her muscular arms bulged. Round her waist was a belt of human skulls.

She flew at him, lips drawn back exposing her teeth, screaming a sort of war cry. She held a huge machete, ready to strike.

But still, he couldn't bring himself to kill her.

His first arrow severed her ear. Tataka stopped in her tracks. Then an arrow from Lakshman tore away her nose. With a bellow of rage,

Tataka charged forward again. As she lunged at Rama he sidestepped, stabbing his own blade up into her armpit. Tataka was immense and strong, but untrained in formal combat; she screamed and swung her machete. Rama forced his blade upwards, twisting, severing tendons. Tataka fell in the dust.

"*Kill* her, Rama," yelled Vishvamitra. "If she gets away now, she'll be back at dusk with her men!"

Tataka had struggled back to her feet. Rama lifted his bow. One arrow pierced her neck. With her good arm, she tried to raise her sword again. The next arrow, perfectly placed, penetrated through her armpit into her heart.

AT THE OUTBREAK of civil wars there is a moment of precarious balance, when assassination goes unpunished, when governments prove themselves unable to defend the weak. Outrage is met by outrage, the edifice of civil society topples. This was the moment when I had reached Sri Lanka.

Why dwell on this clash between the Sinhalese and the Tamils? The *Ramayana* is part of the bedrock of Hinduism, the story by which most Hindus are taught the essential truths of life. It isn't a tract or a creed, but a tale, one that does not shirk the human realities. It proceeds through mutilation, kidnap and rape to its bloody Lankan climax, war on a world-ending scale. And its hero is a God. It's impossible to understand Hinduism—which means it's impossible to understand India—without knowing this tale of lust, bloodshed, duty and piety. In fundamental ways, the *Ramayana* has shaped Indian consciousness.

For a quarter of a century in Sri Lanka, two peoples have been locked in a struggle for survival. Some say they're the same two races whose struggle inspired the *Ramayana* 3,000 years ago, pale-skinned Aryans and dark-skinned indigenous Indians—Dravidians. The *Ramayana* may be more than a myth. It may be the history of a guerrilla war, written, as histories always are, by the victors—in this case the Aryans. The story goes that pale-skinned central Europeans arrived in northern India 5,000 years ago and slowly colonized the subcontinent. (The imperial British liked the Aryan Indians, as did

Hitler—they looked European.) As the Aryans progressed south they displaced, flushed out, the locals, whose dark skin and thick hair, products of their Aboriginal origins, they despised. The northern invaders represented their enemies as less than human, and their leader, coal-black Ravan, was depicted as a demon, a monster.

Swap allegiances, and Ravan becomes the hero of a guerrilla campaign, holed up in his redoubt at the end of India. The Aryan chief, noble-to-the-point-of-smug Rama, will ultimately defeat Ravan. And the dark-skinned Dravidians will be physically and metaphysically enslaved in the evil of the caste system.

According to some people, the Dravidians are back in Sri Lanka. They are growing in numbers. They demand their own nation. Will it now be the Aryans, grown lazy on lotus-eating, who are pushed into the sea?

In AERIAL photographs Sri Lanka seems almost to touch India, with a delicate archipelago of sand islands that extend between two out-stretched fingers of land like Michelangelic sparks. Once upon a time Serendib was joined to India by a narrow causeway. ("Serendib", the ancient name for Sri Lanka, is the Arabic corruption of a Sanskrit word, *Simhaladvipa*, meaning "Dwelling-Place-of-Lions Island".) The end of an Ice Age, 6,000 years ago, raised sea levels by thirty metres and the causeway was submerged. But people could still wade across that string of sand banks into the sixteenth century, and even today the sand bars are rarely invisible beneath a swimmer's feet.

I wanted to take the ferry from Sri Lanka to India, but the service had been cancelled and no one had any idea when it would sail again. Suspension of the main transport link between India and Sri Lanka was a disaster for many families and traders. As for me, I couldn't afford an air ticket to India. There were no budget airlines in 1982.

After weeks of rumour, it was announced that the ferry would make one further crossing. The booking office was deluged with locals and foreigners rushing for tickets, but I was among the first to secure one, from a man who sat in an office out of Joseph Conrad, behind a deep teak desk where documents pinned under glass paperweights flapped like trapped butterflies in the gusts from the ceiling fans. Tickets were bound in fat books bulging with sheets of indigo carbon. The clerk stabbed a date stamp, tore along a dotted line and handed me my ticket, a sheet of flimsy yellow paper.

The morning of the sailing announced itself with a pearlescent sky and no wind. The TSS *Ramanujam*, licensed to carry 500 passengers (foreigners on the top deck only) quickly filled. Many of the passengers were refugees, men, women and children en route to new lives in India, their possessions bound up in jute sacking and tied with jute string. I also saw a number of tea chests—tea was still Sri Lanka's principal export.

There were perhaps fifty tourists on board. It seemed that a lot of foreigners had been trapped like me, waiting for this boat to continue their travels. Many were German or Italian, but on the forward sun deck (where only mad, sun-struck foreigners ventured) I met a young couple from the north of England. "Sunshine breaks" to India were still a decade off and this working-class pair were out of their depth. Their only previous trip abroad had been to Spain, they told me; travel in India and Sri Lanka had been an ordeal. They felt intensely threatened by the chaotic human energies around them (the very thing I liked). They were heading to Bombay for the flight home, and their faces showed relief and paranoid watchfulness.

The man turned conspiratorially towards me and undid the central zip of the canvas tote bag he kept at all times gripped in his hand. Under the zip glinted a large carving knife. "Anyone wants to try it on with us they got another think coming," he said.

The ship steamed onto an ocean of placid turquoise water. We stared at the silver horizon, waiting for India.

PART II

CHAPTER 6

Into India

I SAW A clutch of white domes rising from the haze. It was Rameshwaram island, where I'd have to transfer from boat to train and cross a mile-long sea bridge to the mainland. This was the stepping stone from which Rama threw his bridge the other way, across the sea to Lanka, for his troops to carry his vengeful rage to the walls of his enemy's castle.

As the ferry docked, I could see none of the wharves and cranes of a large port. Rameshwaram's *raison d'être* was spiritual: a humble town, dominated by the towers of a temple as big as any chunk of European Gothic. I put my bags in left luggage and walked towards the temple through dust-pale streets that ricocheted with sunlight. No chandleries or louche bars, but tiny shops selling flower garlands and painted plaster gods. The domes resembled snowmen from a distance, with black button recesses in their whitewashed façades. Close up, it was clear that they were narrow pyramids—the sort of shape you'd get if you trimmed two playing cards to taper slightly and leaned them together, then cut the two halves of a third card to fit the sides. The whole thing was stepped and densely decorated with a motif of dome and pillars, obsessively repeated, smaller with each tier, narrowing to a roof that resembled a rolled scroll, with two jaunty incurved devices at each end like the horns of a Viking helmet. The whitewash gave the pyramids the bone-white brilliance that had made them stand out across the hazy water.

The temple entrance was dominated by images of the bull *Nandi*, the mount of the God Shiva. I stepped from humid seaside heat into clinging cool. I'd stayed out of large temples in Sri Lanka, intimidated by their strangeness and my own sense that I didn't belong. But since Jaffna I'd grown bolder, realizing that no one

53

minded outsiders. Hinduism had the self-confidence to declare the Buddha, Jesus and Mohammed reincarnations of Hindu gods—it had no need to feel threatened by a foreign tourist.

Ramalingeshwara Temple was said to be one of the holiest spots in India—every Hindu was supposed to go there at least once. In a booth inside the entrance a spidery old bookseller informed me, as he passed me with his tiny hand a yellowed pamphlet so desiccated I could have snapped it like a wafer, that visiting Ramalingeshwara was guaranteed to cleanse the pilgrim of his sins.

"*My* sins?" I joked, "—or do I have to be a Hindu?"

He laughed. "But *all* are Hindus. You also are Hindu!"

That was Hinduism's claim: it wasn't a religion, or even a way of life, but human existence per se.

The temple had a famous outer rectangle of pillared corridors so long their perspectives receded almost into infinity. They were gloomy at first but, as my eyes adjusted, I realized the stone was riotously carved and painted. There were twenty-two auspicious wells within the complex and pilgrimage involved "taking a dip" in the water of each. The stone-flagged corridors were wet under my bare feet from the pilgrims who slopped from well to well where muttering Brahmins upped buckets over them as they stood, palms joined, drenched. I navigated the dark corridors of carved pillars and ceilings painted with peeling monsters and mandalas, with unexpected triangles of low sunlight and the omnipresent odours of mould and bat droppings. In niches, oil flames flickered on the faces of idols daubed with coloured pastes.

Maybe the old man was right: maybe we are all Hindus. But the temple guardians didn't let me in to see the twin Holies of Holies: the *lingams*.

A *lingam* is the symbolic penis of Shiva, a stub of stone set in an ellipsis, the *yoni* or vagina of Parvathi. After Rama had finally (look away now if you don't want to know the score) killed Ravan, the priestly caste warned Rama that his enemy had been the son of a Brahmin—killing Ravan was technically a crime. (The *Ramayana* is replete with *dharma*, Do This and Do That, at one level it's a vast manual of obligation, dedicated to reinforcing the divine rights, and responsibilities, of Gods, kings and every descending caste, all of it overseen and policed by those canny priests.) Rama was told he had to purify himself at once, by setting up a *lingam* to worship almighty Shiva. He set up two, one moulded from sand by Sita's own shapely fingers; the other brought by his trusty monkey lieutenant Hanuman. Today, both reside in shrines far more ancient than the stone edifice erected over and around them by devout mediæval *maharajas*. Rama gave the town his name, Rameshwaram; the addition of the *lingams* gave the temple its name: Ramalingeshwara. It was still a magnet, annually, for a million Hindu pilgrims, drawn by the enduring power of the tale of King Rama—and by the promise of absolution; freedom from the cycle of rebirth, the epochal ladder by which the pious soul painfully ascends to unity with God—and the sinner descends, to be reborn in a lower caste, or even as a lower form of life . . . No one wants to be reborn as a worm.

HE WAS A soldier-gentleman, cultivated, self-disciplined, restrained. He was a serving officer, an accomplished charioteer, elephant rider, archer; a hunter and an animal lover; a patron of the arts. He was trained in the law and in statehood, the qualities of kingship. His understanding of *dharma* was absolute. But Rama's supreme quality was this: he never lost self-control.

He had recently been married to Sita, the adopted daughter of King Janaka, of the neighbouring kingdom of Mithila. Janaka was renowned for his scholarship and piety, but the circumstances of his encounter with his daughter were remarkable. He had been tilling the sacred field where the food to be offered to the gods was cultivated by the King's hand alone. He had come across a baby girl, lying in a furrow. Her birth was declared by the sages to be miraculous. She had duly been named Sita—meaning, furrow—and Janaka had made her his daughter. Sita had grown into a beautiful and dutiful young woman, an excellent match (when you also took the politics into account) for Rama. But it had proved a good match in every way. The couple were happy and very much in love.

Now that Rama was married, his father was becoming impatient to see him crowned. Dasharatha knew his own powers were failing. In his son, whom the people loved and almost worshipped, he knew his succession was in good hands. So the clan chiefs of Ayodhya and the kings of neighbouring kingdoms were summoned. The atmosphere that day was expectant—everyone had been quietly hoping that the admired but increasingly erratic old King should soon be replaced by Rama. The tall young prince—he had just turned twenty-five—entered the Audience Chamber, knelt in the traditional mark of respect to touch Dasharatha's feet, then took his place on the gem-studded golden throne beside his father's.

The King's heart overflowed as he gazed at his son, a near-mirror image of himself as a young man. "It's no secret, Rama, that you're my favourite. But it's your virtues that have endeared you to the people. Today, before these witnesses, I appoint you Regent!" Then he added, with a significant look at his prime minister, "But I want you crowned soon. I shall sit to one side of the throne and advise you, my boy. It will be an orderly transfer of power! The dynasty shall continue!"

By evening the bells were ringing out across the plains and echoing in the mountains. But even as the people celebrated, Dasharatha was confiding to his son a terrifying dream of meteors blasting from a cloudless sky. "I feel anxious, Rama—I feel I should appoint you Regent now, while your brother Bharat's out of the city. He's a good man, but even good men shouldn't be tested too hard. I've decided—I'm going to crown you tomorrow."

"Yes, Father." Rama bowed his head and laid both hands on his father's feet.

"Now, go, my son. Prepare yourself. You won't be in your feather bed tonight, it's a grass mat for you! Don't ignore the rituals, they matter. You're going to be the king of the poor as well as the rich, Rama."

"I do understand, Father."

"I know you do, my boy. But listen . . . Be on your guard . . ."

"Against what, Father?"

The King looked uneasy. "Anyone. Yourself—even me. Make sure I crown you before I change my mind. Go, now. Still your mind. Tonight, you grow up. The real trials of life are all ahead of you, my dearest boy."

Rama's and Lakshman's mother was the King's first wife; Bharat's mother was his last. Her name was Kaikeyi, and she was still, at thirty-eight, a beauty, who held the old sensualist in an erotic trance.

It was Kaikeyi's personal servant, Manthara, who fired the Queen's fears and ambitions. With the bells ringing across Ayodhya, Manthara strode straight into Kaikeyi's apartments and snapped, "Get up, you clueless idiot, how can you lie around when Rama's about to beat your son to the throne?"

But the Queen wasn't in the mood tonight to indulge her tiny servant's conspiracies. "Manthara, you know I love both Princes as though they were mine. And much as I adore Bharat, I'm not silly enough to think he should become king. No one would stand for it. Besides, Rama's ready, the people worship him. If, God forbid, he should die, my Bharat will be in line. So please shut up and spare me the back-stairs gossip, just for once."

Manthara would not be silenced. "How long do you think you two will last once Rama's on the throne? Obviously the royal family have kept you in blissful ignorance of their history. I give it a year, and Rama will either have slit Bharat's throat, or had him banished."

Kaikeyi gave that languid, throaty chuckle that was so much a part of her erotic appeal to the King. She walked over to her dressing table, picked up a jewel and handed it to her favourite servant. "You're mad, Manthara, but you've always cared about me more than anyone else—"

Manthara hurled the gem at the marble floor. "You grin and hand out baubles. Try imagining Bharat lying at the bottom of a well with his throat cut. How funny do you find *that*?"

Kaikeyi was unsure whether she should take any more of this or have her servant thrown into the streets.

"My lady," Manthara hissed. "Listen to me, and there's a chance your son will sit on the throne, with you beside him. Not ending your life as a poxy whore in some north-western barracks, wondering if all this was a dream!"

A little later, Manthara approached the King and murmured that his favourite wife was threatening to end her life. He rushed into her apartments, to find Kaikeyi prostate on the cold stone floor. He knelt beside her. "My darling—has someone hurt you? Should I call the doctors?"

Kaikeyi made it clear that the hurt wasn't physical. "After the battle with the *Asuras*," she asked, "who nursed you back to health? And what did you promise me?"

"It was you who nursed me, darling. And I promised you, in return, two boons, two wishes, to be redeemed whenever you wanted."

"Do they still stand?"

"On my life! By all the Gods!"

Then she broke his heart.

ॐ

I SEEMED TO recognize this little loco—wasn't it Kind Edward from *Thomas the Tank Engine*? The narrow-gauge train, a long way from its birthplace in the Swiss Alps, puffed patiently into the Nilgiris Hills. Cumuli of steam intensified the tropic heat in the open-windowed carriages behind. They were cream and blue-liveried, with varnished wooden benches. A permanent picnic was going on—saried matrons endlessly unwrapping knotted bundles of home-cooked curries and *rotis* and sweetmeats. Children clambered from knee to indulgent knee. Young men hung on outside, savouring the breeze and dropping off for a cigarette whenever the wheezing train halted to pick up passengers or to engage the Meccano kit of cogs and ratchets with which it had been dragging itself into the Nilgiris for the best part of a century.

Bulbous jackfruit hung from trees. Monkeys crawled four-footed at the roadside, grabbing any discarded food, looking for the main chance. As we climbed, the air freshened. Frantic jungle foliage gave way to cultivation. Moulded hills looked as though someone had trepanned them to reveal green cerebella—eventually I realized they were covered with tea bushes, not dotted in rows as in Sri Lanka, but in dense, swirling plantations. Just as in Sri Lanka, there were strips of terraced bungalow—"line houses"—for the tea-pluckers.

The plump humps of tea yielded in turn to groves of eucalyptus, slovenly-looking trees with their bark and leaves hanging off them like a teenager's school uniform. An occasional cleft in the hills gave a glimpse of the plains below, ever more bleached and hazy.

At last, at midday, the train chugged into a terminus in what might have been the Scottish Highlands, with gabled Victorian cottages and a looming coronet of peaks. This was Ootacamund, the colonial hill station that trumped Nuwara Eliya—Ooty had been the *queen* of hill stations.

Ootacamund had been the south-Indian summer capital, where the imperial administration decamped from the plains during the intolerable dry months. It had been said to combine latitude and altitude in a sort of eternal English summer—the writer Malcolm Muggeridge called it "the best climate in the world". For modern Indians it was one of their most exclusive resorts, a place where the new ruling classes had effortlessly assumed the privileges of the departed Brits. And somewhere, in moralistic India, that gambling was legal.

No one knew I was coming. I'd taken an overnight express from Rameshwaram and joined the miniature train at dawn at Coimbatore. Trying to telephone would have meant spending hours in some suffocating post-office booth, but anyway, in Rameshwaram, I had simply forgotten. I gave the address to an autorickshaw driver. He jerked a lever that resembled a handbrake but was the starter handle for his two-stroke engine. We hurtled into tunnels of foliage, climbing Betjeman B-roads with steep views down to the hippodrome at the heart of Ootacamund. The driver jerked us to a halt outside a wooden gate. Half hidden behind a wall of vibrant shrubs was a whitewashed bungalow with a tin roof. Beneath us on a tree-ringed lake, pedalos placidly circled. A bright-faced, barefoot boy in khaki shirt and shorts padded to the gate and lifted a latch. I asked if it was where the Buckleys lived.

I hadn't given my parents a precise date, but they'd been expecting me for weeks. I saw my mother first. She was sitting in a wicker chair on the lawn, surrounded by immaculate flower beds. She wore a pale-blue sundress and a broad-brimmed straw hat, and was reading a newspaper. She looked up—and I saw a shock of pleasure pass across her face. She half folded the newspaper and dropped it beside a tray of tea things. Eyes shining, she smiled tolerantly. I kissed her. "Turning up out of the blue as usual," she said, with a reproachful grin. I grinned back sheepishly, aware that I was disorganized and inconvenient, and too proud to admit it. She looked at her watch. "Have you had lunch?" she asked.

"Not exactly. A lot of people gave me portions of picnic on the train."

"You came up by train? We haven't tried it yet. Is it as beautiful as they say?"

"It's wonderful. Very, very slow."

"Shivaraj—" She introduced me to the boy standing expectantly beside us. He looked fifteen, but was apparently nineteen, the shorts and bare feet undermining his attempt to make himself older with a moustache. I was struck again by the expression on his neat, hand-some face, an openness, his eyes bright under quite heavy eyebrows, his mouth instinctively parted in a smile. "Shivaraj, would you bring out some sandwiches, please?"

"Cheese and tomato, Ma?"

She nodded. "And another pot of tea?"

"Yes, Ma." He turned smartly on his heels.

We sat on the wicker chairs and I talked about Sri Lanka. Shivaraj brought tea and a plate of sandwiches cut with geometric precision. My mother told me how she and my father were adapting to India. I felt exhausted, and infinitely relaxed. The weeks of novelty and uncertainty were over and, safe in my parents' home, I could let go. It was a long, pleasantly warm day—as almost every eternal summer Ooty day would be. At dusk, crimson clouds the size of ships steamed towards us, ran us down, soaked us in mist. The clouds turned purple, then battleship-grey and finally they left us in their wake. The peep of a car horn sent Shivaraj scampering to open the gates and a Hindustan Ambassador pulled into the drive. My father appeared, Leonard Samuel Buckley, a massive, aloof, Edwardian figure. He greeted me without hugs, with a stern reminder that I'd arrived without warning. I agreed that I had. "Hmmph," he said.

An immunologist, an expert in the many global strains of foot-and-mouth disease, he'd been seconded by the British government to a project called Operation Flood. It was part of the "White Revolution", a scheme to flood India with sterile, high-cream milk. Shops usually sold milk from large pans on the counter—somebody lifted a muslin fly cloth, put in a ladle and poured the milk into your can, or a plastic bag, which they sealed for you with a knot. The rural masses often got their milk unsterilized, watered down and infected with a rich variety of human and animal bugs—warm milk is a wonderful medium for the culture of bacteria. The White Revolution was going to change all that. UHT Tetrapac technology was en route from Sweden, but they needed better milk. The boffins believed that in the Nilgiris they could eliminate foot-and-mouth disease—the small number of roads into the hills made an infection barrier easy to erect. The cattle inside it could be inoculated and an "island" free of infection be created—in theory. My father was in charge of the labs.

I had been planning to come to India after university. That my parents should also happen to be planted in the country for a couple of years was a massive coincidence. If they hadn't been posted to the deep south, I certainly wouldn't have begun my journey in Sri Lanka. Indeed, I probably wouldn't have visited the Indian south on that first trip. Their presence was going to give me the chance to get to know India, and Indians, far more deeply than would otherwise have been the case. The next phase of my Indian odyssey would be the pampered life of the expat.

Showered and refreshed, Len Buckley reappeared. I was bursting with news, but he sat down with a cup of tea and the newspaper; he was a man of rigour and routine. Savoury smells drifted from the kitchen where Mary, the cook, was preparing our evening meal. Sivaraj laid the table. As we ate (lamb curry in a coconut sauce, which my parents enjoyed, though my mother was, she told me, slowly teaching Mary English cooking), I poured out more of my Sri Lankan experiences. My father frowned a lot, though his air of disapproval was no doubt partly a mask for parental anxiety. Of his own activities he said precisely nothing. As usual. After supper there was coffee in the conservatory. At a certain moment my father lifted the dust sheet from a broadcasting-quality short-wave radio to which he'd attached a fifty-foot copper aerial—when he did technology, he did it *right*—and "Lili Bolero" thrummed out, announcing the World Service news. The doors to the garden were open and powerful scents flooded the veranda. Below us, lamps made a necklace around the lake. Night birds called. The sky above Ooty was jet-back and star-studded.

MY TOUR BEGAN with that small portion of the lake you could drive around. "There was an Englishman called John Sullivan, hiking up here in the 1820s," my mother said.

"Probably hunting tigers," I said.

"Well, the Company—the East India Company—was busy surveying for land. Tea turned out to be the big success here."

"Like Ceylon."

"Oh, it was very much bigger in Ceylon, wasn't it? Anyway, the land here belonged to tribal people called Todas. Ootacamund means 'stone village', apparently—it's what they called the first British-built house, because the Todas made their houses of woven reeds. They still live in the hills here and there's one of their houses in the botanical garden—it's very elaborate. I'll take you to see it. So, this John Sullivan was the Collector down in Coimbatore."

"The what?"

She laughed. "The district heads were called Collectors."

"Of tributes?"

"Of taxes, I suppose. Anyway, they weren't *distributing* money, that's for sure." I grinned. My mum had a social conscience. "And according to the books, this Sullivan paid the Todas one rupee an acre for the land he took."

She asked Shivaraj, who asked the rickshaw driver, to stop at the rather shabby boathouse. Newly-weds, shy to the point of paralysis, were hiring pedalos, saried and bejewelled brides stepping into them with put-on girlish timidity, allowing Western-clad husbands to help them with protective masculine competence.

"The other day", my mother said, "I actually saw them pulling a body from the lake."

Ooty was a popular honeymoon spot. But caste and arranged marriage produced a steady supply of star-crossed lovers, and Ooty, where Bollywood shot its dance numbers and the rich lost fortunes on the gee-gees, was also where the heartbroken came to end their lives, individually and sometimes, more tragically, in suicide pacts.

Close to the lake was the bus stand and above it the station, where, amidst shunting noises, clouds of white vapour billowed into the air. Beyond, Mum told me, was the golf course where my golf virgin father was attempting, with the help of a pro, to develop a swing. Opposite the bus stand was the racecourse, the heart of colonial Ooty and the source of its income during that colonial overhang, the Summer Season. Driving around its perimeter we saw grooms exercising horses. We might have been at Epsom. But not quite.

Twice a week my mother went "marketing" with Shivaraj, and that was the serious purpose of this morning's expedition—with a hungry son around, she wanted to stock up. We began at Chellaram's department store, the only place in Ooty to sell such Anglo-exotica as butter and cheese, chocolate and mushrooms. We climbed from the shabby street into a long, gloomy room, with fans slowly turning on the ceiling. It was built, like many buildings on

Ooty's steep slopes, on stilts, and through wide gaps in the floor-boards you could see the daylight. The establishment was devoid of customers and bizarrely overstaffed. Assistants straightened their backs and beamed obsequious smiles of welcome. Shivaraj made straight for the cold meats counter, followed by Mum, as I ran my eyes over the dispiriting array of goods. In the thirties these glass cases would have bulged with the high-quality manufactures of Birmingham and Derby, Sheffield and the Lancashire mills—brass hurricane lamps, fountain pens, hairbrushes, table linen, canteens of cutlery. Now, mouldy velvet trays held mud-brown earthenware, and knives and forks of appalling cheapness. There were Hong Kong floral thermos jugs and melamine plates—the only imported goods in the place. All over the shop floor assistants were wiping, wiping, removing a day's patina of dust from goods that looked as if they'd been awaiting a buyer for a decade.

Our next stop was a warren of unroofed alleyways divided into zones of spices, vegetables, fruit and meat. The mutton butchers, all Muslims, had their own alley, where men with henna-stained beards stood behind chopping blocks that were metre-high hunks of tree trunk. The beef sellers, Christians, were in a *covered* building, their shame hidden from the public gaze—for while many Hindus ate meat, they had a horror of eating cow.

Shivaraj was put into the three-wheeler, his arms protectively round bulging bags of bananas and beef. Mum and I walked to the top of the town, with its tin-roofed houses and occasional threads of woodsmoke, to where the colonials had planted a squat Gothic church. Inside it, plaques memorialized colonials who died in hunting accidents or giving birth to their twelfth child. Around the church was the administrative heart of Ooty, the Collector's office, Higginbotham's stationers and bookshop, Spencer's store (a lesser Chelleram's with a dusty shelf of colonial "antiques"), the post office and the Nilgiris Library, where my mother was headed. Every day of her life she read for several hours—books were another oxygen.

If all of Ooty was a Victorian stage set, this was its core, a functioning private library that had not changed in any particular since the 1930s. Immense windows illuminated old copies of the *National Geographic*, bleaching them pale turquoise. The previous day's *Times of India*, posted from Bombay, sat primly folded, as yet unopened. In the Fiction Room ranks of forgotten pre-war novels slowly surrendered to the worm, but there was also a large display of racy recent paperbacks. There were the *Encyclopaedias Britannica*, imposing rows of leather-bound *Punch*, *Illustrated London News* and many Victorian volumes on the flora and fauna of the Nilgiris. On the walls hung a series of naïve hand-tinted engravings, made when Ooty was a handful of colonial dwellings dotted on the hillsides round the lake.

I was much less attracted to another vestige of the Raj—the Ooty Club. My parents, who'd spent their first weeks in Ooty at the Club, suggested we go there for Sunday lunch. It stood in its own grounds, approached by a drive that wound through trees past a reedy pond. The entrance was a Greek temple, sandwiched absurdly between two clapboard wings like seaside chalets. Antlers lined panelled walls with framed hunting scenes and a portrait of Queen Victoria. The dining room had table linen as thick as towelling and the china plates, etched with the crest of the Club, were huge and heavy, and had each seen many thousands of servings of meat and potatoes. There were few other diners; indeed, the Club was deserted most of the year, a mothballed symbol of anachronistic privilege. My father took me into the billiard room where a sign claimed that snooker had been invented there when Sir Neville Chamberlain had shouted "Snooker!"—apparently the word for a junior cadet at the Officers Academy at Woolwich. What larks.

"Snooty Ooty" was somewhere ageing colonials too diehard (or hard up) to go home "stayed on". There were still a few of them left alive, including one elderly lady who lived at the Club but was rarely glimpsed. It must have been an alienating, shabby-genteel existence, watching England slough off its imperial past with undignified haste as India seemed to spiral downwards, via decaying infrastructures and civil corruption, into third worldom. But Snooty Ooty still had its "society", an assortment of snobbish Indians who kept holiday homes there, Anglophile Indian Christians like the staff of Ooty's well-regarded boarding schools, and a few expatriates. My dad, a Freemason, received a fraternal welcome from the lodges of Tamil Nadu. As for Mum, with Ooty's stock of memsahibs dead or moribund, there was a grave shortage of ladies to give their time to charitable activities. She was promptly embraced by the Horticultural Society and the Lady Willingdon Homes for Orphaned Girls, roles for which a long secretaryship in the Women's Institute had prepared her well.

I settled into Ooty life. After breakfast my father would set off with his chauffeur Mano. Just once I persuaded him to take me to the labs, a jagged, modernistic complex a few kilometres outside town. Len Buckley was an imposing man, but what impressed itself on people were his rigour and egalitarianism. His closest colleagues had become friends and were regular visitors, as was the man in overall charge of the Ooty labs, Dr Rao. He was an avuncular figure with a mischievous eye, who took to me as much as I took to him. He'd been brought to Ooty from dusty Hyderabad and installed with his wife—who hated the cold—in one of the colonial bungalows down in town. The place was falling apart—*but they didn't seem to notice.* Their cook inhabited the sooty cave of a kitchen, the cleaners ignored the lofty corners of rooms inhabited by spiders and termites, there were crazy pieces of warped furniture, broken windowpanes and ill-fitting doors. The Raos, warm and human, had a different relationship with *things.* They didn't seem to care about surfaces—their hearts were engaged elsewhere. The surfaces of objects, the smooth functionality of the industrial artefact, did not exist for them. Dr Rao was a trained scientist, a materialist, a man who dealt with objective, microscopic realities. But those realities had not made him like us.

I was keen to see the Nilgiris and I'd noticed that the project vets had been provided with motorbikes for their field trips. My father rejected my pleas that I might be able to accompany someone on a trip, but when I mentioned it to Dr Rao he instantly arranged for me to join Dr Christopher, who was, as his name suggests, a Christian. On the back of his 250 Yezdi (the product of a ghastly India–Eastern bloc collaboration) I bumped down the dirt tracks that coiled through the lush, moist Nilgiris Hills. The farmers hadn't been easy to persuade of the virtues of vaccination, but milk yields already were sharply up, and there was an atmosphere of revivalist enthusiasm. Christopher even let me make myself useful. Holding needles in cows' necks and trying to direct the hot squirting blood into Christopher's sample bottles turned out to be fun.

After my father left for work in the morning, Mary and Sivaraj would throw open the windows, air bedclothes and sweep. Milk was boiled to preserve it and to make yoghurt, vegetables were chopped, meat was beaten. (The kitchen consisted of black marble slabs on whitewashed brick benches. The cooker was a two-burner stove. There was a fridge, an enormous green "Godrej"; and a water filter; that was the extent of the labour-saving devices.) My mother would supervise until eleven o'clock when coffee, Nilgiris-grown, was brewed and she retreated to the garden with a copy of south India's stern English-language paper, *The Hindu*. I would join her.

The Hindu became my first guide to the greater India beyond our sequestered hills. Its editors were deeply suspicious of all things North Indian. The great state of Tamil Nadu and the South in general apparently considered itself more traditional, more respectful of women—in short, more *Hindu*—than the north, and better at English, too: it hadn't forgotten or forgiven the attempts by "the Centre" (the New Delhi government) during the 1950s to impose Hindi as the national language. Southerners, with their half-dozen languages of wholly different roots and syntax, had violently resisted the move (a few protestors had even immolated themselves, something of a tradition in the south). Legal structures to protect the southern languages were put in place, and a flourishing southern cinema industry meant that only the biggest Bollywood blockbusters broke into the south. My dad's driver Mano took me to the cinema one night, a Christian Tamil extravaganza at the climax of which the infant Jesus appeared miraculously—at the head of a heavenly staircase surrounded by clouds of dry ice—to save the victim of a car crash. Baby Jesus was almost indistinguishable from the butter-licking baby Krishna so beloved of Hindus. So this was how India's competing cultures had always copied, appropriated, overlapped.

The Hindu's smudged, close-packed columns advertised cinema houses, matrimonials, tuitions and, reflecting Tamil Nadu's agricultural *raison d'être*, a great variety of generators and pump sets. Advertising was of the 1950s variety in which products did not propose lifestyle enhancements but proclaimed their durability. Such claims were usually false.

Many products of British companies that had operated in India into the 1950s were still being made, using the same worn-out dies and the same brown or green hammerite paints. It was a time warp. My father's brand-new Hindustan Ambassador was a 1960s Morris Oxford, still in production (it still is). It was unreliable, as were the Enfield Bullet motorbikes some of the vets used. Precisely three models of camera could be purchased in India then, all of them bulky, bakelite and black. Colour processing had just arrived, but portrait photography was still in black and white, retouched into blue-orange half-life at the photographic lab. Of the multinational companies that retained an Indian presence, Phillips produced industrial valves and domestic radios the size of televisions, Remington made cast-iron typewriters. Coca-Cola had been kicked out and the battle for brand loyalty, fought against Pepsi Cola across the globe, was slugged out in India by the local brands Campa-Cola and Thumbs-Up.

Jawaharlal Nehru, the fastidious upper-class Anglophile who fathered Indira Gandhi and gave his name to the collarless jacket, famously and fatuously described vast hydroelectric dam projects as "temples of progress". Photographs showed these temples under construction, with gigantic webs of scaffolding made from lashed bamboo poles and thousands of labourers crawling over them like flies, carrying wet cement in baskets on their heads. Socialist India's progress was more rhetorical than actual. Its undeniable achievement had been to keep its democracy on the tracks. But its Soviet-style command economy was a basket case.

There was pathos in all this. Hinduism was depicted by the British as preaching fatalism, quietism. In modern India accepting one's lot meant accepting a world where no man-made device would function as it had been designed to do. And yet, I found I was starting to value the fact that in a non-consumer society, objects had inherent values, were *not* disposable. A bicycle was beyond the reach of half the citizens of Ooty, and those lucky enough to possess them could often be seen oiling and polishing them. There were a number of brands, like Hero, Hercules and Atlas, but they all looked exactly the same— big, black, heavy machines that hadn't changed since the 1930s; there were no racers, there were no coloured bikes, or if there were, they existed only for the urban rich. Cars were never junked, but end-lessly rebuilt and somehow kept on the road. The West's remorseless appetite for novelty was terrible for the environment, but in Ooty, our sturdy English shampoo bottles, once empty, were gratefully taken home by Mary.

We were free of the pressures of the consumer society. There was no central heating; most people cooked on wood-burning stoves (the trees of Ooty, constantly plundered for fuel wood, resembled half-plucked chickens). Men wore worn tailored suits and wrapped scarves round their heads to keep the night-time chill at bay. Women wore sari-and-cardigan. The citizens of Ooty weren't governed by *things*. Any surplus resources were concentrated into certain small symbols of display, for women some gold, for men a hand-winding Indian wristwatch. Hinduism taught that things were *maya*—illusion—but that rarefied concept did not, I suspected, loom large in the lives of most Hindus. They might not have possessed much, but that didn't mean they lived in a world of metaphysics—the things that preoccupied them were lentils, rice, antibiotics, school books, dowries.

And yet: that slowness and fatalism went hand in hand with deeply suppressed resentments: mobs could spark into violence at the slightest provocation, as my parents had experienced when Mano accidentally struck a man in a village they passed through and the locals had tried to drag him from the car. The roads were a public forum where people could express themselves freely, and they were utterly undisciplined. Then there were those movies—so often revenge dramas in which a young man, denied liberty or property or opportunity by some corrupt middle-aged landowner, wreaked his revenge in an orgy of shooting or slashing. In October, the Festival of Dasara was joyously celebrated in Ooty. We learned that in the nearby city of Mysore, Dasara traditionally had primacy in the annual calendar over all the other Hindu festivals—it was the local equivalent of Christmas. What Dasara actually marked was the defeat by Rama of the evil Ravan. The *Ramayana* again, scored deeply into Indian consciousness. Great "cars", floats bearing statues of guards, were dragged through the streets by hand. I saw people racing barefoot across red coals, shoving knitting needles through their flesh and literally whipping themselves into a trance. As I took a photograph of one of these men while he lashed himself, his sweat splattered me. Here was religion as a medium that allowed you to express the inexpressible, the deepest, darkest human emotions, as a violent and garish ritual.

ॐ

RAMA DROVE THROUGH streets of cheering people. When they caught sight of the gold-leafed carriage they joined their palms respectfully, but their faces revealed their elation. He was still wearing the finest ceremonial robes, his face and limbs were smeared with rarest, sweet-smelling sandal paste the colour of boar's blood. As Rama entered his apartments, his attendants' faces lit up. He went directly to his private chambers.

Sita had been with her own attendants, preparing her clothes for the coronation. When she went to see Rama, she saw that his face was pale and beaded with sweat, and she felt her stomach turn.

Rama took her hands in his. "My darling, you are going to have to be very strong. I don't have to explain *dharma* to you—it's ruled both of us all our lives. If *I* disobey, the people feel *they* can disobey—the next thing will be chaos."

Sita could feel panic rising in her breast. "What has your father told you to do?"

"He's banished me—to the forest—to live as a hermit. For fourteen years."

Sita gasped. "But you're going to be *crowned*! What . . . *Why?*"

"I'm a threat to Bharat. In the eyes of his mother."

"*What?*"

"It's inexplicable, Sita. We had the procession to the palace, the whole city cheering, people everywhere I looked, *feverish*. I met Father and Kaikeyi alone. She has power over him, it dates back to two boons he granted her, public obligations."

"What did she say?"

"That Bharat has to be crowned in my place. She thinks that if I'm crowned, I'll imprison her son."

"But what about your father?"

"He looked as though she'd put the final nail in his coffin. He'd made vows before God. Now he's publicly renewed them."

"When do we leave?" asked Sita.

"*We* don't. You have to stay here, you have to represent me, and look after my mother—my father, too, if this humiliation doesn't kill him. I'm leaving at dawn. For God's sake, Sita, promise me you'll be careful around Kaikeyi and Bharat."

"I'm coming with you."

Rama smiled. "You can't. There is no choice. You have to stay."

Sita was a soft-spoken woman, temperamentally almost incapable of raising her voice. But now a raw fury flared inside her. "I'm not the wife of my mother-in-law, my father-in-law, my parents, or anyone else. When you leave, I'm leaving *with* you!" She threw herself against him and began to beat his chest with her fists. "If you make me stay here, I'll kill myself. I'll throw myself into a cremation pyre."

Rama held her tight and, suddenly, her sobs diminished. "I would reject heaven itself if it made you unhappy, darling, you know that." Rama spoke softly. "Our lives will be utterly different in the forest. No marble palace, no servants . . .

"Go and instruct your attendants—you have to give away everything you own. We leave this place at dawn, as beggars. Armed beggars. I'm taking my weapons."

Next, Rama went to see his blood brother, the hot-headed Lakshman. "Why d'you think Father made Kaikeyi these ridiculous promises?" Lakshman asked, furiously. "She nursed him back to health? She did something the doctors couldn't? She was sixteen and he was fifty-six. I believe the healing process is known as lust."

"Lakshman, it's taken her twenty years, but she's made her move. She's impulsive and stupid. She has the makings of an excellent tyrant."

"But she won't be Queen, she'll be the mother of the King. And Bharat's your youngest brother! He worships you! He's a decent kid. Does he even know what's happened yet?"

"No, but by the time he does hear, I have to be several days from the city."

"*We* do," said Lakshman.

Rama could take no possessions, no retinue. But his wife, his own brother—that was allowed. Lakshman was as yet unmarried.

"I accept your offer, brother. We're not allowed to bring any possessions, but I want you to get our weapons together, Lakshman. The two best bows, arrows, coats of mail."

By dawn, the citizens of the town had gathered on their verandas and packed the streets to watch a spectacle very different from what they'd anticipated. "Look at that," said a voice in the crowd, "the last time I saw Prince Rama he had four divisions behind that chariot."

"Look at Princess Sita!" a woman hissed at her young daughter. Sita habitually moved through the streets in a covered palanquin. "We used to say that even the birds couldn't get a glimpse of her. Now she's getting eyeballed by every urchin."

The murmurs of dissent became louder.

"What's Dasharatha playing at?"

"Must've gone gaga!"

When Rama reached the palace, the King gabbled about how he'd been enchanted by Kaikeyi, trapped. He begged Rama to arrest him, to take over as King. "Stay in Ayodhya, son! I'll give you anything you want!"

"Father," Rama said mildly, "your first order, made before the Gods, cannot be revoked."

Kaikeyi appeared. Rama saw her expression and thought, "Why does this woman hate us?" But Kaikeyi hated no one: she had tasted victory, she was drunk on power and nothing was going to stop her now.

A sort of wailing started among the courtiers as the exiles made their way back across the audience chamber. It had been decided that they'd take a chariot as far as the hills, to put some distance between themselves and the town. As the little entourage left the palace, the King stumbled, wailing, down the steps. "Let me see my *son*, my darling *son*!" The packed crowd would not let the chariot move. Rama was terrified to look back at his mother's face. She, weeping, tried to run to the chariot. Rama snapped at his charioteer to whip the horses forward. As the horses finally broke into a trot, the King fell on his knees. When Kaikeyi grasped his arm and tried to help him up he screeched at her not to touch him, never to come near him again.

Beyond the city limits the exiles were greeted with noisy cheers. The people assumed there'd been a palace coup and were making it clear whom *they* supported. Lakshman grinned from ear to ear. "It's you they want, Rama."

Rama turned on him angrily. "When are you going to understand, Lakshman? There can be no mutinies, no jungle insurgencies. We must do *nothing* to encourage the belief that we're going to resist. If Kaikeyi gets a hint of that, anyone close to us will be finished! Kaikeyi's a vindictive little girl. Provoke her and she'll bring down a tyranny on Ayodhya."

AFTER SEVERAL LAZY weeks in Ooty's time machine, I repacked my rucksack. I spent my first night away in Bangalore. The drive down to the plains took nine hours and I arrived at my hotel after midnight. The place had been imposed on me by the twinkling Dr Rao, who'd arranged a lift in a field jeep going that way. He'd been adamant that only a pricey establishment would be good enough for his colleague's son. That might have been true of his own son, but it showed how different our worlds were—the picaresque adventures of a young Westerner just out of college was something no decent Indian lad would ever be allowed to experience.

The driver stood behind me in the hotel reception looking exhausted. I told him to leave. I hadn't reserved, as it would have taken hours to get through on the phone from Ooty. Now I learned that the sprawling, multi-storeyed hotel had no free rooms. Two neat young men in wine-red blazers told me helpfully that there were several times of year when it was hard to find a room in Bangalore— and this was one of them. The jeep had disappeared. The hotel was on the edge of town and beyond its floodlit gates was darkness.

"You *must* have a room!"

"No, sir. Sorry, sir."

"A place this size? *Nothing* left?"

"No, sir. Very very sorry, sir." Their foreheads puckered to show how sorry they truly were.

"Anything will do. I'll sleep in a cupboard!"

The receptionists were kind young men, and anxious that they might have before them the son of a VIP. After an earnest conclave they conceded doubtfully, "We do have just one room, sir. But . . . you wouldn't like it, sir."

"You *have* a room . . . But you don't want me to have it, because I wouldn't like it?"

"Correct, sir."

"Does it have a bed?"

"Of course, sir."

"I like it."

After thirty more minutes of form-filling and unaccountable waiting, I was led by back staircase to the room. It was smaller, with more squashed mosquitoes on the walls, than you generally expect in a posh establishment, but I was too tired to care.

I woke at three, feeling feverish. I groped for the light switch, and almost flew off the bed in horror. The sheets were covered in blood—*my* blood—hundreds of red dots of astonishing uniformity. An entire town of bedbugs had dined on me.

I dragged the bed from the wall and heaved off the filthy mattress. The wooden head and toe boards were probably infested too. Furiously, noisily, I dismantled the bed. Then I climbed on the metal frame, wrapped myself in the polka-dot sheets and was instantly unconscious.

At 7 a.m., the blazered boys were still on their shift. I raged; they were sullen. "Sir, we *told* you you wouldn't like the room."

"You mean you *knew* the bed was infested?"

"Sir, it is a *staff* bed, sir, not for guests." A tone of offended moral superiority. They'd had the goodness to help out the spoilt Western kid, and all he could do was whinge.

I became angrier. "So your magnificent hotel has a room with a bed you *know*'s infested with bed lice?

"It is staff quarters, sir," they told me stiffly. "Because of your situation, exception was made, sir."

"*Which* staff use it?"

They exchanged a sheepish look. "Cleaning shift, sir."

Cleaners, *dalits*, untouchables—the higher-caste white-collar staff wouldn't have used the room, that was certain. But a foreigner, outside the rigours of the caste system—you could stick him on an untouchable's mattress. Probably they'd turfed some unfortunate cleaner out of bed to make way for me. That would explain the delay, the back staircase.

"So it's OK for cleaners to get bitten to pieces, is it? Sleep in filth? You don't bother to disinfest the mattress, because *they don't count*?" I was yelling now. Hatred entered the receptionists' eyes.

I would come to see that in many ways this was a typical Indian situation. There's a known problem—in this case infestation—but some kind of inertia prevents it from being addressed. And the spectre of caste always hovers close by.

I took an auto to the station. I wanted to travel to Delhi, but there were no tickets left—no reserved ones, anyway. The ticket clerks told me I could travel, if I was desperate enough, Second Class

Unreserved. My ticket, an inch-long plectrum of pink cardboard, was issued.

Unreserved train travel was cheap. It gave India's impoverished millions the opportunity to navigate their subcontinent. I'd arrived in Bangalore a VIP and slept in the bed of an untouchable. Now I found myself in a railway compartment designed to seat eight—but there were seventeen of us in the compartment. Between the bench seats, where people were supposed to put their legs, were immense jute bundles with cardboard suitcases piled on top. People squatted on the bunks and luggage racks.

I made the two-night journey to New Delhi sitting cross-legged on a luggage rack, my stooped head brushing the curved compartment roof. A caged fan churned stale air inches from my face. I shared the rack with another man—we slept with our heads at opposite ends. He had no shoes. His feet were splayed, blackened, shaggy with split flesh the thickness of shoe leather. They smelt of something worse than sweat. It was enough to give many a high-caste Hindu nightmares for life—Hindus have a particular horror of the caste pollutions associated with feet and shoes. Yet what I most remember about my travelling companion was his passivity, his acceptance of absolute poverty. He was at the bottom of a society he barely understood. All I had to put up with was the sensation in the night of his toes brushing the hair on the back of my head.

For three days I barely moved—or ate or drank. One visit to the public toilet at the end of the corridor persuaded me not to go again. The train was an artery through which flowed the gaunt and the obese, the ragged, the zany and the deformed. The masters of ceremonies were the ticket collectors, sharp-eyed, straight-backed men who somehow conducted this lurid human performance. Improbably—it was an astonishing symbol of formality, like the English colonialists who wore dinner jackets in the tropics—they were dressed in black blazers, which must somehow have held in their bodies' heat, for I never saw one of them sweat. At frequent halts there entrained or detrained an army of vendors chanting "Chai-caffee-col-dlinks!", newspaper vendors, fruit vendors, shoe-shine boys and tinkers selling padlocks-and-chains, combs, talcum powder and cheap perfume. The deformed, with the greatest horrors of their deformity artfully exposed (Indians are prudish but one particularly successful beggar was a boy who kept one taut and shiny testicle exposed—it was bigger than a football). Otherwise healthy young children thrust stumps in my face—my mother had already told me that professional beggars mutilated their children to provide a source of income.

There was one gaunt, sad-faced woman in a green nylon sari who held a sleeping baby in her arms and sang. The poignant tune never left me and later I tried humming it to friends, but could never discover what it was. After two years I was sitting in an autorickshaw in Delhi, when that tune came out of his stereo. Excitedly, I grabbed the driver's arm. It was a song from an old movie, he told me, called *Bobby*: "*Meh Shaayar Toh Nahee*": "I'm Not a Poet".

> *Meh shaayar toh nahee,*
> *Magar ayeh hasee—*
> *Jab seh dekha, tujhko, mujhko,*
> *Shaayari aa gayi . . .*

> I am not a poet,
> But Oh, beautiful one—
> From the moment I saw you,
> I *became* a poet . . .

CHAPTER 7

Spiritual Tourist

I HAD NO plans, although a typical pattern would emerge—smoke dope with a pot-bellied *swami*, sleep with an Australian backpacker; visit the cremation pyres at Varanasi and gawp at sizzling flesh the way a tourist in Paris gawps at the Mona Lisa.

I went as far north as Lahore in Pakistan, where I reeled at the sight of Muslim women clad in an extreme form of *burkha*, engaging with the world through a square grid sewn into the front of a hood. My first instinct was that they were lepers, or that they were being punished. Punished because men wanted to look at them.

I avoided the tourist hot spots—Goa, Rajasthan, the Taj Mahal. I'd boned up on my Indian history—civilization evolved from an Aryan invasion, Hinduism and Buddhism born, the two great empires of Ashoka and Gupta, Alexander arrives in the north, Christianity invades the south, the Muslims invade, the British invade and finally Gandhi, non-violently, kicks them out. But the India I wanted to meet was spiritual. Ideally, it would conclude with meeting God in the Himalayas.

Spirituality, that overused word. I was one of those vague seekers who'd been pitching up in India since the sixties, demanding enlightenment. I was about to learn that India, in many ways, *is* spirit. It doesn't live at a particular address, it needn't be exactly sought. Open yourself up, *and it finds you*. The trouble was that opening myself up was the hardest thing to do. I was a member of one of the world's most emotionally unopen peoples. I wasn't promising spiritual material. But I was a believer . . .

Aggressive rationalists should stop reading now. My first sensations of otherness, of being myself and yet not wholly *of* myself, began in my teens. Teenagers are narcissistic; one day I was staring at my hand, its pale surface, the blue suggestions of blood vessels, the sparse hairs. And suddenly, with a sort of ripple, I felt I wasn't me, but something else *observing* me. It was a sensation of giddiness, almost euphoria. It quickly passed. But a residue remained and it suggested to me there was some other reality, akin, perhaps, to the mad, visionary impulses of William Blake, whom we'd been taught at school, and taught nothing. There was little in the culture around me to suggest that the mystical transports of a Blake or Clare were legitimate or in any way worthwhile. But I felt otherwise.

At university I'd begun to read, for myself, the novels of Aldous Huxley. In the 1920s they had been the quintessence of everything it meant to be young, to reject everything that was old, to *rebel*. Huxley was the *enfant terrible*—and so much cleverer than his enemies. Huxley's novels defined the way a generation thought. Sixty years later his heady world of impossible wit and erudition filled my mind, in contrast to the dull campus reality around me.

It was Huxley's fourth novel, *Those Barren Leaves*, that (as they say on book jackets) changed my life. The hero, Francis Chelifer, is staring at his hand when a kind of metaphysical revelation envelops him. We read novels in the hope of encountering ourselves. I had encountered myself, and I had found a guru. I began to read about how Huxley was punished for his interest in mysticism. The voice of the post-WWI generation left London for California in the late thirties and was attacked for staying away from wartime Britain out of funk (although, nine-tenths blind since a childhood illness, he wouldn't have been much use with a Lee Enfield). He spent the war in the Mojave Desert and in that arid, perfect light—in which he felt he could *see* again—he found his *inner* vision improving. The London intelligentsia never forgave their fallen hero for losing faith with rationality. He began to write about consciousness and became the midwife of the LSD generation, which definitively marred his reputation. But above all, he discovered in Vedanta—the mystical writings of Hinduism—what seemed to him a perennial wisdom, the key to comprehending the human condition in any age.

I tried reading Huxley on Vedanta, but the concepts were too alien. At university we were reading aesthetes like Rimbaud, Baudelaire and Proust, who strained towards sublimity for art's sake.

I envied them and tried to emulate them, but I suspected they were missing something. I experienced states of altered consciousness in others. An ex-girlfriend turned up on my doorstep at the start of a nervous breakdown—a fortnight of derangement that nearly dragged me over the edge with her. Her alternately hellish and radiant visions seemed like inadvertent glimpses of a supernatural destination. It was as though, on a cross-country car journey, she had crashed off the road, smashed through bushes and glimpsed some fantastic mountain castle; reversing back onto the highway she continued her journey, but there were no more glimpses, no road signs or indications of any kind that a magical destination was so close—obscured by the obvious landscape.

I met a man called Michael Roth, who'd also suffered a break-down, been subjected to the routine tortures of the mental health system and published a visionary rant called *A Bolt from the Bleeding Sky*. Roth put me onto R. D. Laing, with his claim that the babbling of psychotics could contain meaningful, even beautiful, truths. Somewhere I read that the schizophrenic brain could produce chemicals similar to those produced by the lysergic acid—or LSD—of Huxley and his followers. In a health food shop in Fulham Broadway, in a cardboard box of reduced-price books under a noticeboard fluttering with ads for yoga classes, I found a Californian volume that had been knocking around for a decade, *Getting There Without Drugs*. For millennia, it asserted, people had reached altered states of consciousness without ingesting chemicals. All fine and dandy, but getting there was bloody hard. On the other hand, the Indians had apparently been getting there for millennia. India was clearly the place to go.

"Ram, Ram," said the man at the bookstall.

The Western hippie chick with the pierced nose clapped her hands together and replied, "Ram, Ram." The grinning trader, having elicited the response he wanted, turned to another customer.

"What was that?" I asked.

The girl turned to look at me. "Rama", she said, "is one of the Indian gods."

"I know—I was just wondering if there's a particular reason why he said that to *you?*"

"'Ram, Ram'? No—it's a greeting. It's sort of a way of saying 'hello'. You hear it all over India."

"Oh."

Liz was an Australian, twenty-three, with a pointed nose and thick golden curls. She was a little on the heavy side but unselfconscious about it. She wrapped her solid flesh lightly in diaphanous cotton, and the jewel in her freckled nose was a rare sight among Westerners then, even those on the hippie trail. We were standing at a stall close to the iron bridge that crosses Ganga—the Ganges—in central Rishikesh. It was the first time I'd glimpsed the river that, according to the *Ramayana*, is itself a Goddess—

> Whose waters cleanse and save,
> Roaming at pleasure, fair and free,
> Purging all sinners, to the sea.

At Rishikesh, Ganga is narrow. She has emerged from behind a curtain of ice—a cave at the mouth of a glacier—a place known as Cow's Mouth, or Gaumukh, at 14,000 feet in the Himalayas. (I took a dip there some years later, swimming among lumps of melting ice.) From Gaumukh, Ganga carves her way through deep gorges to the plains.

This is her story: a megalomaniac king, Sagara, aspires to become a God. He decides to carry out a Horse Sacrifice (like the one that opens the *Ramayana*) and Indra, worried by the power this ritual will give Sagara, steals the horse. Sagara sends off his sons (he has 60,000 of them) to track it down. They search the entire planet and find nothing; so they begin to burrow inside the earth. This is hubris. Deep in the earth they encounter another God, Vishnu, and beside him is their stallion, happily cropping grass. The princes rush at the imagined thief—Vishnu—who incinerates them. Sagara now learns that only Ganga, the river that runs through Heaven, would be capable of rehydrating the ashes and returning his sons to flesh. But even if she could be persuaded to descend from Heaven, her supernatural torrent would shatter the earth. At last, the God Shiva is persuaded to break the force of the goddess—in the tangled coils of his dreadlocks. (Shiva is the personal God of more Indians than any other deity, and therefore, of many of its holy men. He's famous for his matted hair and fondness for marijuana—and so are they. Shiva himself is invariably depicted with a jet of water spouting from his locks.) King Sagara never becomes a God; but his sons are returned to humid life and India gets the Ganges—its multiple tributaries the coiled dreadlocks of Shiva. To enter Ganga's waters is to interpenetrate divinity itself.

I told Liz all this. She was impressed. We went off to find a cup of tea.

Rishikesh had no shortage of tea shops, where pilgrims leaned over glasses of sweet milky tea and swapped spiritual gossip. The town had a long history as a stopping-off point for saints and seekers en route to Himalayan holy spots. In recent decades new ashrams had been established by stars of the spiritual circuit, like the Beatles' Maharishi. They represented various strands of Hinduism, different lineages, alternative varieties of yoga, paths that committed themselves to this god or that guru. Large complexes had grown up with temples and pilgrim accommodation, shops, canteens and even printing presses attached. If the town was a spiritual shopping centre, it had excellent service and loss-leading prices. Westerners turned up with the belief that their own spiritual traditions were trashable and no idea where to find an alternative. Anti-establishment at home, they were ready to give great authority to Indian gurus. But you couldn't spend your life wandering around India. The cycle swung back to the West and to the shallow depths of the New Age and self-help.

I couldn't quite trust Rishikesh. Perhaps it was an innate Anglo-Saxon scepticism or the materialistic belief that anything worth having wouldn't be given away. One evening I was drawn by a wave of the hand of a pot-bellied *swami* into a little temple compound somewhere down by the gravel river banks. Oddly enough, for Rishikesh, there were no Westerners around, just a half-dozen of the *swami*'s acolytes passing around a *chilum*, a pipe of hashish. I joined them, exchanged smiles with them, grew as glassy-eyed as they, and woke up the next morning with no sense whatsoever of having penetrated esoteric mysteries. I passed through the gates of ashrams, and felt as confused and alienated as I did by the varieties of cornflakes in a supermarket. Where was the discrimination, which subspecies of religion did you sign up to? And theoretically, it was all One . . .

Liz had already stayed at three ashrams. I found her credulous, too ready to try anything, and I wondered if she was playing with the spiritual thing. (I was convinced, of course, of my own Huxleyan seriousness.) I was under the influence of the Western method that focuses the beam of its analysis ever more narrowly until it identifies the nub, the nugget, the atomic speck of truth at the heart of the matter. Then there were those squabbling Mediterranean monotheisms, all insisting that they alone had the path. As for the ashrams of Rishikesh, they couldn't *all* be right, could they? So who was? But I was using one of my typical delaying tactics—not to see the forest for the trees, and so to defer the investigation.

On the yoga course we jointly signed up for, it was obvious that Liz was way ahead of me. Twenty spiritual aspirants filed into a large room after breakfast; Liz would cosily settle herself on a cushion in the lotus posture, straighten her back, close her eyes and slip into a contented, deep-breathing trance. For me, it was more of a struggle—every adjacent rustle or note of birdsong disturbed me. I didn't want to keep my eyes closed. My mind could conceive of nothing duller than to concentrate on the tedious sensation of air passing in and out of my nostrils. My subconscious tormented me by sending up a steady stream of images of sex or revenge. I grew stiff, my knees ached, my stomach rumbled. The minutes became years. I was not a natural meditator.

I asked Liz what the secret was. "Oh, I dunno—you just kind of give it all up and sink into a kind of place, y'know?"

I didn't know. "But what's the *point* of this place? I mean, where is it—where are you when you're in it? What's it *doing* to you? Is it making you a better person? Is it making you better able to cope with life when you're *not* meditating?"

"No, look, the thing is, this is an ancient path, right, and for like thousands of years they've been teaching that you have to get beyond this play of the mind, all the incessant mind-games—all that stuff isn't real, Martin—and what you're doing when you meditate is you're tuning into kind of like the universe, in a way, and yes I think that it does make you a better person . . ."

I'm being unkind to Liz. She didn't have the answers. But I was asking the wrong kinds of question. Liz was Birgitte's polar opposite, emotional, uncritical, undemanding of the world, deeply at home in her physical substance. She had something of the goddess about her, the earth mother. She smelt of musky Indian unguents, sandal, neem, patchouli, ambergris . . . I found myself picturing her like a Greek goddess, holding out her arms in a gesture that could be both welcoming and somewhat . . . *over*-encompassing, even entrapping. Liz wasn't chthonic, dark, she was Australianly healthful, friendly and practical. Aroused, a switch threw and she became brooding and animal. Making love to Liz was like penetrating some dark subterranean cavern, the wisps of her hair cobwebs that brushed my face, her flesh, her substance, heavy and essential. But fundamentally she was healthy and sane. She was not troubled, tormented, confused. It was an enviable state.

We left Rishikesh together and travelled east, down the Ganges. We were approaching the sites of grand opera in Hinduism. It had its Himalayan hermits meditating against the all-obliterating whiteness of the snows but it also had its spectacle, the epic use of sound and light, the orchestrated human masses. Our first stop was Varanasi, the Indian Jerusalem. Unlike Rishikesh, this wasn't somewhere where people went to *find out*, it was the epicentre for people who *knew*. See Varanasi and die: to expire there was said to achieve instant *moksha*—enlightenment. It was, as a result, a vast twilight community of the faithful, jammed with OAPs and the terminally ill.

The city itself was a dense mediæval maze, narrow, unnavigable, dirty and decayed. The stone walls of collapsing buildings seemed held together by hand-painted name boards and peeling posters. I saw replacement fan-blade shops and hair oil shops, and a man selling coal, weighed out on a set of hanging scales, from a sort of under-shop with a ceiling just four feet from the ground. Electricity poles leaned at angles, propping up crazy tangles of cables, suspending yellowish low-watt bulbs over thoroughfares of narrow shops. Gnarled trees erupted improbably from corners, paste-smeared bepetalled idols squatted in niches, abrupt, narrow passageways led into gold-domed temples. Humans, cows, bicycles and handcarts eddied through alleys that were broken to reveal effluent and a cloudy disinfectant that presumably kept cholera at bay. When people passed through these shopping streets carrying the bodies of their relatives to the funeral *ghats*, the bodies brushed bonily against you. (When I took a boat along the shore, the wooden hull bonked hollowly against what sounded like a large coconut—it was the head of a corpse, sewn into white muslin: those who can't afford to cremate their dead simply slide them into the water.)

The epicentre of the town, its *raison d'être*, reached by alleyways so sinuous you were unlikely to stumble on them accidentally, were those burning *ghats*. Bodies were cremated inside cages of branches and their ashes raked into the river. No one minded onlookers—there were even tourists hovering nearby in rowboats. It was hot, the roaring heat trapped by ancient stone buildings. It was night and the light of the flames danced on the faces of the thin, grim-faced, unsentimental men who sweated profusely as they worked half-naked, tending the flames with their long poles. Their essential task was one of India's lowest-caste activities. There was the noise of human fat sizzling, the smell of barbecued meat. Frail corpses, the muslin-bound empty shells of the very old, were hastily delivered, the flames consumed them, the glowing ashes were raked into Ganga. Perhaps, in some fourth-storey window in a tenement behind us there was the scream of a newborn. The cycle of life: emerge, live, die, burn, dissolve in the river that was a God.

Varanasi was not like Venice, dead and then resuscitated as a tourist spectacle; this, its real life, had carried on undiminished for millennia. The city was alive with a sense of purpose, even urgency. To understand its scale, you had to climb into a boat. For a mile, Ganga was flanked by elaborate stone temples with great flights of steps descending to her water, where thousands of worshippers in various stages of undress waded or tottered in. It was strange to be a tourist floating on the stuff, the deity, in which these pilgrims were immersing themselves. They never looked up at you, were wholly unaware of themselves as spectacle. And you respected the fact that this was an intimate act on their part, which you should politely ignore. Yet it was odd, in prudish India—all those drenched saris—women who on public transport would be twitchily careful not to expose an inch of flesh were here indifferent to the fact that a soaking made them as good as naked. (I had yet to learn the role that the "wet sari" played in Hindi movies and in the erotic imagination of the Indian male.)

In Varanasi I was close, I knew, to Ayodhya, but I didn't go there—Western travellers didn't, and still don't. There are better guides to India these days than the *Lonely Planet*, but that fat, superficial volume, indispensable then to the English-speaking traveller, informed me that Ayodhya was dusty and uninteresting. But I can't blame *Lonely Planet* for my not going. It appealed to me to see the seat of the Prince of Ayodhya, but I was still in the gravitational field of Liz's substantial mass. Our itinerary turned west, towards Allahabad and Bodhgaya, the birthplace of the Buddha. I was pursuing not Buddhism but orgasm—not the ineffable, but the effable.

As I TRAVELLED, I wondered how much of India was woven into the myths of Hinduism. It seemed that every hill and Lake had some spiritual significance, was mentioned in some holy text or other and subsequently patinated with temples and officiating Brahmins and festivals and pilgrims, and an ultimate commercial layer of souvenirs and veneratory paraphernalia. Hinduism *was* India, a self-contained system that explained itself *to* itself, physically and metaphysically. You almost *had* to be brought up in the faith if you wanted to decode its profusion of Gods and symbols, legends and obligations.

My backpack was filling with books on Hinduism. Several dated from colonial times, reissued as pulpy reprints by cunning Indian publishers who tried to pass them off as new works—an illusion that lasted as long as it took you to open a gaudy cover and read,

> Mr Garrett, Director of Public Instruction at Mysore, published in India a few years ago a "Classical Dictionary of India", but it is of that very miscellaneous character, and embraces a good deal of matter relating to the manners and customs of the present time. It has not obtained favour in Europe . . .

That was John Dowson's *Classical Dictionary of Hindu Mythology and Religion*, an excavation so detailed it made me feel I was crossing a continent with super-scale maps showing tumuli and footpaths, but with no idea about cities, trunk roads, railways. There were *so many* Indian Gods, almost always multiple-limbed, frequently blue and sometimes reincarnations of themselves—therefore the same, yet different; they went by alternative names according to region and regional language, had multiple spouses, and their iconography was so similar that it became a sort of visual noise. It also didn't help that half the imagery seemed to be shared interchangeably with two other religions that had swelled and declined at different times, Buddhism and Jainism. It *did* help that each God rode around on a different animal; once you learned to spot a cow, peacock or eagle, life got easier.

The Hindus I encountered enjoyed an effortless mastery of their mythology—an enthusiasm for it, too—learned at their grand-mothers' knees. I had my copy of the *Ramayana* with me. The mere fact that I was struggling with their great, central myth, using it as a sort of primer to Hinduism and the larger culture, gave them an intense and touching pleasure. In truth, I was still only halfway through it, with its painful English translation, but I knew it held a key to Hinduism. It was clearly one of the world's great myths, a book entirely overlooked when I'd been taught about the *Odyssey*, the *Iliad*, *Beowulf*, the Arthurian legends. Yet this subtle and poetic story, produced by Indian civilization when my ancestors were running around in rabbit skins, was infinitely more alive than any of them.

People would answer my questions with a barrage of rapidly enunciated names and stories that often left me feeling more con-fused. Still, if the lurid universe of Hinduism really did make sense to them, it raised the possibility that the larger chaos around us, India itself, made sense—was, in some esoteric way, patterned, orderly. It was easy to sneer at the country's inefficiencies, inequalities and inconsistencies, and I was meeting plenty of Lonely Planeteers who sneered their way across India. But I was steadily falling in love with India—and Indians. It's quite possible to fall in love with someone's eyes, and Indians had large, soft eyes that didn't avoid mine but seemed to open themselves up, expanding and palpating like discreet, sentient organisms. Indians moved slowly, as though the concept of haste was alien. They weren't sprung with tension like *us*, there was a kind of languor, and their limbs looked weighted when they came to rest. They were at ease with themselves, an ease born perhaps of complacency; indeed, a millennial complacency that placed each of them in his caste and community, with all the inequality that implied. But I was starting to feel comfortable with them. I felt they possessed something my own civilization lacked. I sensed something of the erotic tension that had bound the British and the Indians for well over a century.

Somewhere I bought a tatty Penguin of *An Area of Darkness*, V. S. Naipaul's hate letter to India. The Anglo-educated Caribbean of Indian descent had gone there in 1962, aged thirty, to discover his roots. He found filth and chaos, and a degree of cultural disjuncture that deracinated him all over again. To me, Naipaul seemed to have been so thoroughly colonized by *an idea of Anglo-Saxonness* that he recoiled from India—the opposites-attract syndrome didn't work in his case, he merely loathed the place. I'd only been in India for a few months, but his picture seemed to me cold, intellectual and intolerant. He had missed the point.

I picked up an idiot's guide to Hinduism. By scribbling and cross-referencing, I began to get a handle on its bewildering pantheon. There were said to be 330 million deities and daemons (Hinduism liked superlatives). But at the heart there was a Trinity, which any Christian could get his head around. Brahma was the Supreme Being, the Creator, though few temples were dedicated to him and, like the Christian God, he was rarely *seen* in images and iconography. Far more visible was his female vicar, Devi, the Mother Goddess—a sort of moral policewoman who took the terrifying forms of Durga (Goddess Beyond Reach) and Kali (Goddess of Destruction), both possessed of eight arms and tooled up with heavy weaponry.

Brahma had Big-Banged the universe and withdrawn. He left the day-to-day management to his Number Two, Vishnu, Protector of Humanity and Preserver or Maintainer of the Universe. Vishnu's multiple incarnations, or avatars, included our hero Rama, as well as Krishna, the hero of the other great Hindu epic, the *Mahabharata*. (Vishnu's ninth avatar was—according to Hindus—the Buddha.) Vishnu's wife was Laxshmi, whose four hands were said to represent four spiritual qualities, but who was venerated principally as the Goddess of Wealth, invariably represented with gold coins cascading from her palm. She was worshipped with intense enthusiasm.

Third in the Trinity came Shiva, who bracketed creation as simultaneous Destroyer and Creator. He was sometimes represented in what seemed to me the most beautiful and potent icon I'd encountered—as Nataraja, the King of Dance, dancing within a circle, a ring of fire. His magnificent posture implies a control both aesthetic and metaphysic. The ring of fire symbolizes life and death—perpetual metamorphosis, new forms in the play of creation. Crushed under his dancing feet, the gnomish figure of Ignorance writhes. Shiva's wife Parvathi, or Shakti, was also much appreciated by Hindus; her equanimity was a natural balance to his fieriness, rather as in Roman mythology Venus tempered Mars.

Rama's own personal deity was Indra. Pugnacious, amorous and fond of taking hallucinogenic *soma*, Indra had been a great God of early Hinduism. In recent millennia his star had waned somewhat. Last in the big-time pantheon now were Ganesh and Hanuman. Ganesh, the elephant-headed son of Shiva and Parvathi, was the God of Success. Hindus prayed to him at the start of any new venture and invariably had his portrait near the front door of their homes. As for Hanuman, the Monkey God, he was the servant of Rama and an avatar of Shiva. He was the ultimate embodiment of service, of immense force honestly applied to helping others. Like Ganesh, he was universally adored. What this meant in terms of the *Ramayana* was that its twin heroes were actually Vishnu and Shiva, the two big-time Gods of the Hindu pantheon. It was like recasting Arthur and Lancelot, or Robin Hood and Little John, as Jesus and John the Baptist. It was mind-blowing. The living continuity of this pantheon, long after the Zeuses and Apollos and Wodins were junked, seemed miraculous. Within this glorious and baroque show was—according to Huxley—the world's most sustained attempt to grapple with the mysteries of existence. You could argue that metaphysics is present in Christian civilization—but *where*? The Church has spent centuries expunging it! It was hidden in Europe, embarrassing to the Church, condemned by rationalism, inconvenient to capitalism, banned from television and the university curriculum. In India, it was in my face.

THEY REACHED HOLY River Ganga and found a glade of soft grass to spend the night. The water was transparent and clean, there were swans and cranes and fresh-water dolphins.

The next morning Rama sent back the chariot with his driver, Sumantra. A knight in Dasharatha's court, Sumantra was high-born, a man of integrity and a great warrior. The warrior wept and begged to be allowed to stay with the Princes. "You stay with us and Kaikeyi will start killing people," Rama said. "You're probably now the best friend my father has, Sumantra. The King is in shock, so make sure that anything he orders is acted on quickly, and make sure nobody challenges him—that will lead to disaster. But don't underestimate Kaikeyi—I mean the power she has over my father. Listen: I'm giving her the pleasure of seeing her son on the throne. You need to take that message, and this empty chariot, back to Ayodhya."

Hot-blooded Lakshman was in a fury. "A great king makes a ridiculous vow to a courtesan when she's supposedly healing him, which the whole world knew was an excuse to spend four months in bed with her. Our father has abandoned his sons for a whore."

It was very late when Lakshman finally closed his eyes.

It took Rama another two hours to calm Sita enough for her to fall asleep. Then, he took a few handfuls of sap from a *nyagrodha*, or banyan tree, and began to mat his hair, as hermits, in imitation of Lord Shiva, must do. Thus Rama took the first steps along the ascetic's path. Then, he began to cry. He did not sleep.

The next morning they reached the confluence of Ganga and the River Yamuna, where they found another lovely river bank, the water rainbow-hued, embraced by broad, grassy flood plains where waterbirds waded, and beyond, the glossy forest. From here it was a short walk to the hermitage of the great sage Bharadvaja.

GODTOWN, OR ALLAHABAD, where Rama, Sita and Lakshman passed on their way to exile, is a little to the east of Varanasi. We arrived in mid-afternoon and by night time were watching impromptu theatre on an epic scale—thousands of worshippers launching flickering candles on leaf rafts into the Bible-black Ganges, as drums were banged and trumpets tooted. Hinduism, I was realizing, while it touted the notion that all was *maya*—illusion—was nevertheless extraordinarily sensual, accomplished in the manipulation of the earthly senses.

In Varanasi we'd stayed in a cheap, small lodge with inspiring views across the broad Ganges; Liz and I now found ourselves in a particularly squalid guest house in downtown Allahabad. We went for an early breakfast, then to see a fussy white building that looked as though it ought to be the visitors' centre at the Brighton Pavilion. This was the ancestral mansion of Prime Minister Jawaharlal Nehru, father and grandfather of two further PMs, Indira (assassinated 1983) and Rajiv (assassinated 1991). Mahatma Gandhi (no relation), Father of the Nation, had his own room here at the Nehru home. I was fascinated to see the upper-class, bookish, Anglophile lifestyle of the politicians tolerated and almost groomed by the British to be their replacements.

Allahabad is periodically the scene of the *Kumbh Mela*, the largest religious festival on earth, when seventy million people assemble in the course of three weeks at the time of year considered to be most auspicious. Liz and I walked along a broad flood plain where the *mela* is held. There weren't seventy thousand or even seven thousand pilgrims present that morning, but there was a modest bustle on the waterfront. We climbed aboard a crowded boat to be sculled to a point where holy Ganga meets the holy Yamuna and a third, sub-terranean river—the invisible, mystic Saraswat. This is the Triveni Sangam—*Sangama* being the Sanskrit word for confluence, *Triveni* meaning Three Rivers. Ganga's water was said to be browner and the Yamuna's greener (while the Saraswat rises invisibly from the depths), but the mid-morning sun was so bright that squinting hard, willing the waters to be bichromatic, all we got was a pain in our temples. Our on-board *pandits* babbled their way through Sanskrit prayers and instructed their clients to repeat lines, make gestures and throw coconuts and flowers overboard when instructed. Liz had invested in a modest ceremony, complete with a coconut and a pile of petals on a little raft of dried leaves. We were told categorically that a dip at the point of the Sangam would wash away our sins *and free us from the cycle of rebirth*. I wondered how precisely, doctrinally, metaphysically, the advantages of this dip differed from Varanasi's guarantee of *moksha*, or Rameshwaram's identical guarantee to wash away one's sins. The shallows were crowded with bathers, but I had a particular European fear of unveiling my naked body. If I'd believed my sins would be cleansed, of course, and that a swim would guarantee that I wouldn't be reborn as a lower life form, it would have been a different matter. Even Liz, a more committed spiritual tourist, refused the invitation to enter the waters. I think it was a health scruple: for all her rude vigour, her readiness to eat street food, she had concluded that the waters of the holy Ganges were not—in a materialistic sense—pure.

Liz was an unlikely companion for me, and I had enjoyed her company hugely. I realized I was an experiment on her part, an experiment about to fail. She was warm, generous and almost wholly without intellect. It's a problem with people like me that the contents of our minds can seem more real than external reality. Liz seemed to understand herself at the cellular level. We didn't belong together, but I was grateful. Diving into the dark pool of her sexuality gave me the sense that sex was a trance, an enchantment, illusion, *maya*. You looked up at the surface of the water above—that was reality and you knew you were going to break out into it; but for the time being here you were, submersed in this other realm, breathing this other element.

India remains a prudish land (though it's slowly becoming, like Britain, tawdrily *sex-obsessed*). The Victorian British are often blamed for this. In the *Ramayana*, the old King is portrayed as a victim of lust, yet the book is free from *pudeur*—sex is shown as healthy and enjoyable, and the book even has passages almost of bawd. I discovered this recently, not from reading that first copy, which was a sort of school edition that, like most editions on sale today, was bowdlerized, chastened. Valmiki doesn't apologize for depicting Sita as the quintessence of Indian feminine beauty. He relishes her golden skin, her delicate wrists and slender fingers, her fine waist, her full hips, her swollen lips, her breasts like mangos.

Liz and I separated in Allahabad. I have never parted so lightly from a lover, before or since—it was a question of Australian practicality on her part. For all her interest in mysticism and her swathes of cotton gauze, she had an unmisty view of what she wanted. And she didn't want me. In fact, it had been pretty clear that her interest had shifted to an Austrian bloke in Varanasi who'd been a few doors down the corridor from us and had accompanied us to Godtown. I felt an inevitable twinge of jealousy, but deeper down relief and gratitude for her clarity and decisiveness. They carried on, to Khajuraho, where no doubt their lovemaking took inspiration from the many varieties of erotic imagery carved so enigmatically all over the temples.

I headed south.

KAIKEYI WASN'T PRESENT when her husband died. He had been with his first wife, Rama's mother Kausalya, who reproached him bitterly. Even though his spirit was already broken, the old man reacted as though she had stuck a knife in him. "I need to tell you something," he murmured.

And he confessed that, as a young man, hunting in the forest, he had loosed a poisoned arrow into the undergrowth at what he thought was the sound of an elephant. Instead, he had hit a boy of about seventeen. The arrow had sliced through his genitals and pierced the femoral vein in his thigh. Blood spurted like water from a burst pipe.

Nearby, Dasharatha found the boy's parents. They were blind, decrepit, like the two old geese in the palace gardens that no one had the heart to kill. They'd been dependent on their son for everything. The Prince had led the father, blind, tottering, to his son's body, where the old man fell across the corpse. Rocking his son's head on his lap, he whispered, "Who'll I hear reciting the sacred verses in the morning in a voice so pure and sweet it rises straight to heaven? How will I care for your mother? Stay with us longer—a little longer, my darling boy! Don't leave just yet! We will be with you soon! We're ready to come!"

With his son's blood on his lips, the old man turned to Dasharatha.

"He couldn't even see me," the King told his wife. "But he told me I too would lose a son one day. He said I would die grieving. I brought them to the palace, but it made no difference, they did not live long. And I was cursed . . ."

The King died around midnight. He'd been standing at a window, staring blankly across his city. He gave a cry, threw out his arms and gashed his forehead on a table as he fell. Blood collected in two pools in his eyes. He opened his mouth one last time—and cursed Kaikeyi.

But she had already brought a curse upon herself.

Two days later Bharat arrived in Ayodhya, found the city in mourning and learned from his mother the great treasure she had procured him. "You have murdered your husband, and my father, woman! Are you *insane?*" He turned to the courtiers. "Get her out of here! I never want to see this woman again!"

He went through his father's cremation ritual, and on the thirteenth day he wept as he withdrew his father's bones from the ashes at the cremation grounds. He had his mother's plotting servant dragged before him. Manthara screamed like a trapped animal. Bharat had her thrown into a fire. Then he assembled the army and followed Rama south, with half the population of Ayodhya trailing behind.

Lakshman saw the dust of the army when it was still two days away. "He's coming to finish us off, Rama. We have to move deeper into the forest. Or make a stand here. I'll get him with an arrow, I promise you that! Then I'm going after his mother. I'll kill the whole family—"

Rama smiled at his hot-headed brother. As he predicted, Bharat approached them alone and on foot. He threw himself at Rama's feet. "I've brought you your army and your people. I shall never speak to my mother again, Rama. Command your army, King of Ayodhya. Lead us home."

Rama pulled his half-brother to his feet and embraced him. Having listened impassively to the news of Manthara's punishment he said, "I can't come back. If I fail to do our father's bidding, I undo the knots of *dharma* that hold us all in place. You're a good man, Bharat. Fourteen years will pass in the blink of an eye, you'll see. Don't exile your mother, either, but make sure you deny her any influence. Remember *dharma*—it binds us together." Rama smiled kindly. "No, don't cry, Bharat. We'll soon be wondering where the time went. You have to be strong. For our father's sake."

Bharat realized he could never talk Rama into returning. Only then could he bring himself to break the news that Dasharatha was dead.

The sound of Rama's cries was heard by soldiers camped ten arrow-drops away.

Another fragment of the *Ramayanan* puzzle fell into place on my way back to Ooty.

I had not achieved enlightenment; after three months circum-navigating India on a shoestring, I was ready to return to the easy life in Ooty. I'd caught on about the trains: every long-distance express had a compartment set aside for tourists, to ease their occidental suffering.

I found myself sharing an apartment with Bill, a sort of Australian tramp, and his five-year-old daughter. Roaming Thailand in the days before mass tourism and the sex industry, Bill had experienced it as a sexual paradise. He reminisced about the Thais' lack of sexual fear and guilt, claiming that travellers in remote villages would be offered sexual partners for the night—not prostitutes, but the daughters of mine host. It seemed too good to be true. Anyhow, Bill had eventually married a Thai woman and the product of that union was little Annie. After the divorce he'd been given custody and decided to take off. It was hard to know which of Bill's tales to believe, in part because his connection with reality had been permanently impaired by a ton of mind-altering drugs. Nervy, affable, he was one of those people who seemed capable of rational communication, yet whose mind ran at a tangent, you never quite managed to sync-up, to find an identical wavelength. But maybe it was just ex-centricity, in the geometric sense of the word: possessing a different centre.

Bill saw no need to wash. The middle-class Indians in our carriage shunned him in alarm—the more so because he was in charge of an *enfant sauvage*. He dressed Annie in grimy T-shirts and never brushed her hair, and she ran wild, giggling and screaming and scrambling from lap to lap. Nevertheless, Bill was travelling with a heavy bag full of Australian home education school books and the two of them assiduously set time aside to study. Annie was a brilliant creature, bright, curious, always laughing, with a gap-toothed smile as wide as her face.

I'd had my *Ramayana* out, struggling again with the leaden trans-lation. Bill said, "Important Buddhist legend, that. Gets performed in Thailand all the time."

"Are you joking? The *Ramayana*'s a Hindu legend—about as Hindu as you could get."

He grinned and jabbed the wire-framed glasses up his nose. "Ah, but you see, in Thailand it's a *Buddhist* legend."

It was my first inkling that the *Ramayana* was more than a purely

Hindu, Indian phenomenon. In Thailand it has leapt the barrier between religions and installed itself in the very heart of the culture. Bill told me the kings of Thailand even called themselves Rama (he was right, they take it as a supplementary name—the present monarch is Bhumibol Adulyadej, *Rama IX*).

An Indian man sharing our compartment suddenly spoke out passionately. "*Ramayana* is a plot against south Indians," he said. We had no answer to that. He was a stocky, dark-skinned man with thick, curly hair—a typical south Indian. "When Aryan invaders from north came to south India," he carried on, "they found the south Indians, dark-skinned people with our own language, our own religions. They waged war on us, destroyed us. They imposed Brahminism, that was the vehicle for the destruction of our religion, our culture. They imposed their filthy caste system. The *Ramayana* is a colonialist text, it is racist, it calls the south Indians monkeys— southern people who help Rama find his wife, we are *monkeys* in the eyes of the Aryans. These Brahmins, these high-caste Hindus, they're almost all from north India, you know that? There are very few Brahmins in south India. You know what the *Ramayana* is? It's the story of our resistance, and our defeat by traitors within. And who is the hero of *Ramayana*? I will tell you—it is Ravan, the southern king, who fought a guerrilla war and held out against the northerners, the Aryan invaders, for so many years!"

MY LONG-SUFFERING mother found me returning home with Bill and Annie in tow. Mum was of course horrified by the state they were in and got little Annie straight into a bath. Within two days Bill was clean, beard trimmed, his sandalled feet, habitually encrusted with black, revealed as merely tanned, his body now clothed in starched and ironed shirts. As for Annie, my mother washed and trimmed and brushed her hair, and bought her pretty new clothes. The urchin was suddenly gorgeous, her little bare legs flashing under flared cotton skirts, her finger- and pink toenails clean.

My father was less pleased with the uninvited house guests, but for once was overruled by my mother, who, like me, had fallen in love with Annie. "It's worrying to think of him being left in charge of that child," she ruminated, "—she needs a home, school friends, a mother—not being dragged around the world like a nomad and getting nits in her hair." Then she added, "Still, you can't take the cares of the world on your shoulders, can you?"

I WANTED TO stay in India.

Back home, friends were setting their feet on the first rungs of career ladders. I sat in a garden in the town with the most perfect climate in the world and tried to be a novelist. This presented practical as well as creative challenges—it was impossible to find good paper in Ooty, or even reliable ball-pens. I bought hard-bound notepads whose marbled cardboard covers soon went spongy and limp. The paper's weave was cloudy and ink-resistant, like the shiny institutional toilet paper of my youth. Indian ballpoints dribbled a sort of blue mucus that wiped off the page. But I did discover, disinterred from God knows what long-forgotten godown (Raj-speak for warehouse), ten Venus HB pencils, "Made in England" in the 1950s, wrapped in wax paper inside an elegant tin bearing the image of bare-breasted and unarmed Venus de Milo.

In these beautiful objects with their precision of manufacture—their needle sharpness, the emerald craquelure of their enamel paint, the fragrance of hardwood when you opened the tin—I found a fetish, a symbol of the world of quality manufacturing of which I couldn't quite let go and to which India could barely aspire. Yet the country had an atom bomb, it assembled jet fighters. A younger generation was somewhere in the wings, MIT-educated, sensible of the wider world, aware that in maintaining its anti-capitalist stance, throwing in its lot with the Soviet Union, accepting a moribund economy that mired its hundreds of millions in poverty, India was in economic oblivion. How long could Mrs Gandhi, the articulate and iconic international stateswoman who squatted atop the world's largest democracy—its most sluggish, corrupt and unequal democracy—how long could she maintain her grip? As I sat in my mother's garden reading *The Hindu*'s scathing scepticism of north India's corrupt, Hindi-speaking political élite, it was impossible to imagine that Mrs Gandhi's life would end within a year, in a hail of automatic gunfire from her own bodyguards.

I began to write my novel. Shivaraj brought freshly made lemonade to the desk I set up in the garden. But it was time to move on. My parents would be returning to England in a year and I knew I didn't want to go back. To my father this was procrastination, a putting-off of the inevitable, unpleasant day when I'd have to find a job in England. My belief that I might find work in Bombay struck no chord with him. But I wasn't looking for a career—I was looking for a way of staying in India. England was an exhausted and cynical country under the grip of its own matriarch—Margaret Thatcher— who would re-energize the country, in the process making it oddly harsher and coarser. I felt I knew all about that; but India was a kaleidoscope of the unknown—though with its widely spoken archaic English and vestiges of Empire it mixed the familiar with the zany, like a dream. It was irresistible.

LIFE IN THE forest began well. The three new hermits lived close to an ashram and were at first accepted warmly.

Then, Rama began to notice a few sidelong glances. It seemed that Khara, the brother of the Lankan King and Emperor Ravan, had set up a camp a few days' march to the south. His men had let it be known that they would welcome a chance to take on the Prince of Ayodhya. Rama was unwilling to endanger the lives of the hermits by his presence. So he, Lakshman and Sita duly continued south, deeper into the great Dandaka Forest.

It wasn't long before Rama had to make his first kill. It was dawn in a forest clearing. The creature—was it a man, a demon?—was immense, draped in a tiger skin, decorated with the heads of tigers and wolves, and made even taller by the lion's head he wore as a helmet. He carried the newly decapitated head of an elephant like an obscene standard at the end of a spear. The creature was smeared with grease and blood. Skulls dangled from a belt round his waist. He was flanked by a semicircle of similarly clad and armed, smaller versions of himself. He spoke.

"You come into this forest with the matted hair of a holy hermit, fully armed, with a wife in tow?"

Rama waited a moment. "I am Rama, Prince of Ayodhya," he called. "I am travelling with my wife Sita and my brother Lakshman. We come in peace. If this is your territory, we'll go back the way we came."

The creature laughed. "We've heard of you, the exiled prince, the would-be king. Your road ends here, Rama. It's true about your wife, she's a beauty. Her, I'll have. As for you two, I'll drink your blood straight from your throats."

Lakshman was amazed to see that his brother had turned pale. Rama's eyes were wild. "So is Kaikeyi getting what she wanted, now?" he murmured.

Lakshman didn't hesitate. Faster than the eye could see he loaded two arrows on his drawn bow and dropped into the stance of an archer. A ripple of unease went through the militiamen. Rama dropped beside him, yelling, "Sita! Flat on your face, *now*! Lakshman, *go*!"

With superhuman speed, Rama released a wave of arrows into the centre of the row, while Lakshman took out the flanking militiamen. The leader, whose name was Viradha, was hit by seven arrows. In a few strides Rama and Lakshman were beside him and in two strokes their swords lopped off his arms.

The clearing was quickly a slaughterhouse, the rays of the sun catching steam rising from hot blood. Viradha wasn't dead yet. Bubbling blood, he muttered that it was good to be killed by the great brothers of the Ayodhyan crown. "I was at the court of Indra," he slurred. "Knight . . . musician . . . courtly arts." There was a large pit in the clearing, an elephant trap with thirty sharpened stakes, a staircase, even a space to butcher the animals. Rama and Lakshman dragged the big man by his heels. "Was tricked by an enemy, you see," he mumbled. "Exiled . . . this is . . . curse . . ." They swung him into the pit.

A CURIOUS RELATIONSHIP existed between the hermits and the savage bands that roamed the forest. The hermits relied on protection from the surrounding kingdoms, but help was rarely at hand. At the same time the jungle militias were superstitious of the hermits' supernatural powers. Atrocities stayed at a sort of acceptable minimum. Now, Rama was pleaded with to provide protection to the hermits for as long as he stayed in the forest. With lordly hauteur he agreed.

That evening, Sita took him to one side. "This is a place of savagery," she said, "beyond order and reason. Rama, *please* don't fight—even wicked men—just because you can. What *we* have to learn here are the skills and cunning and diplomacy the ascetics use to survive!"

"I promised to protect these holy men," Rama firmly responded, "because they asked me to. Now that I've given them my word, I can never go back on it."

A few days later they reached the hermitage of Agastya, a legendary sage, who presented Rama with a fantastic jewel-encrusted bow and an ancient arrow of a metal so hard that it could pierce metal. "These belonged to the gods, they say. A holy man shouldn't have weapons like this anywhere near him. But after many years, the right person has come along. A fighting prince—or should I say a fighting monk?" The old man's smiling eyes turned to Sita. "I am pleased to see that she has stayed with you, Rama. She is a good woman.

"But I don't want you to go back into the forest. Travel to Panchavati—it's twenty miles from here, on the banks of the Godavari. It's peaceful there."

Sita experienced an overwhelming sense of relief. But that feeling would be short-lived.

CHAPTER 8

Bombay

As we turned the corner, a hundred men dropped to their knees and swung forward until their foreheads touched the ground.

"It's a conference of entomologists," I said.

Ravi frowned.

"Entomologists," I said, "—they study insects."

"I *know* what entomologists are, *baba*." He looked peeved.

"Well, I thought that was funny."

They were back on their feet, now, the overflow from Friday prayers. Ravi bit his cheek—as he did when he was thinking hard—and his heavy eyebrows beetled down. "You shouldn't mock religion, *yaar*."

In a Muslim wave, they dropped back to their knees.

"I'm not *mocking*, I'm *joking*."

It was the autumn of 1984 and I was senior subeditor at *Business India* magazine, "India's premier business journal". The job title sounded impressive, but there were no *junior* subeditors—I was on *BI*'s bottom rung. I'd shown some visual flair; with the exception of movie fanzines and a couple of news weeklies, Indian journalism inhabited a pre-visual age. So Rusi, our editor, had tasked me with enlivening the grey look of the thing. I'd been put in charge of layouts and Ravishankar Sujir was the picture researcher, my right-hand man. It helped that we got along. Everyone else called him "Shanks", but I called him what he'd introduced himself to me as: Ravi. He was friendly, funny and constitutionally incapable of unkindness—indeed, he became angry when he encountered unkindness in others. He was also, discreetly, religious.

"You shouldn't undermine other people's faith, *baba*," he continued.

"Oh, I'm not *undermining* anything!"

We'd been round the corner for lunch in one of the narrow *dabhas*, the hole-in-the-wall restaurants dotted around the Stock Exchange. Boys in shorts ran barefoot on the marble floors, spooning curry from steel platters onto your *thali* dish, leaving receipts, tiny petals of numbered paper, that stuck to the wet tabletops. Eaters yelled over the crash of platters and the roar of fans. It was hot in those joints—hotter than the humid streets—and we sat as close as possible to oscillating wall fans, which kept the temperature just this side of unbearable. There'd been a power cut today, the strip lights had shuddered and expired, the fans had clattered to a halt and we'd felt as though we'd been shovelling coal in a tramp steamer.

Dalal Street is synonymous in Mumbai/Bombay—like Wall Street in New York—with the stock market. The Exchange had recently been rehoused in an immense skyscraper (still on Dalal Street) that was incomplete and largely untenanted, with debates raging over whether it actually had planning permission. It zoomed above the financial district's tight grid of decaying colonial buildings with dripping air conditioners bolted into their windows. *Business India* operated from one of these ancient hulks—Wadia Building, 17–19 Dalal Street.

We stepped from sunlight into the grimy interior of Wadia. The lift door was open and its operator, an immense man resembling a melted candle, sat in his filthy uniform behind the open lattice gate.

Suddenly Ravi stopped and raised a finger skywards, like a figure in a Renaissance painting. "I forgot the prints," he said.

"Which ones?"

"Hindustan this-thing. Cement Corporation."

"I thought they were already with you. You said the pics arrived before lunch."

"The *negs*, *baba*."

"Have you seen them?"

"Hmm."

We were back in the sun-bright chaos of Dalal Street. You couldn't walk the narrow pavements for all the lamp posts and signage randomly cemented into them, the parked bikes, handcarts, emaciated men in singlets squirting sweat as they manhandled heavy machinery through narrow doorways. The little taxis called *Pad-minis* (an automotive joke—Padmini is a common girl's name) hooted at the handcarts. Cyclists impotently rang their bells—yet were, by some extrasensory miracle, heard. Everybody yelled, incessantly. As for the humidity—inhaling was like being waterboarded.

"I hope they're good, Ravi, they're all we have for the cover story."

He showed me his palms, pouting slightly as he always did when he was being ironic. "*Anth bhalaa, toh sab bhalaa.*"

"Which means?"

I'd made sporadic attempts to learn Hindi, but I didn't even hear it spoken much—English was the language of *Business India* and the only way our polyglottal family of north Indians, Tamils, Gujaratis, Bengalis, Keralites and what-not could hope to communicate with each other.

Ravi raised his right hand, pinching thumb and forefinger together. "If end is good—" his hand flattened, palm facing me "—everyt'ing is good." He rocked his head complacently side to side, his voice a sing-song parody of your ordinary salt-of-the-earth Indian.

"All's well that ends well," I said. "And don't forget that a bird in the hand is worth two in the bush."

He cupped his hand drolly. "Don't worry, *baba*, those birds will be in this hand in just two minutes!"

The photo lab operated out of a wardrobe-sized space at the back of a Xerox shop at the end of Dalal Street. Certain types of shop had particular colours associated with them—public phone booths were blue or red, depending on whether they had a local or an STD line, while the Xerox boys had adopted egg-yolk yellow. Dalal Street was rich in purveyors of commercial stationery, the stamped official forms required to buy and sell shares. Wizened typists were poised in shopfronts ready to hammer out the details for you on their ancient typewriters. The shops were open to the street and many, like this one, had their photocopiers on the pavement. Groaning and clattering, they emitted the odour of Xerox ink and a vile blast of hot air that caught you on the shins.

As we stepped inside, the shop owner clattered a fistful of ball-points against his glass counter and, with a conjurer's casual wrist flick, wrapped a strip of newspaper round them and bound it in place with two deft twists of a rubber band. He held out a flat palm to receive a note from a customer, inverted his hand and slammed it flat against the counter, simultaneously with his other hand pulling open the drawer of a wooden cashbox. He opened his mouth (red and green with half-chewed *betel* and *paan*) to reply to a question from his colleague at the back of the shop, and acknowledged our presence with slightly raised eyebrows and a half-rock of his head. All the time he nervously shook one knee—the compulsive and ubiquitous gesture of the Indian shopkeeper.

We squeezed (the shop was eight feet wide) past jammed cabinets. In cosmopolitan Bombay certain Japanese stationery items had penetrated the import barriers and we loved them—ballpens that wrote, erasers that erased, staplers that did not decompose at first use. Ravi pulled some grimy rupees from the breast pocket where he kept them (crisp new notes were a rare tactile luxury; rupees were inevitably limp and filthy, and sometimes actually warm and wet; when you paid anyone you gave them the filthiest notes and kept back the newer ones; when notes finally fell apart, you gave them to a beggar). A receipt was scribbled. We stepped outside and Ravi handed me the brown envelope like a crack barrister flourishing a clinching piece of evidence. I ripped open the envelope and extracted two black-and-white photographs. The first showed a piece of scrub ground that might have been anywhere in the world. The second was different—the scrub ground had some barbed wire in the foreground and a stunted tree.

My mouth opened and closed. Words took longer to come. "Ravi, the article is about India's most advanced new cement factory . . . These are pictures of a *field*."

He tugged nervously at his beard. "Site pix—where the construction will be. It's what they gave me, *baba*. They told me it's all they have."

"*They* told you? *Who* told you?"

But it didn't work like that. Ravi never divulged his sources. Maybe it guaranteed that he'd remain indispensable, but I think it was something else: his professional mystery. Ravi was a man of mystery.

Doing my best to inject some pictorial life into our dull columns, I was wholly dependent on Ravi to visit companies who'd never before been asked for pictures of their plastics units and jute mills. His job was to bring back something—anything—visual. *Business India*'s staff photographer Ramu went into the city and snapped sour businessman in bulging safari suits. Many of the companies and state corporations we wrote about illustrated their annual reports with a few grainy photographs, bleached images of fractional distilleries and handfuls of cotton fluff, and upon these meagre resources we depended. But sometimes we faced an eight-page cover story with nothing to enliven it but portraits of unphotogenic fat men. This was when Ravi was supposed to come into his own. We'd brainstorm— how can we illustrate this goddam thing?—and Ravi would set off into the decaying rancid maze of Bombay to visit trade organizations, trades unions . . . I had no idea where he went. As the week went by and our press date bore down, he responded to my frantic demands by lightly laying the splayed fingers of one hand on my chest and calmly assuring me that all would be well. But often all wasn't well, at mid afternoon on press day there were black holes in big articles and I'd start yelling at him and he'd start yelling back.

Right now, we were twelve hours from putting *BI* to bed. "Oh, God. What do we have on file, Ravi? Cement mines? We've already used them at least twice."

"Cement mixers," he said. "Bags of cement."

"We need more! Plans for the factories! Some pix of machines that make cement. Those long conveyor belt things at cement factories look nice. You'll have to go out again! *Now*, Ravi!"

His brow furrowed. "I'll just get my bag from the office, *baba*."

Two peons were gossiping by the lift as we walked in. They slid slyly to one side, avoiding eye contact, wary of being given work. Our melted candle of humanity with his filthy khaki uniform and smallpox-pocked face cleared some tar from his throat as he jammed shut the lift gates and slammed the elaborate cast-iron handle that set the ancient lift in motion. He never looked at you, the old man, never read a newspaper, was always impassive in the midst of a group of babbling peons. But for me he was the object of some meta-physical speculation. He so obviously *was*, this man-mountain—to feed his physical needs he kept a thermos and some *parathas* shop-wrapped in greasy newspaper tucked beside his battered wooden stool. But what *exactly* was he? All he did was impassively slide a metal gate and push a handle. *Was there* more to him than that? It was an uneasy line of thought.

We reached the top floor and stepped into the narrow, brightly lit ad department—the only part of *Business India* to have A-C, the only part to be adorned with pretty young women. Ravi opened the door into the art department—and the earth moved. We threw our hands and feet sideways to keep our balance. Gasps of alarm. Lights flickered. A crucifix that hung on an anglepoise lamp swung—its arc a meter needle recording the force of the quake. Lorraine, the office administrator, sprang to her feet with a squeal and her fingers splayed, as though she'd seen a mouse. Silence. Six, eight seconds passed before the second shudder, the aftershock—and some kind of indecipherable answering grumble from the building's elderly bones.

Lorraine was in the middle of the room now, her melodic voice producing a high-pitched cry. But it was a trusting sort of sound, fear combined with an appeal for support.

We loved Lorraine. She was unusually tall and had a sweet open face with a mass of heavy curls. She was in her mid-twenties, substantial but not overweight, with well-modelled arms and elegant hands. She dressed superbly; gold lay on her throat and jangled on her strong wrists. She was *vigorous*. She resembled those gods you saw on cheap posters all over the place—in a country of undernourished people, where film idols were plump, *real* idols were even more admired.

"We have to get out—into the street!"

Raphael, the eldest of the graphic artists and a fellow Christian, came to her aid. "It's all right, Lorraine, it's over. Finished, *yaar*! No danger! Just a small this-thing."

"This-thing" meant "whatsit" or "thingummy", but for Raphael it was a verbal tic employed every time he spoke. Sometimes he abbreviated it just to "this"—"Martin, where's my this?"

Lorraine stared at him uncertainly. The entire art department now formed a reassuring circle around her.

Ravi was the first person to come to. He came out of the art studio with his shoulder bag. "I'll be back, *baba*," he told me.

"Soon!" I called after him, pointlessly. I knew he'd return, possibly with useable pictures, some time before 2 a.m. when we were supposed to put the magazine to bed.

ॐ

THERE WERE OTHER earthquakes too. Usually political ones. One October morning, phone calls from Delhi brought the astounding rumour that Indira Gandhi, the icon who for two decades had run India as legitimate PM and occasional dictator, had been assassinated—by her own Sikh bodyguards. Soon, the tickertape machines began to jump. (These fat grey machines brought us the news of the world, via the wire services—Reuters, AP—typed onto fine paper strips that ran through your fingers to form immense curls on the floor.) The atmosphere became feverish—not least for our two Sikh employees who rightly anticipated reprisals. I remember a female Sikh colleague getting up from her desk grim-faced, speaking briefly with the editor and making straight for the door. The next forty-eight hours brought savage riots nationwide, Sikh homes sacked and burned, something like 1,000 killings. Senior members of the governing Congress Party were credibly accused of helping to orchestrate killings. Indira's son, Rajiv Gandhi, was infamously quoted as having said, "When a big tree falls, the earth is bound to shake." It didn't bode well.

If a big story broke and we were in the first week of our fortnightly cycle, all we could do was try to offer the most authoritative analysis. But if it broke a few days before we went to press we were in real competition with the daily papers. India's English-language papers were largely regional and didn't enjoy deep pockets or teams of investigative journalists. We were fat on earnings from the job ads that were indispensable to every Indian exec. A frantic race would begin to get our journalists on site, to sign up the best commentators and beat our competitors with the best coverage. A month after Mrs Gandhi's death, a Bhopal subsidiary of the American Union Carbide Company oozed poison gas into the night, killing hundreds of sleeping people. It was a national catastrophe and within hours of the story breaking our journalists, including my friend and colleague Arun Subramaniam, were en route to Bhopal. There was no Internet then; international phone calls, which had to be dialled through operators, were maddeningly slow. On Bhopal we got the science right and Arun swiftly made contact with top American experts on corporate accountability; our coverage was probably the best in India. It made us proud—it meant the house journal of Indian capitalism was playing a concerned and liberal part in the evolving story of India.

Economically, India was asleep—the existence of decaying factories that could poison sleeping populations merely seemed to prove the fact. After Independence in 1947 India's Congress Party governments had ordained a state-socialist, self-reliant India, protected by rock-steady trade barriers. India helped establish the "Non-Aligned Movement", a loose confederation that hoped, in partnership with freelance dictators like Egypt's Nasser and Yugoslavia's Tito, to challenge the world's division into two Cold War blocs. It failed utterly.

BI's proprietor was Ashok Advani, one of the visionaries leading the call for capitalism. He was a bright young Sindhi barrister who'd rush in from his chambers on press days, sit on a big old rattan armchair with his leg crooked over the arm and, running his fingers through his beard, dictate his "Letter from the Publisher". These were not masterpieces of rhetoric or construction, but they hammered away at Ashok's theme: India's need to open up her economy to the outside world. The young Turks in the wings—they knew.

The instrument of change turned out to be Mrs Gandhi's younger son, Rajiv. His older brother, the manic Sanjay, apple of his mama's eye, had killed himself in an aerobatic plane. Rajiv was a pilot, too—more prosaically, an airline pilot—who'd trained in Britain as an engineer. He was a mild, shy, unpolitical man, happily married to an Italian woman called Sonia. When Indira went down in that hail of her bodyguard's bullets, images of a white-clad Rajiv lighting the funeral pyre were broadcast around the world and there was no doubt that he would do his duty. The Congress Party and the Gandhi dynasty must go on.

The Rajiv regime's first budget sent a thrill around the *Business India* office. The leftist Congress Party was inaugurating market reforms! Inward investment! Foreigners allowed to take large equity shares in Indian companies! State socialism on death row! Within months, the multinationals were queuing up to form partnerships with Indian companies. Honda, Suzuki, Krupp, Formica, Durex, Cherry Blossom . . . The Mr Clean of Indian politics, the man with no political past, Rajiv sacked his mother's cronies. He even promised—gasp—to bring computers to India.

By the late '80s the collapse of the USSR—India's major trading partner—and Gulf War hikes in oil prices caused a balance-of-payments crisis in India. In 1991 Prime Minister Narasimha Rao and Finance Minister Manmohan Singh initiated full-scale economic liberalization, abolishing the so-called Licence Raj—the centralized licensing of investment, industry and imports. Many public monopolies ended—and inward investment rocketed. India has not looked back. Circa 2033, it will have the world's third-largest economy.

As for Rajiv, his political honeymoon had ended all too quickly. Mr Clean lost power amidst accusations of corruption in a mammoth arms deal with Bofors, the Swedish arms giant that gave Alfred Nobel his wealth. Rajiv's lawyers would no doubt have ensured that he survive the scandal—but in 1991 he was vaporized by a Tamil Tiger suicide bomber.

In accordance with the warped dynasticism of the Nehru–Gandhi family, Rajiv's widow is, as I write, the most powerful person in India. Sonia Antonia Maino, a girl from a poor family that lived near the north Italian town of Vicenza, was studying English at a Cambridge language school when she met Rajiv Gandhi, a student of engineering at Trinity College; they married in 1969. Sonia Gandhi has chosen not to take up the post of prime minister; but when the Congress Party is in power, she runs the country.

THE ARYAN KINGS of the northern kingdoms maintained armies stationed along the southern fringes of their dominions. And gradually they extended their reach, followed by settlers, trading posts, priests and schools . . . Only the faintest memory survived of their arrival from the north-west, when the rich lands around the Indus and Ganges had belonged to the *Rakashasas*, the dark-skinned peoples they'd slowly pushed back into the mountains and jungles. These people had a very different narrative: they hated and resented the word "*rakashasa*", which meant "demon"; they saw their overlord Ravan as the defender of the faith—the old civilization—everything the pale-skinned northerners wanted to extinguish. It seemed to them they had no choice but to use terror to win against the Aryans' cavalry troops and their ranks of disciplined archers. This jungle barrier between the Indians and the Aryans was a lawless battleground, with constant wars of attrition and insurgency fought by mercenaries, criminals and psychopaths.

The sister of Ravan, herself a warrior, had been warned by her scouts of the three exotic hermits. When she first saw Rama—she fell in love. His chest was broad, his shoulders massive, his body perfect, his skin like honey. She instructed her men to find a time and place when she could meet Rama alone.

When it happened, Rama was startled to see a woman similar to the creature he'd killed ten years earlier, the demon Tataka. He drew his sword.

"We don't have to fight," the woman confidently announced. "There are better ways to amuse ourselves. My name is Princess Surpanakha, sister of Ravan, Emperor of the Indians. You look good enough to eat, my Prince. I've seen your little Sita, an ugly little mouse. You deserve better. I'll show you how we make love in the jungle."

Rama smiled grimly. "I'm very content with things the way they are."

"You think I'm hideous, don't you, Prince of Ayodhya? But that can change, believe me. I can be anything I want to be." Surpanakha waded into the shallows. Unselfconsciously she threw her girdles of weapons and her clothes on the bank and began to wash. Unlike Sita with her fleshy curves, Surpanakha had the form of an athlete. She was tall, dark-skinned, her thin lower legs had tough cups of calf muscle and her thighs swelled with hard muscle. When she lifted and bunched her wet hair behind her neck her breasts were firm. Her face wasn't soft and round like the women of the Ayodhyan court, but chiselled, though her lips were full. Her eyes were dark and wild. Surpanakha grinned at him. "Not bad, eh, Prince? Good enough for you?"

Unexpectedly, Lakshman emerged from the bushes and halted in his tracks. "By God—" he said.

Rama felt a blush rise to his cheeks. "Princess, this is my brother, you should try him for size. He's a good-looking young man—and unattached."

Surpanakha turned haughtily to Lakshman. "I might consider it," she said.

And then, Sita arrived on the scene. She stared open-mouthed at the sight of the naked figure.

"Get dressed," Lakshman told Surpanakha harshly. "Get out of here, you rebel whore."

The woman grabbed a dagger, then dashed towards Sita. Rama blocked her path and threw her to the ground. It wasn't easy.

With her free hand Surpanakha tore a bracelet from her ankle, which concealed a small dagger. Lakshman hurled himself on top of her, pinning her arms, while Rama grabbed her ankles. The woman had incredible strength.

With his own dagger Lakshman sliced at the woman's nose, then her ears. Surpanakha stumbled screaming to her feet and ran naked into the jungle.

Rama turned on Lakshman furiously. "What the hell is *wrong* with you, man?"

"Dear God," said Sita. "What is happening to us here?"

That night, Rama sat alone and tried to meditate. For the first time in his life he felt he was losing his self-control. The jungle was testing him in ways he'd never imagined. And he felt he was losing.

IT TOOK SURPANAKHA three days to reach the camp of her brother Khara. Doctors did their best with needle and thread, but her face was swollen and purple.

Khara called for his captain of the guard. "Get a platoon of your best men ready to move in an hour!"

"I want to drink their blood fresh and frothing from their necks," hissed Surpanakha.

The squad set off an hour later, accompanied by Surpanakha, travelling on a palanquin carried by sixteen fast runners who took turns in eights to carry her.

Anticipating reprisals, Lakshman and Rama selected an ambush point. They left Sita at the ashram, with instructions of what to do if they were killed. But Sita had a plan for that eventuality: she would take her own life.

Lakshman prepared arrows; Rama was a better scout, but was nearly caught out by the stealth of the experienced jungle fighters. Dressed and daubed in black, they moved through the undergrowth like panthers. Rama circled back to the ridge and the two brothers waited.

But then, with foolish bravado, the panthers stepped out into the open and hurled spears at the brothers.

Rama's iron-tipped arrows could outdistance any spear. He decimated Khara's men easily. Flailing, they looked, Lakshman thought, like snakes plunging into an anthill.

WHEN SURPANAKHA RETURNED to her brother's camp, she threw herself down in front of him and howled.

"Don't tell me my men are *dead?*" Khara asked incredulously. "*They're* the ones supposed to do the killing!"

"Your flesh-eating warrior élite are virgin girls," Surpanakha sneered. "This Rama would finish you off, too. Forget it, you're no match for the Aryans. Better run home to our big brother and beg him for an army. Maybe five hundred of his best men would be a match for two Ayodhyan princes lost in the forest."

Khara reacted predictably to the taunt. He took five hundred men with him. Rama waited at the neck of a gulley, in the shadow of a great tree that offered protection like a cobra's hood. Khara ordered fifty men to rush him. Most went down. And Lakshman strode among them, lopping. Khara ordered forward more troops. Men fell to the earth screaming, heads and bodies split open, weapons scattered around them. The battlefield was a swamp of flesh and blood. Now Khara desperately threw himself into the last wave of terrified, screaming men. Arrows caught him and his blood frothed. Maddened by the smell of blood, he was one of the last to get anywhere near Rama. Rama reached down to a brazier on the ground beside him and pulled an arrow from it. Khara stared, fascinated. It buried itself in his guts and as he sank to his knees, still mystified by the rout of his men, he breathed smoke.

Can mass extermination be called victory, be heralded as a good? Rama doubted it, but he was trembling with an excitement beyond any sexual pleasure. He and Lakshman could not rest, uncertain if another wave of attackers was on its way. Blood-drenched, they prepared themselves to do battle again.

MY SOCIAL LIFE in Bombay revolved around *Business India* or the Bombay Press Club, a pleasantly seedy establishment on the edge of the big open space of the *maidan*, the city centre cricket ground. There were soothing breezes from across the cricket ground, cheap beer, and noisy fights at midnight between drunken journalists who invariably made up afterwards. Other times I went out on the town with Ravi and two of the graphic artists, Mukesh and Bertie, evenings that revolved around Kingfisher (beer), Wills Honey Dew (cigarettes), immense meals and sometimes a movie at one of Bombay's impressive art deco cinemas. The films were usually Hollywood blockbusters with the sex snipped out. There were very rarely any girls on our nights out—girls went home after work.

Sex before marriage was uncommon in Bombay, but within weeks of arriving I had been seduced by Susanne, a student at Sophia's, a girls' boarding college whose clients were in large part prosperous expatriate Indians. Sophia's inmates were adept at using tips and flirtation to slip past the half-witted guards on the dorm gates.

Susanne, at eighteen, deplored her virginity. She propositioned me very frankly: if she gave herself to an Indian man, the word would go round and she'd be called a whore, but I, as a Westerner, would be sure to take a more "modern" approach. So how about it? We were at a party. After an hour or two, Susanne led me to the car park and into the back of a parked Ambassador, where she pulled off her shirt. Technical consummation occurred in Colaba, close to the Royal Yacht Club, the colonial establishment where my father stayed when he was in Bombay. Susanne and I took a room in a more squalid and affordable hotel in the narrow, sinful streets behind. After that, we met every Saturday afternoon for six months in the *Business India* guest flat where I'd been given a temporary room. When I was asked to move out, I discovered the harsh realities of Bombay life. Rents were astronomical. The best I could hope for was a rented room in somebody's apartment. The moral police were on constant watch and my amatory adventures were soon curtailed.

RAVI AND I called him Chatters behind his back, for he never stopped yacking. A former captain of industry, Mr Chatterjee had been brought in by Ashok to give *Business India* the benefit of a view from the top. I can't remember which dead limb of a remote Western multinational he'd worked for—I've a feeling it was Shell. Anyway, he'd stand around at the office being pompous to anyone who'd give him five minutes of their time, stopping journalists getting their work done. People soon began to avoid him. But when he first arrived I'd heard he had a room to let. His apartment was central, a ten-minute walk from the office. I didn't suspect that Mr Chatterjee, who wore cuff-linked shirts to the office and bore the emblem of a gold Cross fountain pen, was a pathological miser.

The apartment, shared with Mrs Chatterjee, was gloomy and dank. Nothing had been spent on it for decades. My accommodation deal included breakfast—a boiled egg, toast, butter and tea. Mr Chatterjee rose early every morning to prepare this for me. He purchased tiny loaves of snow-white polystyrene that came in a greased paper bag. Chatters would extract three slices, toast them and bring them to the table with a tiny smear of butter. Tea was served in a small teapot with a precise measure of milk. It was made clear to me that I shouldn't expect anything more. Just to make me feel even more welcome, as soon as I finished eating Mr Chatterjee would drop my plates into a bowl of blood-red potassium permanganate—a disinfectant.

Eventually I realized that Chatters kept two loaves and that my slices always came from the older of the two. The tropical climate made bread go off fast—it had already been sitting on some shop counter open to the street for God knew how long. My three slices were sometimes actually green with mould. When I pointed this out to Mr Chatterjee, he expressed surprise.

One morning I got up early and disingenuously helped myself to bread from the newer pack and butter from the fridge. Chatterjee arrived twenty minutes later, hair awry, a look of distress on his face. He stared wildly from the table to the place beside the toaster where the newer pack stood unwrapped, then goggled at the butter dish on the table, from which I'd taken a modest curl. He almost ran to the fridge, where he counted the eggs.

So began our cat-and-mouse game. The following morning it was satisfying to hear him bumbling around the kitchen at the crack of dawn, and to see the rings under his eyes as I sallied in for breakfast later than usual and greeted him with an innocent smile. I did this for a couple of days. Then, when he thought he had my rhythm mapped, I pre-empted him again—for the sheer pleasure of seeing his haggard panic. Another morning Chatters was emerging from the bathroom just as I was going past it; he rammed the door open and ran, with shocking speed for a man in his seventies, to get to the toaster before I could. This was the high-powered executive who daily conducted pompous, prolonged phone conversations with his broker.

The final phase of our campaign saw Mr Chatterjee waiting in the crack of his bedroom door every morning for me to pass, so that he could barge out just before I reached the kitchen. By now we cordially hated each other. My main pleasure consisted in tormenting him—like entering the kitchen at dawn, only to emerge with a glass of water. But Chatters asked me if I wouldn't mind not entering the kitchen until 7 a.m., as my early-morning sorties disturbed Mrs Chatterjee. The only ploy left to me now was to provide my own bread and butter, to ignore his dire self-regarding conversation and stick my nose in a book.

He was agreeably offended by *Prick Up Your Ears*, a biography of the homosexual playwright Joe Orton, whose campaign of pasting lines of pornography into middlebrow novels at the Islington lending library gave me courage in my campaign against my landlord. I was now leading a double life. There was no hope of smuggling Susanne into Chatters's flat. Even when he and the memsahib were out, I was watched by the servants. But I'd managed to find a place on the seashore north of Bombay, favoured by adulterers. Getting there—by train, taxi, ferry and taxi—took an entire morning, but the contrast with seething Dickensian Bombay was absolute. There were simple, clean rooms with pitched terracotta roofs and sheets that smelt of salt and sunshine. The beach was always deserted and the little restaurant served fish caught at the fishing village just a mile away.

I WAS LEADING a kind of double interior life, too. Chatterjee was an Indian whose own culture had been destroyed for him by Western education. His put-downs were the usual ones. He sneered at

Hinduism's superstition and its claim that all was illusion. I didn't dispute the hard truths of the material world—my father was a scientist—but I did question science's triumphalism. There was, I knew, another view. In India, pesticide use was uncontrolled and excessive. The unbridled prescription of antibiotics was reducing resistance to disease. Groundwater levels were dropping due to uncontrolled deep-well pumping. As for the West's dominion over the invisible world, I had read Janet Malcolm and Bruno Bettelheim on the flaws in the hegemony of Freud. I'd also been reading Jung, who said he *knew* there was a God. Even if you read that in its weakest form—that humans have a tendency to intuit the idea of a first principle, a pattern—it made Western philosophy's aggressive desire to kill God seem, as Freud would say, neurotic.

I had two piles of books in my bedroom, the mainstream and the mystical, mostly procured on Sunday morning trawls of the dusty second-hand bookstalls around the University. I was still working on the novel I'd started in Ooty, frustrated by the fact that I had no typewriter and couldn't possibly afford to buy even a second-hand one. I read novels and the biographies of novelists—Robert Lowell, Malcolm Lowry, Ernest Hemingway. The product of a Western literary education, I'd studied artists who had taken drugs as well as liberties. But you must not deviate from the bourgeois norm. Be so bohemian as to hand a couple of essays in late and the whole weight of the institution comes crashing down on you. Still, I was taken with the Romantics, the Symbolists, the Surrealists, the Dadaists. I was never late for work—but I believed myself a bohemian.

The second pile of books dealt with philosophy. Inevitably, I was coming at mysticism from the direction of empiricism—which placed me a long way from any mystical union with God. The book that helped me most was a shabby Pelican, its spine dried out by the Bombay heat—*Mysticism* by F. C. Happold. I still have it, yellowed, loose-paged and scribbled-in. In the course of his analysis, Happold showed how mystical experiences struck individuals in every class and culture. These curious visions were often feared, often valued, and were the bedrock of many religious traditions.

But I wasn't experiencing the ancient, pervasive mysticism that surrounded me. I was ill at ease with *advaitha*'s vocabulary and the garish trappings of faith, and flummoxed by the relentless insistence on illusion. It didn't help that I lived in the country's commercial capital and was working close to the heart of Indian materialism. But *advaitha*'s claim that all things were fundamentally united, were ONE, struck a chord with me—since my teens, I had felt that to be true. Fate moves in mysterious ways, and fate had given me for my closest colleague and friend, a man who had found some of the keys to Hindu mysticism.

I've said that Ravi was generous and benign. Let me describe him. He was short and stocky, rather pot-bellied for someone in his early twenties—he had something of the look about him of Ganesh, the chubby elephant-headed god who's cherished in Bombay more than anywhere else in India. Ravi wore *khadi*, or hand-loom clothes, as I did. Hand-loom was a mark of solidarity with the Indian villager, for village weaving had been intended by Mahatma Gandhi to provide income to the rural masses. I wore it because the loose-weave cotton was wonderfully cool. City dwellers who wore *khadi* were usually Communists or, as with Ravi, were demonstrating a feeling for the continuity of Hindu tradition.

I've also mentioned that Ravi was a man of mystery, not only about the sources of his photographs. I had picked up that some strand of mysticism played a key role in his life, but he never spoke of it overtly—although, unlike most in our office, he did wear explicit signs of religious practice, like the set of *rudraksha* beads round his neck, and often he turned up with his forehead smeared with paste, showing that he'd attended early morning *aarthi*, the Hindu equivalent of mass . . . We were friends, but it took us a while to get each other's measure, in particular for Ravi to realize that my interest in his spiritual world was genuine. He'd been amazed to find the *Ramayana* and a pile of books on Hinduism beside my bed. That had sparked the first of several long discussions on the role of Rama and Sita as the quintessential exemplars of Hindu man- and womanhood. Ravi was acute enough, too, to have picked up on the quirks and ambiguities in their two characters, as well as the unexpected flashes of goodness and conscience shown by Ravan. The *Ramayana* was a complex moral tale, with many shades of greys to supplement its blacks and whites.

The first time Ravi took me home for dinner, I found the Sujir family almost shocking in its uncomplicated warmth. With two brothers and a sister all of similar ages, the meal was exuberant. But the governing framework of respect for parents and tradition was also plain. It was drummed into Hindu children that—as taught in the *Ramayana*—their father, mother, teachers and any visitor to the home should be revered like gods. Television was absent from the Sujirs' home, as it was from most Indian homes. Television sets cost a fortune and the output of Doordarshan, the Indian state broad-caster, was unwatchable. Their small flat was in an apartment block, within a compound, inhabited entirely by members of their own Hindu sect, the *Saraswats*. Family life ebbed between ritual, school and home. Mr Sujir was an Elder who officiated at Hindu ceremonies, so that Ravi had been saturated in the ways of his religion since infancy. His appetite for devotion was evident. But he was also hooked on another form of religion.

He kept a framed picture beside his bed, a montage of gurus. Who were they? On that first occasion I learned nothing.

It was his brother, Anand, who first mentioned Ravi's guru. This man, who had died two years earlier, was considered by many to have been one of the greatest twentieth-century incarnations of the Hindu tradition. He lived, in utmost simplicity, not far from the Sujir home. In his late teens Ravi had begun to creep to the back of the old man's *satsangs* (his public audiences), which anyone was free to attend.

Ravi was reticent about Nisargadatta. It wasn't so much shyness as maybe something to do with pearls before swine—though without the arrogance that implies. Ravi knew the futility of discussing a subject that didn't interest most people and that struck others as foolish or even crazy. Eventually, I got it out of him. We were sitting in the bedroom he shared with his brothers, a small square space with cheap furniture and dusty piles of now irrelevant school books.

"I had heard of this man and I began to go and sit in his *darshans*," he explained. "I was so *shy*—I used to sit at the back and hide myself! There were always some of his older devotees sitting up front, discussing, taking notes." Ravi grinned. "I was overawed, *baba*. Then, one day, he called me forward. I wanted to wriggle away, but it was no good, he made me sit with him. And so, I began to know him. I began to learn . . ."

It was like that too in ancient Greece: students sitting at the feet of their teachers. It's supposed to be like that at Oxford.

There are many accounts of Nisargadatta chain-smoking his way through his *darshans*—after all, the old man had earned a living as a cigarette vendor. If it killed him at eighty-four, he'd had a good run for his money. Photos taken late in his life show a man with a round face, a broad nose and a small, puckish mouth with a pugnacious lower lip. It's his eyes you can't escape from—they radiate extraordinary power and warmth, it's easy to imagine that to have been in the presence of this man would have been electric.

Nisargadatta died in 1981 of throat cancer and Ravishankar had helped care for him, wash him, nurse him through his final illness.

Ravi didn't try to summarize the teaching of Nisargadatta. Although he'd become close to a man many considered one of the spiritual giants of the twentieth century, Ravi was in awe of the teaching itself, still attempting to digest what it might mean to him personally. Even for a devout Hindu, the insights taught by *advaitha* present a massive challenge to the psyche.

I was delving widely—Zen, the Sufis, Julian of Norwich, Holderlin. A collection of conversations with Nisargadatta had been published in English as *I Am That* and Ravi had a much-thumbed copy beside his bed. He told me I could buy one at Bombay's main outlet for spiritual literature, Chetana's, just round the corner from our Dalal Street office. In fact, Chetana was the publisher of the heavy volume, bound like my *Ramayana* in renunciatory orange. But I couldn't get more than fifty pages into the book; Nisargadatta's assertion that life is unreal, that human beings inhabit a stream of mental states that are ultimately meaningless, was too alien to the mind of a film-loving, novel-loving, sensualistic, self-styled bohemian. The book stayed at my bedside nevertheless—a talisman, the unintelligible map to a country I knew I'd visit some day.

Ravi's focus was far narrower and more meaningful. But it wasn't clear to either of us how the spiritual search should proceed. Nisargadatta had no anointed successor in Bombay. But another man came to fascinate us.

In Bombay, many families had gurus who even spent time in their homes, living symbols of the family's faith, who taught the tradition to the young. Anyone who had a leaning towards the higher, mystical realms of religion was considered to be in pursuit of something legitimate and even enviable. Some gurus played the role of, say, a fashionable New York psychoanalyst. Our editor at *BI*, Rusi Engineer, had a guru at Almora, up in the Himalayas, whom he visited annually. Rusi shared his guru with some quite notable characters in the Bombay media world and, in particular, the Calcutta intelligentsia. Ravi and I discovered that this guru, one Ashish Da, was a highly improbable figure—an upper-class Englishman who'd travelled to India during WWII as an RAF engineer and ended by taking *sanyass*—the vow of poverty, the wearing of the saffron robe. He had become the acolyte of another Englishman-turned-guru, the late Shri Krishna Prem—who had been, even more fantastically, a Spitfire pilot, by the name of Reginald Nixon. Ashish Da, this fusion of England and India, was reputed to combine a razor intellect with a mastery of vedantic philosophy. Rusi had access to an inner circle that was denied to kids like us. He would reply to our expressions of interest with gnomic half-smiles. So the guru fascinated us from a distance and we made do with pamphlets of his writing, sold by Chetana's. Neither Ravi nor I had the freedom or resources to leave Bombay and travel to the Himalayas. But we dreamed of it. We felt sure that an appointment awaited us in Almora.

Our *BI* friend Mukesh married and his first son was born. The art department bunch of us—Andrew, Ravi, Bertie, I—had been to see the baby in the suburb where Mukesh lived. It was late evening and we were heading back into town, the four of us crammed into an autorickshaw. I was conscious of the high-pitched drone of the two-stroke, the stink of the Bombay night, the heavy warmth, as our rickshaw weaved dangerously through the traffic. Motorbikes and scooters swerved around us, lorries and buses loomed. There was a bang; the auto went over. We were all lying in a heap, me on top of Bertie and Andrew. We picked ourselves up, Andrew clutching his hand, looking shocked and angry. He'd been hurt. Walking round the auto, I caught sight of Ravi on the ground. An oncoming car had hit us and Ravi, who had had one of his legs sticking out of the side of the rickshaw, had been struck. His brown leg looked as though it had been unzipped, his foot was smashed open, bone and yellow fat exposed, his blood oozed onto the road. He was staring upwards.

It took half an hour, I think, for the ambulance to arrive. It was a metal box with a stretcher in it. The two ambulancemen didn't want to get blood on their hands or clothes. I yelled at them to get hold of his shoulders and I helped lift the rest of him onto the stretcher. I sat beside him in the ambulance and kept talking to him for the eternity it took to reach the "hospital". The emergency ward resembled my worst imaginings of the Crimean War. Ravi was put into a bed and given fluids. I went into the nearest toilet and found an unlit, stinking sewer, its walls coppery with urine, the stench suffocating. The doctor was young and abrupt, with tired black-rimmed eyes behind wire spectacles. He wouldn't talk, explain anything, he was almost dismissive—I know now that he expected Ravi to die, of shock. This information he did give me: the driver of the car that hit us was dead. He had been having a race with another driver. Both had been drunk.

We waited. I talked to Ravi. Some of the time he was half-conscious. Minutes crawled by. I was holding his hand when he died. His cheerful round face became flat and no longer his. I asked if anyone had telephoned his parents. Andrew and Bertie were both in shock and useless, neither had had the courage to put fifty *paise* in a payphone. I had to do it. "Mr Sujir, sir, I have to tell you something. There has been a terrible accident . . . Ravi is dead."

"Oh."

The sound of that flat, gentle exhalation has stayed with me to this day.

It took Ravi's parents an hour to get to the hospital. Composed, almost awestruck, they approached the bed where their dead son lay.

The next day the news spread through the office like a frost. Ravi's loss was keenly felt. Rusi, our editor, wrote about Ravi in a black-bordered box underneath the "Letter from the Publisher" that week.

I'll never meet another Ravi. But when my son was born almost twenty years later, I gave him as his second name Ravishankar. A name should be something you grow into and I could think of no finer example to live up to than Ravishankar Sujir.

I remember standing in my white *kurta* when Ravi was cremated, as *pandits* muttered prayers. His father, wearing only a white *lunghi* round his waist and the Brahmin thread over his shoulder, circled the pyre, barefoot, pouring ghee on the mound of branches. He tried to concentrate but looked almost wildly disconnected from the reality that he was burning his dear son's body. I stood to one side, shaking, and the tears poured out of me.

I MADE IT to Almora eventually; it was a year after Ravi's death. Buses were toiling up *ghats* and swinging perilously into bends. Like the journey up to Ooty, the road passed through tropical forest, where monkeys and vast jackfruit hung from branches, before reaching the cooler altitudes of the Himalayan foothills. I paused at the hill station of Almora before deciding it should be possible, just, to reach Mirtola before nightfall. The bus dropped me at dusk beside a steeply ascending track. I began to climb, lost my way and was soon scrambling through woodland in pitch darkness. I thought I saw a light. Dogs began to bark. A man carrying a torch emerged from the wood ahead of me and asked furiously who I was. He was David, accompanied by a dog wearing a large spiked collar. He told me I was a fool, there were wolves in these woods.

I had obtained permission from Ashish Da to visit but, with typical disorganization, I hadn't fixed a time or found out exactly how to reach the ashram. David led me past more barking dogs in an outhouse to a building set back from a small garden. Inside, by the light of oil lamps, half a dozen people were sitting in a circle. There was a pleasant hum of conversation and an odour of woodsmoke and pipe tobacco. I was introduced to Shri Mahadeva Ashish, better known by the Bengali diminutive of his Calcuttan devotees, as Ashish *Da*: Papa Ashish.

He was a tall man with plentiful white hair that began in a peak on his forehead and was brushed straight back. He had a strong nose, a narrow mouth that seemed to hover between hardness and amusement, and penetrating eyes. He spoke English with a crisp, pre-war upper-class accent. David's irritation was not echoed by Ashish Da. He asked if I had eaten, and a beautiful, dark-eyed girl called Chitra scrambled to her feet. It turned out that she was David's wife. Later she showed me to my room, a tiny cabin, cold but clean, with an oil lamp, a coarse wool blanket and little more.

The next day I had an audience with Ashish Da. He was sitting in a comfy old armchair in his study on the first floor of a simple wooden building. A portable typewriter was by his side and there were packed shelves of books behind him. He wanted to know what I hoped to find by visiting Mirtola. I told him about Ravi. I said I longed to find this spiritual dimension that I sensed existed, but which my mind denied. He sat, wrapped in his faded saffron *khadi* robe and a threadbare cardigan, puffing on his pipe. He was still a restrained, public school-educated Englishman of the 1930s—upon whom there lay a mantle of *sanyass*, renunciation.

"Stay a while," he said. "We'll talk again."

IN THE THREE weeks I remained at Mirtola, I came to know its little cast of characters, the people who'd relocated from the city to be close to their guru. David, Ashish Da's adopted son and anointed successor, was a taciturn, pent-up man with big worker's hands. He was comfortable with the hard, physical business of running the ashram's farm but seemed ill at ease with language. In general, there was a rigour about Mirtola—beyond the unheated rooms, the cold that made you hop as you pulled on your clothes and rubbed your arms and legs in an effort to get warm. There was none of the ease that I'd encountered in Rishikesh. Whatever it was, the spiritual path these people had committed themselves to, it wasn't *easy*.

Chitra was an inspiration—quick-witted, funny, working all day long with passionate energy, sweeping, cleaning or chopping vegetables. We had breakfast together, early, sitting on the hard kitchen floor, a huge brass beaker full of tea and hot, freshly baked *rotis* with butter and apricot jam. People ate hugely, something I didn't quite grasp the first day, until I discovered that there was no lunch. After breakfast, people launched themselves at the fields like furies. I was given softer tasks—churning milk to make butter, or mowing grass—and showed myself to be lazy and inept.

Every evening came *aarthi*, with blown conches, waved fly whisks and the banging and rattling of a variety of instruments, as David led the propitiation of the ashram's household god, Krishna, the God of Love. The ashram's founder, Krishna Prem, had believed love to be the key fact of the religious life. I gathered that Ashish Da had moved beyond ritual devotion; for the rest of us it was deemed necessary.

I was granted only a couple of brief private audiences with Ashish Da. I got to know him better in the course of the evening chats. There was an intellectual elasticity about him, a humanity and generosity, but an intolerance of lazy thinking and self-indulgence. He would listen to people with an amused smile, sucking on his pipe. When he intervened, he cut to the chase—but he rarely laid down the law.

Although I admired Ashish Da, I began to feel low. The *aarthis* seemed empty and the physical work was unpleasant. I felt oppressed by David's taciturnity; he didn't exemplify any notion I had of spirituality. I felt tormented by the beauty and vivacity of Chitra. But it was the death of Ravi that lay on me most heavily. I had no sense of direction or motivation—at Mirtola, or in my life. I didn't know what I was doing there, or where I was going next, and I didn't *care*. I had this stubborn spiritual aspiration—if that was what it was, this nagging yearning—but no idea how to realize it. And no one at Mirtola, least of all the guru, seemed inclined to give me any help.

Ashish Da told me, with characteristic aristocratic understatement, that "it wouldn't be a bad idea" to read that book of Ravi's guru Nisargadatta—*I Am That*. I found an ageing hardback copy in the ashram library. I was being eased back towards the Hindu insistence on the emptiness of everything. I tried to read it again, but its stress on the fundamental unreality of all things still struck me as wrong.

Late one afternoon I climbed the steep slope behind the ashram to where a path crossed the ridge between our valley and the next. There was a dramatic view to the not-so-distant snow-capped Himalayas. I decided to head towards a little peak that looked climbable. I noticed a figure behind me, a girl of about fifteen, in a sari, carrying on her head a shallow basket of vegetables. She couldn't see me. As she reached the point of passage between her valley and ours, she paused and dropped her eyes, putting her hands together in *namaste*. It was a moment of private, ancient belief. I felt a searing pain in my heart, for I was witnessing a simplicity of spirit I could never find in my own soul.

After she had passed, in a sort of panic I ran up the hill, struggling through the copse, grabbing hold of branches, leaves brushing my face, muttering as I went, "I am that, I am that." At the brow of the hill there was no vegetation. The little white dome of the ashram's *mandir* was clearly visible among the trees below. The sun had lost its intensity of whiteness and begun its transition to red. I sat and crossed my legs. The sun hung before me and I stared at it, still reciting, in a kind of desperation, "I am that, I am that . . ."

Quite suddenly the sun zoomed towards me, growing in size. It entered me, it *was* me. My heart exploded. I fell flat on my face and began to writhe on the ground, delirious, muttering prayers, at the same time wanting to make love to the warm, dry earth. Then I fell unconscious.

When I came to, the sun was back where it should be, in the sky, and late-afternoon bronze in colour. I was exhausted, but ecstatic. With a sort of joy, a feeling of love for everything I could see surging through me, I scampered back down to the ashram.

I asked to see Ashish Da. He listened to what I described and said, "You're on the way." He was a man who gave no lectures, no explanations, he wanted you to make discoveries by yourself. I had no idea what "the way" was and he didn't seem inclined to illuminate me. For several days I was filled with a sense of the oneness, the interconnectedness of everything. I was well disposed to everyone I met; indeed, to existence itself—I was in love. Something had happened, a kind of divine boot had kicked open a door in my consciousness. I didn't know what it was, but I did know that it felt good, that I was experiencing, actually *feeling*, love—not for someone, but as a kind of general state, abstract, boundless. This was something the mystics wrote about. It very evidently was not a state of emptiness, a fear of which my readings of *advaitha* had sparked in me. The sensation stayed with me for about three weeks, diminishing a little every day. I had been searching for something and I had found . . . something. But was it a path, or a map, or a compass? Or another delusion? I had absolutely no idea.

PART III

CHAPTER 9

Of Mosques and Mandirs

JUNE, 2005. Twenty-five years had passed. The path to salvation was steep and narrow, lined with snares to snag the pockets of the faithful. Stalls hawked a profusion of spiritual ephemera: garlands, incense sticks, tracts, devotional cassettes, *roli* (protective threads to tie round pilgrims' wrists), icons of Hinduism's best-beloved Gods, beads, *bhindis*, brassware, blankets, beach balls . . . It was like the Via Dolorosa in Jerusalem, the path Christ trod on His way to crucifixion, lined now with gaudy souvenir stalls. Christ threw the money-lenders from the temple, but surely trade and religion, fundamental human activities, must coexist. It is puritan wish-fulfilment to believe otherwise.

A man was spreading lime in a gutter to disinfect it. A sort of al fresco Madame Tussauds showed figures posed in key scenes from the *Ramayana*—noble Rama, evil Ravan . . . A man fed lengths of sugar cane into the cast-iron cogs of a crusher, cranking a handle and catching the bilious juice in a glass. Hawkers pressed on pilgrims packets of *prasad*, tiny white sugar balls, to be purchased and offered—via a *Brahman*—to the Gods, and returned to them blessed, a holy nibble, combining sweetness with auspiciousness.

As I climbed the narrow way I had views across Ayodhya of many temple spires, near and far, spiking the cloudless sky. The city was a spectacle of decayed wonder. It was surprisingly green, too. As at Varanasi, broad staircases descended to a gleaming glassy broad river, the Sarayu, that might almost be an inland sea.

There was a deadness here, though. I'd spent the morning wandering among rotting buildings with decaying arches and falling walls. Domes presented themselves at every turn, onion-shaped or elongated or swollen pyramids, sometimes vibrant with shiny paint, sky-blue with highlights of crimson, yolk, salmon and jade—but just as often unpainted, unmaintained, unloved. Ornately carved doors hung peeling in their frames, temples had become cow byres, once-proud mansions were inhabited by ragged squatters.

Faith itself, however, was spectacularly alive. Ask the locals how many temples there were in Ayodhya and their answers varied from 5,000 to 8,000—for not only were there hundreds of formal temples, many of them resembling private palaces, but famously, every home in the city was supposed to contain a shrine, some of them as large and elaborate as a public temple. Stroll through the city at dusk and the tinkles of bells and the steady chanting of *"Jai Sita-Ram"* came at you from endless doorways. And, amazingly in a city of a thousand decaying temples, new ones were under construction, ranging from tiny shrines for shanty dwellers to multi-storey town centre complexes.

On the path up the hill, a huge crowd pressed towards the temple dedicated to Hanuman. A lesser stream continued on to the *Ram Janmabhoomi*—Rama's Birthplace—the site where a few years earlier a huge mob had demolished a defunct mosque built in 1528 on the spot where some believed Lord Rama had been born. This was India's Dome of the Rock, a place of extreme holiness, where religions clashed.

Where the slope levelled off I came to a metal barrier and a police post set up in an ancient doorway. Policemen lounged in the shade like emperors, knees crooked up, bare feet flat on the soothing cool marble. This lotus-eating vision was spoilt by another group who stood in aggressive feet-apart stance, tooled-up to the teeth. I was spotted, pulled from the crowd and body-searched. I'd asked for no special privilege, but an officer shouldered his rifle and led me forwards, past the queuing faithful, past the blackened façade of yet another defunct religious structure, to a doorway crammed with another contingent of cops. There were some shrewd-looking plain-clothes men here who took their time examining my passport and visa details, which they scrupulously recorded on a scrap of envelope from someone's back pocket.

I was led further along the street, to a third checkpoint, where I was relieved of my bag and subjected to a yet more thorough body search. Accompanied by the plain-clothes men I now turned left and stepped through a metal detector into a long alleyway lined with metal grills fifteen feet high. To one side there were decaying brick walls where cows tugged at tufts of sun-scorched grass. The alleyway of grills became a snaking maze, a device to prevent stampedes—though, with cows wandering around, it bore an uneasy resemblance to a feedlot.

We approached a fourth police post, where I was searched again, with even greater vigilance and this time had a small penknife taken from me. Another cop appeared, a tall, plain-clothes man with a permanent sceptical frown. He led the way, the other two following at my heels. They ushered me into another alley, long and narrow and lined with corrugated-iron sheets, ending in a roofed pen—and yet another metal detector.

It was near the middle of the day and all was sun-bleached dust. But the tall policeman told me in heavily accented but accurate English that I'd chosen the best time to come—there were few pilgrims now. From this vantage point I could see, on a slope some way off, a village of khaki tents.

He followed my eyes. "That is our camp," he volunteered. "It is very big. More than one square kilometre."

"How many of you are here?"

He shrugged. "Seven hundred, maybe."

"Why so many?"

"You must understand, this is very dangerous place. These Musselman people, you see. They are maybe twenty-five per cent of population here. Anyone who comes can be Musselman—how can we tell? They can come here with gun, bomb—start many troubles. This is the danger."

I was taken aback by his readiness to characterize every Muslim in Ayodhya as a potential terrorist. The enemy within. Until Ayodhya was politicized by Hindu hardliners, Muslims and Hindus were supposed to have lived in harmony here.

We turned into yet another corridor, this time walled in billowing purple cotton, which led in a rectangle round what was evidently an archæological dig. This was the site of the vanished mosque, the Babri Masjid, destroyed by hard-line Hindus with hammers and bare hands. A 200,000-strong mob had broken through police cordons. Apparently rehearsed in the skills of demolition and well equipped, they had first knocked down the three domes of the mosque, then torn at the bricks, totally demolishing the building. The government had brought in hundreds of extra police, but, according to eyewitnesses, they stood by and allowed the destruction to proceed. Other sources claimed that the police had killed some 300 people. Walking through the ruins, I wondered how the hardliners could have achieved such total destruction without earth-moving equipment. And where had all the rubble gone?

The Mughals were said to have built their mosque using two rows of black stone pillars from the original *mandir*, traditionally believed to have been brought by Hanuman from Lanka. Would the mobs have destroyed them, too? Surely not. Early Muslim rulers had been fascinated by Hindu spirituality, and had practised and encouraged tolerance. But later rulers had reversed this trend, showing no pity for "idol worshippers". Iconoclastic Mughals in their zealotry had demolished thousands of *mandirs*, often building mosques on the same locations and incorporating parts of the *mandir* fabric— according to some historians it was a deliberate strategy, to show the Hindu building *translated* into the higher, victorious Islamic form.

It was unfortunate that a mediæval building had been destroyed; but wasn't it ironic, given the orgy of destruction the Mughals had wrought on Hindu temples, that there should be such a hue and cry in modern India about the destruction of one defunct mosque in which no Muslim had worshipped for fifty years? You might take a long historic view and argue that the restoration of a key Hindu relic, the healing of a kind of religious wound, seemed like a reasonable request. But that conclusion would be politically naïve. It would ignore the religious tensions in the country—the bombings, the riots, the stand-offs with Pakistan, the danger that an elected Hindu nationalist government would be seen as acting against the interests of the Muslim minority. It would ignore the fact that, prior to the current controversy, the Hindu masses had *not* been clamouring to visit Rama's birthplace. And what would be the message, in India and abroad, of a regime that destroyed even *one* mosque to allow its replacement by a *mandir*? Who was to say that that wouldn't establish the precedent for a whole series of mosque demolitions? Minorities had to be protected. The courts had to be free to ensure that the law was observed and to call politicians to account when it wasn't.

The object of the archæological dig was to verify (or dismiss) the claim that a temple had existed on the site before the construction of the mosque. I'd read news cuttings from many responsible sources asserting that there was no tradition and no evidence of an earlier temple. Journalist friends of mine had snorted that "absolutely nothing whatsoever" had been found. Commentators jeered that the whole affair was absurd—Rama was a fictional character, therefore any debate about his birthplace was nothing but a joke. Others suggested that there was not even clinching proof that modern Ayodhya occupied the same ground as the historic Ayodhya of three or five millennia ago. In general, a vociferous section of the media hated the whole Ayodhya controversy and was eager to side with the wronged Muslims. My own readings of the published data had convinced me that some kind of structure *had* stood on the site. There was also evidence from the British colonial archives of an established tradition: Hindus in Ayodhya resentfully believed that the Babri Masjid did stand on the site of the *Ram Janmabhoomi*.

Even if you accepted the argument that fundamentalist thugs, urged on by cynical and manipulative politicians, had violated Muslim sentiments, the fact remained that Hindus were seeking to revive a tradition, while Muslims were seeking to retain a defunct building on principle, and out of the desire not to lose a political advantage. I found myself wondering what it had been like in those years prior to 1538, as Muslim invaders flooded across India, putting down Hindu resistance with utter brutality, convinced in many cases that Koranic *jihad* made the murder of heathens not just acceptable but obligatory. Jews and Christians were considered deviant, but Hindus were utterly benighted. They were hanged and beheaded by the hundreds of thousands; they saw their temples razed to the ground.

But then, slip back 2,000 or 3,000 years, and I had that image—planted in my mind by the Tamil I'd met on a train—of an earlier wave of invaders, pale-skinned Aryans, sweeping south, destroying the culture and gods of the dark-skinned indigenous Indians. They set up altars to Shiva and Vishnu. The holy horns of these cow-loving pastoral invaders supplanted the wood spirits and water spirits of the jungle dwellers. Yet it hadn't been a total victory for the cow worshippers. Somehow, all this conflict had been fused together into the great catholic family of interwoven cults and traditions that was Hinduism, which still managed to combine the most ancient elements of spirit worship with one of the highest philosophical-mystical religious traditions the world has produced.

I peeped through slits in the worn fabric. Sections of ground were marked off with lengths of string, and figures knelt in trenches. This was curious, because the official dig was supposed to be finished . . . The published report had already recorded evidence of a pre-existing structure—the evidence pounced on and denounced by a broad cross-section of sources. The policemen didn't object to my taking a good long peek through one particularly large rent, but when I pulled out my pen and notebook the leader firmly told me to put them away—"All this place is for Lord Rama. No one is taking photograph or writing or recording. That is not for here. Here is only for worship."

But what exactly were we supposed to worship?

Leaving the third aisle of the purple cloister, I found myself facing a raised mound of packed earth. This was probably the site just outside the mosque where, hundreds of years earlier, as zealotry cooled and Hindus and Muslims learned to live alongside each other in harmony, the Mughals had permitted Hindus to raise a platform and set up idols. For centuries that raised platform had been the focus for Hindu pilgrims to Rama's birthplace.

There was a sort of marquee atop the mound, where two *pandits* sat. One of them received donations, tucking them for all to see into a large perspex-sided chest. The other *pandit* received and doled out those little bags of auspicious sugar sweeties.

"Sri Rama's birthplace," the cop confided to me.

The flaps of the marquee were propped open. Through the triangular slit I could see the shrine, a five-foot statue of Rama, gold-leafed, standing on gold, draped in gold.

Ten days later, on 5 July 2005, six Muslim terrorists blew a hole in the wall around the Ayodhya temple and tried to bomb that golden shrine. They were killed after a ninety-minute shoot-out with security forces, having failed to achieve their goal. Coverage of the attack was quickly put into the shade, for two days later Islamic extremists targeted London buses and tube trains, killing thirty-five people.

Surpanakha at last reached Lanka and the great castle of her big brother, Ravan. The Lankan King and ruler of a wide empire received her seated on the throne in his Audience Chamber. His white teeth and gold ornaments gleamed against his black-brown skin. People reported that he had ten heads and twenty arms—meaning, perhaps, that his eyes, ears and armies were everywhere. He reigned over several wealthy lands beyond the seas. He was a great king, famed for sponsoring scholarship and building libraries—but he had a far darker side. He had broken treaties and sacked cities. It was said that he had raped the wives of close lieutenants. But all-powerful Ravan was about to face his greatest challenge. Surpanakha slyly described to her brother the matchless beauty of Sita, wife of the upstart Ayodhyan who had slaughtered their brother, Khara. Ravan's sister knew that he rarely remained indifferent to reports of a beautiful—and available—woman.

Like King Dasharatha, Ravan would be undone—by lust.

Sita was sure that the scream she heard from the forest was Rama's. Anxiously, she asked Lakshman to go and find out what was wrong.

"He's deep in the forest, Sita, that wasn't his voice."

"It was *him*, I *swear*! Lakshman, *please*!"

"Sita, calm down; he'll be back. I'm supposed to guard you when he's away."

"Did Bharat put you up to this? Don't for a moment think I'll have either of you if you kill Rama. I'll kill myself first—"

She was hysterical, and venomous. Lakshman was shocked: he had never before heard her speak in such a tone. The tensions of life in the forest were eating into all of them. Warily, he reached for his bow and climbed to his feet. "Just remember to keep the door barred."

"*Go*, will you!"

Ravan waited about twenty minutes before approaching the hut. Sita was standing outside, staring towards the forest. She wasn't in the least surprised to see a bearded hermit approach her.

Sita herself had not entirely followed the injunction to poverty. She wore a gold silk sari, one of several she'd managed to bring with her.

She kept her hair long and well-brushed and decorated with flowers. Jewellery glittered on her throat, her wrists and ankles. The arrows of love, they say, pierced Ravan immediately. Dry-mouthed, he asked for water.

"Please—sit," Sita said. She brought a plate of wild fruit and, as tradition dictated, water for him to wash his feet.

But Ravan couldn't stay in character for long. "Who are you?" he asked. "It's very rare to meet a beauty like you in this wilderness!" He praised her hips, her thighs, her "good, full breasts".

Sita felt panic rising in her.

"Am I embarrassing you, Princess? Yet the way that necklace is placed, it's *supposed* to draw the eye to your breasts, isn't it? That's what female adornment is all about, after all, to *allure*." Ravan gave a hoarse laugh. "What are you *doing* here? I mean, anyone who left you unprotected would be mad, wouldn't he? This jungle is full of wild animals! And I'm not talking about lion and jackals—I'm talking about *men*!"

Sita jumped to her feet and tried to dart past him. But he grabbed her wrist. "I am Ravan," he said. "Emperor of the South. The animals in this jungle obey *me*. But my capital city, Lanka, is a paradise. Your little Ayodhya's a village by comparison. Come, I'll take you there— now. My palaces are like nothing on earth—I have jewelled paths leading to summer houses, ornamental lakes, fountains. You would have five thousand women waiting on you."

"You *fool*," mocked Sita. "Rama is a lion next to you. Your men are gorillas. Two Ayodhyans cut them down like corn."

Ravan was not in the mood to argue. He dragged her to the *Pushpaka* and barked at his charioteer. The magical machine took off. Sita ripped off her shawl, her jewellery, letting them fall in the hope that Rama might somehow find them and follow her trail. As heavy bracelets struck the branches below, five huge monkeys looked up and saw the *Pushpaka* flash past—and a woman with her hair streaming. Sita's pearl necklace snapped and slipped between her breasts, twisting to earth like Ganga descending.

Back in Lanka, Ravan summoned his generals and told them to find Rama and kill him. Then he dragged Sita around his palace, determined that she should admire its insane opulence, the private zoos, the pillars of gold and lapis, the vast pleasure gardens.

"There's no way off this island," he told her. "But you could be the Empress of the greatest kingdom on earth!" He leaned closer. "Youth is short, Sita. Enjoy it!"

Sita plucked a blade of grass and placed it between them. "I warn you," she said, "never again come closer to me than that blade of grass."

"Listen to me, Princess," Ravan snarled, "if you don't submit to me soon, I'll have you chopped into pieces and served at my breakfast table."

Sita gave a sour smile. "What became of the courtly love, Lord Ravan?"

The ruler of Lanka stormed back to his attendants. "Take her away," he said. "Be attentive, sympathetic—then: threats, isolation. *Break her.*"

CHAPTER 10

I Am Indian, Therefore I Am Hindu

AFTER LEAVING INDIA in the winter of 1986, my first decent job had been at the BBC. I joined a programme called Network East, 'East' referring to the mythic land from which I'd just returned. The programme was directed at the Indian and Pakistani diaspora in Great Britain. For many years the BBC had served them a diet of well-intentioned, dull public information films, Urdu-language advice about visiting the dentist, that sort of thing. Network East was supposed to ring the changes, with a strong news agenda, and broadcast in English by second-generation migrants. It would abandon boring geriatric Indians and Pakistanis who spoke bad English, tapping instead into hip, happening Asian yoof culture, *bhangra* music, Bollywood. We had three older producers who'd been working there for years. One had a heart attack and died, another had a catastrophic stroke. In general, the misery levels were extreme —at one point the entire production team downed tools to demand better conditions (without success). I'd moved from India, where paternalism and humanity abounded in my workplaces, to lovable Auntie Beeb where managerial ineptitude, egotism and bullying flourished.

Reluctantly pandering to the older generation, the "Asian Unit" decided in 1988 to broadcast a TV dramatization called *Ramayan*. Indian TV was still a moribund propaganda vehicle for sitting prime ministers. Television ownership was slowly spreading among the middle classes, but swathes of the country had no TV at all—or even an electricity grid—although it was not uncommon in the countryside to encounter, at night in a darkened village, some flickering black-and-white TV wired to a clattering generator. Pre-televisual India was in thrall to the colour and drama of cinema, but also of popular religion. So it was appropriate that the first attempt at a big TV drama series should take on the country's big religious myth. But no one could have predicted its impact. Streets emptied during the transmissions, life came to a halt, the owners of televisions found their living rooms packed with visitors. The stars of the show were lionized and even treated as incarnations of the God, most notably Arun Govil, who played Rama. Indian television is now a deregulated dog's breakfast of news-lite, soaps, celeb-chat and sport. Back then, with the explosive impact of Ramanand Sagar's *Ramayan*, there was the revelation of television as a force for good. A new version of the *Ramayan*, produced by Sagar's son, hit TV screens in early 2008 and was an immediate success. But in today's multi-channel TV environment, nothing will ever match the series that, two decades ago, united a nation around an incandescent retelling of its best-loved story.

In fact, *Ramayan* did much more than that: it highlighted the cult of Rama at the very moment that politicians were about to make His birthplace the epicentre of Indian political debate. To the staff of Network East, *Ramayan* was kitsch, its acting wooden and its special effects pitiful. The cultural shift required to comprehend the power of the series was beyond anyone who hadn't known and loved India. Writing this, I have beside me a few of the trinkets from a goodie bag the producers of *Ramayan* sent the Network East office. A Hindu-style necklace of plastic orange beads, various badges, a *Ramayan* key ring with the stars' faces imprisoned in Perspex. Why did I keep these ridiculous trinkets? What could they have meant to me?

Returning to India every year or so, I witnessed a rapid trans-formation. The Congress Party was losing its grip. Mrs G had ruled India by a sort of *droit de seigneur*, but in the aftermath of her Machiavellian leadership the Congress grew weaker, undermined by a series of scandals. National politics was beginning to be dominated by nationalism. And Ayodhya was its focus.

The issue of Rama's birthplace had been disputed for centuries. The Mughal emperors had moved to suppress the worship of Rama. His name had the power to provide a rallying call to the conquered Hindus, so the cult must be crushed. The Muslim Emperor Babur raised a mosque, the Babri Masjid, on the spot where Hindus believed that Rama had been born. But the story hadn't ended there.

The Masjid had a curious history. When the Brits took over India and were called upon to adjudicate, with typical British pragmatism (and lack of finesse), they built a barrier down the middle and told Hindus and Muslims both to worship there. In the course of the nineteenth century a tradition duly developed that both religionists worshipped side by side. In time, the Masjid fell into disuse and no Muslim appeared to have worshipped there since the 1920s. The Hindus had it to themselves. In the 1970s an organization called the VHP, the Vishva Hindu Parishad (World Hindu Council), began to campaign to reconstruct the ancient temple. Their protests were initially peaceful, but by the late 1980s they were calling for the demolition of the mosque, a demand exploited with considerable skill by the political party called the BJP (*Bharatiya Janata Party*, Indian People's Party).

The BJP went in for a conservative domestic agenda and steroidal rhetoric on defence. It had come into existence with the support of a phalanx of Hindu nationalist organizations known as the League of Indian Nationalist Organizations,[1] notably a somewhat dubious paramilitary group called the RSS.[2] The architect of Hindu nationalism, Vinayak Damodar Savarkar (1883–1966), had spoken of *Hindutva*, or Hinduness. Now, the Big Idea was that all India was a *Hindu rashtra* or nation—the *rashtra* was an umbrella that covered every bough to have sprung from Indian civilization, including indigenous religions like Jainism, Sikhism and Buddhism, but also the two newer arrivals, Islam and Christianity. *I am Indian, therefore I am Hindu.* All the peoples of India were to be seen—culturally—as Hindu. (*Hindu* in fact simply means "inhabitants of the land of the River Sindhu", now the Indus in Pakistan.) The BJP wanted to foster a modern Indian state inspired by ancient Hindu values, where all learnt to live in accordance with the scriptures' four phases of life: *kama* (gratification), *artha* (wealth), *dharma* (faith), and *moksha* (spiritual release). But an overt and rather sinister nationalism overshadowed the BJP's spiritual line. A nationalistic rhetoric was employed to woo the country's majority Hindu masses, in part by demonizing the Muslim minority. Hindu hardliners resented Muslims because, they said, a sort of Political Correctness was featherbedding them, to the

[1] Sangh Parivar.
[2] Rashtriya Swayamsevak Sangh.

disadvantage of the Hindu majority. Hindus were losing out in their own land! Democracy was failing the majority.

The Rama temple issue became the BJP's rallying cry. Rallies were held in Ayodhya. The TV *Ramayan* had powerfully reassociated in public consciousness the idea of Rama with his birthplace. The man who turned this popular religion into a national political programme was the politician L. K. Advani, who, by skillfully playing on the fears of Hindus, released the genie of religious fundamentalism into a democracy that had, as an article of secular faith, done everything to keep it out. Ayodhya propelled the BJP to victory in the 1991 state assembly elections in Uttar Pradesh, India's most populous—and a key electoral—state.

The following year the BJP's political shenanigans reached their messy climax: 200,000 Hindu fundamentalists ripped the Babri Masjid to bits. Images broadcast around the world showed men swarming over the ancient three-domed mosque, attacking it with hand tools. There followed a country-wide explosion of Muslim anger, murder, counter-murder, looting and burning: two thousand people died. In the aftermath of that communal violence, the Worldwide Hindu Council was banned and several leaders of the BJP were charged with involvement. Many people felt that the secular foundations of modern India had been gravely threatened. Meanwhile, the political power of the BJP continued to grow rapidly.

> Despite barbarism from the Islamic hordes of central Asia and Turkey [went a BJP press release], Hindus never played with the same rules as Muslims . . . Thousands of years of anger and shame, so diligently bottled up . . . [were] released when the first piece [of the mosque] . . . was torn down . . . Hindutva is here to stay . . . the guiding principles of Bharat [India] will come from two of the great teachings of the Vedas, the ancient Hindu and Indian scriptures.

I have read pamphlets of Hindu fundamentalism that go much further. They accuse the constitution of having been rigged in such a way as to favour Western-style liberalism and secularism, which play into the anti-Hindu hands, favouring Christianity and Islam.

The Christians are making 1,000 conversions a day, they claim; the Muslims are multiplying with the aim of creating a north Indian vote bank and ultimately to secede as the state they call Mughalstan. The Nehru–Gandhi dynasty, the Congress party with its readiness to forge political alliances with Muslim parties, are in league with the devil.

Such nationalist fulminations have only fueled the anger of the secularists who for fifty years had the debate about Indian national identity all to themselves. Just as in France, where *l'état* is a kind of secular deity, the holy writ of Indian secularism had glued together the disparate parts of the country since independence. The left-leaning Congress, the Western-influenced media élite, the country's influential Marxist historians, the Muslims who stood to lose a lot from any desecularization of India—nobody wanted to see the rise of Hindu nationalism. Maybe they were right. Many historians considered it almost a miracle that India had not fragmented in the course of the twentieth century, although certainly it had experienced its share of communal strife, as well as wars with neighbouring Pakistan, which undeniably had their roots in religious divisions.

The common criticism levelled at the BJP was that its assertion of Hinduness as a basis for politics smacked of racism, even fascism. It didn't help that some of the supporters of the nationalist cause were a brutal rabble and that some of the senior politicians permitted themselves to make crude and inflammatory statements. This continues. In 2002, two thousand Muslims died during orchestrated assaults by Hindu fanatics, and some members of the state's BJP government have been implicated by the police; senior politicians have refused to condemn the killings and Hindu fundamentalists can easily be heard to say that—in essence—the Muslims "had it coming".

The BJP briefly formed a national government in 1996 and 1998, before serving a full five-year term from 1999 to 2004. It tested nuclear weapons, making India an undeclared nuclear state. It unleashed economic reforms—privatizations, deregulations—speeding India's advance towards superpowerdom. Yet the BJP did not, despite the fears of its critics, aggressively pursue the Ayodhya agenda. Ayodhya did, nevertheless, remain a flashpoint, a fulcrum of nationalist sentiment, a pungent provocation to Muslims.

In 2001, after leaving the BBC, I went to India to present a TV documentary for Discovery Channel about the Ganges. The film crew began its journey at the Cow's Mouth, the gaping cavern of ice where Ganga is born and where I took, for the benefit of the cameras, a pneumonial dip. A couple of weeks later I stood, with the programme's Indian fixer, an imposing character called Vishvanath Sharma, looking across Ganga at Varanasi to the green land beyond.

"The jungle used to be out there," he said to me. "Somewhere to the south of here, Rama began his journey to Lanka. I'd like to make that journey. It seems weird that nobody does it—I mean, there are so many pilgrimages in India but you never hear of anyone setting out to trace Rama's journey to Sri Lanka—it's probably not even safe, now, with the war over there. And yet every Hindu loves Rama and Sita. Every time I come here, to the landscape of the *Ramayana*, I have this very strong sense that . . . the jungle started beyond the Ganges. Then, after Sita was kidnapped, Rama had to cross this vast jungle with its wild animals and barbaric tribes to try and find her. All the way there are traces, temples where his memory is revered. I'd love to do it one day. It is an incredible story. It would make an incredible journey."

CHAPTER 11

The Road to Ayodhya

THE MOTORBIKE I'D been following for fifteen kilometres stopped dead in the road—I had to do an emergency stop to avoid him. My front wheel locked, I skidded and almost smashed into the Hero-Honda; its driver didn't notice, or didn't care. Overladen lorries plunged around us like enraged bull elephants. I cursed, booted the Bullet back into first and pulled round the stationary fool.

It was June 2005. I was on my way, for the first time, to Ayodhya. An hour before dawn I'd left the Young Women's Christian Association guest house, which makes me sound like Count Dracula, but the YWCA is, and long may it remain, the best cheap accommodation in downtown New Delhi. I sped towards Old Delhi, past the Red Fort as a hint of red entered the sky, over a multi-lane flyover beside the River Yamuna—the shock of the Indian new. I had a five-hundred-mile drive ahead of me to Ayodhya, mostly by the Trunk Road, an overloaded lane designed three centuries earlier for horse traffic. How long would this first stage of my journey take me? Three days? I hoped, two. It took four.

Some time after nine I was shocked to encounter a tollbooth, heralding an anything but phantom motorway: four smooth black lanes, almost empty. I sped along. Here was the brave new Indian infrastructure that was going to compete with the Chinese. Later, someone told me truck drivers wouldn't use the motorways—they wanted to save money, and anyway, the motorway network was vestigial. And had no whorehouses.

After an hour, the freeway ended and I was dumped back into the Trunk Road's manic free for all, with its twin torrents of trucks and buses cleaving flotsam like motorbikes, as swifter vehicles—mini-buses and private cars—suicidally weaved. Only it isn't suicidal, it's what they used to call in the days of nuclear stand-offs MAD: Mutually-Assured Destruction. That, I already knew. Ravi's death had taught me that.

The bright green blur in my peripheral vision was sunlit cultivation. It was broken occasionally by a hut or some squat little *mandir*, with gaudy streamers or a string of light bulbs and perhaps a glimpse of a tubby man sitting cross-legged, or a stooping woman raising a little dust as she flicked her switch from side to side. Sometimes I glimpsed an older structure, its whitewash gone, sandy bricks dissolving like a heap of brown sugar lumps. I was crossing the Gangetic Plain, the wide swath of alluvial earth deposited by the Ganges, Ganga, the holy river that rises in Himalayan glaciers and descends south-east, skirting foothills where it's joined by many orange torrents from the Himalayan forests, to ease its way across this flat land until it reaches the great mangrove swamp where it fuses with the warm salt water of the Indian Ocean. This landscape *is* old India. It's where the Vedic civilization that became Hinduism continued its spread from the plains of the Indus. This silken soil, this rich fertile farmland, gave early kings their fortunes. They decreed a mythology, one that positioned them at its apex, almost on a par with the God Indra. The bards, Valmiki and his ilk, co-operated. This is where the *Ramayana* was born and where those ancient kingdoms are buried.

The only way to see India is by motorbike. It gets you down rutted lanes too tough for a car and alleys too narrow for a 4x4. But how wise is it to undertake hundreds of miles of Trunk Road by so vulnerable a means of transport? It wasn't wise, I knew that. I learned never—NEVER—to take my eyes off the road ahead for more than a couple of seconds.

But I must have turned to glance at something. (On some stretches of the Gangetic Plain a little bridge, a clump of trees, a meandering stream, a barefoot five-year-old goatherd, combine into a scene so picturesque it could have seduced any wandering eighteenth-century landscape artist.) I swivelled my eyes back to the road ahead to see three vehicles coming at me, abreast—two lorries, one overtaking the other, and a car overtaking the overtaking lorry. I was in the car's way. I jerked my handlebars left without even looking where I was going. As the Maruti hatchback, its suspension bouncing on the

143

rutted hard shoulder, blurred past a few feet away I caught a glimpse of the driver's manic face. I crashed into the dust and went over. The bike, all 168 kilos of it plus the weight in my panniers, came down on top of me. The Bullet squashed my left leg and a pain shot through my knee; I *was* wearing—the only motorcyclist in the Indian heat who was—leathers, providing protection I was suddenly very grateful for.

It was a quiet stretch of road with no roadside stalls and there was no one to help me. I wheeled the bike a few feet further from the road, stuck it on its side stand and limped to a tree. I took a long drink of water. I did not feel happy. Crossing India by motorbike is romantic, indeed is glorious—if you can avoid the Trunk Roads.

IN CENTRAL FAIZABAD a cow lay in the middle of the street. It sported on one horn a plastic bag from rooting in a waste bin. In its shadow lay an emaciated dog, panting, slimy after climbing out of a cooling puddle. Cows in India are respected, indeed spoilt (the BJP would like to make it illegal to slaughter them). Between this one and a crowded pavement, Faizabad's commuters, squeezed to a single lane, attempted to thread.

This bustling provincial city is just seven kilometres from Ayodhya. I hadn't found an hotel in Ayodhya. The holy city had pilgrim lodges but nothing resembling an hotel with phone lines and so on—nothing so secular. Faizabad, a Muslim-dominated city, was where business was done. Hotels could be found. I drove though the old civil lines where the British colonial institutions had been—the church, the college, the barracks, all still there in their acres of lawn, institutions of privilege still, mock-Gothic, demarcated by rows of whitewashed stones. Two miles off was their opposite: the old Muslim city, a dense labyrinth of textile retailers, electric motor rewinders, visiting card printers. Between these two poles was a jungle of signboards, broken urine-stained walls, men manoeuvring scooters into dusty alleys, students stepping over broken gutters—a typical Indian town, undifferentiable and chaotic to an outsider, logical and lovable to the native.

Ayodhya, so close, did not do business. It squatted in inaction, decay. The only action was devotion. The only business—and it did pay, I supposed—was fleecing pilgrims. The only parallels I could think of were . . . Lourdes? Knock? Mecca?

It was five days since I'd checked my emails. The receptionists at my Faizabad hotel treated my enquiry about an Internet connection with contempt. They said they thought there was some place a kilometre up the road. Eventually I found it, a dingy shop with crates of empty Coke bottles gathering dust in the doorway. Out back was a row of partitioned plywood cabins. Clients went in and—despite the suffocating heat—shut the doors behind them. It took minutes for a page to load, or fail to load. An hour and a half to read and send a half-dozen emails. As the plywood cabins were all occupied, I was invited to use the main computer beside the till. Inside the cabins young men masturbated. The Internet, mirror on the world! In another cabin a couple appeared to enjoy some variety of furtive sex.

I ducked past a squawking three-wheel share-taxi into the gloom of a restaurant. After the brilliant white of the day, the gloom was good, was luxury. It was a Muslim restaurant—"non-veg". Everything inside was the colour of a meat curry. Brown nylon curtains flopped over windows whose panes had been painted over, in brown. There were massive dark hardwood chairs and tables, and even the walls had been daubed a nauseating shade of khaki-streaked brown, in ghastly imitation of woodgrain. I ordered *aloo palak* and *dahl*—potatoes in spinach and lentil stew. Both were dark-brown— or was it just too gloomy to discern colours? Someone came and asked to take one of the chairs from my table. He wore a friendly smile and carried a very long rifle.

When I returned to the hotel I found a man waiting for me in the lounge. He was short and round, and wore a belted orange safari suit. A broad splash of crimson paste across his forehead declared his piety to the world. He stood up stiffly and introduced himself: Mr Tiwari.

We'd only spoken previously by phone. I'd spent two days in Ayodhya trying to find someone who could be my guide. I had hoped to find a local historian, an enthusiast, but calls to colleges and libraries drew a blank. Then, a prominent businessman I met told me he knew the very man. He asked where I was staying in Faizabad and I gave him the name of my hotel. Now, I thought I should check that the arrangement suited Mr Tiwari.

"It is my duty to help a stranger," the small man responded glibly, conveying the precise impression that a duty is by no means the same as a pleasure. I offered him a get-out, but he wouldn't hear of it. Some bond, or perhaps the hope of favour, made him eager to fulfil the big businessman's request.

I needed to change my clothes. With a sniff of displeasure, Mr Tiwari accompanied me to my room. He sat at the coffee table, refused a glass of water and told me he was an English teacher. "But although I may have devoted my life to your English literature"—he enunciated the syllables of this last word with sing-song precision, lee-terra-*tyou*-er—"I have given my heart to those works of our Hindu tradition—the *Vedas*, the *Mahabharata* and so on—which speak to man's spiritual part. Without a spiritual life, it is certain that man is nothing."

He spoke like someone addressing a heathen ignorant even of the *possibility* of a spiritual dimension to life. Then he looked very pointedly at his watch.

"It's really very kind of you to help me," I said hastily.

"It is my duty, thank-you please," Mr Tiwari replied, looking towards the door.

He insisted that it would be best for us to travel by his scooter. I climbed on the back of the battered Bajaj and Mr Tiwari jerked it into the crazy Faizabad traffic. Zigzagging towards Ayodhya, he yelled a commentary and I strained forward to hear him.

"Tomorrow, as you know, is *Ram Navami*, annual celebration of our Lord Rama's birthday. A wall of people will fill Ayodhya."

"A *wall*?" (Surely he hadn't said "wall"?)

"Fifty-one *lakhs*, the radio had said."

"Wow!" A lakh is 100,000. Times fifty-one, equals . . . *five million*! Surely not.

We left the outskirts of Faizabad. The sister towns are only separated by a handkerchief of bleached countryside dotted with the towers of temples and mausolea. Along both sides of the narrow road people were streaming into Ayodhya.

We passed a modern-looking concrete temple painted cream and terracotta. "This is known as Birla Temple," said Mr Tiwari. "You know him? He was a capitalist of India. It was a tax write-off."

I laughed. "Is that your judgement? Of a great act of philanthropy?"

Mr Tiwari held up two short fingers. "Number one, it gives them name and fame. Number two, it saves them money!"

"You're a cynic!" He couldn't see my grin.

"Perhaps I know a little of the world I despise. Of the rich, of the politicians." Polly-*tea*-she-anns.

"What's your view of the great debate?"

"*Ram Janmabhoomi,* you mean? Pure foolishness. There is good harmony here between Hindu and Muslim. But politicians do not want that there should be peace. For them, there is nothing of the spiritual in this place, they see it only as a chess piece, no? They are despicable." Des-*pea*-kibble.

We reached the centre of Ayodhya, the narrow road crowded with pilgrims. Mr Tiwari parked his scooter beside a tea shop and didn't so much ask as instruct one of the waiters to keep an eye on it.

"You will climb this way to Ram Janmabhoomi."

"No, I went there yesterday. I want to see the rest of Ayodhya."

Mr Tiwari looked irritated. "And you had seen temple of Lord Hanuman?"

"No."

"You must see it. This way, please." I followed him through the jostling crowds. "It may surprise you, sir, to see that all of these pilgrims are village people"—his lips twisted with humour—"rustics, as it were. You will see here no city dwellers of any kind."

In the gutter at our feet lay a baby beggar girl, shaking a rattle. Beyond her, older beggars sat in a row, as though it was their pitch, alongside the stalls of the sweet and trinket vendors. I leaned forward and laid down a few coins.

"You should not do that," said Mr Tiwari severely.

"I know." I couldn't help myself—I pitied her. That's how it works. I wondered which pair in the row of ragged professional mendicants were her parents.

Mr Tiwari seemed to me like one of those characters in novels of the nineteenth century: devout, orthodox, proper, blinkered.

We climbed the narrow road that had reminded me of the Via Dolorosa, but quickly forked left towards a tall building set slightly back from the road. Several hundred people were jostling up a stone staircase. People pressed forward, hands cradling garlands and card-board boxes piled with sweetmeats. At a tall iron grill they paused to remove their shoes. Here, they were scrutinized by troops of India's élite Rapid Action Force, part of the Central Reserve Police Force. The RAF is a dedicated anti-riot force, carefully screened, recruited from all religions and sections of Indian society, and trained to manage delicate communal situations where tensions can flare quickly. They're trained in the use of non-lethal deterrents like shock batons, rubber bullets, stun grenades and tear gas—also, automatic weapons. The RAF has only been in existence for fifteen years or so and is considered something of a success story in modern India. To my eyes, they displayed a carriage and alertness that set them apart from the average constable with his paunch-filled khaki shirt and bamboo baton trailing in the dust. They wore fetching indigo and light-blue camouflage uniforms—hard to see quite where the camouflage would be effective, unless they were hiding in the sky, but the unusual colour achieved what I imagine was its primary purpose, high visibility. Mr Tiwari glared at one of the RAFs, who stood with his assault rifle lowered. The man nodded me forward.

"I shouldn't," I faltered to Mr Tiwari. "I should be queuing too."

"You are our *guest!*" he said, with undisguised exasperation.

Obediently, I removed my boots and passed though the gate. Dozens of faces watched me. None showed hostility, merely curiosity. Mr Tiwari followed me in. We mounted the steps, where I stared in shock at the spectacle of Hanuman being mobbed. It wasn't a Hollywood or even a Renaissance idea of spirituality. There was very little formal drama. The aesthetics of the situation were negligible—real religious fervour doesn't need theatrics. Yelling and shoving *Brahman*s kept the pilgrims moving through a grill that channelled them past the entrance to the shrine. No one had more than an instant to direct his or her adoration through the doorway. But through that doorway was the living idol, the incarnation of adorable Hanuman, Monkey God, devoted servant of Rama, exemplar of the highest *human* qualities! The devotees' offerings were torn from their hands and at once thrust back into them as they were jostled forward by the swell of the crowd behind and the strong arms of the *Brahman*s. But *darshan* had occurred. The devotee had made the journey, bought new clothes, sweetmeats, presented himself before the God. *Hanumanji, I exist, do not forget me!*

Mr Tiwari kick-started his scooter and we wove through the

crowds at a walking pace in the direction of the river. We had to cross a major road choked with trucks to reach the banks of the Saryu, a branch of the Ganga. A long, many-arched road bridge stretched across the river for perhaps a kilometre. We parked the scooter on a pavement, from which bathing *ghats* led down to thewater, two dozen or more flights of broad, shallow steps where the faithful could wade into the holy water to—as Mr Tiwari put it—"take holy dip". Grass-roofed huts owned by *pandits* stood here and there, and a clutch of *pandits* waited for business. "People take dip, get some *tilak* [the splash of sandalwood paste dabbed on their foreheads] and with that service these *Brahmans* are supporting their families." He paused. "The water has miraculous properties, you know."

"Really?"

"I tell you, sir, you take a drop of this water, your cough and cold will be gone! It is my personal observation!" Ob-sair-*vay*-she-on. "You can keep this water of this river for one year, two, three, four years, without it becoming stale."

"Because it's fast-flowing?"

"*Fast-flowing? No!* Because it is *holy water!*"

I watched a middle-aged man wrap a *lunghi* under his bulbous breasts, with their frostings of white hair around the nipples, and wade in. Mr Tiwari returned to his theme of the rich-poor divide. "It is the village people of India who sustain religion, not the urbanites and intellectuals. This festival is alive because of illiterate people. You will not find a single person belonging to upper tens."

"'Upper tens'?"

"Upper ten per cent of society. Rich persons, aristocrats, politicians and the like. For some reason, they will have nothing to do with these 'bogus' things."

"I'd have thought the reason is pretty obvious," I ventured. "Rationalism, the breakdown of the conservative values of rural life. Economic migration to the cities. And isn't there another factor in India—don't cities give people a way to escape from the restrictions of the caste system?"

Mr Tiwari pursed his lips.

"You *don't* consider it bogus?" I persisted.

"I think it is the most essential thing of life!"

149

"Religion?"

"No, not religion—*God*! The rich have to suffer more than the poor. They will get only money, nothing more! And where there is money, there is no religion. They think what they have is their own attainment, not given by God. Oh, but when they get ill, when they suffer—*then* they remember God!"

He led me along the shore to another, lofty-domed temple. "This is Nageshwarnath Temple, supposed to have been established by Raja Kush—younger son of Lord Rama. It is the most important temple in Ayodhya."

"Why's that? Considering that the whole town is devoted to Rama."

He shot me another irritated look, then shrugged. "These other places are historic; but it is believed that Lord Shiva himself lives here. It is *alive*."

The same was true in Varanasi's principal temple. For all the worship of Rama or Krishna, incarnations of Vishnu, most of India was nowadays "Shaivite" (or Shivite)—predominantly it worshipped Shiva.

We passed into candlelit gloom, where in the midst of a frantic swirl of worshippers a stone *lingam*—symbolic penis of Shiva—was splattered with gold and crimson flowers, and awash with coconut milk and ghee. Juices and petals filled the elliptical tray in which the *lingam* was planted, *yoni* grasping *lingam*. Only when the phallus is surrounded by the *yoni* can procreation take place and, from that cosmic copulation, the world arises. It's a common sight in temples, worshippers spilling libations over *lingams*, caressing them.

"Male and female," intoned Mr Tiwari, "—lower part symbolizes Parvathi, wife of Shiva. Circle is female organ, womb. External as well as internal. *Lingam* is Lord Himself. God gave a blessing that Shiva should be worshipped in shape of *lingam*. On *shivrathri* in March, the anniversary of His marriage, He presents himself to His devotees, only they can see Him. A man who has belief, the divine eye, the spiritual eye—he only can see Him."

"You worship Him?" I asked.

"I worship Goddess Durga, because without energy nothing is possible. When I suffered from acute disease—I'm a chronic diabetic

—I discovered that worshipping her is the only way to get better. Doctors say I'm an acute diabetic, yet now I have no symptoms of diabetes."

We watched the energetic *pandits*, shaven-headed, stripped to the waist, a cotton thread round their shoulders, splashing and scattering with quick, practised hands.

"To be perfectly frank," said Mr Tiwari thoughtfully, "I am not sure even these *Brahmans* have seen the God they worship. All that glitters is not gold. Appearances are deceptive." I looked at him, waiting for more.

"The corruption in some of these temples is boundless, you know that? The most popular temples are money-making machines. Donations are diverted into the pockets of unscrupulous priests. They are *not* priests—they are scoundrels. Come between them and their ill-gotten gains and they would not hesitate to kill you. Did you know that?"

"Are you *kidding*?"

He gave my question the scornful look it evidently deserved. Mr Tiwari did not *kid*. He shrugged. "I do not say *all*, I say *some*. But even the working temple *Brahmans*—religion is providing their bread and butter. I'm not criticizing them, I am praising my religion! All are a family and God is the father. My God is Creator, He is preserver. God says, you give me something, I give you something. Less leads to less, more leads to more. Everything leads to everything. Partial surrender means partial attainment."

"Mm . . ." I said. I stared at him quizzically.

"God has sent me to help you," he stated.

"I see. And why do you think that is?"

"So that you may not be deceived by those people who are known as thieves and thugs. We are puppets. The guest is God—even Bernard Shaw has written this thing in *Arms and the Man*."

I nodded, but I still wasn't sure what he was getting at. He sensed this, and if, in the course of the afternoon we'd spent together, he'd often seemed impatient with the task he was having to perform, now, as evening was falling, he seemed to be striving to tell me something that mattered to him. And for the first time he was behaving as though *I* mattered. I asked if I could buy him a cup of tea and suddenly I saw how weak he looked. I remembered the diabetes. We climbed up into a small, open-sided tea house. Boys brought sweet tea in glasses; small bowls made from pressed leaves held peanuts and slices of dried coconut in chilli. In the street underneath our toes, a man had a cart loaded with glass bangles displayed on poles, glittering columns of ruby, emerald and gilt.

"Many people come to Ayodhya," Mr Tiwari said. "Some of them for a picnic, a day out, a holiday decreed by tradition. Because they do not have any spiritual power, they do not feel the presence of God. The temple is empty, the God is absent. They feel they know this. I know their mental and spiritual state—their mental and spiritual *weakness*.

"You see, if a man has spiritual power, he does not roam—he does not need to wander from temple to temple. These pilgrimages—it is fallacious.

"In *Gitangali*, Tagore writes that God does not live in temples. I go there because he meets me there. If he does not meet me there, I will not go there."

He looked at me soberly. "I am a *pukha* religious *Brahman*, not by body but by mind, not by caste but by practice. I take my bath every morning at four, then meditate until six. Then I am ready to start my day. I am proud to have been born a *Brahman*, but in truth that is beside the point—what is more important is, do I *live* as a *Brahman*? You understand that?"

"I do," I said.

Traditionally the *Brahman*s were the guardians of the temples and officiators in all the ceremonies that mark the passages of life and death. They were educated, literate, the repositories of lore and law; and they were *privileged*—though not necessarily in a financial sense. Making money was beneath them, but their caste superiority was worth infinitely more than mere gold.

It has been argued that by the time the British came to govern India, the *Brahman*s presided over a decadent social order that favoured them utterly and subjected the lowest orders in society to a form of subjugation that was all the more brutal for implying that they had earned their low status through transgressions in previous lives— the *Brahman*s, by the same logic, had *deserved* their superior status by performing meritorious deeds. Many in India today still revile the *Brahman* castes for the power they once yielded so callously.

Although the *Brahmans* are a minority in India—three per cent of the Indian population (Uttar Pradesh, where Ayodhya is, has more *Brahmans* than any other Indian state, at around nine per cent), they do not easily forget their ancient status. But as their influence has waned in post-Independence India, they have become a minority group like any other. Today's *Brahmans* are more likely to be professors, journalists, artists, politicians or scientists than *pandits*. *Brahmans* have a reputation for a certain cunning and drive, the ability to maximise their opportunities. Yet as the country has increasingly favoured its business classes, the phenomenon of the "poor *Brahman*" is talked about more and more. Impoverished *Brahmans* forced into the cities to find work sometimes become rickshaw drivers or even—gulp—*cleaners*. The most surprising aspect of *Brahman* existence in India today is that tens of thousands of them have been forced out of Kashmir by the war with Pakistan, which is in many ways, de facto, a war of religion; the exiles live as refugees in Delhi and elsewhere.

Clan, *jati*, caste, tribe—these terms will stay in Indian life for centuries to come. For the present, they still play a powerful role, one that is by no means Politically Correct. Hinduism has four traditional *varnas*, or castes. Each has its own duties, rights, diet, traditional occupation etc. The highest *varna* is the *Brahman*. Next come the *Kshatriyas*—the rulers, aristocrats, warlords of society. After them are the *Vaisia*, landlords and businessmen. Lastly are the *Sudra*, the peasants and working classes who work in *non-polluting* jobs. Lowest of all are the *dalits*, traditionally "untouchable" and spiritually polluting, who work in cleaning, sewage etc. (The British colonials naturally attached themselves to the *higher* castes—who are, to this day, the most "Europeanized" Indians. By the way, it's worth noting that Indian Muslims and Christians also observe caste, often in just as discriminatory a way as the Hindus.)

The system is impossibly complex and seems likely to have very ancient roots, which may have *their* roots in some form of colonial apartheid, or perhaps even a rational division of labour far less pernicious than what it eventually became. Suffice to say that in parts of rural India the system's rigidity still discriminates severely against the Untouchables (known by the government as Scheduled Classes —i.e., scheduled for state assistance, a category that includes India's seventy-five million tribals). The "scheduling" of these disadvantaged castes has meant setting aside quotas for university participation and even numbers of Air India stewardesses. It has led to massive resentment among the higher castes. To which the answer of the lower orders is: "Tough." Recently, the *Sudras* have at last begun to form a significant voting block. The various intermediate castes squabble interminably about their relative status. As for the *Brahman*s, no longer do they dominate the ranks of senior politicians, as they did at Independence. Their days of innate superiority have passed.

Mr Tiwari had asked me if I understood what he meant when he said that he lived as a *Brahman* and I had presumed to say that I did.

A shadow crossed his face. "My children cannot understand it. They have no notion of these things, they are busy, simply studying and studying. My eldest son—I desire that he should be religious-minded, but also coping with present conditions, the conditions that prevail in India today. It is fast-changing, you know, it is almost bewildering. Where will he go? Lucknow? Bangalore? I cannot say— it was inconceivable that I should remove myself from the presence of my parents, but I have no idea where my own son will go—he *wants* to go to America. He is doing an MCA in computer science. But wherever he lives, he should not lose his religion, his contact with God. That is my fear. I have risen from utter poverty. All my life I have done tuitions after school in order to earn money. At present, I have a double-storey building. I own a scooter. But money is nothing to me—I do not hoard. I have many people to support. Naturally, I want that my children should not know poverty. My son wants a car—Papa is riding an old scooter, but *he* wants a new car. He does not know how he is going to manage that car, to pay for petrol or mechanical upkeep. But he is in dreamland. He dreams of El Dorado. He believes money will come to him. Perhaps it *will*—India is growing rich. But will he lose God? Can he *find* God in this new India? What chance could he have in . . . *America?*"

THE NEXT DAY, I steeled myself for the short journey into Ayodhya. Mr Tiwari had warned me not to go. There was a danger of violence. But I'd travelled a long way to see Ayodhya on its Prince's birthday. I took one precaution: I dressed in a *kurta-pyjama,* a collarless shirt and trousers made from *khadi.* I hoped they'd make me look a bit like a pilgrim.

I had to park the Bullet on the edge of town. I left it in front of a friendly tea shop and continued on foot, moving through a dense press of people. On fields outside the town, people had camped in canvas tents and under nylon tarpaulins. The press of people made me feel uneasy and I was glad I'd worn boots I'd be able to run in if I needed to, instead of the *kolhapuri* sandals I usually wore. I couldn't shake off fantasies of a crowd panic, where people would be crushed underfoot. I kept close to the gutter where I could dive into the safety of one of the small shops if necessary.

When the riot came, I wasn't anywhere near it. But I heard the crackle of gunfire. The packed crowd reacted pretty much as I'd expected—the way you see a shoal of minnows change direction instantly, as one. But they didn't all turn and run away from the sound of gunfire—they ran chaotically, some from the left-hand side of the road to the right, some from the right-hand side to the left. People froze, gripped children, cannoned into each other, stumbled —some even flinched or ducked. I was about half a kilometre from the site of the gunfire. I dived into a little grocery store and wondered what to do. There were a couple of customers, chattering anxiously. More people crowded into the shop, pushing me towards the back. The owner began to yell. We heard more gunfire, like distant firecrackers. A wave of people surged away from the centre of Ayodhya.

I squeezed to the front of the shop and looked out. The crowd was moving steadily away from the town centre, but now there was no panic. I stepped out of the shop and returned as quickly as I could to my motorbike.

The following day the papers reported that an angry crowd had pushed against a scaffolding tower, from which a policeman had fallen to his death. Although this may seem a callous observation—a death toll of one was unexceptional, compared to the 13,000-odd lives consumed by the Ayodhya affair since the early 1990s.

I decided to go into Ayodhya at once, before the sun grew hot, before the streets filled again with crowds. I could see no sign of damage or struggle of any kind—though few shops in Ayodhya have glass windows. In the event of trouble all the traders have to do is drop their metal grills. There were some parked buses that had presumably brought in the police reinforcements, but even the police presence on the streets didn't seem excessive. By mid-morning it was clear that most pilgrims had left town. The population of Ayodhya was barely a quarter of what it had been the previous day.

THE FIGURE THAT emerged from shadows to unlock the grills was as slender as a man can be. He wore a cotton singlet, underneath which his breastbone stood out against the taut skin of his chest. He did not seem pleased to be disturbed, but I produced the name Mark Tully, and it proved to be a passport. He invited me into a small office, with a dark-green metal desk reminiscent of the 1950s, an anglepoise lamp of similar vintage, two chairs and a bed that seemed to be serving as a bookcase. "So, you know Mr Mark Tully? He's a friend of yours?"

"I've worked with him—we used to be colleagues, at the BBC. I met up with him last week in Delhi. I'm writing a book about the *Ramayana*. Mark told me you might be able to be—perhaps in some way—a guide to Ayodhya for me."

"No, not at all," he said quickly. "I know nothing about Ayodhya. I never leave this temple. I take no interest in the communal dimension. I quite possibly know even less about Ayodhya than you do, my good sir."

I laughed nervously. "Do you know anyone else who might be able to help me?"

"Not at all," he said quickly. "I know no one here. This is a small town, you know. Very few people speak English. Ayodhya has no intellectual life of any kind."

"You don't perhaps know a student, someone who might be able to take me around . . ."

"I know no one at all, I'm afraid," he said with finality. "Have you read Mr Tully's book? It's a very good book. He mentions me, you know."

"Yes, of course."

"A *very* good book." He reached behind him. "I have my copy here, look. See, he dedicated it to me." He opened a hardback copy of *India in Slow Motion* at the title page. "A very nice man. And his, er . . . Gillian, isn't it? She speaks excellent Hindi."

"Yes." I was feeling weary.

"I'm an author myself," he said.

"Really?" I now felt desperate. I knew where this was going. I was about to have—as so often happens—an amateurish manuscript thrust at me, autobiographical witterings or an unreadable novel.

"Yes, I have published two books privately, here in Ayodhya. It is very expensive, it has cost me a great deal of money. And the printing is appalling. Sadly, I have no copies here, or I would show you one. Well . . ." He looked at the watch on his bony wrist.

"Hm," I said, getting the message. I stood up, ready to leave. "What", I added politely, "are the books about?"

"They have nothing to do with the contemporary life of Ayodhya, nothing could interest me less. They are translations—one of the Tulsidas *Ramayana*, the other is of a collection of writings dedicated to Sri Hanuman. Books of devotion, you know. Have you heard of the *Ramayana* of Valmiki?"

"Of course I have. I've read it several times."

For the first time since I had entered the room, Ajai Kumar Chhawchharia looked at me with interest. "But do you know the *Ramcharitmanas*, the *Ramayana* of Tulsidas?"

"I do," I said. "I have a reprint of the nineteenth-century translation, by Growse."

"*Ah* . . . You surprise me, sir. It is almost unknown. In English, I mean. Tulsidas *is* the *Ramayana* to the Hindi-speaking masses—not Valmiki's work, which has been endlessly translated but which is rarely read by ordinary people. Tulsidas's work is probably the best-loved and in many ways the most significant book in Hinduism. He is the greatest Hindi poet, his significance is such that you could almost call him the Hindi Shakespeare! And yet it is an enigma to most English-speakers. So, I have made it my life's work. To bring this, perhaps the most loved work in the whole canon of Hindu literature—to make its beauty and power available to the reader of English."

WE STEPPED OUTSIDE. The afternoon was hot. Ajai Kumar carried a fine cane, Chaplin-style. "It is for the *monkeys* only!" He pointed to a pair of them, hazelnut-brown, crouching slyly nearby. "They are a menace, they are a *scourge*. Later we must put your motorbike away safely or they will rip the seats to pieces."

He led me towards *Kanak Bhavan*'s accommodation wing. "Our rooms are almost all empty, it's one effect of all this controversy—pilgrimage has fallen off, visitor numbers have dropped precipitously. Some of these big suites used to be taken by wealthy people. We don't specify a payment—they make a contribution when they leave—but on this the wealth of this temple was highly dependent. This is an old building, the cost of the upkeep is high, we have staff to pay . . . The House of Rama has fallen on hard times."

Kanak Bhavan, literally, House of Gold. It was a nineteenth-century palace, built by a rich maharani as a conceit—located on a traditional site, it was venerated as the palace where Rama and Sita lived immediately after their marriage. The big ring of keys in Ajai Kumar's hands jangled as he unlocked and opened grills—principally designed to keep out the monkeys. He threw open doors and showed me rooms, anterooms, private kitchens, extra bathrooms. The rooms were large, half-tiled with pleasant geometric designs, but otherwise sparsely furnished and plain. "This is our best suite. You're quite welcome to it. No charge, no charge—if you feel like it, when you leave, you make a contribution, we're not a commercial enterprise." He barked a couple of syllables at the man accompanying us, who began at once to attack the dust under the low wooden beds with a switch.

We moved onto the balcony, squinting from the *Bhavan*'s high vantage point across the rooftops of Ayodhya. "We used to be able to see it from here, you know. The Babri Masjid, its three domes—just there, a few hundred yards away. Mr Tully and his BBC crew, I think they filmed it from here. The destruction. Such a foolish outcome. Such hypocrisy! The demonization of Muslims! Muslims and Hindus have lived here, more or less in harmony, for hundreds of years. Yes, they were our masters, then the British were our masters. Does anyone talk of tearing down the churches? No, they don't, although perhaps they would if it gave them some political advantage. The Muslims here, there are no differences between communities. Muslims will say '*Namaste*' when greeting you. They tailor clothes, they labour—they even work in temple construction. The flower gardens all belong to them, they make the garlands and rosaries we offer our gods! If some of the *Brahmans* are so adamant about the Masjid, why are garlands from Muslim hands being offered to the Lord? Where is the consistency?"

THE NEXT MORNING I moved into *Kanak Bhavan*. I hoped Ajai Kumar might spare me some time that day, but he said he was too busy. I can't have hidden my disappointment very well, for he quickly added, "I have my duties for the temple, and certain other obligations of my own. I have little time to socialize, I'm afraid. But I will try to spare you an hour or so in the late afternoon. Say, at four?"

Sensing that he was a man of rigid discipline, I turned up promptly. We walked into his little office and he offered me a glass of water. "It isn't ice cold, I'm afraid, I have no refrigerator. It's from the *ghara*, an earthenware pot, it's kept cool by evaporation—"

"That's cool enough for me," I said, wanting to press on.

He handed me the steel beaker. "So, my good sir. I have no interest at all in politics, you know—"

"That's fine—I'd like to hear more about Tulsidas."

Ajai Kumar handed me copies of his two books. They were self-published—cheaply printed pamphlets.

"They are very crude," he said. "Local printers. Poor paper. All I could afford. It cost 25,000 rupees to print one, you know, and 10,000 for the other. And what am I to do with them? How can I distribute them?"

I flicked through the first volume. "You described the Tulsidas *Ramayana* as the best-loved and most-read book in Hinduism. And in the West, very few people have even heard of it."

"How many versions of Valmiki are available in Britain?"

"Well . . . I own ten. Add together the new Berkeley translation, various devotional and children's editions . . . I'd say at least two dozen."

"And of Tulsidas, none."

I shrugged. "None. There's a clear need for your book."

He gave a wan smile. "Well, the Valmiki is an important ancient epic, while Tulsidas is a mediæval poet. But still . . . they are a duo, as it were. Valmiki is historical, Tulsidas is far more devotional. Valmiki writes in Sanskrit, the language of the priestly caste, but Tulsidas wants to make Rama's story accessible to the common man. You see, Valmiki's *spiritual message* was too abstract for the masses. Like Christ, he embodied religious principles, and slowly his message became ritualized, and the philosophy became abbreviated, truncated."

I wondered if I agreed about that. It seemed to me that there were very few religious principles in Valmiki's *Ramayana*. Was there some underlying mystical symbolism, like Arthur and the Holy Grail . . .? I wasn't sure. But undoubtedly Valmiki's Rama *had* been ritualized, *religionized*, as it were. Tulsidas had perfected and completed that process.

"Tulsidas", Ajai Kumar went on, "was basically a devotional poet. He thought Rama probably had the most righteous *dharma* of any person who had ever lived—that's why he selected him to be the subject of his writing. His Rama was absolutely an incarnation of God. What *I* learned from Tulsidas is that it wasn't Rama's body that was holy, but his *soul*. So we can all be Rama if we can suppress the demonic in ourselves. He is a blueprint for human perfection, for human happiness. This is his power. People consider Tulsidas a saint, now, they say he was divinely inspired. They call the *Ramcharitmanas* the fifth *Veda,* you know—it would be like calling something the Fifth Gospel."

Ajai Kumar's face was lit up, now. "My mother was a very religious-minded woman. She taught me to read one line of Tulsidas every day. When I graduated, she told me, 'This is God's work, not yours'! But you know, Tulsidas has an intensely vivid narrative! His pen pictures are far superior to Valmiki's. The war is wonderfully painted. And his Hindi is so beautiful and so memorable! So grammatically correct! These are the qualities that still endear him to the Hindi-speaking masses."

The text the *Ramayana* is most frequently compared with is the *Odyssey*. I tried to imagine several hundred million Europeans daily reading, reciting and quoting Homer, the market place witticism, the improving epigram for the child. I failed.

"When he was writing," Ajai Kumar went on, "Hinduism was in a period of sharp decline. It was under severe pressure from Islam. With this one work Tulsidas gave an immense impetus to a Hindu renaissance whose effects we feel to this day."

He launched into the story of Tulsidas's life. As a child, the saint had been orphaned and adopted by the priests of a temple. He married early and a colourful story is told of the ascetic's attachment to sex as a young man. His wife had received an urgent message to visit her parents in a nearby village. Restless at the thought of a night without her, Tulsidas left home. It was raining heavily and the Ganges was flooded. Unable to find a boat or swim, he caught hold of a passing corpse and used it as a float. He reached the house late at night and decided to enter by stealth, from the roof. Trying to drop down into his wife's room, he caught hold of a rope—that turned out to be a snake. He dropped it and collapsed on the floor of his wife's bedroom, soaked through and stinking like a corpse. She was disgusted. "You're always going on about Lord Rama, but if you were half as interested in him as you are in my body you'd have met him by now!"

Tulsidas was, Ajai Kumar continued, tormented by the *Brahmans*. "They wouldn't allow the translation of Valmiki, because they didn't want the common man to have access to the story. Tulsidas says God is in your heart, you can obtain salvation just through chanting His name. The *Brahmans* thought that if people can have contact with God in their homes, they'll keep away from temples! So they stole the manuscript. And after that, he couldn't find a publisher! He was forced to go to an ancient press in Bombay . . ."

I had told Ajai Kumar I intended to include an abridged *Ramayana* in my own book. "You will put Tulsidas into your narrative!" he said.

"Well, it would become a bit of a cocktail . . ."

"But it will be a very unique cocktail! When you have guests, you do not put out one type of biscuit, but five or six types!"

(In the event, for the sake of clarity, I avoided cocktails; my abridgement is almost neat Valmiki.)

I CONTINUED my explorations of Ayodhya. In every street there were several temples. During *aarthi*, at dusk, I would glimpse in the space of five minutes a score of shrines, their devotees filling the air with the sound of bells and the chanted words, *Sita-Ram, Sita-Ram* . . . At the same time the city confronted me with the bewildering and often depressing spectacle of a once-glittering spiritual metropolis in the last stages of decline. It had been rich, you could tell that—not just the palatial temples and the sheer number of domes and spires that dominated the skyline, but the evidence in every street and alleyway of substantial, ornate and highly decorated houses and *dharamshalas*—pilgrim rest houses—many of them now in advanced states of decay. The city had the misfortune to be in corrupt and impoverished Uttar Pradesh, and there was little evidence that the politicians who'd recently done so much to put Ayodhya on the political map—and to promulgate grandiose plans for a new temple to straddle the site of the demolished mosque— were spending any money improving the rotten fabric of the place (though a beautification programme was slowly transforming the edges of Ayodhya where rubbish-strewn slums met the holy River Sarayu). As I walked around Ayodhya I stepped from one piece of shattered, uneven paving to another, the cracks and missing flag- stones revealing black gutters awash with sewage, or merely the opaque soapy water from ablutions. There was the smell of dis- infectant, too. The town's little army of Untouchables were labouring to keep pollution and disease within acceptable limits. No map I'd found made any sense of Ayodhya's tangle of tiny alleys. Sometimes it felt like a kind of ruined Venice—impenetrable alleyways, then an unexpected view of a broad, hazy Lido. The town was too sprawling and too hot to explore on foot—I was constantly in a state of heat exhaustion, needing to sit down with a cold drink. So I prowled by bike, stopping to climb a staircase or enter a temple or peer into the ruined compounds of some decaying edifice.

I was lost in a network of alleys close, I'd thought, to the river. I took off my helmet and met a profound silence. Set in an open courtyard was a tiny, decaying mosque with an elegant, slender minaret. Bushes grew from the roof. It was set in a delightful courtyard, cooled by the leaves of several trees. I had arrived in one of Ayodhya's Muslim quarters. A few questions asked of the inhabitants of the crumbling houses nearby led to an old man tottering forward with a key ring in his gnarled hands. The elaborately carved wood of the doors was grey with age. We stepped into a dusty, perfectly proportioned space, with sunlight sneaking past closed shutters in narrow vertical shafts. As my eyes adjusted they took in the perfect proportions of the little mosque, its *minbar* (pulpit) and stone flags, and the trails of the termites descending the walls like dried drips. A few chairs and newspapers lay around, thick with dust. I asked the old man a foolish question: if the mosque was ever used. He shook his head. Too old, he said, and no funds to restore it. Sad, I said—it was beautiful. He shrugged and pointed to some newer concrete structure where the faithful now met. The old one waited for collapse, or perhaps for some new wave of fashion, or prosperity, to lift Ayodhya up from the swamp of neglect. Allah alone—Peace Be Upon Him—knew when that would be.

ON THE RAILWAY station side of Ayodhya there was a large godown where sections of stone were cut and carved, and piled in layers twenty feet high. This was the new temple of Rama, under construction. Nearby stood a symbolic brick wall, a fund-raising exercise—each brick had been "purchased" by well-wishers, and many were engraved with their provenance in Europe, the Far East or America. The new temple being funded by this generosity would be hewn from solid stone, making use of no steel or concrete, held in place by the force of gravity alone. But whether the temple would ever take its place on that dusty mound where the Babri Masjid had stood seemed in doubt. A court order was preventing—and seemed likely to continue to prevent—construction to commence.

Nearby was the compound of the fundamentalist VHP, or World Hindu Council, where a model of the proposed temple was on display in a shed. If the building were ever completed, it would be an impressive structure. Inevitably, the model was expected to be treated with reverence—I had to remove my shoes to walk round it. People entering the shed bobbed and blessed it as though they were entering an actual sacred space. Which, in a sense, they were. Indian sacred spaces do not have to be consecrated by some remote archbishop in order to become "legit". They are sacred as a result of being *regarded as* sacred. As such, they give the devotee permission, as it were, to venerate. This is how Hinduism is. The state of veneration, the ability to experience a religious emotion, is never far away.

The offices of the VHP were a red-brick building opposite the shed. The man in charge was Prakash Avasthi, who offered me a cup of tea and said he was willing to answer any questions I might have. A few years ago he had suffered from a stroke, and when he smiled only the right side of his face moved. His disabled left hand, which he held with his right, was curiously smooth. I found him a pleasant enough man; and utterly dogmatic. Our exchange went something like this:

Q: Do you really believe that your great new temple will ever be built here? Won't the national politicians' need to find compromise keep it stuck in the courts for decades?

A: India has had strong Hindu politicians in the past; another may come. If God wills it, the strong man will come.

Q: Do you have any regrets about the way things turned out in Ayodhya, and all the killings that followed?

A: We have no regrets.

Q: But hasn't the whole controversy set back the cause of Hindu politics and given the world the impression that India is an intolerant society?

A: We are compromising! The Muslim invaders destroyed thousands of temples; we have asked for the demolition of three mosques in the whole of India. How is that intolerant? And please, let us not call that structure in Ayodhya a mosque. No sacraments had been performed there for thirty years, so how is that a mosque? It was a *former* mosque!

Q: Shouldn't everyone observe the rule of law, though?

A: Were the Muslims who invaded this country and slaughtered and demolished observing any laws? Did the Emperor Babur observe a law when he demolished the Rama temple here and built his mosque?

Q: But shouldn't you be behaving better than that today?

A: The Muslims have an opportunity here to make amends

for historic crime. They should apologize for their past crimes, as other regimes around the world have apologized for past genocides. As a gesture, they should accept the demolition of a tiny handful of mosques in places that are particularly sensitive to Hindus. That will be the basis for future communal harmony. Hindus were temperamentally too passive in the past. Our scriptures taught us tolerance and renunciation. That allowed the whole culture to be threatened. Now that has changed. We have too many sects in Hinduism, too many different Scriptures and holy books. We have to unify. The Muslims are unified all over the world. We have to follow that example if we want to protect ourselves.

Q: And do you feel regret for the recent violence in Gujarat, when 2,000 people were killed?

A: In a war, there can be no compromise; innocent people will suffer. The Muslims needed a bashing. Are they not uncompromising and aggressive? They want to convert the whole world to Islam, it is a tenet of their faith! Everything is calm in Gujarat now because we hit back at the Muslims. Only when a slap is answered with a counter-slap will people learn their lesson!

OPPOSITE MY WINDOW the wall of the derelict palace or temple had recessed into it an elaborate biscuit-bitten Mughal arch, pierced by several ogeed windows. Beneath them an imposing double door had been permanently obstructed by a mean row of lean-to shops, no doubt illegally constructed and resembling a row of garages, each of them just six feet wide, with tin roofs and metal shutters. Only one of the shops was functioning—as a barbershop. A man dressed in white sat himself on the hard wooden seat and contentedly examined his face in the mirror, while the barber slopped up some shaving foam in a mug. He flicked his brush to remove the excess foam and it splashed onto the pavement. In one of the elegant ancient windows above them sat a monkey. The monkeys are clearly accelerating the decline and fall of Ayodhya. I watched the creature absent-mindedly pluck a half-loose brick out of the wall and let it fall onto the tin roof below, where it joined a little mound of previously dislodged bricks. The barber looked up in annoyance at the bang, then continued with his work.

It was seven p.m. I walked over the *Bhavan*'s central courtyard towards the evening *aarthi*. I was inside the temple in shoes, which Ajai had told me was acceptable in the main courtyard. But I heard a sharp, "Sir, *sir!*" and I stopped guiltily, assuming someone was ticking me off about the shoes. An instant later my bag was plucked from my hand by a monkey. The animal skittered away from me and the contents of the bag erupted in an arc across the courtyard. All I was carrying were books, pens and notebooks. Disgusted, the monkey darted away.

I removed my shoes. At midday the stone underfoot had been painfully hot and the air humid, but now the evening was cool and the stone was merely pleasantly warm, and the drone of voices was soothing. The air was thick with cicadas. I trotted up the marble steps of God's palace.

About twenty people were seated before the idols, some chatting, some swaying, some clasping their hands in prayer. I sat before the open curtain and looked into the shrine. A devotee clad all in white prostrated himself on the carpet, then squatted beside me, gazing expectantly at the Gods. Another man sat to my left, impoverished, poorly dressed, shaven-headed but for the tiny *Brahman* tuft of hair on the back of his cranium, and the twin moustaches growing from his ears. We were at the head of the men's queue; to our right were the women; a larger group of devotees was gathering in the hall behind us.

A portable accordion played, cymbals tinkled between thumbs and index fingers. Drums and horns began to sound. Devotees approached, fingers intertwined in prayer, stepped over a low rail and bowed and prayed to the God who inhabited a small marble statue, His eyes outlined in black, His tiny mouth lipstick-red, His forehead orange with sandal paste, His head crowned with gold, His body garlanded with flowers in a rippling ocean of orange silk. His lovely marble consort was beside him, next to them stood Lakshman and Hanuman. Men and women stooped to touch their foreheads to the step before the Gods, then brought their joined fingers to their foreheads, then their hearts. Some kissed the floor.

A wave of human energy was focused on the idols, who seemed to radiate something back to us. I found myself suddenly responding to the beauty of the little Rama, His sweet face, His gorgeous panoply. Something stirred in my heart. The *pujari* walked very delicately, with his arm turned up and fingers pointing at the sky. He shot a golden curtain across this tableau, then a saffron one. The hall had filled with people now. Big drums were beating a heavy bass note from the corners of the hall. The golden curtain closed again, starting quickly, then teasingly hovered, before closing, denying us the sight of the Gods. Then it opened one more time, before slowly, steadily, closing for good. The *darshan*, the seeing, was over.

Now the *pandit* walked around, with his curiously light gait, hands raised at the wrists, ferrying *prasad* backwards and forwards between the worshippers and worshipped. I accepted a twist of the sweet rice and began my circumnavigations of the shrine, via a corridor that passed directly behind the Gods, allowing worshippers to pause close behind the throne and put their foreheads to the wall.

THE NEXT DAY I followed Ajai Kumar across the paved courtyard and through a pair of wooden doors to the left of the altar, into a private chamber. "I sit on the floor here and work. In the old times a man called a *munim* sat on the floor with a sloping desk and a bottle of ink, he was responsible for all the master's paperwork. I am the *munim* of the deity. I feel Rama has accepted me! Each day for the last eighteen years, I've been cleaning this room with the belief that if I clean His room, He will clean *my* sins. If there is such a thing as many lives—we have to believe what our elders and what the Scriptures say—*if* it is true, then each passing year here will clean so many of my lives—I don't mean I really believe such things, but in case it *is* true . . ."

He laughed, then pointed to the wall. In cupboards, bolts of costly silks were piled to the ceilings. They were the robes of the Gods. "They wear a different colour every day. White on Monday, the colour of the moon. Red on Tuesday—Hanuman's day—the association would be Mars, wouldn't it? Wednesday is green—Venus?—and so on. Sunday is yellow, the colour of the sun.

"Apart from the temple accounts, my main work is to set out the Gods' clothes every day. The *pujaris* do the dressing, the decoration. But through the cloth I am in touch with the Gods—and it's better that way. There's a saying in Hindi, *It's better to keep some distance from your guru.* There's no danger that I might touch the skin and find that it's as cold as a corpse. People like me, intellectual types, we experience doubt—'*Ahah*, so there's no life in it!' I'm trying to bypass my own scepticism—fully aware of what I'm doing. I am consciously fooling myself! But you see, analytical, intellectual thought is pretty limited. It's mechanical. Religion is non-mechanicality, it is direct experience. And those who have witnessed, *experienced*, God are changed by the experience. They cease to be shallowly intellectual, and they aren't obsessed with money and possessions. Purposedly I want to keep my eye closed—because that gives me peace. I am serving My Lord, you see, even though He is not everywhere, even though He is not warmly alive, in the flesh, in the idol."

I had attended several *aarthis*, but I had yet to see Ajai there. "No," he said, "I do not attend. I don't believe in rituals."

"Rather an unconventional view", I said, "in a building full of people murmuring mantras and chanting hymns twenty-four hours a day!"

"Yes, people ask me '*Why* you don't put the *tilak* on your forehead?' I tell them, 'The Lord is inside me. You want that I should worship *myself?*'" Ajai Kumar laughed. "Rituals are not necessary to reach God. Idol worship is a drag on spiritual progress. It's even forbidden in the *Upanishads*[3]—not many people know that! Other, better ways exist to reach God. Devotional prayer should come from your heart. God is peace, He is where your soul finds rest.

"*But*", he went on, "ritual is a *first step*. Show a toddler how to take his first step and later he'll teach others how to walk. Ritual evokes an atmosphere, it reminds you of what you have glimpsed before, it invokes a state of potentiality. So you just sit down before the idols for a while, and absorb the atmosphere. That is very much a part of spirituality, isn't it? You lie in a bath and *soak*. You do the

[3] The *Upanishads* are part of the *Vedas*, the Hindu scriptures, and form their spiritual core.

same thing when you visit a place with a powerful spiritual atmosphere, you *soak it in*. If you are devoted, in time you will experience the bliss of meeting God. Then the task is to make your attachment to bliss permanent."

"And what is bliss?"

"Bliss? I have known bliss. I was experienceless. All my feelings vanished. I was devoid of sensation. The *Koran* calls bliss a white angel on a white horse. Seventh heaven. Dazzling light. You have a wound and the doctor comes along and relieves your pain—that is bliss for a few seconds. But we mean by bliss—Hinduism means—a higher plane of the soul. In Hindu texts there is a tradition of saying that God *isn't*. He is what remains when every illusion, every attachment to this material world, is gone. Then, you realize that you and God are one. That is bliss."

He smiled. I wanted to know more about the experience he was referring to, but somehow it seemed too intimate to pry into. Then I wondered if that experience had occurred during some meditation on Rama, if it was what had brought this highly wrought intellectual man to Ayodhya.

"I have taken a religious vow not to go outside the boundaries of Ayodhya municipality," Ajai Kumar told me. "That is my *jidh*, my commitment. If you die here, they say, you will obtain salvation. Certainly the atmosphere in this town is holier than in other places. But Ayodhya has no intellectual life, no scholarship or debate. There are these contradictions in my character. If you ask me why I have isolated myself in such a shallow place, I would say it is because of my Rama, my beloved Rama. I say God is inside us, is everywhere— yet I isolate myself here. Don't ask me to explain. There are some things you can't explain!"

A small boy poked his nose into the office and said the monkeys had been at my motorbike. "That's all right," I said, "there's nothing there."

"Please go and take a look, sir."

When I reached the locked grills, I saw they'd been pushed apart enough to make a gap a monkey could squeeze through. The boy told me with great politeness that a monkey had escaped with "camera reels".

"Not possible," I told him, "there were none on the bike."

He lowered his eyes deferentially. At this point I noticed that the lid of one of the rear panniers was open. I was sure there had been nothing in it but some heavy tools, but I unfastened the padlock, heaved open the grill and looked in the pannier.

I pulled out a greasy plywood box that had held spark plugs. One of them was lying on the ground. "It was one of these," I said.

"No, sir, it wasn't one of those," the boy said quietly.

Then I saw a scrap of cloth on the ground. In the gloom, I couldn't make it out. Then I realized it was the bag I kept my films in. Evidently I had dropped it. And my slide films were missing.

I felt a rush of anger against the monkeys, but also against myself for arrogantly assuming that I knew best when I had insisted that the boy was wrong. I tried humour. "I wonder where they are now?" I grinned.

The boy, who evidently did not hold my know-it-all attitude against me, smiled. He lifted his palm, cupped but with the fingers open, and half twisted his hand. It was the Indian gesture that means "I don't know" or "who knows". He gave a sweet smile. "A long way away, sir."

PART IV

CHAPTER 12

Across the Ganges

IN THE WEST, the cradle of individualism, artistic borrowings are suspect—and plagiarism is a crime. Scholars unpicking the influences on Shakespeare sometimes imply that he weakened the value of his art by using borrowed plots. But the story of Rama is a current that flows across frontiers and cultural barriers, adapting itself to every human plight. The tale has even crossed the religious barrier—into Buddhism—not only in Thailand but in Burma and elsewhere. Some researchers claim that the story of Rama originated in south-east Asia and migrated to India. It's a minority view.

Versions of the *Ramayana* are found in Tibet, China, Japan, Malaysia, Cambodia, Laos and Java. It has inspired sculpture, bas-relief, painting, textiles, popular fiction and, in 2007, a computer game. Currently it can be found as poetry, prose, drama and puppet plays; in Bali, it's incessantly performed as a dance drama.

Valmiki's *Ramayana* is the version most usually translated into English. But as I mentioned earlier, many more Indians know and venerate the *Ramcharitmanas* (literally, The Lake of the Deeds of Rama), which is sixty per cent Tulsidas's own work. South India has its own *Ramayana*, too, written 900 years ago by the great poet Kambar. Turn to Jainism, the world's most non-violent religion (it developed in parallel with Buddhism during the sixth century BC) and you find that it too has seen the need to grapple with this universally loved text. The Jain *Ramayana* is rational and peaceable, and—like many of the alternative versions—it puts Ravan at the centre of the plot, as a tragic anti-hero. This isn't a flesh-eating monster, but a great man, undone by the human passions he is unable to resist. In one œdipal Jain version, Ravan lusts after Sita—without knowing she's his own daughter.

Numerous tribals and subgroups have folk *Ramayana*s in their own languages. There's an Untouchable version in the Kannada language, where Ravan greedily eats a magic mango that has the power of childbirth, comically becomes pregnant and gives birth to Sita himself, later to lust after his own daughter (incest is a common theme in Indian literature). In some folk versions of the story it's told almost exclusively from the point of view of Sita. It can readily take a feminist spin, representing the plight of women in a male-dominated society.

For many Indians (including those unable to read) the oral tradition is still alive—they heard the *Ramayana* from a parent or grandparent. Others have retained vivid memories of the TV version (the new TV adaptation has up-to-date special effects and a contemporary emphasis on Sita's point of view). The differences in style and tone are boundless.

In Thailand, the story of Rama isn't a religious text and exemplar of ideal male and female behaviour; war and romance are to the fore and it's love, not lust, that makes Ravan pursue Sita. The hero of the Thai *Ramayana* is Hanuman—who isn't the selfless divine of Hindu tradition, but a rogue with an eye for the ladies.

There's a long tradition of asking, *How many Ramayanas have there been*? The answer is often given as a kind of metaphysical riddle, like this:

Rama drops his ring, which burns a hole in the ground and disappears. Faithful Hanuman, dispatched to bring it back, shrinks himself to the size of Rama's finger and disappears into the hole. In the Underworld he finds the King of the Spirits, sitting next to a platter piled high with rings—thousands of them—all Rama's. "Pick *your* Rama's ring," says the King. Hanuman replies, "But I don't know which one it is." "Ah," says the King, "*every* incarnation of Rama loses his ring. Take one back—but you won't find the Rama you knew. That incarnation has ended. Another is about to begin."

This codicil reinforces the concept of reincarnation and suggests that the flow of *Ramayana*s will never end. There's no ur-*Ramayana*, no correct version. It has endlessly been told and will always be retold. In my abridgement I've diminished the fairy tale elements, but emphasized the human observation and naturalism that make the *Ramayana* such a vivid account of kingship and war. Before

Machiavelli, Valmiki presented the responsibilities of kings with a pragmatism that verged on cynicism—tempered by *dharma*. His descriptions of the human body when it cries or bleeds show that he was a real observer of the human condition; he had seen people die—violently; he had seen blood sports; he had savoured the female body. These are difficult issues for some of the devout, since Valmiki has been turned into a kind of Gospel writer. Parts of my version may upset orthodox Hindus brought up in the blandest of puritanical Rama traditions; but I believe I am firmly within the tradition when I look into the *Ramayana* and draw out of it those elements that speak most strongly to *me*. Just as Shakespeare's plays have survived being set in Harlem, Japan and the Wild West, the *Ramayana* can take it—and continue to inspire.

THE TRUNK ROAD was two lanes wide. On either side of the tarmac was a shoulder, a strip of dust or rutted dirt colonized by tea stalls, grocery shacks, bicycle repair men, truck tyre shops. Trees, often immensely fat and ancient, warty, frothing with leaves, lined the roads—except where they'd been illegally felled, and there were many signs of that. The solid tunnels of shade I remembered were getting patchy and there were long stretches where the sun beat down uninterrupted.

My plan was to visit the sites around Ayodhya that have the strongest traditional connections with the *Ramayana*—the places Rama, Sita and Lakshman passed through en route to the small town of Chitrakut, then Panchavatti, where Sita was abducted by Ravan. With the passing of time, many of the names in the *Ramayana* have vanished, and settlements, rivers and mountains have become impossible to identify. But a number of sites within a hundred-mile circumference of Ayodhya are, beyond any doubt, those Valmiki had in mind. Several sites claim a connection with Valmiki himself, too. And since meeting Ajai Kumar I'd become interested in Tulsidas, the mediæval devotee of Rama who kicked off a religious reformation with a book that's still loved in almost every Hindi-speaking home. I decided to seek out the little ashram in Benares where Tulsidas lived and worked.

But first I was heading west—back to Lucknow. The Bullet had been playing up and needed to be serviced by someone who knew what he was doing. En route to Ayodhya it had given up the ghost about sixty miles short of the town of Bareilly, and a local roadside mechanic had spent half a day trying to repair it. We'd then boarded a bus to Bareilly and visited a shifty spare parts supplier who provided a new magneto that very obviously was not an original manufacturer's part. I had spent the night in an unspeakably squalid hotel, which left me with the strongest desire never to see Bareilly again; and in the morning we took a taxi back to the mechanic's village, as I didn't want to spend another three hours jolting in the back of a bus. I wanted the bike repaired and to be well past Bareilly by dusk. The repair was completed before an audience of at least twenty people. I'd had a feeling that for all his apparent friendliness, the mechanic saw me as a meal ticket, a plump chicken ready to be plucked. He ripped me off more soundly than I think I ever have been in India, presenting his bill with a flourish to a hushed silence from our audience. I paid up, cursing my trusting stupidity in not having negotiated his rates before we started. The illusion of friendship was maintained, there were handshakes and grins, and I got sixty feet up the road before the bike stopped working again. Two hours of further fumbling passed. And then, gingerly, I was off once more.

From Ayodhya, I'd hoped the Bullet would get me across country to Allahabad, 150 miles to the south, where I could find a serious mechanic. But after a few miles the bike began to hiccup again and I decided to head for Lucknow—if the bike gave up the ghost completely, I'd be better off on a main highway than stuck in the backwoods halfway between Ayodhya and Allahabad.

So I was back on the Trunk Road, driving defensively, expecting the unexpected. In addition to the dangers from other road users, a child might step out from behind a roadside shack, or a rut, invisible until I was on top of it, might catapult me into the path of some oncoming leviathan. When drivers wanted to stop they did so abruptly, without indicating—the onus was on the vehicle behind to notice and react. When lorries broke down, as they often did, they stayed on the road, with a few large stones around them as a warning signal, while the drivers slithered underneath. Repairs completed, they roared away without removing the rocks, which became a particular hazard for me, especially at dusk. (In general, the advice to motorcyclists is *don't drive at night*.)

If something caught my eye and I wanted to look at it, I had to check what was behind me, slow down, *get off the road*, turn, cross two carriageways and drive back. It was a palaver—so I rarely paused; I pressed on. It was hot and dusty. The odometer seemed to be on a go-slow. As I negotiated the pitted tarmac and death-waltzed with fellow motorists, it was almost impossible to get above thirty-five or forty miles an hour.

When I needed to eat, I usually stopped at one of the modest roadside joints. The food had flavour and the people were human. The building would be little more than a big shack, open to the elements. There'd be wooden benches and a few plastic chairs arranged under spreading branches. Sometimes I'd have to wake up waiters who were deeply asleep on a bench, their limbs outstretched and limp. Or else they'd be wandering in from the outside shower, bare-chested, with a checked *lunghi* folded back above their knees. An older man, in a *lunghi* and a cotton singlet full of holes, would be preparing the food, standing behind big pans of rice, curries, *dahls,* pulling the flat lids on and off the steaming pans and using a fan made from woven leaves to keep off the flies. The waiters were thin young men with fine noses, thick hair and large hands that made you think they'd spent a few years with hoe and rake before they entered this world. They had soft eyes—smiling, curious, communicative eyes. To look into them was to know that Europe was more than just a plane ride away.

New (and supposedly hygienic) restaurants were springing up along the Trunk Roads, gated compounds signalled by long, Coca-Cola-logoed walls. I decided to try one. The car park was crammed with the little saloon cars of the nouveaux prosperous. A man in shorts was diligently watering a half-dozen rose bushes. I went through the smoked-glass door, ordered tea and "sweet bread", and found myself next to a family of seven, each of whom had the face of a frog—from mother-in-law to babe-in-arms, the same moon face, down-turned mouth and prodigious, sagging jowls. It was only mid morning, but morosely, silently, they stuffed themselves. It was the very model of passive-aggressive petit-bourgeois complacency.

The rich in poor countries, I reflected, often seem to believe that only systematic gluttony will keep poverty at bay.

The hall was air-conditioned and well-mopped, but brash and ugly, a *desi* take on a Western fast food joint. India is rich in vernacular styles and decorative traditions—so why was so much new design so phoney? I found myself thinking of the *babus* satirized in colonial times for their spats and collar-studs—their absurd eagerness to ape the colonial masters. For all its new-found success, India lacks the confidence to be *itself*. And in a country with many competing identities, an external influence can represent a kind of neutrality, avoidance of conflict.

India is absorbing foreign influences wholesale, with insufficient irony and caution, and often with unhappy results. Something of the country's distinctiveness and pride is disappearing. Delhi is becoming full of people in hideous Western clothes—not so much the Anglophone élites as the lower middle classes and the poorer clerks and workers, who are increasingly indistinguishable from the drones of Beijing or Brasilia. At New Delhi airport two female employees of the budget airline Kingfisher—an offshoot, unpleasantly enough, of the beer brand—waddled past me in red miniskirts, looking like Mexican tarts. The Kingfisher brand defines itself as modern, it is young male-aspirational and its unique selling point is a kind of leering, naff sexiness (it even publishes a Pirelli-ish calendar). This is modernity defined as men having money and women having tits. The company's Chief Executive, the liquor baron Vijay Mallya, had himself photographed for London's *Observer* magazine as a vast paunch, a whale asea in the turquoise of his swimming pool, one hand gripping a bottle of beer. Mallya was recently nominated India's eighth most influential man: "Because he embodies the high life and hard work of young India."

I HAD REACHED an area of industrial strip development on the fringe of Lucknow where there were no cosy roadside eateries. Hunger pangs made me pull up at a truck halt, a two-storey building in the middle of a row of welding shops. At the centre of the establishment the cashier, an obese, scowling man, squatted on a table behind a great vat of boiling oil in which he deep-fried *samosas* and *parathas*. A sour-faced young waiter threw a couple of the *samosas* in front of me on a paper plate. The oil had had the goodness boiled out of it a year ago and had penetrated the pastry, leaving a pattern of soot grains on the surface. It tasted the way sump oil must taste. When the waiter returned I told him to take the food away. His uncurious eyes showed nothing.

As I watched the life of the place go on around me I suddenly realized it was a brothel. India's truck drivers have efficiently distributed AIDS around the country, infected by prostitutes, then passing the disease on to other prostitutes, to their own wives and to their unborn children. Many of the prostitutes are eunuchs and anal sex is commonplace. Condoms are not. Truck drivers are pretty prosperous, but are nowadays acquiring an unpleasant reputation— in some parts of India, marrying one is considered socially unaccept- able. So I sat and watched men trooping into the "bath house" and other men leaving. A kind of anomie hung over the entire establishment.

I drove on. Ten miles out of Lucknow an ancient motorcycle pulled alongside me on the inside. There were two policemen on board. The pillion passenger waved me down with a peremptory flap of his hand, hopped off and indicated that I should get down.

I stayed seated and raised my eyebrows. "*Kyun?*" I asked. Why? I was feeling half starved and tense about the bike, which was threatening not to get me as far as Lucknow.

"Check," he said irritably.

"*Kyun?*" I repeated.

"Check, *check!*" he yelled, enraged that I hadn't automatically and swiftly obeyed. He took a step closer—too close—near enough for me to smell the *betel* nut on his breath, and observe his red-stained teeth and the smallpox moon-cratering on his face.

I pulled off my full-face helmet and frowned. "*Ap kohn heh?*" (Who are you?)

His face showed vaudevillian disbelief. He pointed at the badge on his cap. "*Meh* ufficair *hoong!*" He flourished an ID card showing his face and a lot of Hindi printed in purple, having been typed using carbon paper. It was so amateurish that for a moment it crossed my mind that it might be fake. But no. With his swagger and paunch and malicious eyes, he was the very model of an Indian cop. And he might have been an *ufficair*, but it was obvious from his uniform that the younger man on the bike was the senior partner.

He demanded my papers again. Trying to reproduce the disdain upper middle class Indians use when dealing with the lower orders, I repeated, more haughtily than ever, "*Why?*" His face became a mask of fury and he lifted his weighted bamboo baton.

I turned to his senior, who was sitting on the bike, his hands on the handlebars. "*Meh jahnlist hoong.*" (I am a journalist.) I flashed my own ID card, with a mugshot and the word "PRESS" in large letters. Simultaneously, pock-face gave a roar of fury and swung back his stick. A bark from his superior stopped him. The officer told him to get back on the bike, which he did with the petulant expression of a misunderstood child. The younger man gave me a flap of his hand, telling me to move on. I turned my back on them and made a show of consulting my map. At last they moved off, their low-powered bike wobbling in low gear, my aggressor watching me over his shoulder with a look of explosive rage that I found very satisfying.

They were going to touch me for a bribe. Indian policemen are commonly corrupt and violent. Of course, police thuggery is rarely directed at foreigners. My full-face helmet had allowed me to experience some abuse of power first-hand.

RAMA AND LAKSHMAN entered the jungle.

There was no chance they would ever find Sita on their own. They needed allies. This advice came from the *rakashasa* militiaman, Kabandha, who made the mistake of confronting the brothers on their first day heading south into the forest. They were spoiling for a fight. Kabandha was big and tough, but he fell victim instantly to their slick combined swordsmanship. The militiaman fell screaming to the ground.

But at least they agreed not to leave him to be fought over by jackals. They agreed to cremate him. The man's big frame was thick with fat and he burned like a flare, for hours. But earlier, to repay their kindness, he told them this: "Head south-west, up into the *ghats*, where the monkeys are. King Sugriva has been ousted by his brother Vali, he needs military help. Vali kept his wife, too. Sugriva will do anything to get his power and his wife back. Help him—get his support—and you'll have an army behind you."

The monkeys: those mysterious, half-civilized creatures with thick hair and sunburned skins. People called them monkeys, but many claimed they were human. The Princes had known the "monkey" ambassador in the Ayodhya court. He was an exotic figure, but as human as either of them. Violent and impulsive, the monkeys were masters of the jungle. Some said they could move through the crown of the forest without ever touching the earth, that they built homes in the trees. Some said they ate their enemies and wore their skins as trophies. Certainly the monkeys dealt with intruders quickly and without pity. And they were Rama's only hope.

I WAS LOST in rush hour, somewhere near Lucknow railway station. The dual carriageway was hell for a motorcyclist—trucks and buses careered along intersecting parabolas that only by some miracle of aberrant geometry failed to meet. A grey, slab-sided truck veered at me like a monstrous predator, swerved round me, then swerved again—this time to avoid a man who was dragging across the road, on the end of a string, a dead dog. He was using a string because he didn't want to touch the body, presumably, but who he was and why he should be dragging a dead dog across a dual carriageway at rush hour was anyone's guess; this was India, where the unexpected and inexplicable are merely commonplace.

At last I found the address I was looking for: the Bullet service centre. It wasn't a garage recommended by Royal Enfield, but a backstreet joint a Bullet enthusiast had told me I could trust—a filthy little lock-up halfway up a muddy alleyway in Old Lucknow. But I could tell from the large number of bikes in various stages of repair and several shiny machines waiting to be collected by their owners that these guys knew what they were doing. One of them jumped on my Bullet, jammed it into first and took off into the mêlée of traffic with a speed and dexterity I could only have dreamed of. Five minutes later he was back. He'd diagnosed the problem, he said. The bike would be ready the following evening.

I took an autorickshaw to the Carlton, a colonnaded, stuccoed, colonial institution popular with travellers with a taste for the shabby genteel. The place was owned by an aristocratic family (Lucknow is famous for its *Nawabs*), but had been falling apart for years. At the same time it had a staff of insanely enthusiastic old retainers. The lawns in front of the Carlton were popular with Lucknow wedding parties, which probably kept the place going. But I was shocked to see that all around the hotel a forest of concrete pillars was rising. The land had been sold, the owner later told me, not without melancholy, to build "a mall".

I took a ground-floor suite. The rooms were enormous, with elaborate (but holed) mosquito screens, the colonial origins still visible under a bizarre mix of mid-twentieth-century furnishings. On the wall were framed 1960s chocolate box lids. A small black-and-white TV set with a coat hanger for an aerial sat on a vast air conditioner in a plywood frame in the window, obscuring the view of the mall-under-construction. The suite's *pièce de résistance* was the bathroom, which, despite its de-enamelled bath and Made in Birmingham bath taps that hadn't run for decades, was spacious and evocative. When I put my bare feet on those cracked tiles I felt the ghosts of the past moving around me: colonial officers loosening their celluloid collars and gargling Listerine, pale colonial wives in their white muslin shifts (Lucknow was famous for its exquisitely fine cottons) applying powder to their sunburned noses. Peering into the liver-spotted art deco mirror felt like looking through a glass darkly, straight into history—and not history resurrected and theme-parked: this was a time machine. But even in unfashionable, off-the-tourist-beat Lucknow, the Carlton was unlikely to resist modern India much longer. The next time I saw it, it would be tight in the embrace of the new mall with its mobile phone shops and preening, noisy teenagers. An oasis of peace was about to vanish.

On the terrace outside the hotel bar I met an Englishman, slim, blond, about my age. I will call him Anthony. He was an NGO worker, moving mountains 200 kilometres or so to the south.

"We do water resources. It's vulnerable land, subject to flooding in the rainy season, yet very arid the rest of the year. Land degredation—the loss of topsoil—is a huge problem. The people are incredibly poor down there—I'm talking about by the standards of an already very poor state. This lot have the environment working against them, too. We're trying to stabilize river banks, that sort of thing. New wells for fresh drinking water. New sewers to protect the drinking water. Glamorous work."

He was the sardonic type.

"I can't believe you come so far north for R & R," I said.

"No, I couldn't justify that. My nearest big town is a place called Jabalpur, and believe me, it's no Monte Carlo. And some of the partners are up here in Lucknow. They don't like to come to me—being Indian bureaucrats they naturally prefer to sit in an air-conditioned office, considering that it's beneath them to see how the money's actually being spent. I try to avoid meeting them, to be honest, but when I have to I take advantage of a long weekend and enjoy the limited cultural delights of Lucknow."

"You sound rather jaded," I said.

"So would you, believe me," he said. "So would you."

"Do you know the *Ramayana*?" I asked.

"Well, I've read the Penguin abridgement, the one by R. K. Narayan. Why?"

"Did you know that somewhere near your project is supposed to be Lanka—where the *Ramayana* ends?"

"Fabled Lanka, one of my blighted hills? Surely not! What about *Sri* Lanka?"

"According to a lot of the academics—Western academics, anyway—the population of northern India in Valmiki's time didn't know anything about the island we call Sri Lanka. They reckon the story has its climax on an island in a lake, bang in the middle of India."

The previous year I'd discussed it with an esteemed professor of Indology, a man so crippled by the risk of making an unambiguous statement he had trouble uttering two connected syllables. He wouldn't be drawn on anything to do with the possible historicity of the *Ramayana*—or even if Valmiki had actually *existed*. But he did bring himself to say that the place the authors of the *Ramayana* had in mind was somewhere in Middle India, in the hills between Jabalpur and Allahabad.

"Do you believe it?" Anthony asked.

"Who am I to argue with eminent Indologists who've spent their entire careers studying the *Ramayana*? Hundreds of millions of Hindus believe that Lanka *was* Sri Lanka—but it could well be a myth, unprovable, like the location of Atlantis. The academics seem to think that Valmiki had no precise sense of the geography beyond the Ganges. To me, that doesn't feel quite right. I think there's evidence that civilization extended further 3,000 years ago than we can prove—or than it's currently fashionable to believe. I want to keep an open mind . . ."

We sipped our beer and stared at the lawn. Controlled and neat, it had an oddly soothing effect: it offered a relief from India. The way an air filter sucks impurities and odours into its spongy innards, that half-acre of green seemed to filter the heat and din out of the Lucknow evening sky. We chatted on, absent-mindedly scratching mosquito bites, congratulating ourselves on our good taste in choosing this heap of rotting Raj over the hideous business hotels that have sprung up all around it.

"It really is so much nicer than efficient air-conditioning and satellite TV," said Anthony. "Nostalgia's the English curse, of course. Bad enough at home with its paralyzing class system and fucking mock-Tudor hypermarkets—nothing like India, of course, with its caste system and the fucking mall they're building all around us here."

I laughed. "And how can we justify nostalgia for a time when our ancestors ran this entire subcontinent as a racist imperium? Because we planted lawns? Because we ran the Indian railways even better than Mussolini could have done?"

Such are the questions with which strangers divert themselves over the second and third bottles of beer. Like me, Anthony had been travelling to India for more than half his life. I asked him, "Do you still remember how it first struck you?"

"I do. Every delicious bit of culture shock. What about you—did you keep a diary?"

"Yup. From the first day I climbed off an Aeroflot plane in Columbo."

He grinned. "Me too. Does it embarrass you now?"

"No . . . It isn't a question of *embarrassment,* more a sense of wonder—that that boy fresh from university, who scribbled a journal on his knee in jolting buses, could be so different from the 'I' who writes today."

"You can say that again! I feel exactly the same thing. It wasn't *me*, it was someone else . . . Someone I'll never meet again." He paused. "Would you like to go to Lanka?"

AS THE BROTHERS reached the tall ridge where the deposed Sugriva was living in exile, spring was in the air. They saw great vistas with forests of immensely tall trees. Gigantic pink and crimson blooms erupted around them, velvet-fleshed, open-lipped.

"This landscape is almost erotic!" Rama told Lakshman. "It's so beautiful and so *lush!*"

"Like a good wife!" Lakshman grinned—and immediately realized his mistake. "Rama—"

"It's all right, Lakshman, stop punishing yourself."

But Lakshman wasn't sure he'd ever be able to do that.

Sugriva's scouts reported the approach of two men, dressed like hermits yet heavily armed. His first instinct was that they must be mercenaries, sent by his brother to finish him off. Squatting on a bluff to observe them, he started to tremble—a year on the run had not been good for Sugriva's nerves. "Just look at those two! They could take on a regiment of us!"

His most loyal adviser, Hanuman, tried to calm him: "My Lord . . ."

"Get down there!" snapped Sugriva. "Find out what they're doing here, armed like that!"

Unarmed, Hanuman approached the men. They were a puzzle: matted hair, saffron robes and heavy armour. Superb bodies, unworn by work. They clearly weren't hermits—or mercenaries. He introduced himself: "I am General to the deposed King Sugriva."

The bigger of the two men laughed. "Well, I've been looking for the King—and *he's* found *me!*"

The story of the exiled Prince of Ayodhya had already reached the jungle. And Hanuman realized the support of these aristocratic northern warriors against Vali could be decisive. Rama and Sugriva had both lost a kingdom—and a wife. Perhaps they could help each other . . .

When the Prince and the King met, they shook hands and embraced. Hanuman lit a sacred fire, lowered his head in prayer and watched the deposed leaders walk around the flames to mark their alliance. Then he and Sugriva told Rama the stories of a flying chariot, and a woman shedding jewels.

Rama gave a start. "Where did he *take* her?"

But Sugriva could tell him little more. "Ravan's kingdom is the south. His militias pass us on their raiding expeditions into your territory! He has territories oversea, too, and a fleet of ships . . ."

"And his army?" asked Rama. "They say it's huge?"

Sugriva nodded. "Yes, many of his soldiers are foreign mercenaries. And he's unassailable. Lanka's a castle, the sea is its moat."

Rama took all this in grimly. Sugriva could offer him little real assistance. Suddenly Sugriva started, as though Hanuman had given him a kick. "Er, but be sure of this, great Prince! Help me, and we'll leave our forest! We'll punish this despicable Ravan! You will meet your Princess again!"

How Rama killed Vali is much retold—and much debated; the controversy never subsides.

Rama suggested that Sugriva challenge his brother to a duel, to decide the succession once and for all. They met in an open space on the edge of the forest. It was a brutal fight. But as the brothers rolled in the dust, Rama took aim from a distance and coolly shot Vali between the shoulder blades.

Pandemonium. But Hanuman had carefully sewn the seeds of a coup. Vali's remaining supporters were rounded up. The dying King lay alone, face-down in the dust.

Hearing footsteps, Vali twisted his head. "Who are you?"

"Prince Rama. Of Ayodhya."

"Rama . . . the *dharma*-lover? The coward who shoots men in the back!"

"I killed you as an animal, not a man," Rama said contemptuously, "*How* I did it is irrelevant. The day you usurped your brother's crown and climbed into his bed with his wife, you died. And you have condemned your own wife, too—your whole family. Did you ever consider that?"

Vali coughed up bright blood. "Listen, Prince," he gasped. "My wife—Tara—she can look after herself. But I have a son, Angada . . . Be compassionate to my boy, Rama."

"He'll be treated as well as *dharma* dictates."

"You'll protect him?"

Rama nodded curtly. Two attendants gently turned Vali on his side. His wife Tara was shrieking with grief, held back by female courtiers. Angada, a boy of eighteen, rushed forward and threw his arms round his mortally wounded father.

As Vali struggled to lift his hand onto his son's head, he saw his brother Sugriva, whose eyes were bright with tears. "It is *karma*, Sugriva," Vali said. "And now I'm dead. Be good to this boy." He bared his teeth in a last grimace of pain, his eyes rolled upwards, and he died.

Angada clung blindly to his father's clothes. Attendants pulled the arrow from Vali's back and his body oozed blood. Tara's screams became even louder. Rama told her roughly, "That won't help him now. Get on with what you have to do next—prepare the funeral." He turned to Sugriva. "Have yourself crowned king at once. And anoint this boy your heir. It should be enough to unite the two factions once more."

ॐ

An hour or so out of Lucknow I reached the scene of a crash. Nothing new in that—I was passing such sites every few miles, with the twisted hulks of vehicles stripped of anything valuable left rotting at the roadside. Every day the road would be blocked somewhere or other by buses and lorries that had lost the chicken run, the game of hair's-breadth avoidance. Their offside corners would be crumpled like silver foil, the vinyl drivers' seats puddles of blood and windscreen glass.

It was early morning, the air still fresh. Changing down to first gear, I slowly overtook the line of stationary vehicles until I reached a T-junction that was the source of the delay. Several vehicles were at odd angles in a kind of bizarre tableau, the traffic slowly weaving past them. It appeared that a truck had been overtaking another truck when it struck a jeep that was pulling across the road. The trucks had scrunched and skidded and shed their loads, the jeep had been catapulted down an embankment. The police were there, waiting for ambulances to take the dead away. Bodies were lined up, covered in blood-soaked sheets. About fourteen people had lost their lives, according to a thin young cop standing beside them. He was holding his carbine in a nervous way as though under orders to shoot anyone who came too close. He looked sick—and I couldn't blame him. The jeep had been a long-wheelbase model with a canvas roof that provided no structural strength—it had compressed like an accordion. Those not killed by the impact had been squashed as it rolled. Blood oozed from it like jam from a doughnut.

It was a typical morning on the Trunk Roads. In his novel *Kim*, Rudyard Kipling called the Grand Trunk Road a wonderful spectacle, "a river of life as nowhere else exists in the world", running straight, "bearing without crowding India's traffic, for fifteen hundred miles". It began in the sixteenth century when the emperor Sher Shah Suri built a *Sadak-e-Azam* (Great Road) to connect his capital Agra with his home town Sasaram, 500 miles to the east. During the Raj, the Grand Trunk Road traversed British India from Peshawar on the North-West Frontier to Calcutta, gaining the jokey nickname "The Long Walk". Today, India has over 65,000 kilometres of Trunk Roads, or highways, two per cent of the total road network, but carrying almost half of the country's traffic. They are the most dangerous roads in the world. India has over 100,000 road deaths a year—nearly 300 a day—growing at four per cent a year. The country's rapidly expanding middle class means that small cars are pouring onto the market, crowding already overcrowded roads (the Tata company recently launched the world's cheapest car, priced at US$ 1,300). The little hatchbacks' nifty acceleration tempts drivers to dart past lumbering trucks; their fragility means that in collisions, car passengers often stand little chance.

Many Indian road users demonstrate an indifference to the possibility of accident that can seem homicidal; but it may have more to do with naïvety and a simple lack of imagination. Indian friends tell me their fellow countrymen drive so badly because they believe in destiny—if your time has come, it has come. Indians, they say, can't conceptualize accident *avoidance*. Of course, there are less patronizing explanations. Many drivers have little or no training; licences are often purchased or forged or non-existent. Village boys who've never piloted anything more powerful than a bicycle abruptly find themselves at the wheels of a powerful machine and are as reckless as teenagers on a Gameboy. I think Indian road users are more skilled than those of the West, because they have quickly learned the arts of high-speed overtaking, swerving, braking. But why, in a country so notable for its people's softness—why the *aggression* on the roads? On a motorbike, I was pushed off the road several times a day. I wasn't surprised; I had vivid memories of being in a long-distance taxi whose driver *deliberately* forced a man and woman on a scooter off the road, for the hell of it—to show who was boss. He'd grinned nastily as he watched them fall over in his rear-view mirror. I knew what I was letting myself in for.

In Lucknow I had visited the Residency, where 2,000 British residents (and loyal Indians) died in the course of a three-month siege during the 1857 Indian Mutiny (now renamed the First War of Independence). Fifty miles south of Lucknow is Kanpur, an industrial town whose main claim to fame is the pair of massacres that took place that summer—the worst violence of the uprising: 400 British men, women and children were ambushed as they boarded boats on the Ganga at *Satichaura Ghat*; 200 were butchered— apparently by genuine *butchers*, who were called in to perform the task when soldiers balked at it. The British reprisals, Old Testamental in their fury, were almost equally brutal—though they did not target women and children. Kanpur is a dull industrial city today and little remains of the sights connected with the 1857 massacre. But I wanted to see not Kanpur, but a small town called Bithur, on the banks of the Ganga a little to the north.

I checked into an hotel near Kanpur station called the Grand Palace, that was predictably neither grand nor palatial. Then I looked for somewhere to eat lunch, ending up with an egg curry at a Muslim joint. I drove north-west, along a road that follows the west bank of the Ganges, towards Bithur. The significance of this small, ancient town is simple: it claims to have played a key role in the *Ramayana*. Oh—and it is the centre of the universe. This boast has its roots in a charming story in the Hindu *Puranas* (an important set of medieval mythical texts) that Shiva, after creating the earth, asked Brahma to make human beings to populate it. Brahma brought certain saints into existence, but they devoted themselves to lives of asceticism and refused to further the race. Brahma then performed a Horse *yagna* (sacrifice) at the most sacred place on earth—the forest of Utpalaranyan (which later became known as Brahma-varta, and was eventually condensed into Bithur). As a result of the sacrifice, Manu and his wife, Queen Satrupa, were born, and became the primogenitors of the human race. Brahma also set up a temple to Shiva, and embedded a nail from the shoe of the sacrificial horse in one of the steps of the temple *ghat*. That nail is still there.

As for the connection with the *Ramayana*, it was said that Valmiki had his hermitage in Bithur. A temple stands on the site, complete with the place known as Sita Kund, where Sita disappeared into the bosom of the earth at the end of her life.

After driving ten miles or so from Kanpur and getting lost, as I always did, and asking several people the way, I arrived in Bithur. I was at once struck by the charm of the place. With its honey-coloured temples crowding along the broad Ganges, it felt to me a romantically abandoned city (though it was supposed to come alive during its annual festival). I was disappointed by Valmiki's supposed ashram, rebuilt two centuries ago by the local lord; I don't know what I was expecting a prehistoric ashram to look like—a modest, wood-frame structure, perhaps, like an ancient European barn; but to imagine the survival of such a structure for over 2,500 years was idiotic. As for the little pool where Sita had entered the earth, I felt a sense of ambivalence. Researching this journey, I'd found half a dozen other Valmiki ashrams and Sita *kunds* scattered across north India, and they couldn't *all* be the sites of the most ancient tradition. My feeling was that this place had a strong claim, given its proximity to Ayodhya.

Bithur receives no mention in the reliably shallow *Lonely Planet*, and even *Footprint India*, once the bible for India travellers, dismisses the town. As I wandered along its crumbling *ghats* (it used to be known as "*Bavan Ghaton ki Nagari*", City of Fifty-Two Ghats, though it now has only twenty-nine), I knew I had stumbled into a secret place.

My time in Bithur was to be curtailed. I felt a strange pain in my guts, a sort of nauseous wave, echoed by a pain in my right temple.

I sat down beside the river. The sensation passed and I was hailed by a friendly boatman who offered to carry me along the *ghats*. The sun was moving behind the town, darkening into silhouette the line of holy buildings crowded, shoulder to shoulder, along the shore. There were ruins lining the river bank, which were the other reason for an Englishman to be interested in Bithur. Nana Sahib, the leader of the Kanpur massacres, was pursued by the British to his palace here. According to the *Encyclopædia Britannica* and Wikipedia, the British levelled the town. This appears to be a wild exaggeration. There was artillery on both sides, and damage was done to Nana Sahib's palace and the temples around it. The defending sepoys around the palace put up spirited resistance but, as usual, couldn't match the superior organization and weaponry of the British. But far from razing Bithur to the ground, the British rapidly withdrew to Kanpur after their victory, returning later to scour the palace grounds for hidden treasure. In one eyewitness report a British officer remembers walking around the palace after the sacking and comments that it was in pretty good condition under the circumstances—he even found some unopened letters. As for Nana Sahib, he apparently faked his drowning in the Ganges, but how he ended his days—there are rumours that he fled to Nepal—nobody knows.

All that has nothing to do with the *Ramayana*, but I was intrigued by the mystery over the Battle of Bithur. That investigation will have to wait for another trip to India. I had asked the boatman to scull further north, beyond the town limits and against the current, to where I thought there was a small temple dedicated to Rama and a large, derelict mosque allegedly built on the site of a demolished Hindu temple. But suddenly I felt a ghastly sensation in my guts, accompanied by the feeling that I was about to faint. I told the boatman to take me back to town at once. Almost in a panic, I climbed on the bike and retraced my route back to Kanpur. I nearly didn't make it. When I reached the hotel, I gave the astonished doorman a hundred-rupee note and instructions to look after the bike, and stumbled blindly to reception to claim my key. I don't know how I made it up to my room. I spent the next twenty-four hours in feverish hallucinations. As I tossed and turned on the bed, that egg curry was luridly projected, magnified a hundred times, all over the walls and ceiling of the room. At seven the next evening I staggered outside to find a pharmacy to buy ciproxacillin, and to grab some water and a couple of bananas.

TWO DAYS LATER I reached Chitrakut. After leaving the main highway to Allahabad it was a gentle, if bumpy, journey, following tree-lined backroads through fertile countryside and occasional villages. But I arrived in Chitrakut feeling drained. It was a kind of Bithur—another miniature Benares—with temples clustered, this time facing each other, on either side of the Mandakini, a tributary of the holy Yamuna, that was here about a hundred feet wide. Chitrakut did pilgrim trade on a scale that dwarfed Bithur, holy mendicants in beards and saffron robes and wooden clogs wandered, their coins dangling in testicular cotton pouches, pausing at street vendors' wheeled stalls to buy a chunk of sweet bread or a half-pound of grapes or a cone of groundnuts. Across the river was a statue of Hanuman thirty feet high. The roads were lined with little shops flogging religious paraphernalia, stonemasons where boys chipped at hunks of marble that were to become statues of Rama, Sita or Hanuman, and nasty, opportunistic hotels.

Although the ciproxacillin was doing its work, I had taken to the road too soon—I was still weak from dehydration and from not having eaten sufficiently. My guts were being held together by Imodium. I kept meeting touts who seemed aggressive, although the stomach bug was making me hypersensitive and irritable. I found it hard to keep my mind on my purpose in being in Chitrakut. This haven for our exiled threesome is one of the few geographical locations that even the most arid scholars concede *is* the same place as the one Valmiki had in mind. But my resolve was faltering. I felt lonely and ill, and in need of the familiar.

That evening I walked along the Ramghat, where canopied boats plied backwards and forwards across the Mandakini, and the sun turned to copper and the sky to a kind of metallic pink and the river, slowly, to black. The next morning I puttered early to the Rama temple on the far side of the bank, but I felt no enthusiasm. All I wanted was the comfort of a decent hotel—and I knew a place, just under a day's drive away, in Khajuraho. I drank several cups of sweet, strong, milky tea and hit the road.

I spent four days at Khajuraho, one of my favourite spots in India. One needn't get too carried away about the extraordinary—and, as far as I know, unique—erotic statues to be found in the midst of the many other more conventional Hindu carvings that seethe over the surfaces of the temples. Exotic theories have been propounded about the temples' function as an aphrodisiacal device to repopulate the landscape during a time of unnaturally low birth rates. The proponents of that theory are unable to explain why the furtherance of the race required instruction in quite so many gymnastic and occasionally zoophile acts of sexuality. We don't have the history that could answer these questions; my own theory is that the kings of this land came under the influence of a Tantric sect and for a while, for the kings and their intimates, Khajuraho must have been an exciting if ultimately exhausting place.

The temples are set in a well-protected and verdant park in the midst of what's still a small country town, well off the beaten track—though God knows, the new railway line to Khajuraho will change that. For now, it is one of the best places I know in mainland India to take a break. I checked into the place where I'd stayed once before, far more expensive than my travelling budget allowed, but this was an emergency. That first night, I slept for thirteen hours.

At Khajuraho I drank a lot of *lassi* (a sort of natural yoghurt milkshake), ate good, clean, plain food and felt my strength returning. I visited a man I knew who ran a small souvenir shop and who, whenever I visited, remembered me and pulled from under his desk one or two "genuine" antiques that were within my price range (*not* of such rarity and antiquity as to endanger India's patrimony . . .). This time he took me to a nearby village where a friend of his had a little lean-to structure on the side of his house, full of modest, dusty little curios. I chose what seemed to me to be an object of unusual design—a sort of Sphinx, cast in bronze—with a little lid on its head that meant that it could have served as an inkwell, although, given the object's apparent religious significance, it seemed more likely to have been used to contain some substance of religious significance. It was a mystery to be resolved.

FROM KHAJURAHO I drove towards "Lanka", where Anthony's NGO was based. It was a long drive, along progressively worsening roads. As I climbed, the landscape became drier than I'd expected—far more arid than the soft alluvial earth of the Gangetic Plain. All a function of water tables and water management, I'd been told. Much of southern India had been jungle—the British decimated it for teak to build ships and sideboards—but this area had drier, arid-zone vegetation, with wispy acacia trees that flourish on poor land.

As ever, I got lost several times over and wasted a couple of hours trying to find my way across a river and asking directions of locals who had no idea what I was talking about. I was using a GPS and the largest-scale map of India available, but it was impossible to navigate the back roads without frequently stopping to ask the way. I'd been warned against travelling by night due to the very real danger of dacoits and by 11 p.m., when I found the project, I was again exhausted.

Anthony greeted me with an ironic grin, and I tried to shrug off the last four hours spent picking my way in darkness along deserted, potholed roads. He inhabited a single room in the compound, a simple building, purpose-built, its crude wooden furniture and whitewashed latrine contrasting starkly with his laptop and satellite phone. I was put up in one of a row of little guest bungalows. Although we were in a gated compound, Anthony had the security guard wheel my bike into an outhouse and padlock it. Then, for the first time in well over a week, I accepted a beer. I felt in need of a familiar face, the sense of being in the company of someone I could trust. Anthony was the best I could do.

The next morning I was introduced to his two Indian colleagues and two pink-faced "volunteers" from the UK, wearing slovenly T-shirts with the NGO logo on the chest.

"What are they like, the co-workers?" I asked as we drove away.

"All right," he said. "Sanjay's a Marxist. It takes all sorts. They're fine—they're committed. Unlike the enemy—the bureaucrats, I mean."

We drove for half an hour to one of the project sites. I'd expected there to be earth movers, but all I saw were a couple of dozen men scraping at the beige landscape with large hoes. "Labour intensive," said Anthony. "Brings water *and* employment—helps the local economy twice over. Double whammy." I suspected I was getting the standard VIP itinerary; perhaps it had occurred to Anthony that I could provide him with some good publicity.

At about eleven he suggested we meet some of the people who'd benefited from the project.

"I wonder what they think about the Lanka theory," I said.

"It's hard for them to find time to attend academic conferences," said Anthony. "What with struggling to stay alive and all that."

I grinned at him. "Don't deliberately misunderstand me. The myth was born here—the most powerful narrative in India, still going strong three millennia on! I want to ask if it means anything to them!"

AS THE 4×4 pulled up by an impoverished-looking collection of small houses, a dozen smiling women and children emerged from various doorways and clustered around us. One of Anthony's Indian colleagues, a woman called Kalpana, was already there. "Talking to the women about contraceptive matters." She gave a smile. "All part of the job!"

We were invited to step through a low doorway into a small house. There were a couple of wooden stools, but we crouched on mats on the hard-packed mud floor. Kalpana joined us. A stove was lit and we were brought tea in steel beakers. The women wore saris, arranged to cover the crowns of their heads as well as their bodies. Kalpana had the standard left-wing 'look' of the Indian NGO worker—a village-spun *khadi shalwar* to show her solidarity with the masses, jeans to show her commitment to Western empiricism, and a bad hairdo and cheap watch to emphasize her lack of personal vanity and her fundamental seriousness.

I asked those present—there were women and children, no men —if anyone in the village had ever made a pilgrimage to Ayodhya. There was vigorous shaking of heads. So I asked whether they knew the *Ramayana*. This time there was an enthusiastic response. One woman, more confident than the rest, appointed herself spokeswoman. She said she knew the *Ramayana*, so I asked her if she could outline it for me. She gave a shy look, but that seemed more a reflex than anything, for she promptly launched into the story. Everyone listened to her avidly, women and black-eyed children alike. What a compulsive passion we humans have for narrative, I thought. And these were people who possessed no televisions. Most of them could not read. I watched her hands—hard-working hands with ingrained dirt and tiny scribbles of tattoo, the nails cut short and stained red with *betel*. Beside her a child played with a tiny green bird, a sort of living version of a mechanical toy. Its wing feathers had been trimmed and its tail feathers were held together with a stitch of cotton. It skittered around the hard floor, pursuing a metal bottle cap. When it seemed it might run out into the yard the child, who was chewing a piece of straw, smiled and extended a crooked finger to redirect it.

"And what do they—" I said to Kalpana, who was translating, then caught myself. I turned to the woman. "And what do you feel about Rama and Sita?" Kalpana translated.

"They are our gods," the woman replied simply. "We have to pray to Sita-Ram, Hanumanji. We believe that if we pray to them, they will help us." A toothy smile suddenly animated her thin, lined face. "*Jai, Jai Sita-Ram!*"

"*Jai, Jai Sita-Ram!*" came the echoing cry from all around her.

THAT EVENING I shared a meal with the NGOs. The food was brought to us on stainless-steel platters by their cook, a smiling, gracious woman. Simply watching her, beaming shyly from the kitchen doorway as we ate, I could tell that she was grateful for her work and took pride in it, that her simple kitchen with its running water and implements scrubbed and arranged like scalpels in an operating theatre was an escape from the hut she lived in with a husband and however many children and relatives. That quiet, shy smile has stayed with me.

During the meal, I learned that the project was in its final phase.

"They're shutting us down," said Anthony.

"Our funding comes mostly from the EU," explained Chris, a

volunteer. "They've changed their funding priorities. The budget's going somewhere else."

"We've been working on a five-year plan, here," said Anthony. "And it works, and it's delivering a real, verifiable improvement to the lives of some of the poorest people in India. So the bosses", he added with heavy irony, "decide *not* to let us finish it."

"Why have they changed their minds?" I asked. "What assessments have they done?"

"It's nothing to do with assessments! Some Kafkaesque bureau in the entrails of the EU decided to change its funding policy. Free up some cash for an orphanage in Baghdad—I don't know."

The meal ended, with people muttering about early starts. Anthony turned the exhalation of a lungful of cigarette smoke into a long sigh. He stood up, walked to the tall fridge and took out two bottles of beer. "Four more months and I'm finished here. Then it's a fortnight in Thailand. Then it's back to London. Then a new project. One step forward, one step back. Do you know, I've been in this game for a few years now, and I've spent a big chunk of the last four years here and I don't think I've ever managed to implement something so effective—something that's actually managed to change, improve, the lives of a considerable number of people in the back of bloody beyond. The local officials are totally ineffective, corrupt to a man. I don't mean our people, they're bright and they work hard. But the ministry and local government officials are dyed-in-the-wool, one hundred per cent-proof shits. They couldn't give a flying fuck if this project succeeds or fails. The people we're helping are invisible, whether from the perspective of India or Brussels. So it's goodbye and good luck."

"The mood is changing towards NGOs, isn't it?"

"How do you mean?"

"Governments are questioning whether the best way to help people in the developing world is to parachute in outside help. The fashion now is to work with governments and local people, isn't it? Micro credit. Help people help themselves. India's in the process of turning itself into a superpower. Handouts are an insult."

He looked at me gloomily. "Tell that to the people here. Tell them that's why we have to go, to stop digging wells and keeping the water clean to help reduce the appalling levels of waterborne disease and child mortality. We know all about the economic miracle—the big issue is going to be how the cake is divided up. India may be developing a super-rich class and a petit bourgeoisie, but the lives of many of the rural poor will take *decades* to transform, believe me."

"Perhaps I could write something about the decision to close this project," I said. "The EU's a public body, it's accountable, it responds to pressure. Let me try to place an article about this in one of the papers."

"D'you think you could?"

"I could try. Give me your email address."

"You give me yours. I'll send you a load of stuff."

I suppose he had second thoughts. Perhaps he'd just needed to let off steam—and criticizing his masters in public could have ended his career. But I never heard from him.

Allahabad—Godtown—the very evidently Islamic name for the prosperous bureaucratic city that is still known to many Hindus as Prayag, Confluence. It's the place I'd visited more than twenty years earlier in the company of Liz. It's where the Ganges and the Yamuna merge, and the mystic river, the Saraswati, surges invisibly and intangibly from the depths. Recent archæological evidence had suggested that in something like 5,000 BC there was a real river where today's mystic one meets those other holy rivers (it would have disappeared when natural forces diverted its headwaters); could it be that the memory of a vanished river has stayed in Indian folk memory for 7,000 years?

I went to the home of Mahendra and Urmilla Jain, the parents of my next-door neighbour in London. A retired librarian and journalist (Urmilla is a well-regarded travel writer), they lived in a pleasant house near the university. Although, as their surname implies, they're members of the pacifist, fiercely vegetarian Jain religion, Urmilla and Mahendra had a lively awareness of the Hindu traditions of which Prayag was close to the heart. Mahendra at once asked me if I'd heard of Shringverpur, where Rama, Sita and Lakshman crossed the Ganges.

We set off after breakfast, travelling north-east on the Kanpur road. It was a continuous thread of shops and workshops and colleges, festooned with advertising hoardings painted onto the walls of buildings and little tin signs nailed to the trunks of trees. TEST-TUBE BABY LAB declared one sign bluntly. Allahabad, seat of a university and a high court, considered itself a keen-witted sort of a town, and currently its colleges were cashing in on the demand for English-language call centres. CALL CENTRE TRAINING—JOB 102% and COME HERE 2B THERE were emblazoned alongside photographs of blonde women wearing cordless headsets. I particularly admired the signs declaring SPEAK BRITISH— TEACHER FROM DELHI and SWISS SCHOOL OF SPOKEN ENGLISH.

In the flat farmland between the road and the Ganges rose the gherkin chimneys of brick kilns, billowing black smoke. Also in the fields were men at work on a new highway, part of the imposingly named "Golden Quadrilateral", a network of roads shaped like a kite—a diamond with a central cross—that will interconnect India's principal cities. We turned left, crossed the trajectory of the new highway and carried on towards the Ganges. A tractor was pulling a trailer on which sat perhaps twenty people, mostly women dressed in poor clothes. It was a funeral cortège. One woman, sitting at the back of the trailer, wailed. With one hand she wiped her eyes with the sari covering her head, her other hand resting on the corpse that lay across the back of the trailer wrapped in a cheap, tinsel-fringed cloth. Beside its head a cone of incense burned.

"They must be on their way to cremate the body," Mahendra said.

We came to a small collection of buildings where the road suddenly dipped to a wide grey beach. A few hundred yards to the south, smudges of smoke drifted into the sky where bodies were being cremated on Mother Ganga's shore. We were promptly accosted by a couple of guides, who led us to wooden benches where we could receive some shade from the sun. The most talkative of the two was a man called Ram Murat, a jovial fellow with sparkling eyes, and splendid white moustaches and chops on his cheeks. This place, he told us, was the site of Rishyashringa's ashram. (He, you may remember, was the unblemished young hermit who had to be seduced to guarantee the success of the Horse Sacrifice intended to bring sons to King Dasharatha.) Here, Ram Murat told us, Dasharatha's three Queens received the blessings of Rishyashringa before returning to Ayodhya to give birth to their sons. Twenty-five years later, on his way into exile, Rama stopped here and sent his chariot with its driver, Sumantra, back to Ayodhya, before crossing the Ganga. And sure enough, on a tall pedestal behind us, over-looking the river, was a life-size statue of a chariot drawn by two magnificent horses and carrying a charioteer and the three exiles.

An entire book could be written on the subject of artistic representations of the faces of these three, depicted always to embody the special qualities of each—pugnacity and loyalty in the case of Lakshman, devotion and duty for Sita, and as for Rama, the absolute ideal of nobility, honesty and masculine resolve. Sometimes they're represented with extreme sweetness, even as children; occasionally, their pain is allowed to be seen. In this case, I thought the artist had seized his opportunity to bring that precise moment into being, the uncertainty, the determination of three young people cast out of their home, obliged in this very instant to abandon privilege, about to cross the broad Ganges and proceed on foot towards the jungle, and whatever destiny and fourteen years of exile had in store for them. Hanuman enters their story much later, but there he was beside them, a statue two storeys high: in that quintessential image with which he is so often portrayed, he is gorily ripping open his chest and there, upon his heart, sit Rama and Sita, as happy as two larks.

In ancient times Ayodhya, then a massive, fortified city, derived much of its influence not only from the wealth of its hinterland but from its position at the nexus of a web of trading routes. A major one of these routes ran south to Shringverpur and Prayag/Allahabad. In other words, this point has been used to ferry passengers across the Ganges for many thousands of years.

Ram Murat pointed to an impressive wooded promontory that overlooked the Ganges a kilometre to the south. "The king's palace was there," he said, "*Nishadraj Kila.*"

For a moment I assumed that he meant King Rompada, to whose pouting, pulchritudinous daughter Rishyashringa had been hitched. Then I remembered that Rama had been given the blessings of King Guha, the Nishada King, at Shringverpur. King Guha's kingdom was on the edge of Ayodhyan civilization. His Nishadas were a tribal people (albeit a friendly one). Beyond the river were the jungle, hostile tribes and the lands where the writ of Ravan ran.

When we climbed to the mound I was surprised to see the excavation of an immense series of brick buildings, including a complex system of drainage channels and pools, apparently designed to capture rainwater and filter off impurities, to result in a tank of clean water. Datings of pottery in the area of the mound indicate that it was inhabited at least as early as 500 BC—approximately the time when Valmiki is believed to have produced his written version of the *Ramayana*.

Another kilometre or so to the south we came to the village of Sigraur, or Ram Chaura, where the exiles spent the night before crossing the Ganges. A walled temple compound contained two marble pedestals, one marking where, it was said, Lakshman slept, and the other the spot where Rama and Sita spent the night. The *pujari* was a tall and very lean man of forty-something years, by the name of Babaram Gopal Das. He wore the untrimmed beard and the simple saffron *lunghi* of his calling. But he did not exude calm—the man had a passionate, high-voltage quality to him.

His slender limbs were covered in minute, meticulous arrow-shaped markings made from the same pastes of ash and ground bark and stone used to mark the forehead—in the case of Vishnu devotees (Rama being an incarnation of Vishnu), three vertical stripes on the forehead.

"Here", he told me, "Rama came wearing princely dress. Here he changed into simple dress."

"Like yours," I said.

That was clumsy. He put his palms together and dropped his eyes. My mentioning him and his Lord in the same breath was too much.

"So how", I asked, "does it make you feel, living in such an auspicious place?"

"It's good here. It's quiet, it's simple. It keeps the mind calm and pure."

Moustachioed Ram Murat echoed him. "To live and work in this place is *anand, anand,*" he said. Absolute bliss.

ॐ

WE HAD RETURNED to Prayag. Night had fallen. Mahendra and I were climbing an alleyway, past a large open-air workshop where tall painted clay statues of Hanuman and elephant-headed, tubby Ganesh gathered dust, waiting for their next appearance in a public festival. We reached a row of small temples, in each of which the idol, quivering in candlelight and incense-stick smoke, was not some recognizable deity, but a bearded ancient. This was the ashram of Bhardwaj.

It was a warm, but not unpleasantly hot, evening. A middle-aged, comfortable-looking man climbed to his feet and asked if he could be of help. He said he was Shivji Goswami, the president of the temple's management committee.

"After they crossed the river," he told us, "the three came to Prayag on foot. This place was on the river bank in those days, you know, the *ghat* was just at the bottom of this alleyway. Anyway, they stayed here for three days. They visited the Prayag, of course. Rama asked *Shree* Bhardwaj-*ji*[4] for his advice on a place for them to stay and he recommended the hill of Chitrakut, about sixty miles away, as somewhere that was isolated, but a beautiful and very spiritual place. So from here they went to Chitrakut. And from there they went to Nasik near Bombay, to Panchavatti, where Lakshman cut off the nose of Ravan's sister and subsequently Ravan abducted Sita.

"Lord Rama came here a second time, you know," Mr Goswami continued. "After he'd come back from Lanka. Ravan was a *Brahman* and, in killing him, Rama had committed a sin. So he came to Bhardwaj-*ji* to absolve himself of the guilt."

He smiled and stepped to one side, to reveal his wife, Madhu, sitting wearing a sari on the white-tiled steps of one of the temples. "My wife is a very devout woman," he added with a smile, "a great traveller, a great expert on this *Ramayana*. She has made three long pilgrimages around India, to the sites connected with Shree Rama." Mrs Goswami rose and went to a shelf on the wall of the little temple. From behind a clock she pulled a tiny scroll, which she presented to me. "Please take it," said Mr Goswami, "it is a gift, it may be of help to you."

---

[4] The prefix and suffix *Sri* (*Shri*, *Shree*) and *Ji* are often singly or jointly added to names, to imply respect.

I thanked him. We made a small contribution to temple funds and ambled away into the humid darkness. Back at the Jain's house, Mahindra and I unfurled the little map, which was pierced by a couple of dozen tiny bookworm holes. Compiled by one Dr Ramautar (I later found him described as Dr Ram Avatar—the *incarnation* of Rama!), it purported to show the journeys of Rama through India and Sri Lanka. Dr Avatar had made an admirable effort to note almost every temple or site in India that claimed a connection with Rama, and to plot a feasible itinerary. Where the work stumbled, inevitably, was in its inability (and unwillingness) to distinguish between different sites that made identical claims—or, crucially, to support its identifications with scholarship of any kind. But no one could deny that the assembly of temples and sites that claimed a traditional connection with the *Ramayana* made for a remarkably consistent and in many ways credible route—the early life around Ayodhya, then Rama's long journey south, following the line of the Western Ghat range, to Rameshwaram and Sri Lanka beyond.

Personally, I was convinced—now, having visited these sites around Ayodhya, more convinced than ever—that the *Ramayana* had been set in a *real* landscape, by a creative artist who knew that landscape. For me, this strengthened the likelihood of Rama having been a real person. But I had to admit I thought it probable that the majority of Rama traditions post-dated the popularity of the epic, and in some cases were simply the result of duplicated name places— I was dubious, for example, about the claim of Nasik's Panchavatti, close to the western coast, 600-odd miles to the south-west of Chitrakut, to have been the place Valmiki had in mind when he had his exiles reaching a place of that name. He makes it sound a few miles off, not two-thirds of the way across a subcontinent.

As for the case against Sri Lanka, my own instinct told me that Valmiki *had* heard of an island called Lanka off the south-east coast of India; even if he wrote about it not as an historian but an artist, using his imagination and such knowledge of geography as he had to fill out the canvas of his epic poem, it somehow legitimized the case for our keeping Sri Lanka in our minds when we read the *Ramayana*. As I have said, many scholars strongly disagree with the identification of Sri Lanka with Valmiki's Lanka. It can't be *proved* one way or another, and to try to do so is absurd. And yet, that is exactly the debate going on in the Indian courts, no less, as I write this book. But more of that very soon.

CHAPTER 13

The Gospel According to Tulsi

MR AND MRS JAIN had introduced me to Dhirendra Kumar, a Ph.D. student in English Literature at Allahabad University. He was also a devout Hindu who'd already explored, for his own benefit, the tradition of Rama around Prayag. He'd been born a few dozen kilometres to the east, on the outskirts of Hinduism's holiest city, Benares or Varanasi. He offered to accompany me to the sites in the area that I had yet to see.

We decided to head first towards Chitrakut, which I'd passed through in something of a haze, while gastroenteritis passed through me. I wanted to visit two sites that were almost equidistant from Chitrakut: the hilltop where it was said that Valmiki had his ashram (bearing in mind that I had already seen its competitor in Bithur) and the spot where Tulsidas had lived, and where part of his *Ramayana* manuscript, four centuries years old, was said to be kept.

We travelled in slanting, early-morning light through some desolate-looking country, arid and unfarmed. I saw signs of sand and gravel extraction, and, among some mean-looking shanties and godowns, a cross over the door of a sort of shed.

"The Christians, they're making so many conversions among the poor," I said. "They've always found it easier to prey on the lowest castes, haven't they—the people squeezed out and neglected by the Hindu mainstream. They're easy pickings for the missionaries. I read somewhere that they're making, across India, 1,000 conversions a day. I read it, come to think of it, in a VHP propaganda leaflet, so a grain of salt may be in order. But how do you feel about the conversions, as a Hindu?"

"I follow my religion very strictly," Dhirendra replied judiciously, "but if politicians talk big about religion and they're not uplifting the daily lives of the poor, then I don't think they have much to complain about."

On the other side of the road, a tractor pulling an empty trailer stopped to give a lift to a bunch of schoolgirls, aged eight or nine, wearing neat bottle-green skirts and white blouses. They clambered familiarly aboard.

"Being a *Brahman*," he went on, "I've seen occasions when my grandparents and father didn't want to eat the foods of lower castes. This hurts these people and alienates them from you. This kind of casteism is a decadent and warped manifestation of Indian life, it has nothing whatsoever to do with being a good Hindu. There's no doubt about it—the caste system is an abomination."

As we passed a small lake I saw, on its far bank, a ruined temple of pinkish stone. At the hamlet after the lake we turned and followed a narrow, twisting lane that came out beside the ruins. Up close, we saw that over a dozen men were at work on the temple. Scattered all around, or projecting from excavated mounds of dirt nearby, were carved slabs of stone. Only a few columns of the central sanctum stood, but men were busy restoring the ground-level platforms, inserting and decorating new slabs of rock. No electrical machines of any kind were in evidence, no generators—here, in twenty-first-century India, temples were being built and rebuilt the way they had been a thousand years ago. Beneath the temple, on the shore of the lake, an elderly woman sat, her old breasts dangling, while a girl of six or seven soaped and scrubbed her back with a wood-handled brush.

The supervisor told us the temple was a fourteenth-century structure. Ninety per cent of the original stone was still on site, he said, but barely half was usable, the rest of the temple would be built anew. The government was paying for the work.

I noticed that there were very few statues around and wondered if they'd been pilfered. Well, he said, more than half the statuary had been removed for safe-keeping to Kalinger Fort, a hundred kilometres away (where the workers came from, too—they were allowed home to see their families once a fortnight). As for the rest of the statuary, it would be carved anew. The stone they were using came from a quarry about twenty-five kilometres away. And as for the presiding deity, it was a Shiva temple.

I was surprised. An enormous statue of Mahavira, the Jain saint, stood propped against a wall. No, he said—they'd found him in a field a couple of kilometres away, nowhere near any ruins. That seemed extraordinary and it begged the question—had this temple previously been Jain, or had a Jain temple perhaps been demolished and the stone recycled in the construction of this one? And how, then, had this one been destroyed? Most likely, it had been a casualty of the Mughals.

We continued along the road to Chitrakut, stopping at the abrupt hog's-back that was said to be the site of Valmiki's ashram. There were only a couple of impoverished-seeming roadside stalls selling the means for pilgrims to make—as they invariably did at every holy place—the conventional offering of a coconut, flowers, incense sticks. We climbed a short flight of stairs to where a woman in a sari walked barefoot around the outer terrace of a *mandir*, freshening it with water from a bulbous jug she held under one crooked elbow.

"Take a couple of kids with you," she called out with a smile. "And a stick for the monkeys!"

We began to climb, in the late morning sunshine, the cement staircase that led up the hillside. We passed a rubble of ancient carved stone, but of the ancient structure from which it must have come there was no sign. Another casualty, perhaps. Two small boys and a dog scampered ahead of us, up the stairs. Dhirendra and I paused once to get our breath, then, chastened by the energy of our younger companions, we pushed ahead.

At the top of the hill, immense boulders lay around like marbles casually dropped by giants. Someone had placed stone slabs with carvings of the sage Valmiki being saluted by Rama, Sita and Lakshman. They were evidently modern. At the very apex of the hilltop was a small stone cell, which we were to believe Valmiki had inhabited. We scrambled into gloom. As always in such shrines in India, however small or remote they were, there were no signs of desecration; just an idol—in this case, Shree Rama—respectfully smeared with orange pastes, and to one side a little pile of burned *agarbatis* and cracked coconut shells.

The smaller boy, who can only have been three or four, stared blankly at us, a fat oyster of mucus clinging to his upper lip. His brother, who looked about eight, knew what he had to do—he cracked our little coconut in two, placed half of it in front of the

God, tore the rest of it up with his grubby fingers and passed it to each of us. The incense sticks were lit; we sat for a minute or two in silence, then stepped back into the light. As we descended, the shameless monkeys came for us, reaching up with their sharp claws to grab at everything we were carrying. With sticks and yells we fought them off.

We paused a mile or so down the road, where a stream passed Valmiki's hill. It was here, perhaps, that he bathed before having the mystic vision of Brahma, the Creator, who instructed him to begin work on a poem to celebrate the life of his great contemporary, King Rama. Two middle-aged women whirled saris round their heads and brought them down, *slap!* on a flat rock, the time-honoured way in India to wash clothes. A young woman stood in the stream, washing her infant daughter and splashing her own face and bare breasts. It seemed as ancient a scene as anything we'd encountered that morning.

Lunchtime had come and we stopped at a roadside eatery. For a few plates of *dahl*, spinach, rice and chopped tomatoes the owner charged us what we would have paid for dinner at an upmarket Allahabad restaurant. I felt furious—I hadn't asked for the prices before we sat, because I wasn't used to being so blatantly fleeced. I protested, but the proprietor belligerently held his ground. Dhirendra looked sheepish. Other patrons, who might have intervened, just gawped at the sight of the foreigner being taken advantage of. Perhaps, I thought, India was changing. Then I reminded myself that I was close to a major pilgrimage site. They'd been fleecing people here for centuries . . .

I realized the real truth of that a couple of hours later. We had visited, in Chitrakut, a lovely temple dedicated to Bharat, the dutiful brother of Rama. Two gum-chewing attendants brazenly *instructed* us to give money—we refused. We drove a few miles out of town to what seems very likely to be the mountain described to Rama in such glowing terms by the sage, Bhardwaj. It is dominated now by Hanuman Dara (*dara* means stream), a hillside shrine dedicated to the Monkey God, and a "kitchen" where Sita is supposed to have cooked.

The countryside here felt like parts of the Italian south—there were low hills and cottages whose terracotta roofs were made from handmade clay lozenges that only loosely interlocked. Dozens of hawkers pitched at us. When we came to the staircase that led to the top of the hill, each one of the 400 steps had a number painted on it, in descending order, next to a logo of the Allahabad Bank. In such a place it was crass—but worse was in store.

We crowded with thirty others into the cave, around which had been built walls with grilled windows to keep out the monkeys. In the recesses of the cave the sacred stream gushed from a length of pipe. "No one knows from where it comes, and no one knows where it goes," one of the attendants informed us portentously. A sort of *puja* was conducted by a fat man stripped to the waist, his hair dread-locked, his eyes dull and indifferent from a life spent in empty repetition. At either end of the cell his assistants slid shut grills that might have been meant to keep out the monkeys, but made me feel as though I was being kept in. Both men, who resembled mafiosi more than churchmen, fidgeted with boredom. Overhead, electric fans turned. The dreadlocked *pujari* told us a cock-and-bull story about how Hanuman had returned from Lanka with fire in his belly, and Rama had had to fire an arrow into the hillside to create a stream to quench the flames. We were then brought forward, to be fleeced. Each pilgrim was expected to hand over a ten-rupee note. Prayers were muttered, interrupted by the repeated *Crack!* of coconuts, and a club like Hanuman's was laid on every shoulder in benediction. There was one conservative-looking metropolitan family among us, but most of the pilgrims were very poor, dressed in their best pil-grimage weeds. The women wore nylon saris, but the men, dressed in a rag-tail assortment of probably second-hand Western clothes, looked like a bunch of shambling vagabonds. One unfortunate man tried to get away with offering only five rupees, and the attendants demanded ten, snarling at him, "What good will *five* do? The God wants *more!*"

Dhirendra and I watched this from the back with sinking hearts. "These pilgrims are highly innocent people," said Dhirendra with cold anger, "—uneducated, superstitious, they look up to these temple attendants and believe they have contact with the Gods. They're labourers, or even poorer—look at them, how thin they are, malnourished. And *still*, these *pujaris* aren't embarrassed about exploiting them, telling them they'll anger the Gods if they don't hand over more money! It's *despicable*. This is found everywhere nowadays. These people are *destroying* religion!"

It was our turn. Dhirendra's prostrations were impeccable. (He performed the same meticulous ritual at every temple he entered.) Then he handed over our offering: an exquisite long garland of flowers for the idol—no money. The *pujaris* began to protest, but Dhirendra shook his head firmly. He grinned at me when we got outside. "They thought you'd be a good customer—worth fifty rupees at least!"

We climbed another long flight of steps towards the top of this stone mound. The view across to Chitrakut town was picturesque and I was hit with another spasm of plausibility: yes, this was an ideal place for an exiled prince to stay. You could see anyone approaching when they were miles off (and Valmiki describes the dust of Bharat's approaching army). The caves were virtual houses, there would be innumerable hiding places, secret paths down to the plain below, and there was a year-long spring close to the summit.

We were hustled through a couple of little grottoes, one of which was said to have been a spot where Sita prepared food. Why shouldn't such a myth arise? Prehistoric men would have been living here, cooking, blackening the rocks with the smoke from their fires, long before the time of Rama.

In every grotto we were greeted with a sort of coarse, gum-chewing joviality by a bunch of chubby and cocksure young attendants who reminded me of the Romanies you meet in European fairgrounds (the gypsy bloodline, of course, leads, via Romania, straight to India). At each of four shrines they demanded money (we refused it). One of them, attending a long row of Gods, looked as though he was running a coconut shy. There was nothing spiritual, religious or even minimally reverent about any of them.

As we walked away, I told Dhirendra a fantasy had presented itself to me: the ancient *Brahman* families who ran these temples—some of them, doubtless, very rich—had been killed or driven away by organized crime. Now the place was run by hucksters. Dhirendra looked gloomily at me. "You know what Krishna says in the *Bhagavad-Gita*? 'If you want to bring me an offering, what pleases me most is clean water, green leaves, the petals of a few flowers.' It goes without saying that nothing is said about extortion."

The sun was dropping low and we had one more trip to make before nightfall. We headed out of Chitrakut on the dusty northerly road to Prayag, the road I'd used to reach Chitrakut on my previous trip. That time I'd driven straight through Rajpur (Kingtown), an anonymous large village on the banks of the Yamuna river. Yet Rajpur was said to be the birthplace of Saint Tulsidas.

It was dark by the time we reached a shrine that stood above a *ghat* with steps down to the Yamuna. An old man sat in the light of an oil lamp (there was a power cut and Rajpur was in darkness). He was, he told us, a tenth-generation descendant of a disciple of the saint. He brought two ancient wooden clogs from a niche and held them to our foreheads in benediction. When I tried to make an offering, he gestured vaguely at the temple's offertory box on the far side of the room.

The extant pages of the Lake of the Deeds of Rama are kept in a tiny adjacent temple. Another bearded ancient sat in an open porch, chanting Tulsidas from a large volume open on a lectern. He was a little put out when Dhirendra asked, with sublime politeness, what hope there was that we might be granted a glimpse of the great book. At last, with a forbearing sigh, he stood and led us into the back room, and sat on the floor behind a low table. He began to tell us in painful detail the biography of Tulsidas—how he started writing at 76 and lived to be 126. At last, he turned to the wall behind him. A great blue-painted metal safe inscribed with the maker's name "Godrej" was set into the wall. "It was installed in 1948," he told us, "—you know that the whole manuscript had been stolen? That was much earlier, 200 years ago."

With a groan he twisted round and unlocked the safe, taking out a cloth bundle. From its size, I anticipated an enormous tome, like one of those fat, leather-boarded old Bibles you find in a gothic parish church in England. But then he began to unwrap it—layer after layer of velvet. "These wrappings were all donated by devotees, you see." At last, the final layer of onion skin was unpeeled and we beheld a stack of white cards, or *frames*, each of them sealed into a thick polythene envelope slightly larger than foolscap. "They were conserved recently, by the Department of Archæology," he told us. "It's Japanese paper, it has no chemicals in it, it can't affect the manuscripts in any way." He held one of the pages up in front of us.

The framed manuscript pages were brown, covered in lines of neat handwritten Hindi script of an archaic, mediæval form. "It isn't possible for us to read, but if you learn to substitute the ancient characters with modern ones, it becomes easy enough." It was very obvious from dark watermarks that the pages had been wet at some point. "Yes," he said, "the person who stole it 200 years ago was a *pujari*. When they caught him, he threw it in the river! This is all they managed to recover—the second canto."

So, cupidity among *pujaris* was nothing new—though the two *pujaris* here had shown no interest in money at all. Still, I found myself wondering about the man who had stolen these pages. I saw this village in the Middle Ages, the *pujari* dressed in saffron running along the grey foreshore, pursued by the other men of the temple, and desperately casting the irreplaceable pages into the waters of a holy river. Had he just wanted money, or had he been mentally disturbed in some way, obsessed with and weakened by the power and beauty of this religious artefact, like those lunatics of our age who've attacked with hammers or shotguns the sublimest productions of devotional Christian art, Bellini's *Pietà* or Leonardo's cartoon of the Madonna and Child?

THE NEXT MORNING we set out for Varanasi. Tulsidas had lived and worked there, at Asi Ghat, one of the many temples with their great flights of steps that extend for over a mile along the banks of the Ganga. Asi Ghat is at the extreme southern end of the *ghats*, where the River Asi joins the Ganges (the Asi is one of five rivers pilgrims should bathe in daily). We sat where the Saint once sat, beside a small temple with a view across the river. It was a pleasant spot, little frequented and serene. Here sat the man who recast the *Ramayana* story in the language of the common people, who rekindled the fire of Hinduism when it seemed to be guttering and wrote a book that, 500 years later, would still have much of its power.

Dhirendra asked, "Shall we go to Dasaswamedh?"

It is the main *ghat* in Varanasi—the holiest *ghat*. We walked along the shore, where fishing boats bobbed and fishermen in loincloths stepped ashore, looking like supermarket shoppers, only they weren't carrying plastic bags but small bundles of net alive with silver fish. A man, near-naked, crouched on the steps of the temple and emptied his bowels. "Insane," said Dhirendra, "he must be—can you imagine what people would do to him, being so filthy on the steps of a *temple*?" I wondered; the last time I'd been here, five years earlier, I'd witnessed the same sight.

Boys played cricket next to a half-dozen tourists dressed in ugly T-shirts and sandals, dazed spectators to the cremations at Harishchandra Ghat. Wooden boats propped up on bricks were being repaired or recaulked, and the smells of hot tar and roasting flesh mingled. Here, five years earlier, this, my own book, had been conceived.

At Dasaswamedh (Ten Horse Sacrifice) Ghat, we purchased two unfired clay pots for a few pence each and knelt by the river, wiping aside the skin of garlands to find clear water to fill the pots. We heard drums and the wail of pipes, and a parade led by musicians approached. "Newly-married couples seeking the blessings of Lord Shiva and Mother Ganga," Dhirendra grinned. The men wore turbans, the women shyly covered their heads with their saris, showing hands entirely covered in gold jewellery.

We walked up the street, passing a vegetable market where men crouched on the ground beside their produce, cycle rickshaws tinkled by and wandering cows flicked their tails to keep away the flies. Bollywood soundtracks blared from speakers set on the counters of music shops. A group of schoolgirls in elegant grey uniforms passed us, passing also a man pissing (well, his back was towards them) into a gutter. We entered the crowded alleyways with their shops selling sweets, sandals, school uniforms—then coconuts and garlands: this was the entrance to the Vishwanath (Lord of the Universe) Temple. Here, Lord Shiva is believed to be alive, and the temple throbs with religious fervour. I felt excited: I had always been told that this was one of the temples to which non-Hindus find it hardest to gain access. We had to leave our valuables in little boxes for which we were given the keys and our shoes went onto racks underneath. We continued barefoot, up the wet pavement, glimpsing the solid gold of the temple dome, undergoing four body searches, before passing through an ancient doorway into the church of Shiva. It was by no means the rush hour, but it was Monday—

Shiva's day—and people pushed and shoved each other forward, and a policeman snapped at us to "Move along!". We ignored him as we poured our oblations of Ganga water upon the *lingam*, adding too the milk we'd just bought, watching it run through the channels of the embracing *yoni*, finally adding our garlands to the rich, sticky, gorgeous, adored mess of Hinduism's holiest ithyphallus.

We circumnavigated the sanctum. After the human press had expelled us back into the street, Dhirendra said, "Do you want to see the mosque?"

This site was at least as politically potent as Rama's birthplace in Ayodhya. The temple we had visited was relatively new; the original had been demolished by the Mughals. We walked around the *mandir*, past another half-dozen armed and suspicious soldiers, to a suddenly unpopulated square. There were two mosques nearby, barbed-wire-ringed and heavily militarized.

"Can we go in?" I asked.

"We won't be welcome," said Dhirendra.

Perhaps he was right; but now I wish we had at least found out.

We returned to the narrow, crowded alleyways to reclaim our shoes and coins and mobile phones. "I love this town," Dhirendra told me suddenly with an eager smile. We were close to Benares Hindu University, where he had spent several years as a student. "I *like* other places, but the spirit of Varanasi is unique—the role religion plays in the lives of people here—the ordinary citizens. They'll queue for a *darshan* at Vishwanath in their thousands, then go down to the water for their bath, at dawn. Can there be another city like this on earth? I know of none."

CHUNAR, TWENTY-FIVE miles south of Varanasi, is a small town on a bend in the Ganges, dominated by a fort built on one of the few really massive defensible hills that jut into the Gangetic Plain. It has long been a stronghold, but the present fort was constructed by the Mughals and modified only slightly by the British after they took it from them in 1772.

The evening was setting in when we reached Dhirendra's "native place" (as Indians say) on the edge of Chunar, close to the banks of the Ganges. We went up a narrow alleyway and through a stone archway into a walled compound of about half an acre, where maize and mustard were growing. A smaller area was planted with parsley, coriander and other herbs. In one corner, onto the street, stood a two-storey building that looked from the ogeed niches in its plaster walls as if it had been of Islamic construction. Its roof was broken, beams were falling and a wall had collapsed.

The delighted face of Dhirendra's grandmother, Hiramani Devi, appeared. "Dhiraj, Dhiraj!" she said, using his nickname, and he embraced the small, wizened woman. She led us into a low, single-storey building where two rope beds faced each other. It was dark inside—there was a power cut—and oil lamps were lit. Grandma bustled off to bring us tea and a snack, and various cheerful faces appeared to greet Dhiraj, who hadn't been to his "native place" in a while. A couple of free calendars with religious images decorated the room. A big disused pumpset sat on the floor and an ancient fuse box with a perilous nest of wiring hung on the wall. Dhiraj turned to me. "My family are very simple people. Cultivators. No one speaks English here."

"Please, Dhirendra, I'm delighted to be here."

"Still, explanation is a good thing, no? This is our family compound. My grandfather built this building, fifty years ago. There are two rooms—the kitchen is next door. He was a wonderful man, my grandfather, a man of substance, you could say—everyone in the village knew him and respected him, they turned to him for advice . . . He was wise, but he was not worldly in the financial sense. He lost a lot of family land because he wouldn't stoop to squabbles over such things. Money meant little to him. But he was punctilious and well-organized, and since he died, ten years ago . . . Well, my own father has his affairs in Allahabad, he can't spare the time to manage our property and our land . . . So things have been allowed to slip . . ."

Dhiraj's grandfather had been a man of influence, but not wealth. A traditional *Brahman*, a member of Hinduism's élite *pandit* caste.

The online free encyclopaedia Wikipedia contains an entry on Chunar, cheerfully observing that (*sic*): "people of all communities live together with peacefully and took part in the each other communal festivals. Chunar and surrounding villages are majorly populated with *Kurmi Kshatriyas*, contributing more than 50% of the population."

Click on *Kurmi Kshatriyas*, and a Wikipediast informs you that Kurmi ". . . is the name of one of the *Jatis* (*castes*) of the Hindus. The 'Kurmi' is known as the chief ancient agricultural caste of India. . . . Kurmis are the direct descendants of the wellknown Kshatriya dynasties of Lord Rama."

Ah—the business of claiming a family connection with Rama has preoccupied many of India's influential bloodlines. As for the term Kshatriya, it is, as I mentioned earlier, the second of the four traditional Hindu *"varnas"*, or castes—the *Brahmans* (religious scholars), *Kshatriyas* (nobles), *Vaisias* (bourgeois) and *Sudras* (the rest)—and beneath them all the "Untouchables".

But to return to enchantingly non-PC Wiki World:

The physical appearance of the *kurmis* tends to support the view of their *Kshatriya* Origin. According to the Reverend Sherring, "The *Kurmi* has a strong, bony hand, natural to a man of his employment. He is frequently tall and powerful, manly, outspoken and independent in manner and is altogether free from cringing obsequiousness."

Colonel Dalton regards them as the descendants of some of the earliest Aryan Colonists—a brown tawny coloured people, of an average height, well-proportioned and with fair amount of good looks. They show well-shaped heads and high features and except when they have obviously intermixed with aborigins, they are unquestionable Aryans in looks. Grey eyes and brownish hair are sometimes met with amongst them. The women usually have small and well formed hands and feet.

Sir George Campbell, speaking of the *Kurmis* of Hindustan says, "they are on an average darker and less good looking than the Brahmans and Rajputs, but still quite Aryan in their features, institutions and manners."

The link between Kshatriyas and agriculture has been justified on the grounds of linguistic affinities between the root "ar" (bravery, heroism, found in English and Greek *hero*, Russian *geroj* and Sanskrit *arya*) and other words for cultivators i.e. those who labour nobly (Russian *oratel* or ploughman, Airga in the Zend-Avesta), as well as in the legend of King "Prithu", who tamed the earth to make fertile again. It is for this reason that the Sanskrit word for "earth" is "Prithvi", in honour of the Aryan king "Prithu" who first cultivated the earth. And, in the words of Thomas Jefferson, "cultivators of the earth are the most virtuous and independent citizens." [*sic*]

Wikipedia's contributor is striving rather poignantly to make clear that *ethnically*, the *Kurmis* are nothing like the lower castes—*they* have noble, *Aryan* blood! And although they practise agriculture— a *Sudra* trade—they are nevertheless—*down deep*—warriors and kings. It's ironic, as well as sad, that the racialist attitudes of the Victorians, with their assumptions about the superiority of those descended from the Aryans and inferiority of those with "aboriginal" blood, should be employed by modern Indians to prop up their sense of caste pride. But the contributor himself clearly finds it neither ironic nor sad. In that sense, most Indians are still touched by a system of social (and perhaps racial) segregation that casts a long shadow indeed.

IT WAS DHIRENDRA'S surviving grandfather, on his mother's side, Shree Laxmi Kant Tiwari, that he particularly wanted me to meet.

"He's a *pandit* at a local temple—that's a very old family tradition. When we were kids he used to recite us long chunks of the *Ramcharitmanas*. I grew up in Allahabad, but we spent our vacations here, and every evening in the summer we kids would all sit on the floor and listen. I used to love it. These recitations would take place, with people playing the harmonium and the *tabla*.[5] My grandfather would entertain us by reciting chunks from memory."

In a second small house across a narrow lane, Dhirendra's grandfather lay on a bed. Dhirendra joined his palms, then quickly touched the old man's feet. His grandfather pushed him away (it is a common convention, when someone touches your feet in this traditional mark of respect, to encourage them back to their feet,

---

[5] A type of drum.

indicating that you don't consider yourself deserving of such reverence), then sat up, pushing back his blankets. I protested that we were disturbing him, but he brushed the suggestion aside and pushed me into a wooden armchair at the bedside. Another lamp was brought into the room and we were joined by the Laxmi Kant's wife Umravati Devi, Dhirendra's maternal grandmother.

As we told them about my interest in Tulsidas, two fat family copies promptly appeared. The old man held the larger volume, which was broken-spined, its boards peeling, the binding string just about holding its quartos in place. "An ancient book!" he said to me. (It was not, in fact, quite as ancient as he was—he appears to have bought it just after Independence, when he was fifteen years old. First published by the Gita Press in 1947, it was, in fact, the first accurate, scholarly edition of the *Ramcharitmanas*.)

Laxmi Kant's wife was a handsome woman who looked about ten years younger than her husband. She was wrapped in a dark-green sari and wore rings on her ankles and toes. She opened her own copy of Tulsidas and their son and daughter-in-law, Bal Krishna and Pratima, trained torch beams on the two books. The old couple, cross-legged on the bed, began to recite the same passage from near the end of the *Ramcharitmanas*, he, running his finger over the curled Hindi characters, a little more falteringly than she. Insects danced in the intersecting beams of the torches.

When they paused, I asked what the story of Rama and Sita meant to them.

The old man said with gravity, "It brings merit." It was a claim I'd heard before—indeed, it is one of the claims Tulsidas's work makes about itself in its closing pages. "It cleanses you," he went on, "it provides you with an ideal against which to measure your own life, your own conduct. It's a wonderful ideal. I recite some lines of the *Ramcharitmanas* every day."

"It's the story of a struggle," his wife added. "That's what it teaches: that life is full of struggles, and even rich and privileged people like Rama and Sita will have to face the same hardships as the rest of us. It teaches acceptance, and determination."

"Is it still *relevant* today?" I asked her. "Does the book have a future?"

"Oh, *yes*. Because of its connection to daily life. I'm not sure about the future of other Scriptures, but I feel sure that Tulsidas will survive—because of our tradition that he's recited in every home. And people do that because they actually enjoy the way he wrote so much."

I turned to her daughter-in-law Pratima, a woman of just twenty-six years, not yet a mother. "Sita is the ideal woman for me," she told me, "in that she never disobeyed—she always did whatever her father-in-law and society in general expected of her."

That will be the nitty-gritty for quite a number of people. Tulsidas stands accused of enshrining the servility of women in a way that India is only just beginning to shake off. Indian daughters-in-law traditionally go to live with their husbands' families, where their mother-in-law becomes their ruler and life is often far from easy. (As for Valmiki, one of the crimes laid at his door is his support for the divine right of kings, which his critics say inspired despots into the twentieth century and still provides succour for India's contemporary dynastic rulers.) So here was a modern daughter-in-law using Tulsidas to make the case for abject obedience to those very people—seated in front of her—that she was supposed to obey: her in-laws.

I tried a different tack. "How can the traditions of the *Ramcharitmanas* continue to have relevance in an age when people spend half their lives in front of the TV, and receive many of their values and influences from soap operas, which are competing with each other to come up with the most spiteful plot lines?"

"Well," Pratima replied, "there are still many Sitas in this world and plenty of Ravans—to whom Sita is nothing but an object of lust. And people like him will always be around. It isn't just a question of how well Sita behaves, it's about how she's treated—how women in society are treated. I think society *is* changing for the worse, and movies and TV have a lot to do with it. Urban life is changing so quickly that women in big cities may not be able to cherish the example of Sita much longer. But I think women are changing unwillingly, they feel they have to flirt and seduce men, because society as a whole is losing its willingness to uphold the traditional social structure. Traditionally, people are supposed to behave decently, with self-control, and women are to be respected. But I don't think these changes make Sita *less* relevant—she's still an example of how we *ought to* be living. And the more society changes, the more we're going to need an example to look up to!"

In the course of each of our conversations the others in the room sat quietly, listening. They were calm and polite people, who didn't talk over each other, yet were at the same time unselfconscious, spontaneous and direct. They showed all the traditional virtues that the Indian TV universe with its celebration of greed and spite is so eagerly subverting.

"Tulsidas has left a real imprint behind him," Grandad put in. He added, with the air of someone playing an ace, "Not only on us, but on the world—on *you*, after all, it's because of him that you're here!"

Laxmi Kant was a slight man, with a long face that cracked in two with the sort of merriment that made it impossible not to laugh with him. Dhiraj's paternal grandmother, who'd been sitting in a low armchair observing all this, now asked me a question: "What about your parents? Are they still alive?"

"I'm afraid not," I said.

"They were killed in the war!" said Grandad with a roar of laughter. He was implying that they'd been killed in battle by Indian independence fighters, and this was such a funny suggestion that everybody laughed, including me. The old man had the room, now, and he wasn't going to let go. He changed his tack. "In his country, they kill people when they get to your age," he roared at his ancient sister-in-law. "You eat too much food, so they do away with you!" The room was in uproar now. The old man, grinning from ear to ear, kept repeating his punchlines over and over. "Too old to be of any use, a waste of food! So they'll have you put down!"

It was late—at least, in country time. Dhiraj's aunt had been busily preparing us a meal, vegetarian of course—these were *Brahmans*—and we sat by the light of an oil lamp and ate, as moths tried to break through the glass and immolate themselves in the flame.

After dinner Dhirendra's elder grandma accompanied us indoors. She sat beside Dhirendra on one of the rope beds, plying him with questions. He sat, looming over her, replying with patience and affection. But the gulf between them was clear: he was a man now, highly educated, a city dweller, knowledgeable in the ways of the world. Twenty years ago he had been a little boy here, running giggling around the saris of his grandmother. Now she was eighty-four and, as she sat beside him on the bed, tiny, trusting, her eyes gleaming with love, it seemed poignantly clear that she was more like the child, and that while Dhiraj was patient and kind, a gulf of understanding separated them. He had to go out into this cruel and incomprehensible world and make a life for himself. She could only watch and hope for the best.

It wasn't yet 11 p.m., but beyond the little barred window the darkness and silence were absolute. Hiramani Devi withdrew, and Dhirendra dropped into place the solid beam that secured the door against invasion. I pulled my blanket over me. Dhirendra was in a mood to chat, but I was feeling the irresistible undertow of sleep.

Soon after 4 a.m. the life of the countryside began. The open window let straight onto a street with a dozen households and a couple of shops. My dozing was disturbed by the sounds of cocks crowing, bus horns, people spitting toothpaste and expectorating, street cleaners, switches brushing the courtyard, plates scraped. Dhirendra and I, the city dwellers, clung to sleep the longest. It was a radio that finally roused me. India is embracing FM radio and the manic, fake bonhomie of a local radio presenter, unmistakable in any language, assaulted me from the counter of the shop across the street.

After breakfast, Dhirendra led me along narrow lanes to the shore of Mother Ganga. His own parental home was here, just yards from the holy river. Close by stood an imposing colonial house. It looked to me as if it could have been an early nineteenth- or even late eighteenth-century building—it was all classic porticoes and pediments. It had been subdivided and seemed partly ruined, the curious rounded structures at its corners, like the defensive turrets of a mediæval fortress, crumbling as tree roots proved themselves stronger than stone.

A wide, grassy bank dropped gently to the river. A flight of steps descended to the shore, but the lower steps had been eroded. The water appeared deep. A woman crouched on one of the displaced slabs, washing clothes. She was soaked through and her brown, goose-pimpled skin glowed pinkly with cold.

"They did something upriver that changed the flow," said Dhirendra. "It means that now there's deep water on this side of the river. We used to have a wide beach here, the water was shallow and slow-moving. Still people come down for their morning dip, but as kids we used to roam here freely, to play. We used to swim two to three hours a day.

"Now, it is too dangerous to swim. Two children, you know, members of my family, have been drowned here in recent years. And yet . . . Despite that, people do not in any way hate or resent the river. She is still holy to us."

He picked his way forward and crouched on the lowest step. In front of him Ganga flowed rapidly, hidden currents causing eddies, navels, on her silken skin. But the water did not look clean, and where the steps jutted forward there was a collection of flotsam and an oily, rainbow hue to the surface. Dhirendra leaned forward, wiped away some detritus with the edge of his hand, then scooped a drop of water into his palm. He swallowed it and muttered some prayers. He caught my eye and smiled. "This is what we do," he said. "We believe she is pure. That is our faith."

After breakfast we went to collect Dhirendra's grandad. The old man was still sitting on his bed when we arrived, but then leapt spryly to his feet. When I laughingly commented on this, he jumped on the spot with astonishing athleticism and even a kind of grace.

Dhirendra and his *pandit* grandad took me to visit two temples. At the first of them, dedicated to the Goddess Durga, we were forced, in order to enter the sanctum, to kneel down and crawl through a space barely two feet high. "You see", said Dhirendra, "how you're obliged to approach the Goddess on your knees?" The space in front of the Goddess was perhaps eight feet square, with a wire screen to protect the two seated *pandits* from the eager worshippers who jostled to light their *agarbatis* and press forward their offerings—their coconuts, flowers, fruits and cash.

At the other temple we visited there was less of a crush, but it was in its own way an important shrine, one of few temples in India devoted to Lord Krishna in his incarnation as a child. Lord Rama is worshipped as a child, too, but it is Krishna whose mischievous infant exploits so endear him to Hindus. The temple was a period piece, not heavily carved stone but covered in rotund, curly-moustached figures, like greatly magnified children's toys, typical of the pre-colonial style. With its walled "tank" of emerald water and beautiful rose garden, it was serene. It was here that Grandpa, Laxmi Kant Tiwari, was a *pandit*. And it was here that Dhirendra as a child would scamper freely. I wasn't surprised when he told me that his personal deity was Krishna. (It is outside the scope of this book to detail the relations in the various schools of Hinduism between notions of a formless God and a personal deity; suffice to say, most Hindus adopt one of the forms of either Vishnu or Shiva as a personal deity, making them in essence—since in Hinduism All is One—into monotheists . . .)

They took me also to Chunar's great fort, now an army recruitment centre. There was a huge subterranean dungeon reached by no staircase—the steps ended above head height and the only way out was by ladder. It had been constructed, Laxmi Kant insisted, by the British, to hold prisoners. The other notable contribution of the British was a gorgeous tall-ceilinged bungalow with five rooms and a terrace from which one could observe the Ganges as it snaked round the granite promontory of Chunar.

We saw another sign of the British before we left Chunar. In the shadow of the fortress is the British cemetery, indicated by a bent and pitted sign placed by the Indian Archæological Survey. Many of the obelisks date from the late eighteenth century and have a clean classicism to their design that is superior, to my eye, to the fussier efforts of the Victorian age. But without exception, the tombs are falling, their black marble nameplates are being stolen. No doubt, in years to come, Indian families will be turning Grandma's chopping board upside down and finding letters carved in Roman script, and will wonder at the provenance of the antique. The wall of the cemetery has been pushed over, animals graze inside and the larger obelisks are used to dry cow dung, which is used as a fuel.

"What", I asked Dhirendra, "would happen if people dried dung in a Muslim cemetery?"

"There would be clashes!" he replied. "But the Christians have left!"

PART V

CHAPTER 14

Cooking the Kali

IT WAS LATE evening. Underneath us, the reassuring, hypnotic clack of iron wheels on track. One by one the passengers around us had turned in. The blue night lights were illuminated, the soft grey acrylic curtains drawn. Mothers slept with their hands on the heads of small children, travelling reps slept with their heads on their plastic briefcases.

Even the conductors slept.

The train was headed south from Delhi to Mysore. I was leaving north India behind me, to travel to where Prince Rama is seen not as a figure of devotion but as a hated outsider, an Aryan invader. First, though, I had an appointment—in Ooty, where my parents had lived.

Three of us were still awake. The two young officers from an Indian parachute regiment, heading home on leave, were telling rude jokes.

". . . there was once a fish in a pond, and it sees a fly flying low over the surface of the pond and it thinks, 'If that fly comes down another six inches, I'll jump and get it.' And a cat is watching the fish. And the cat thinks, 'If the fly comes down another six inches, the fish will jump, and then I can grab it in my teeth!' So—the fly comes down, and the fish leaps, but the cat misses him, and it falls in the pond. And the moral of this story is—when the fly comes down six inches, the pussy gets wet!"

They fell back on the blue vinyl benches, clutching their stomachs. A half-bottle of whisky had been discreetly—extremely discreetly—passing between them.

"Is it getting a little late, gentlemen?" I asked.

"Yes, Sir," they both said, responding automatically to the voice of authority. I appear to have reached an age where I can elicit an automatic "Sir".

The younger of the two yawned. "I'll turn in." He climbed onto his middle bunk. The older one crouched cautiously beside me on my lower bunk. "What are you reading, Sir?" I showed him. It was the south Indian *Ramayana*, the *Ramavataram*, written in the twelfth century by the Tamil poet Kambar.

"*Ramayana*, my *God*! *Playboy* is more my level! I'll join you for a minute, Sir?"

"Mm."

"What's your profession, Sir?"

"I'm a writer; a journalist."

"*Really*? You should write about us!"

"Oh?" I said, without enthusiasm.

"Kashmir. You had been to Kashmir?"

"Not yet. The last time I tried to go, they started a war."

"Exactly! That is our job. Our job is counter-insurgency."

"What, you're fighting Pakistani militants?"

"Absolutely! Sir, you'll take a peg?" He grinned sheepishly. "I am out of uniform, so . . ."

"Go on, then." He poured a double Hayward's into a plastic cup. "Cheers," I said. "So—are you actually fighting a counter-insurgency war? Against whom?"

"Militants! Islamicists!"

"I mean *who* are they?"

"They're professional fighters—but not regular forces. Some are coming from Pakistan, but many are coming from Afghanistan. War is all those guys have known. They beat the Russians; then, they lost to the Americans—when the Taliban were kicked out. What are they going to do? Where are they going to go? They look for another war."

"They travel to the Kashmir border. Jihad."

"Jihad. Somebody pays, they don't care who. Pakistani government? Saudis? They just keep fighting."

"And what kind of war is it? I mean, what kinds of encounters take place?"

"We're aiming for area domination. Deny territory to your enemy."

"This is in the mountains?"

"Absolutely. Basically the way we work is, we go out for several days at a time, sleep by day, travel by night. No lights, no cigarettes, anything—that's holy writ, an officer will be bumped down for smoking on an op or the accidental discharge of a weapon. We move very slowly—I mean *very* slowly. We have to be invisible. The point is to circle them—and that's that."

"You take prisoners?"

"No. We circle them and shoot to kill. Finished. Kill more than three terrorists, it will be printed in the media and shown on TV as an Indian victory."

"Meanwhile they're trying to circle and kill you?"

He grinned again. "Correct. You should come out with us some time, Sir!"

I didn't think the Indian government would be very keen on that idea. I said, "I'd probably shit my pants when the firing started."

"No, Sir, not if you understood what was happening. The action never lasts more than five minutes."

"And tell me: do you ever kill the wrong people?"

"*Never*. The problem is to be sure they're militants—they wear this shawl, no?—over the shoulder, which covers and hides the gun. But my boys will see just the flash of the metal catch on the leather strap against the guy's neck. And they never make mistakes. You aim for the chest area—it's a bigger target. One bullet is enough. We use .765 ammo, it makes a small entry hole that as it spins it opens up, it makes a tremendous shock on the arteries, bones etc., it might destroy the lungs . . ."

"So you guys are well equipped?"

"We have the *best*. My weapon is an Israeli weapon—we use semi-autos. It's a beautiful weapon, you just sight it and it's totally accurate. Then we use a Czech gun, a beauty. Drop it in the water, pick it up—and it will still fire straight away. But the weapon I prefer is the rocket-fired grenade—you Brits call it a bazooka—a lovely weapon, *love-ly* weapon. It has a double detonation, the second one goes off at chest height, it's hundreds of small steel balls, basically. Kills anyone around. That really frightens them. That's the one that gets them running for cover. God, I really love that weapon!"

"How do you find out where they—the militants—are?"

229

"Scouting. Tip-offs. Often we can see them moving about on the other side of the valley. But getting close enough to kill—that is a different matter. Also, we work with civilians."

"They crawl around with you in silence for three days?"

"Well, it can be a problem. One time I had a civilian stand up—we were right on top of some militants—he panicked and stood up and yelled, 'Civilian!' Bloody stupid thing to do. They opened fire immediately. Two civilians were killed that day and one of our guys also."

He looked so young, it was hard to believe he was commanding a kind of death squad. I asked, "How did you feel when you first saw somebody killed?"

"I felt very good, I tell you—*very* good. One less guy who'd like to kill me. And my boys, they hate to come back empty-handed. '*Aray*, we went all that away and came back empty-handed!'—they'll be *too* depressed. But get some militants and they'll be *really* high—'OK, let's go and find some more!'—they'll be really buoyed up and keen!"

I held out my cup for another peg. "Dangerous job you have."

"Not if you remember your fieldcraft. Teamwork. The boys are great if they have total trust in their officer. If they don't, they're unhappy. My boys love me. Focus. Encounter. Back to base. And you feel so so high, *yaar!*"

"What do you do then? To . . . unwind?"

"Well . . . We cook—my boys love to cook. Best of all they love chicken. They just pluck them and put them on the fire—even that red thing on top, what do you call it? We call that *kali*, like the goddess, no? That they eat, it's a delicacy, a pre-meal snack, if you like."

"Then what do you do?"

"We play volleyball, chess . . . cricket, even though there isn't really space, but somehow we make some. We read . . ."

"This is my territory. What do you read?"

"Not the *Ramayana*, that's for sure!"

I gave a manly, conspiratorial, whisky-enhanced chuckle. "Then?"

"Porn, *yaar!* Somebody comes and says—Do you have anything to read? And you say—Yes, I have Sherlock Holmes.—Hey, bloody fuck off, man, don't give me any Sherlock Holmes, do you have any porn?—Yes, I have porn.—Then hand it over!"

"What about the locals? Do they resent you a lot? Are the majority Muslims?"

"*Resent?* My boys pay the locals a hundred per cent extra for anything they buy. And an army like ours needs a huge amount of back-up, so we spend a lot of money in the local economy. So it very much suits them to have us there."

"They don't care that it's a majority Muslim state controlled by a Hindu national majority?"

"The locals are *happy* being Indian! They don't care about these things . . ."

"I wonder, from everything I've read, if that's really true."

"Well, I'll tell you one thing . . . This war has been unnecessarily prolonged. It could have been settled years ago—*many* years ago. The line of control should be recognized. More than fifty years have gone by, thousands of deaths, a fortune spent . . . But that is politicians. A couple of years back, we and the Pakistanis were sabre-rattling with nukes! Now, we're friends. Meanwhile, Pakistan built up these Islamic militants for its own purposes and now they threaten the stability of Pakistan itself. They threaten the stability of the whole region. Who knows what will happen next?"

SUGRIVA WAS AS much a hedonist as his brother had been. It was traditional, after a victory, to feast; but Sugriva ate, drank and made love for four long months. His own wife had been restored to him, but he also took his brother's wife, Tara, whom he had always secretly desired. (Rama turned an uneasy blind eye.) Sugriva rarely saw daylight; he grew fat and pale. He turned the running of the mountain kingdom over to his ministers and didn't even consult them.

Hanuman bided his time. When the moment seemed right, he reminded Sugriva of his greatness as a king, and his duty to Rama, who was waiting patiently for the fulfilment of the promise to find Sita. Sugriva gave an order for the country's border commanders to attend Kishkindha within fifteen days, on pain of death. Then he returned to the bedroom.

The rainy season had passed. Rama was sitting on the mountain where he and Lakshman had installed themselves, overlooking the city.

"Now that Sugriva has everything he wants," he said, "he's forgotten his promises. Most of the time he's drunk." He looked down into the valley. "The streams are falling," he said. "Like the poem—'slowly they uncover their pale sandbanks, the way a shy girl shows her breasts'. The rains are over, Lakshman—*now*'s the time of year for an expedition!" His voice became angry. "I think you should go down and tell that rutting monkey that if he doesn't want to die alongside his whole family, he'd better do something!"

Lakshman grabbed his bow. "Don't worry, I'll save you the trouble, I'll kill him straight away."

Rama held up his hands and laughed. "My God, when I see you getting angry it certainly cools my temper! No—we need Sugriva! Just go and remind him of his commitment, as a king, to the Prince of Ayodhya."

But Lakshman arrived at the gates of the city in a rage. In no time there was a stand-off between him and a detachment of terrified palace guards. Sugriva was busy making love to Tara. Her son Angada, who'd been learning archery from Lakshman, managed to calm down the furious Prince. At last, he was led into the audience room where Sugriva, draped in his jewel-studded royal silks, took his place on his throne. His hands were trembling.

"How can we help the brother of our best ally?" he asked.

"You're an ungrateful, lying *monkey*!" The court gave a collective gasp. "You've done nothing to help find Sita! You spend your days squeezing female flesh! Just remember, what killed your brother can kill you!"

Tara intervened. "The King", she said, "has been rediscovering what for so long he missed. I am sure Rama will be able to understand that one day."

"Oh, and when exactly will that be?" Lakshman asked sarcastically.

"You can't kill the *rakashas* without us, Prince Lakshman," said Tara. "The King has already ordered his border commanders back. The matter is in hand."

Sugriva climbed shakily to his feet, his bloodshot eyes gleaming. "Forgive me, Lakshman my *friend*," he said. "But who is there in the world who never offended a friend?"

CHAPTER 15

Slow Bus to Ooty

MOST OF THE magazines at the bus station bookstall in Mysore had images of film stars or gods on their covers. The scattering of English-language magazines offered greater wealth or better orgasms.

I had another pilgrimage to make, here in south-west India. Before my mother died, the previous Christmas, she told me she wanted to leave some money to her former servant, Sivaraj. This was my first chance to make good her wish.

A Dostoevskyan young man in a dirty T-shirt sat across the aisle from me, bearded and scowling, a fat black Bible cupped in his hands. In front of me were two *Brahman* honeymooners. (In the course of the day's journey they were barely to exchange six sentences.) The bus set off and quickly joined a brand-new black-top highway. Where a viaduct was being built across the road, barefoot men carried shallow baskets of gravel on their heads. The roadside was a continuous trail of litter, a silver tidemark of discarded plastic. We passed granite fence posts and spindly trees planted to replace illegally felled ancient ones. I saw a lake with a sandy pink shore where a herd of gaunt cattle wandered in the shallows. A woman crouched on a shoal, washing clothes. A man, his bicycle propped on the scrubby bank, stooped and washed the udders of a cow. Beyond them, across the water, a tree flamed acrylic red, the red of an Indian school cardigan.

After a couple of hours the bus turned onto a narrower, rougher road and began to climb. As we entered Mudumalai Wildlife Sanctuary a sign warned us not to exceed twenty kilometres per hour—a warning unnecessary in our case, as every vehicle on the road was overtaking us. We laboured up even modest slopes in first gear. I watched the sluggish drift of the landscape as we entered the veldt-like landscape of Mudumalai with its clumps of splayed bamboo, like loosely held spillikins seventy feet high. We passed termite mounds and strutting peacocks. A man pointed out an elephant to his son and everyone on board gawped into the bush, where we saw a female elephant and her child. A sign said, "Wild Animals Have the Rights of Way" and another, "Do Not Kindle Fire in the Forest". A third said, "Welcome to Plastic-free Nilgiris". That seemed like a forlorn hope. Where my arm, crooked out of the window, had been continually in the sun, I saw that it was burned. The inflammation felt good.

Roadworks were in progress. Where the tarmac was split, a man placed neat, hand-sculpted granite balls into the cracks, while another poured over them a thin stream of tar. He looked like a chef drizzling balsamic vinegar on *mozzarella di bufala*. Monkeys squatted on boulders, watching us pass. I saw a small, orange-domed *mandir* where a dozen chickens pecked at the earth, a reminder that not all Hindus observed the injunction to vegetarianism—those who abjured meat were either *Brahmans*, or were simply too poor to afford it. The air was becoming cooler. Eucalyptus trees in tight formation—barely six feet apart—marched solemnly past, replaced eventually by the slopes of tea bushes I remembered so well, like giant broccoli with paths vermiculating through them. This was the Liddelsdale Tea Estate.

We weren't going to reach Ooty before dark. The men outside now had turbans or scarves wrapped round their heads against the cold. I was treated to a classic Nilgiris sunset, beginning with the great clouds metamorphosing into mangoes. The sky behind them turned saffron, then turquoise and finally an intense purple-blue, against which the clouds, now a kind of cream colour, stood out with the three-dimensionality of an optical illusion. At last we approached Ooty, everything around us now ink-black. An eight- or nine-hour journey had taken twelve, during which the bus had stopped once for a tea break and once to allow passengers to clamber down and urinate in a gutter.

I climbed into a taxi and gave the name of an hotel I remembered, close to my parents' first home. The Dasaprakash is a rambling Victorian heap overlooking the racecourse, to which dozens of rooms have been added, interlinked by covered walkways to keep off the rain. With their iron poles and gabled, corrugated roofs, they are bizarrely reminiscent of some archaic English seaside holiday camp. The hotel reception smelt of eucalyptus oil and woodsmoke, and I experienced a sudden Proustian moment—for those *are* the smells of Ooty, and in a rush two decades fell away and I was back in a place I knew and where I felt at ease. I took the cheapest room, which wasn't very cheap. I was greeted by a toilet full of stagnant urine, covered by a toilet seat with a band of paper informing me that it had been hygienically cleaned for the benefit of me, the valued customer. I rang reception and asked them to send down some incense sticks— and a heater: the room was freezing.

At eleven in the morning I was to meet Sivaraj, as well as Mr Devasagayam, the now retired estate agent who'd managed the houses my parents rented and with whom my mother had stayed in touch. She had made him a smaller, token bequest.

I met them in reception. Neither of them recognized me—then did so with a sort of dawning horror that I had undergone what was evidently a gruesome transformation. They were both small men; I felt suddenly large and clumsy. I led them to easy chairs on the lawn. Smiling, I looked at them; reticently, they returned my look. Sivaraj seemed almost identical to his younger self, no fatter, with no white hair—but very subtly aged, ever so faintly *creased*, the difference between a fresh apple and one that's a few weeks old. Devasagayam had already been in middle age when I'd known him, and although his wavy hair had a crest of silver now, his face and physique seemed miraculously unchanged. He rejected my astonishment with a sort of amused dismissal. "I still walk up and down," he grinned, "the hills keep me fit."

I told them how my mother had died—of a brain tumour. There were quiet "Oh"s, but otherwise discreet silence. We exchanged a few more mechanical phrases, with Devasagayam speaking on behalf of Sivaraj, who seemed to have lost his English. We emptied our teacups, and with a sense of anticlimax, that was that. I went down to my room to fetch the envelopes containing my mother's bequests and handed them over. There was no display of emotion.

I mentioned that I'd like to visit Sivaraj's home and meet his family. Devasagayam promptly said that this would be a bad idea, that it was not a "good place". I thought he was probably trying to avoid embarrassment all round—discretion again—his conservative sense, as a professional man who'd been used to dealing with rich Indians, in particular the spoilt and haughty ladies of the Indian Money Aristocracy, that for the peace of mind of both parties, the rich and the poor should be kept apart. Or was there a caste dimension? In India, there is always a caste dimension. I offered him a lift into town, where he was going to do some "marketing", but he declined. Then he padded out of my sight, probably for ever.

Sivaraj had gone to hail an autorickshaw. He returned and told me he'd found a driver he knew, a neighbour of his, who wouldn't overcharge. We climbed aboard.

I had said I'd like to see our old houses. The first place was close by, reached by climbing a few narrow lanes. Below—further away than I remembered—was the green lake where, as ever, pedalos slowly circled. Sivaraj sped off to find his father, who was still the gardener. The old man appeared, with a scarf tied round his temples, and joined his palms in greeting. Sivaraj, meanwhile, had become more relaxed and expansive—I realized it was the presence of Mr Devasagayam that had inhibited him. I was invited into the garden. It was a riot of immaculately tended flowers, but smaller than in my memory. Mr Devasagayam had phoned ahead to instruct the house-keeper to let me take a peek inside. I stepped into the chalet, which also seemed on the outside much smaller than I remembered, and gave an involuntary shudder of surprise. Nothing had changed—except that, like some episode from *Alice in Wonderland*, every-thing—the polished wooden floorboards, the stone fireplace, the ghastly M. F. Hussein painting—had shrunk. I couldn't go on; I thanked them profusely and returned to the garden. The front lawn seemed like a strip of grass along the top of a precipitous cliff—as though one wrong step might plunge you into the lake. I had a schizophrenic sense of two realities. My memories seemed to be losing the battle with the present and I struggled to hang on to them. I stood for a long while, staring down at the lake, and at this holiday chalet that had been so absurdly gracious and substantial in my memory. The air, in contrast with the Gangetic Plain, was cool and soothing. Above me, great clouds sailed through the Ooty skies.

Sivaraj and I continued down to the lake. From the chalet, my parents had moved into a bigger house beside the lake, with grounds so extensive that tree poachers would come in the night and fell mature trees—and we'd hear nothing. The house was invisible behind its walls and heavy, locked gates. Sivaraj began to apologize, and I told him not to be absurd.

It was midday. We went to a simple restaurant opposite the railway station and talked about our families. He had two teenage daughters. I, starting on the family path much later, had a small son. I asked how his work was. When they were leaving Ooty, my mother had implored my father to find Sivaraj a job—something better paid than a houseboy. The job he'd managed to find him, in the state dairy, didn't earn her full approval: it was hard physical work. But Sivaraj was grateful, he told me. It was a regular income; it had allowed him to raise his daughters, who were both off to college now.

The afternoon was overcast. We made a tour of the town—the Ooty Club, Chellaram's Department Store, Higginbottoms's book shop, and finally to the top of the town, where the church stood. It's a fussy piece of Victorian Gothic, with a tower that looks too low. The churchyard, unlike the one in Chunar, has not been defiled. Sivaraj had never been inside the church. I asked him and the rickshaw driver if they'd like to take a look, and awkwardly they followed me in. It is an exquisite space, far lovelier than its squat Gothic exterior would have you expect. There are white columns, a timber roof, pews with elegant and comfortable rattan seats. There is some exquisite jewelled Victorian glass. Beyond the altar, Christ is framed in a narrow, vaulted window, the words EMANUEL GOD WITH US inscribed around Him. It is unfashionable to approve of the Raj, but standing in that church once again, I could only feel sympathy with those English men and women who died here, so far from home. Brass plaques, exquisitely polished, told their stories in telegraphese: the Nellies and Corals, deceased wives of planters and Collectors. Georgiana Grace, "an excellent wife, a good, kind and judicious mother", who died at Coimbatore in 1847 aged thirty years, "leaving her husband and seven children to deplore their irreparable loss". And the unfortunate Richard William Preston, Captain first Bombay Grenadier Guards,

. . .who drowned in the Knomund River
while out hunting with the Ootacamund Hounds.
"Thy Will be done"

THE BEARDED MUSLIM butcher gave his cleaver a few strokes
against a sharp, hung the mutton on a hook and began to slice. I
knew many Hindus who never touched meat (mostly *Brahmans*); I'd
been interested to learn that Sivaraj and his family, devout Hindus all,
readily consumed fish, chicken and mutton, but not pork ("not
interested"), and a violent shake of the head at the question, "beef?".
But meat was expensive, he told me—they ate it once or twice a
month. We'd already been to the chocolate shop—chocolate being
an Ooty speciality and my mother having been a regular customer
there. I wanted to offer them a chicken, too, and Sivaraj led me to
another section of the market and his preferred butcher. While he
selected a plump bird, the butcher lit an oil lamp under a stainless
steel drum with an inch of water in it; we waited (I wasn't sure why)
for it to boil. The bird's throat was cut and it was dropped into the
tub, where it danced insanely until it died. I had never witnessed this
ritual before. The brutality of it, the impassive face of the butcher,
numbed me. The now dead bird was beheaded and dropped into a
rapidly revolving drum full of stiff rubber rods. It looked like a lump
of dough, revolving obscenely, shedding feathers, oozing clotted
blood. The butcher meanwhile rinsed his block and wiped his knife
with a torn sheet of newspaper. I realized that I was staring fixedly at
the Tamil characters on the newspaper as it soaked up blood.

Mr Devasagayam's social caution had been needless. Sivaraj and
his family lived in a tin-roofed room built onto the side of a small
colonial house. It was divided into three by hanging curtains. His
wife seemed delighted to receive me, his daughters were full of
teenage enthusiasm. I sat on the hard bed close to the front door and
was served tea and biscuits. When I was last in Ooty, two decades
earlier, these three women had yet to enter the young Sivaraj's life.
The girls lovingly spread out on the bed every card they had ever
received from my mother—the snapshots of myself and my sister
marrying, our children as babies. For his part, Sivaraj never missed a

Christmas card to my mother—he still referred to her as "Ma". Ridiculously, it used to make me jealous; I had to fight back a tear when I remembered that. She had meant a lot to them. My mother, the socialist, ill suited to the role of memsahib, had managed to give her servant a chance in life, to raise him up from houseboy to salary earner. It was not nothing.

Sivaraj *had* changed; the puppy had gone out of him. In repose his face assumed an anxious expression. Perhaps, like every parent, he was brooding on the future of his children. But when he moved to the door and looked out, he became seventeen again: he still stood on one foot and tapped the toes of his other foot against the step, one arm raised to hold the door frame, as he stared out across the valley. He still gave a little cough before replying to a question, or ran his hand over his brush of hair . . . Watching him, I felt a spasm of emotion, as if I was meeting a younger brother after a separation of many years. I swallowed hard.

Our autorickshaw man drove us both down to the bus stand. Sivaraj stood and waved as the bus pulled out and I waved back. We were both crying.

KING SUGRIVA TOLD Rama he was sending out scouting parties to discover where Sita was being held. To Hanuman he said, "If anyone can find Sita, it will be you."

Before Hanuman left, Rama gave him his signet ring. "If you find her, and manage to speak to her, this will prove that you've come from me."

Hanuman and his men travelled south, crossing the region ringed by mountains on one side and ocean on the other. They could discover nothing about Sita. They became increasingly worried—and most worried of all was the son of Vali, Crown Prince Angada.

"Sugriva's ruthless, Hanuman. What happens if all the search parties come back empty-handed? Rama will go mad! Sugriva would have to kill him—and that would start a war with Ayodhya. So Sugriva's more likely to try and buy Rama's understanding by punishing *us*. And whom would he most like to get rid of? *Me*."

Some others in the party overheard. "Sugriva won't just kill Angada,

Hanuman, he'll make an example of a whole lot of us. We're not going back."

It had the making of a rebellion. How long, Hanuman wondered, before Angada began to plot with his mother to kill Sugriva? But spies would inform Sugriva before they returned. He'd have them all murdered, en route to the capital.

And then, reaching the palm-fringed south-east shore, they heard a rumour that a young woman had been carried across the water to Lanka and was imprisoned in Ravan's castle. A rumour wasn't enough, though: Hanuman needed proof.

The sixteen-mile-long chain of islands that led to Lanka was the best-defended strip of land in India. It was like a drawbridge over a moat and it made Lanka unassailable. Some islands were linked by causeways or bridges, while the longest stretches of open water had to be crossed by boat. If Hanuman's men tried to storm the archipelago, they'd be killed before they reached the first island.

The best hope was to reach Lanka by boat—though Ravan's men patrolled the waters. From a palm grove by the beach, Hanuman studied the fat-bellied ships loaded with people and cargo, the tall-masted sloops that carried officers and wealthy traders, the scores of little fishing vessels that drifted with tiny stay-sails, hauling fish from the ocean.

Most of Hanuman's troops volunteered. But Hanuman didn't want the anxiety and uncertainty of waiting for someone else to do the job. He decided that in four nights' time, shielded by the darkness of a new moon, *he* would cross to Lanka—alone.

CHAPTER 16

The Dravidians Strike Back

THE BLACK FIST clutching a flaming lamp stands twenty feet high in a memorial garden in central Madras (or Chennai), on the south-east coast of India. It is—as such torches usually are—the flame of Freedom, of Truth. Why black? Black is the colour of the shirts worn by the members of the movement the torch celebrates, the Self-Respect Movement; black pride.

Close to the lamp is a series of marble slabs, engraved with the sayings of the man who did more than anyone to diminish the esteem in which the *Ramayana* is held in India. One slab reads, "The Epics *Ramayana* and *Mahabharata* are meant to ensnare the Dravidians in the Aryan net, and to make them bereft of honour and rational thought."

Another announces that:

> He who invented God is a fool.
> He who propagates God is a Knave
> He who worships God is a primitive.

A third asks,

> Will rats ever be freed by the efforts of cats? Will non-*Brahmans* achieve equality through the goodwill of *Brahmans*? Even if these impossibilities come to pass, women will never get freedom by the efforts of men.

The author of these pithy sayings was a south Indian Tamil called E. P. Ramaswamy, a social reformer who set out to turn the *Ramayana* from beloved gospel into a sort of anti-Dravidian *Mein*

241

Kampf. He also set in motion the political machine that dominates southern India today. Ironically, the analysis at the core of his rhetoric was borrowed from another set of oppressors—the colonial British of the Raj era.

THE HONOURABLE EAST India Company was granted a Royal Charter by Elizabeth I on 31 December 1600, giving it a twenty-one-year monopoly on trade in the East Indies. It would grow into the most successful company in history, evolving from a commercial venture into a colonial one, with its own armed forces and quasi-governmental power, dominating India. Its dissolution after the 1857 Rebellion (or First War of Independence) led to the creation of the British Raj.

As Britons wrested power from India's rulers, they became fascinated by the country whose wealth they were appropriating. The exotic subcontinent stimulated scientists, too. Science was making great strides in the late eighteenth and early nineteenth centuries—including such esoteric branches of study as philology and lexicography, which were painstakingly unpicking the languages of the world. When British and German scholars examined the languages of India (aided by dictionaries compiled by missionaries anxious to make the Bible available to the speakers of savage tongues) they found, to their amazement, connections between the European languages and Sanskrit. The discovery caused feverish excitement. Could ancient Europe and the Middle East, with their Old Testament stories of migrating tribes, in fact have roots extending through Persia into the fertile valleys of the Indus and the Ganges? If so, it meant that the Vedic tales of the *Mahabharata* and the *Ramayana* contained the kernel of a *common* heritage. India might be the *Urheimat*, the original homeland, of all Indo-European languages—and perhaps, therefore, of Europeans themselves. For a couple of decades a passionate love affair bloomed. For the British, the rich history of the subcontinent was all the richer for suddenly becoming *their own.*

The romance, alas, didn't last—and the end of the affair makes uncomfortable reading. Philologists decided that Sanskrit was *not* the "ur" language, but a sister language that shared roots with some other, impenetrably ancient and almost certainly unknowable, mother tongue. Scholars determined that, far from being the Europeans' ancestors, Indians were the product of two elements: an aboriginal race and Aryan invaders from somewhere in central Europe. The theory helped confirm the colonialists' views of themselves as victors and the subjugated Indians as losers. As the British consolidated their hold on India, they increasingly viewed the Indians as their inferiors. An explicit racism began to mark the way the British thought, wrote and spoke.

The *Ramayana* was seized on as the story of the Aryan invasion—it wasn't some fantastic tale about gods and magic monkeys, but a record of India's conquest by a pale-skinned race. These white invaders had called the jungle-dwelling South Indians "monkeys" as a sort of racist nickname. And wasn't Ravan, the southern King, described as "black"? A few pages back I mentioned some curious lines on Wikipedia where a contemporary Indian has quoted, apparently with approval, colonial soldiers and clergymen on their view that the better-looking and generally superior Indians were those with the most Aryan blood, those least affected by contact with aboriginal peoples. As the nineteenth century advanced, racism became increasingly entrenched across the world; the dark-skinned races were widely believed to be inferior to the pale-skinned. The world's indigenous peoples, from Tasmania to the Congo and the American plains, were oppressed and sometimes even exterminated. In India, twenty million people were allowed to die from famine on the British watch, mostly not because of food shortages but because of deliberate restrictions on the distribution of food.

In the twentieth century, European and American scholars were united by the idea of the Aryan invasion—it came to be known as the "Into India" theory. The evidence they offered came almost entirely from linguistic analysis, microscopic work that tried to reconstruct long-dead languages and deduce, by grammatical analysis and the study of different words for indigenous fishes and trees and so on, where the speakers of putative prehistoric languages might have lived. It is one of the most esoteric branches of academic endeavour, resting on a tiny database and largely unsupported by archæological evidence. Its findings have been variously interpreted to prove that the tribes who first populated Europe and India originated in Iran, Russia or China.

There have been few challenges to the "Into India" theory; but, of course, it was unpopular with many Indians. Early in the twentieth century, nationalists rejected a version of their history that saw indigenous Indians depending on an infusion of "white blood" to make anything of themselves. They countered with an "Out of India" argument, claiming that the spread of occidental civilization had, as those eighteenth-century philologists believed, begun in India. The arguments were often more rhetorical than scientific, as Indian academics lacked the resources to take on well-endowed foreign universities. But very recently more credible arguments in favour of "Out of India" have begun to be made—though the theory continues to be derided and sometimes even accused of supporting a racist-nationalist (anti-Muslim, anti-Christian, anti-secular) agenda. "Out of India" remains a minority position, but one that's being taken more seriously today than at any time in the last century.

A definitive solution to the whole question may come from the harder science of genetics. The analysis of DNA should provide, within a decade or so, more authoritative evidence about the movements of prehistoric populations. A wealth of new archæological evidence, aided by satellite photography, is becoming available too. Future hypotheses about the earliest peoples of the Indian subcontinent will be less dependent on the theoretical suffixes and fish names of non-existent languages.

Nevertheless, there remain significant groups whose interests are served by the "Into India" Aryan invasion theory—notably the "Dravidian" politicians of south India. For them, the *Ramayana* remains a record of the cruel abuse of indigenous Indians by invading, pale-skinned *Brahmans*. They believe (in contrast to most academics) that an indigenous Indian race once existed. The word used to describe it, "Dravidian", is a term more properly used to describe a group of south Indian languages. But for those who believe in a darker-skinned, blacker-haired, flatter-nosed indigenous race, Dravidian is the term that has stuck.

THE SCOURGE OF Rama, E. V. Ramaswamy Naicker (the name Ramaswamy means, ironically, "Rama-Priest"), was born in 1879 into a prosperous (not *Brahman*) trading family. He challenged its orthodoxy at an early age when he drank water with Muslim school friends after being forbidden on religious grounds to do so. He married at nineteen and proved himself a good businessman, though his free spirit constantly tested his conventional family. At twenty-five, he went off without telling anyone and lived the life of an ascetic for several years. Visiting Varanasi as a pilgrim, he found himself denied entry to a *Brahman*-only eating hall—and understood in a flash the inequity of the caste system. He had to fill his stomach with other people's leavings. Changed forever, he would devote the rest of his life to fighting religion, which he saw as a weapon that allowed the priestly class to exploit and enslave the majority of the population. Southern India had many more *Sudras* (peasants) and Untouchables than the north. It made the dominion exercised by a tiny minority of *Brahmans* seem all the more pernicious.

Ramaswamy became a political activist and social reformer, founding his "Self-Respect Movement" in 1925. He was a brilliant campaigning journalist and popular speaker, his caustic wit making his public meetings popular events—even with his opponents. In 1938 he "accepted" the epithet "Periyar", or Great Man, which his followers were in the habit of using—just as the epithet "mahatma" applied to Gandhi meant Great Soul. The Great Man applied himself to destroying something he believed the Great Soul was guilty of accepting: the caste system. Periyar inspired the Dravidian political movement that dominates southern politics to this day, giving Tamil Nadu, India's largest and most populous state, a political voice independent of the north India-dominated political élites. The overtly political agenda was taken forward by Periyar's acolytes; he continued to concentrate on broader social reform, and the cause célèbre he chose to make his own was the assault on the *Brahman* par excellence, Lord Rama. His various writings, never out of print, have persuaded millions of south Indians they've been the object of Aryan-*Brahmanical* enslavement. Rama is a bad guy; but Ravan, in Periyar's reading, is a great Indian hero, wrongly maligned.

IT WAS BY LUCK, not planning, that the offices of the Periyar Society turned out to be just a five-minute walk from my hotel. I'd arrived in Madras in the early hours, checked into the stolid old YMCA and tumbled into bed. I got down to the restaurant too late for breakfast and had to plead with waiters who were clearing away the buffet. Reluctantly, they produced Chatterjee-style toast and some of the red paste, radiant with E-numbers, that passes for jam in India. As I ate, I peered at a map and realized that my destination was just round the corner.

The white of the sun and the paleness of the dust made mid-morning Madras almost misty. I walked past tarpaulin tents where families were living on pavements broken by tree roots and reeking of human urine. Traffic surged by, a taxi or auto stopping every few seconds to offer the mad foreigner a ride. On walls were the graffiti—if one could call these neatly stencilled messages graffiti—"Worship God Alone" and "God is One". Further along, competing stencils read: "Believe in No God". Religious debate, Tamil-style. Tamil Nadu is one of India's most traditionalist states. But, as elsewhere in the country, there's a tension: a multi-storey billboard advertising the *Deccan Chronicle* newspaper depicted a bold-looking woman in a sexy pink dress. The slogan was, "Definitely Courageous". It was Kingfisher Syndrome, modernity equals sex. The editors of one of south India's principal newspapers declare their belief that women in hidebound Tamil Nadu can free themselves from convention, be taken more seriously as people, by looking sexy. In the West this is passé; the icons of sex-as-self-respect are tarnished—Germaine Greer's nipples are not as interesting as they were in 1971, *Cosmo* magazine affects to preach sexual responsibility and Madonna pompously embraces Kabbalah. But India has embraced its own sexual revolution.

At a roundabout close to the offices of the Periyar Society I saw another hoarding, advertising a new movie: *Periyar*. The lead actor was shown white-bearded and beatific, surrounded by people clasping their fingers imploringly, their expressions a mixture of desperate hope and relief. If this was a secular image, it was secular idolatry—Mao sprang to mind; here in India, the tradition of veneration was so entrenched that even the ultimate atheist was canonized posthumously. Bemused, I turned into the dusty driveway of the Periyar Society.

The compound was about the size of a football pitch. At the far end was the little memorial garden immortalizing the pungent sayings of Periyar in black marble. To its right was a repellent modern office block of black glass, more like a Ministry of Fear than an expression of the Society's beneficent ambitions. On its steps a wedding party was gathering, an extended family of grinning siblings and nieces and aunties all done up to celebrate a marriage in best secular style. Two rows of older buildings faced each other across the courtyard, a bookshop bulging with rationalist pamphlets and a typical line of colonial-era bungalows, one of them bearing the sign, "Periyar Museum".

The old man died in 1973, aged ninety-five. He had not achieved the dream of an independent Dravidian nation; but he had done as much as anyone alive to smash the caste structures that denied the lower orders education and independence.

The man at the helm of the Society now is K. Veeramani (the K stands, irony upon further irony, for Krishnaswami—the leaders of India's secular movement were named after its two principal devotional Gods). Legend has it that Mr Veeramani entered the movement at the precocious age of ten, when he was stood on a table to address a meeting and he astounded the adults with his oratory. As I waited to meet him, I flipped through what announced itself as an "infolet", describing forty-odd Periyar institutions ranging from staid educational and medical institutions to the wilder shores of the Periyar Self-Respect Propaganda Institution and the Peryarism Seminary. The current leader's photograph appeared on almost every page and he was eulogized as "a relentless fighter of Social Justice"; there were few mentions of any other official of the organization, nor, when I scanned its website later on, could I find any indication of the structures, finances or voting systems within the several organizations—though a great deal more information was provided about the leader's long list of achievements.

Waiting for my interview I stepped into the Periyar Museum. It was a single room containing a number of the Great Man's possessions, including his bed and, poignantly, an archaic iron wheelchair. The room had a recently retiled floor, the hygienic and banally patterned ceramic contrasting oddly with the ancient volumes, spectacles and fountain pens that filled the display cases.

At length I was ushered into the presence. Mr Veeramani rose from a chair to meet me, a neat, white-haired man whose smooth, plump face gave few indications of his more than seventy years. He wore the movement uniform—a black shirt—and round his waist was a crisp white *dhoti*, his status as leader being indicated by a folded white scarf over his left shoulder. He greeted me with a sort of brisk, polite indifference, ordered me some tea and asked if I'd mind waiting while he dashed off an editorial for that week's newspaper. He was the editor of (along with three monthly magazines) the *Daily Viduthalai*, a rationalist publication whose impressive circulation—two *lakhs*, or 200,000—must be an insight into the power of caste politics in south India. It's the only rationalist daily newspaper in the world. The Periyar publications' favourite international pin-up is Richard Dawkins.

Frowning, clearly accustomed to rapidly marshalling thoughts and arguments, Veeramani scribbled his way through the editorial inside fifteen minutes. With a swift glance at his wristwatch and pursing his lips slightly, he turned his attention to me. What exactly, he asked coldly, did I want?

What I wanted was to know where contemporary Periyarists stood on the *Ramayana* question. Did they still loathe the epic and believe that their ancestors, a "Dravidian" race or civilization, had been crushed by Aryan invaders?

He began his reply cautiously. "Certainly there was an invasion; the culture of the south was—is—very different from that of the north."

"So there's no *racial* difference?"

"There *is* a difference. The south Indian is darker, Aryans are more yellow—they have very different skin." I couldn't help noticing that Mr Veeramani himself had a kind of golden complexion, paler than most south Indians. "But whether there was a Dravidian race or not, the key fact of an invasion is undeniable."

"So to that extent, the *Ramayana* reflects historic fact?"

"It is impossible to know whether a story this ancient is factual and accurate or a concoction. Probably it *was* fiction, but based to some extent on real people or real events. Essentially, the story symbolizes this clash between two cultures, a violent, intolerant assault on the southern peoples. These 'monkeys' written about in the story—they are *people, our* people, the people of southern India. You know, Jawaharlal Nehru wrote a letter to his daughter Indira Gandhi, in which he gave his opinion that the *Ramayana* was based on the fight between the north and the south."

I felt unmoved by the reference to Nehru, the secular Anglophile who notoriously took most of his Indian history from British colonial textbooks. I decided to move on to Ravan, the villain of the Valmiki piece who had been turned into a Tamil anti-hero.

"Do you feel Ravan's represented as a good man, or a bad one?"

"Ravan *is* a positive representation—because he is such a fine gentleman! His own subjects didn't complain about him—he was eulogized! Sita was under his control for ages, but he didn't rape her! He was all-powerful, if he wants he could squeeze her! Why is it she was not molested? Nowadays, so many rape cases are there in police stations. No—Ravan's mistake, his single, great error, was to elope with Sita."

A few later versions of the *Ramayana* have Sita eloping with Ravan; but in the original, Valmiki is unambiguous: she is kidnapped, manhandled and psychologically abused. Like other anti-Ramayanans, Veeramani was rewriting the *Ramayana* to serve his political ends. Or was it possible that he was not familiar with the Valmiki original? In general, I had discovered, both north and south Indians tend to assume that their own *Ramayanas*—the ones they're familiar with, those of Tulsidas and Kambar—are *translations* of Valmiki. In fact, both are original works, *inspired by* Valmiki, but willing to throw away whatever of his that does not suit their own vision and times, and to mould his characters in their own likenesses.

I also found it striking that, like his predecessor, Mr Veeramani spoke of the *Ramayana* as though it were *real*. In part, no doubt, that was a rhetorical device—flaying a living opponent makes for better rabble-rousing than dusty literary exegesis. But such literalism shows how real the characters of the *Ramayana* remain in the popular imagination—love it or loathe it, you can't deny the epic's enduring grip.

Periyar himself had been as much in a thrall to the epic as anyone else in Tamil Nadu, discussing its characters with the kind of passion today's TV viewers often feel for the characters of a soap opera. To this day, criticism of the *Ramayana* is a team game, with Ravan supporters attacking Rama, the Captain of the Aryan squad, and vice versa. A book published recently under the aegis of the Periyar Society, *Epic Musings* (by the Tamil historian N. Subrahmanian), starts out as a secularist demolition of the *Ramayana*, then turns into an infuriated rant against the character weaknesses of Rama and those around him. Subrahmanian's assertions include the eccentric claim that Ravan abducted Sita "only to deprive Rama of his wife and not to appropriate Sita for himself". Anyone who has read, unexpurgated, Valmiki's lip-smacking descriptions of Sita's breasts may conclude that some Tamils are blinded to the reality of the *Ramayana* by their desperation to validate Ravan as the hidden hero of the text. (Periyar cites Valmiki's sexual frankness as evidence of his *Brahman* decadence, and makes his own *pudeur* plain; he condemns Hanuman because "He spoke to Sita in most obscene and slang terms on subjects (even about penis) . . . not to be discussed with women".)

"Academics", I said, "tend to the view that the *Ramayana* is set in a very narrow area of north India, and is purely fiction, but—"

"What they say is manipulated!" Mr Veeramani interrupted hotly.

"*But*," I tried to finish, "—*but*, my own instinctive response is that the text has its roots in a real conflict. I find what seem to be depictions of a guerrilla war very convincing. Perhaps there'd been a conflict lasting long enough to have established its own mythology. Or maybe it conflated a series of events that were preserved by bards long before they were written down. Rama too—perhaps he was a mythic fighter, with whom a series of legendary events became associated, like Robin Hood. But there's a core, a spine, of historic truth—history written by the winners, of course."

Mollified, Mr Veeramani said, "I concur with your view of it being a guerrilla war. There is much evidence of an invading army. I give you one example—as the Aryan kings conquered the south they brought with them *yagna*. *Yagna* is not at all supported by Tamil culture—it was a cultural intrusion." (A *yagna* is the Vedic ritual of pouring oblations into the divine *agni*, the sacrificial fire, an act closer to magic than to worship.)

"The trouble is", I said, "there's pretty much a consensus among academics that this so-called 'Dravidian' civilization never existed. I mean, the very word 'Dravidian' can't strictly be applied to race—"

Mr Veeramani became agitated again. "Hah!" he interrupted. "The academics can be *purchased*!"

"Are you seriously suggesting that academic opinion is up for sale?"

"I am telling you that there is a systematic campaign in the West to impose its views on India! The debate is not balanced, I tell you that!"

This was perplexing. Many Indians feel the West had forced on them the view of an Aryan invasion. But here was Mr Veeramani accusing the West's current *anti*-invasion consensus of being a malicious plot.

I asked, "Is your movement still pushing for a Dravidian state?"

"What we want is a *casteless* society with equality of opportunity. Now, social justice has a momentum. We have seen a Muslim president, a Sikh PM, an Italian woman as leader of the government. Next, we want real federation, more freedom from the centre—from the Hindi-speaking, Hindu élites of the north. But happily the Brahmanocracy—that phrase was coined by Periyar in 1924—the Brahmanocracy, government of, by and for the *Brahmans*, is finished."

"It's interesting that Periyar was in many ways supportive of the British . . ."

"Because but for the British invasion, for their humanism, their education system, Brahmanistical primitivism would have prevailed to this very day! The *Ramayana* blatantly advocates the *Brahmans*! Tulsidas was pro-*Brahman*!"

E. V. Ramaswamy's most provocative act of anti-Brahmanism came in 1956, when he and his followers announced their intention to burn pictures of Lord Rama in public. Political leaders implored him to cancel such a formal desecration, arguing that it would betray the faith in God by which Mahatma Gandhi had won Indian Independence. Ramaswamy, who would later make "anti-Gandhism" one of the five planks of his movement, ignored them, turning up for the demo with a box of matches and a bed roll for his inevitable spell in prison.

How far, I asked Mr Veeramani, was it morally acceptable to go on insulting the feelings of others to make a point? Should *all* Hindus be tarnished by the actions of *Brahmans*—not even *all* of the

Brahmans? Is it morally legitimate to try to destroy an entire religion because some of its adherents behaved badly?

"Listen to me—religion is *lies!* And to protect myself from lies, sometimes I must provoke! Without that provocation, you wouldn't be here!"

I laughed. "I suppose that's true."

"This was legitimate propaganda. Periyar wanted to expose a form of superstition that supports slavery! You ask about morality— morality doesn't mean you have to be a slave!"

I had one last question: "Why did Periyar allow a personality cult to grow up around him?"

He gave a start. "*A cult?*"

"And what about that movie poster out there? It represents him as a kind of saint!"

"You—you have to understand that Periyar is like a god to the people who have benefited from his work—the non-*Brahmans!* Some of them want to deify him. But his disciples, we movement members—we would never deify him. But he is our hero. Hero-worship is not cultish! I love Churchill—but I do not *deify* him!"

CHAPTER 17

Immersions

"KILLING CHICKENS THAT way is a common practice in Indian markets—they're put into scalding water to remove their feathers—usually still conscious after the cut to the throat. Perhaps the increased heart rate causes the body to expel its blood. Just think, millions of chickens tormented every day! Yet that is the reality, I fear."

It's an odd thing, travel. One day you encounter some strange and discomfiting phenomenon; the next day you find yourself sharing a sleeper compartment with the person who can best explain it to you. Mr Kannan had what seemed to me a particularly unpleasant job, and one indicative of the speed of India's transformation: a refrigeration expert, he was setting up on behalf of a chain of fast food restaurants a network of abattoirs, intended to provide a consistent standard of slaughtered animal across India.

"You know, the brutality in Indian animal husbandry and slaughtering is extreme. It is an aspect of national shame. Mechanized abattoirs, government-monitored, will change that."

A soft-spoken man, a Tamil Hindu, full of the quiet south Indian pleasures of tradition and family, he had his own hesitancies about the virtues of introducing industrial-scale slaughter into a country famed for its vegetarianism. "Because, you know, meat-eating is increasing rapidly." He shrugged. "When I was young, we rarely ate meat. Now, youngsters see it as the thing to do. Americans do it. Europeans do it."

The Siamese in old Siam do it. Let's do it. Everyone is eating more meat, the Indians, the Chinese, vast new markets of prosperous consumers demanding, like the wealthy West, animal protein three times a day.

AT 4.30 A.M. the train pulled in to Madurai station, 300 kilometres south of Madras. Mr Kannan solicitously put me on a bus to the main terminus, saving me the forty-five rupees I might have spent on an autorickshaw. It's easy for travellers to count too glibly on the kindness of strangers, which is almost unvarying.

The city bus stand was coming alive with a greasy, metallic light. A driver limped towards the Rameshwaram bus. At first I thought he had elephantiasis of the right leg, a fairly common complaint in southern India, the disease that produces permanent thickening of the leg being endemic there. He wore only flip-flops; sitting behind him I could see that his foot and ankle had been torn apart and sewn back together like so much cowhide. The stitches had been enormous and the result of the surgery was an immense, flattened foot that couldn't flex, but was still good enough to work an accelerator. He'd probably been involved in one of those daily accidents where the offside corners of two vehicles catch each other and the result, if not fatal, usually sees the drivers' right legs crushed. This guy looked as though he'd been lucky—he'd lived and been able to work again.

Courtesy of that Frankenstein foot we roared towards Rameshwaram. We passed enormous piles of tree trunks with wrinkled barks, resembling, in the dim dawn light, mounds of giant cinnamon. Where towns and villages gave way to farmland, every centimetre had been staked out, evidence of India's real estate explosion.

In a four-hour journey we stopped just once, for a quick cup of foaming, sandalwood-red tea. I couldn't sleep. At around nine we reached the end of the Indian mainland and the road became a concrete causeway, threading arrow-straight towards the holy island of Rameshwaram. The British-built bridge had been washed away on the night of 22 September 1964, when hurricane winds and twenty-five-foot tidal waves destroyed an entire town a few kilometres south of Rameshwaram. The island was spared, however, during the January 2004 tsunami—it stopped just a few kilometres south of here.

The bus rumbled off the causeway onto the island and I saw multi-storey hotels under construction. For a moment I feared that the temple pyramids would be dwarfed by ugly new skyscrapers, but then I saw, to the south, those white needles pricking the sky.

I found an hotel close to the temple's north tower. The room's walls and nylon curtains were filthy, but the sheets were crisp. The day was already hotting up. The shower, a broken pipe jutting from the wall, yielded a dribble of water. I washed, splashed water on the mattress—an old trick, the evaporation keeps you cool, even if the latex stinks—and fell naked across the bed.

I woke at midday and stumbled downstairs for tea. The streets were almost deserted. As in Ooty, my memory played tricks—nothing looked as it had done twenty-five years earlier. I remembered the avenue of shops selling garlands and souvenirs made from glued seashells, leading down to the beach where pilgrims took a dip. But the temple seemed to have shrunk. And where was that little cubicle where the old man sold his ancient booklets?

I advanced into the gloom under the temple's south tower. The floors were as wet as I remembered; the pilgrims trooping after their guides would have been wholly conventional if they hadn't been soaked to the skin, hair like seaweed, *kurtas* and saris clinging. Those infinite corridors loomed to the left and right. An elderly *Brahman*, wearing a white loincloth and a thread over one shoulder, with moustaches of white hair sprouting from his ears, showed me a flat palm like a traffic cop. "No sightseeing! Only *Brahman* will be admitted!"

I retreated humbly. Some Indian temples ban non-Hindus, though on dubious grounds, I believe. Hinduism is a big tent, with no universally acknowledged set of laws, and no one has ever shown me doctrinal support for the proposition that outsiders should be denied entry to temples. But *Brahman*s sometimes impose bans, notably at Puri in Orissa. In Nepal, white-skinned Hindu converts were reportedly excluded from a temple recently, along with low-caste Hindus! But it isn't usually difficult for outsiders to circumvent such rules. If they know the right *Brahman*.

Back at the hotel I spoke to the receptionist, a tubby, jovial character with a can-do smile. "I want to see the temple," I told him. "Would they let me in with a guide?"

"You want to go to inner sanctum?"

"Yes, the core of the temple."

"You want to make pilgrimage? You want to take dip?"

A legitimate pilgrimage would probably swing it. "Yes," I said.

"But the important thing is, I want a guide who can explain the architecture, the history—"

"These mens are *Brahman*," he replied, as though *Brahman* were synonymous with "ignorant". For a few moments he thought intensely. Then he grabbed his mobile and barked.

He put the phone down. "Someone will come. Please wait."

"How long will they be?"

"Just—" He held up his hand with the thumb touching the index and middle fingers, the symbol of tinyness that means, in India, "no time at all". "Please sit."

I sat on one of three hard chairs lined against a wall. Two minutes later a young man stepped into the lobby, clad in jeans and a fashionable shirt. He held out his hand and unleashed a vulpine grin. His name, he said, was Vijayakumar.

"I'd like to visit the temple," I said.

"Yes," he replied. "It is for Hindus only."

"I know."

"Sir."

"Yes. But I thought we rang you because you might be able to get me in—I mean, do you mean I *can't* visit it?"

"If you are with *Brahman* guide," he said complacently, "then no one will object."

"*OK*. Then . . . tomorrow?"

"You must be ready early morning, when temple bell is ringing."

By dawn, when the bell tolled, I was washed and shaved and wearing my "I'm Hindu too, deep-down" *khadi kurta*. There was a sharp rap on the door: it was Vijayakumar, clad now only in a simple white *lunghi*, with his *Brahman*'s cotton thread over one thin shoulder. "Come!" he said urgently, "already we are late!"

"I thought you said . . ." But it wasn't worth arguing. Vijayakumar told me to leave my shoes behind. Barefoot, I followed him down the dusty street to the Ramalingeshwara Temple.

Vijayakumar was in his mid-twenties, but his guileless brown eyes and eagerness to please made him seem younger. He didn't dawdle. We plunged straight into the temple's heart, with its alternations of pitch gloom and open-air courtyards. I lost any sense of direction, for we seemed to turn back on ourselves several times and the sun was still too low to provide orientating shadows. The first of the twenty-odd wells was circular and about eight feet wide, with a small retaining wall. Without ado Vijayakumar dropped his personal miniature galvanized pail into the depths, tugged it up brimming with water and, muttering some Sanskrit, emptied it over me. I spluttered and wiped water from my mouth and eyes.

"Next?" he asked brightly, and whisked me on.

The number of anointings varied from well to well. They were distributed in open courtyards all over the complex. Some were your typical wishing-style well, others narrower, yet another was a "tank" the size of a swimming pool. Each had, Vijayakumar told me, different spiritual qualities—and a different flavour, some salty, others sweet; and those with drinking water did not taste the same. He communicated a vivid picture of a network of Gothic tunnels worming their way beneath the temple's foundations and of seawater boiling through caverns numberless to man.

Occasionally, Vijayakumar instructed me to meditate on a subject; sometimes he had me clasp my hands and repeat after him a few scraps of Sanskrit.

There were many groups of pilgrims circumnavigating the temple, each in the company of a *Brahman* who rattled through Sanskrit verses while dropping a bucket on a rope into a well and emptying water all over his own little group. It was done without emotion, mechanically. The lack of ceremony struck me, not for the first time in a Hindu religious setting, as peculiar, and I wondered if these pandits *spoke* Sanskrit or learned it parrot-fashion. (I've been told it's usually the latter.) Surely, if all this *meant* anything, if one were to *believe* that immersion in the soft or salty waters of these ancient wells was capable of bringing about something of such overwhelming, transformational, metaphysical power as a release from sin and the cycle of rebirth—if a man dumping water on you from a galvanized bucket, as he had done for thousands of other pilgrims, were enough to sound the trumpets of heaven and herald eternal bliss—shouldn't there be an expression of awe and mystery upon his face, shouldn't the pilgrim be ecstatic, transported?

No. *Brahman*s and pilgrims alike just went through the motions. It was a formality. They did it because they always had and always would. Or was that changing? A few spoilt teenage Hindu daughters did not, I noticed, allow themselves to be doused. A couple of them—

shock and horror—wore *jeans*. And they were *conscious* of their difference, loudly prattling to cover up their embarrassment. Modern families were more ready to respect the desires of teenage daughters not to spoil their hair or to demonstrate their up-to-dateness by wandering around a holy place in jeans. It was the thin end of the wedge. But Hinduism doesn't mind. It has legendary tolerance; this religion thinks not in terms of earthly fashion, but in æons. Built in is the pessimistic notion that we are passing through Kali Yuga, a decline in human values destined to last for thousands of years. Beyond it— sunshine once more, universal love, universal devotion.

As all this went through my mind, I saw an elderly couple being helped around the circuit, both dressed in white, toothless, in their eighties or even nineties. Their faces showed something I seemed to see less often than I used to, the expression of an *older* India: content- ment, acceptance, the sense of having passed through life's tangle of enticements and illusions, and of being able, now, simply to *be*. After all, Hinduism explicitly teaches that the flesh is weak. In midlife the desire for money and sex—all that flesh is heir to—is not dis- couraged. You are not, despite what Western practitioners of meditation and yoga might think, expected to live like a monk. That is for monks. But in old age, when the flesh is literally weak, when your body is renouncing life—renounce it with your spirit too! That is when, traditionally, people set off on pilgrimages, on the journey away from worldly preoccupations, towards the understanding that all is *maya*—illusion—and towards dissolution and rebirth. Their families may never see them again.

Vijayakumar was padding with mercurial speed over the stone flags he'd known since early boyhood, his long fingers flashing around him as he pointed out a god in a niche here or the height of a *vimana* (spire) there, his eyes quick and warm and trusting. He talked in a gabble and before I had a chance to finish any question he'd give an answer to what he presumed—usually wrongly—the question was going to be. He did it with such innocence and enthusiasm that it was impossible to object. I tried a few detailed questions about the history of the temple, but realized he'd had no formal training in either the history or architecture of the place. And he was in the right: Vijayakumar belonged to a long line of *Brahmans* who'd spent their whole lives within these walls because of what the building *meant*. English parish churches and cathedrals greet visitors, in Betjemanesque parody, with leaflets about the age of their fonts and rood screens. But then, the Church of England is moribund. In India, where religion lives, the onus is entirely upon the worshipper—it's about what *you* bring to the temple, to the encounter with the ineffable, in whatever form it takes.

What Vijayakumar *was* eager to tell me about was Hinduism—how Lord Rama worshipped the two *Shivalingams* here after his victory over Ravan. He wanted to tell me the *results* of a visit to the temple: I'd spent half my life as a non-Hindu; I would now spend the rest of it *as a Hindu*. He told me this brightly, not portentously, not emotively, but as a fact, to be celebrated. He might have been a Christian telling me stoutly that Jesus loved me. We are not shaking with charismatic ecstasies here, we are merely stating joyous facts. And facts, as lain down and reinforced by tradition, outweigh doubt.

We stopped to stroke the temple elephant, a sweet-looking creature that seemed happy in its mottled pink skin. It had a gaily painted face, and evidently it adored the great cakes of basmati rice—each one the contents of an entire pan—that its *mahouts* were feeding it like so many sweeties.

It is the custom, after temple ablutions, to descend the short, narrow road that leads from the south entrance to the seashore. On your way, you stop at one of the many vendors to buy yourself an offering—a coconut, some fruit, some flowers, on a plate woven from shiny banana leaves. You wade in up to your chest and release your offering into the waves, then dip yourself under the water—the final immersion, the completion of the pilgrimage. I joined the hundred-odd pilgrims wading into the shallows that morning. Vijayakumar plunged in next to me, enthusiastically having me launch my little vessel of fruit into the waves, repeat some more Sanskrit, then get my head under the water.

Then he asked, "Tea?"

We sat in sparkling sunlight, sipping sweet tea. I had enjoyed the morning. But for someone who loves the panoply of Hindu ceremony, and for all the powerful symbolism of this place in the *Ramayana* story, I felt oddly unmoved.

WITH HANUMAN UNDER a pile of nets at the front of his boat, almost hidden except for the protruding metal tip of an arrow pointed at the fisherman's heart, the fisherman put to sea. He nervously raised a sail they'd daubed black with tar, and the boat glided easily across the waters towards Lanka, skirting a big cluster of fishing boats whose constellation of night lights could be seen quivering on the swell.

When they were two-thirds of the way across, the boat abruptly slowed. From nearby came a dull sound like the ringing of cowbells. "We've snagged something," said the fisherman.

"An alarm," said Hanuman.

A hundred yards away lamps appeared and a voice called out, "Don't move!"

"They'll kill us!" gasped the fisherman.

"Shut up!" hissed Hanuman. "Drop the sail! This boat is empty, adrift—just get down and hide!" Keeping low, he watched the approach of a vessel five times their size; its lanterns revealed a complement of at least eight men, two of them gripping boat hooks, others with swords ready in their hands. It drew rapidly closer.

At the very last moment, Hanuman leapt from his hiding place, instinctively calculating how much purchase the deck would give him. He landed, knees almost fully bent, on the fo'c'sle, then, with incredible power, leapt again. The fishing boat nosed under him, water rushed in, but Hanuman flew into the air with superhuman force. He landed on the gunwale of the *rakashasa* ship, a sword in each hand, scything, killing two men with two strokes. He catapulted himself forward again, his blades cutting the air in figures of eight. In twenty seconds he had killed everyone on board. Sheathing his bloody swords, he grabbed an oar and battered down at the hull, smashing planks along its length. Seawater rushed into the belly of the ship. He jumped back into the smaller boat and pulled the fisherman from his hiding place.

The man's eyes bulged. "What are you going to do?"

"Swim, obviously," said Hanuman.

"And kill me?"

"No," said Hanuman. "Go home now. Remember, if you care about your family's lives—you never saw me."

"You're in luck," the fisherman ventured. "It's a spring tide, one of the lowest of the year. Low tide's in an hour. The islands are high and dry—you can practically walk to Lanka at this time of year!"

"I don't believe in luck," said Hanuman.

He swam hard for an hour, avoiding Ravan's patrol boats. Reaching shallows, he turned south-east and half-waded, half-swam the remaining three or four miles of the gulf. At dawn, he found himself in the last shallows before the coast of Lanka. He stood and began to wade towards the shore.

Two chariots raced along the strand and swept around him in a pincer movement. Each held a charioteer and three foot soldiers, who leapt down. He killed the first three immediately. Two more men rushed him—he killed one, the other turned and ran back to a chariot. But a sixth man, equal in height and size to Hanuman himself, approached him confidently. Hanuman pulled a heavy arrow from his quiver and calculated where the armour should be weakest. The arrow struck in the perforated space over the man's mouth and he toppled backwards. Hanuman pried back the helmet and pushed in a sword blade. Panic-stricken, the charioteers whipped their horses and galloped off the way they'd come. Making sure that there was no one else around, Hanuman sprinted towards the jungle that began where the white sand ended.

As I WADED through midday heat, an autorickshaw man stopped and asked where I wanted to go. "To the end of the island," I said.

"Please come in, sir."

We negotiated a price and he pointed his rickshaw south along the spit of land that narrows towards Sri Lanka. We passed railtrack, twisted like barley sugar, the aftermath of what he called "the '64 tsunami". We detoured to the left, to the temple dedicated to Vibhishana, the brother of Ravan—who left him for Rama, making him a hero to Rama lovers and a traitor in the eyes of the Periyarists. "Only this one Vibhishana temple in all India!" the driver told me. I went inside and was immediately thrown out by a *Brahman*.

A mile or so on, we puttered up to a collection of shacks, beside an opal-blue sea.

"We can't be there already," I said.

"Sir, road is ending here. From here is sand, sir."

"What . . . Can I walk?"

"Is many kilometres, sir! You must have jeep." He paused, seeing my frustration. "You are not knowing, sir?"

"No, I am not knowing, sir," I muttered sarcastically, feeling tricked. To one side stood a row of light Mahindra 4x4 trucks with big ribbed tyres and canvas backs. "How far is it?" I asked.

"Sir, I am not knowing *exactly*, I am never going, sir." He was anxious now that I shouldn't think him a crook. "Sir, not any taxi or autorickshaw is coming any further, sir—road is deep sand, sir, only Mahindra can go, sir."

"All right," I said wearily.

A man wandered over and asked what was up. The familiar public debate, in which the traveller attempts to referee those competing for his patronage, began. He said it would cost 900 rupees to get to the end of this spit of land—to that uttermost scrap of India. "Too much," I said. He assured me that if I didn't like it when I got there, I wouldn't have to pay. "A likely story," I retorted.

In fact, he was a tout. He led us to someone who *was* a driver—and the two of them proceeded to scream at each other like mortal enemies, with the rickshaw driver translating for my benefit various choice threats. The jeep driver was refusing to take me any further than halfway along the spit, to the ruins of the town destroyed in the 1964 storms. "I don't give a damn about a ruined railway station," I said hotly, "I want to go to the end of the land—I'm interested in the bloody bridge to Sri Lanka."

The fight was stopped by a fourth party, a sort of Godfather figure who pronounced in a basso profundo straight from his sternum (his chest was as round as an opera singer's) that if foreigners wanted to go to the far end of the island, sobeit. He was obeyed instantly. Suddenly, the driver was impatient to be off. "*Chalo, chalo!*" (Let's go!)

The rickshaw driver and I jumped into the back of the truck. It advanced perhaps thirty feet, then stopped, and half a dozen women climbed in. So I was paying for exclusive use of a vehicle, which was also functioning as a bus. It wasn't the first time I'd succumbed to that particular ruse.

The Mahindra slewed heavily in deep sand, passing bleak, impoverished fishing communities. Beyond straggling acacia bushes a line of white foam marked the edge of the sea. The women opposite me sat gloomily, folded five-rupee notes in their fingers, neither speaking nor even staring out at the passing flats, but seeing only their thoughts. One by one, they descended. The rickshaw driver pointed out the storm-smashed station and church as we passed. We rejoined the seawrack-littered flats and carried on, past a wrecked canoe and the bleached trunk of an entire tree that had been washed here from who knew where—the Himalayas, via the Ganga? We passed a military post resembling a shack built by beachcombers, where several uniformed men lolled in the shade and ignored us. Their trousers, hung up to dry, flopped in the breeze.

Finally we reached the extreme end of the spit. From here a succession of sand bars hopped, like skimmed stones, the sixteen miles to Sri Lanka.

My rickshaw driver and I jumped down and walked to the edge of the water. The place seemed so lonely—even the Mahindra drivers didn't want to bring people here—yet a pilgrim had recently fashioned an exquisite *lingam* from the sand, decorating it with a score of petals. I felt more touched by that sight than I had during my holy dip that morning. I turned to the rickshaw driver. "You're a Hindu?" I asked.

"No, sir, I am Muslim."

I smiled. "You know this story? The *Ramayana*?"

"Sir, every pilgrim is coming Rameshwaram for *Ramayana*. Sir, you should take dip."

"Do we have time?"

"You are paying, no?"

Suddenly, the irritable voice of the Mahindra driver cut in from behind us. "*Chalo!*"

We had been there all of five minutes. I turned on him furiously and yelled, "900 rupees for five minutes? You wait until I'm ready to go, or you can have half your money now and I'll bloody well walk back!"

He looked perplexed. There was a brief conversation between him and my Muslim friend. Suddenly smiles appeared. "He says to take your time," said the rickshaw driver.

"I should damn well hope so."

I crouched beside the sand *lingam*. After Rama defeated Ravan, Hanuman was dispatched to bring a stone *lingam* for the victorious prince and his wife to show their gratitude to Shiva. But Sita knelt down and fashioned a *lingam* from the sand with her own shapely fingers. It's an erotic, overtly masturbatory image, except to all those Hindus who've been puritanically protected from the earthy roots of Hinduism and have no knowledge of the *lingam*'s ithyphallic origins, or of Valmiki's fondness for the erotic. What image *could* be more erotic than that—a beautiful woman fashioning a phallus out of moist sand? Yet the image contains other layers of meaning. In a Christian funeral you get your hands dirty, you get dirt under your fingernails as you grasp a handful of damp earth to throw it down on the coffin of the departed. In a sense it's the loved one you get under your fingernails, for he or she will soon be dust—you're in contact with that earth from which we sprang and to which we must return. It is deeply consoling. So here is Sita getting her hands dirty, plunging them into the stuff of earth, which becomes, through her efforts, God Himself. She expresses her gratitude, her hope and in a sense—even though she is a highborn queen, reputedly *miraculously* born—her powerlessness. (As we'll see, the *Ramayana* does not have a happy ending in store for Sita; the earth will swallow her before her time.)

"You will take dip, no?" said the auto driver.

"I think I will."

I stripped down to my underpants and waded in. The sand spit that spat south towards Sri Lanka shelved slowly down and another rose like a basking whale just a hundred feet off. Adam's Bridge, they call it, supposedly after a Muslim legend that Adam, having been expelled from paradise, chose to sojourn in Sri Lanka—the closest equivalent he could find. That and several myths like it are assiduously repeated by the Sri Lankan Tourism Board. The name preferred by Hindus is *Rama Setu*—*setu* is "bridge" in Sanskrit.

It is easy to imagine engineering a bridge across these shallows; the oldest inhabitants of Sri Lanka, its so-called "indigenous" *Veddah* people, crossed from here in Neolithic times, 15,000 or more years ago.

The water was velvet-soft and warmer than a blanket. I let my eyes rest on the fawn horizon, beyond which mainland Sri Lanka began only twice the distance I'd travelled from Rameshwaram. I did feel, in some sense, at the heart of the story of the *Ramayana*. I felt no desire to leave.

PART VI

CHAPTER 18

Lanka

THEY WERE NOT called "monkeys" for nothing. For all his bulk, Hanuman could be nimble, could scale a palm trunk as quickly as any of us could run along a level surface. Most extraordinary of all, he could make himself appear smaller than he was. All these talents were needed when he scaled the ramparts of the city of Lanka.

Built from dazzling white stone atop a table mountain, Lanka floated like a cloud. The lofty ramparts, the lapis lazuli gateway marking the entrance to the city, were far grander than the palace of the kings of Kishkindha. The guards were equipped with exotic weaponry. But no one in Lanka was expecting an invasion, or any kind of challenge to the visible might of their King and Emperor.

It had taken Hanuman a week, travelling by night, skirting towns and settlements, to reach this city in the south-east of the island. At dusk, he'd climbed the walls and seen in the gleam of a slender new moon the city spread before him like a woman, the ocean beyond it shining like the silk of an undraped sari. He paused and considered Lanka's defences. "Even if we could reach the island, what hope would we have of storming this fortress? It's impregnable!"

Lanka was divided by boulevards, lit—astonishingly, to Hanuman— by street lamps. They were flanked by mansion houses and ornamental gardens. Drunken revellers yelled and stumbled in the gutters. The mix of people in the streets was extraordinary, including men who wouldn't have been out of place in his own mountain kingdom—and soon Hanuman was walking about freely. In the days he spent in Lanka he saw offices of state and pavilions of art as well as bars and brothels. He marvelled at the scale and development of the city. At the same time there was—especially at night—a kind of desperate wildness. How could such sophistication and ugliness exist side by side? It was, he realized, the hallmark of Ravan's kingdom. A huge population of armed troops had access to the capital; they were kept happy with a diet of alcohol and endless entertainment. Hanuman saw arenas where elephant, fed aphrodisiacs and dripping with ichor, were kept at that stage of extreme arousal where they can rut madly, race (this being the preferred sport of Indian kings) or, unleashed into battle, hurl themselves fearlessly against any enemy.

When Hanuman scaled the walls of Ravan's castle, he saw, in a central courtyard, the *Pushpaka*, the Emperor's personal transport. It was an immense machine, the size of a large house, lavishly decorated with gold leaf. A movable staircase led up to a door in the fuselage. Four guards chatted there and smoked *bidis*. Hanuman silently climbed the staircase and slipped inside, unseen.

A heavy odour of incense and alcohol assailed him. An image of the Goddess Lakshmi stood, four hands outstretched, delicately holding a lotus between one finger and thumb. Oil lamps flickered along the interior walls. Bulkheads were carved from solid ivory, highlighted with gems. The floors were carpeted with silk rugs and the furnishings upholstered with the hides of animals Hanuman had never even encountered. Sweet song burbled from caged birds (on heat, just as Ravan liked them) in alcoves the length of the plane. Hanuman saw a kitchen, bathrooms and a suite of private rooms. This was the heart of Ravan's world.

Hanuman tiptoed past women who slept, sprawled-out, sated, the vermillion on their foreheads smeared, their necklaces twisted and waistbands snapped, their painted breasts lolling. Some were completely naked, their limbs splayed like a horse that rolls on its back after its saddle is removed. Many lay with their limbs twined round each other, making it impossible to tell whom this arm or that leg belonged to. Some lay with a gauze over their faces, the cotton rising and falling gently with their breath. Ravan had three hundred wives, it was said, all of them schooled in the erotic arts. They were not concubines but women of good birth, obtained by treaty, never rape. Most of them, virgins when they met Ravan, had known no other man, no erotic life but with him and with each other.

Hanuman came suddenly upon Ravan. He too was asleep, lying on his back, his massive limbs at peace, the hands that had made enemies and lovers scream in different ways cupped open, battle scars evident under the blood-red sandal paste that was smeared on his dark skin. Women were draped around him like *apsaras* ornamenting the statue of a god. Could any of them be Sita—using Ravan as a pillow in the aftermath of an orgy? Inconceivable. Hanuman noticed another woman sleeping alone in a canopied bed off to one side. But no, evidently this was not Sita either, but Ravan's Queen Mandodari.

There were hundreds of rooms in the palace. What chance was there of finding Sita, or someone who could lead him safely to her? Where could she be?

IT'S A FAMILIAR sound, the rasp and clang of metal on metal as my mother searches for utensils in a big echoey wooden drawer in the kitchen cabinet.

The noise goes on. Surely she must have found it by now!

I open my eyes. I am not in Pirbright. And Mum has been dead for a year.

Milky dawn light glimmers around the edge of a heavy linen curtain. The fan above me is turning slowly—I remember, I was cold in the night and had to get out of bed to turn it down.

The rasping and clanging continue. I go to the window. Beneath my balcony the nightwatchman pads back from the latrine with his water jug in hand. The noise is coming from the other side of the wall, where builders have already started work. Yes, I remember— life begins early in Sri Lanka.

The noise continues. I visualize short metal rods, undoubtedly in a wooden crate. But exactly what is going on, and why doesn't it stop?

I am still half asleep.

I lift the phone and order tea, then go into the bathroom with its immense avocado-green cast-iron bath, the enamel scraped away, the plug long since vanished. I stuff a fat wad of toilet paper into the plughole and turn the taps. Water dribbles into the avocado cavern.

Back in the room, I reach for a book on the floor and see tiny pyramids of dust under the bed. They have been excreted by woodworms in the frame. This guest house is run-down, but quaint. In a few years it will have been demolished for the value of the land, like most of the villas around it, like the building site next door.

A knock on the door. A man crosses the room, delicately sets a tray of tea things on the table by the window and retreats. I carry the cup and saucer into the bathroom and slide into water that's still only two inches deep.

Another early arrival, another night of missed sleep.

THEY WERE still serving breakfast when I got downstairs, an omelette with chopped chillies, fragrant light Ceylon tea and slices of orange-pink papaya of the utmost melting sweetness.

I had come to Sri Lanka to follow the path of the *Ramayana* wherever it led. So many sites in Sri Lanka claimed a connection with some specific episode from the epic. To the sceptical mind, it suggested spiritual tourism—that opportunistic *Brahmans* had seen the grip the story exercised on people's imaginations, and attempted to cash in. But I wasn't on a quest to prove, or disprove, the truth of any tradition. It was the enduring power of the story that interested me. The cult of Rama had reached its climax in southern India, with a great wave of devotion and temple construction, about a thousand years ago. At that time, it was almost certainly easy to travel to Lanka on foot, or by the easiest of ferry rides. Countless numbers of pilgrims must have done so since then, for the traditions to have remained so strong.

I had another aim: to try to make sense of the war between Hindu and Buddhist that had engulfed Sri Lanka a few months after I climbed aboard the ferry to Rameshwaram. The war for a Tamil homeland had plumbed the depths of human brutality. The Tamil Tigers, under their leader Vellupillai Prabhakaran, had become the most fanatical militia on earth. There had been counter-extremity from the government and armed forces. Insanity and darkness. The struggle had ground to an exhausted halt in the late 1990s, the Tigers in possession of a chunk of northern Sri Lanka (known as Eelam); and a peace process had been brokered by a Scandinavian delegation in 2002. Now, that process appeared to be in trouble. Fighting was breaking out again. I read a newspaper report that eight hundred people had died in the three months prior to my arrival. In 2005 the Foreign Minister had been assassinated.

Recently a woman had managed to blow herself up *inside* Colombo's central army compound, as the country's senior military commander drove past her (he survived). She'd been posing as the wife of an officer—the *pregnant* wife. Her heavy stomach had accorded her a level of respect and discretion from the security men. The bump hid a bomb. The incident seemed to sum up the desperation, cynicism and inhumanity of the civil war. But why should Sri Lanka be ready to return to hell?

The day was already growing hot when I left the guest house and headed for the British Council, passing battered street signs with the names of forgotten Englishmen. Pavements were broken by surging tree roots, ripe smells rose from gutters. I turned onto Galle Road, the business artery that runs south from central Colombo. The pleasant, low-rise city I'd ambled through two decades earlier had all but gone. High-rise, close-packed concrete boxes had supplanted the gabled, terracotta-tiled villas that had given Colombo its charm. Galle Road, which runs parallel to the seashore, had been celebrated for its soothing breezes and smell of ozone; now it stank of exhaust fumes. Traditional dress seemed to have vanished, replaced by cheap Western clothes (seconds and surplus, I learned, from Sri Lanka's textile factories). I saw dourness, ugliness and preoccupation. A country and people that have lived through a quarter-century of civil war.

In England, I'd been unable to find any research exploring the history of the *Ramayana* in Sri Lanka. Given the role of the British in bringing so many Tamils to Ceylon, establishing them as a buffer between themselves and the Sinhalese, my first stop now was the British Council library. I found nothing. Close by was the library of the Tamil Cultural Centre—nothing there, either. I caught an autorickshaw (or, as they say in Sri Lanka, a trishaw) to the civic heart of Colombo, the green spaces laid out by the British, where the municipal library was an angular modern building in an unkempt garden. The staff redirected me to the National Library, up the road. And there, after being frisked, I entered an atmosphere of quiet competence. An enthusiastic lady librarian consulted the library's online catalogue, then dispatched a porter to bring me a pile of books. I sat at a quiet desk; it was pleasantly cool; the volumes exhaled their odours of sandalwood and musk. But there was little in any of them about the *Ramayana* in Sri Lankan life. The country was almost twenty per cent Hindu and littered with pilgrimage sites. But no one had studied them.

DAWN WAS APPROACHING. Hanuman worked his way back along the ramparts, towards the walled pleasure garden. He saw a group of what appeared to be old women sitting round a fire, singing and laughing. Then, off to one side, he made out the shape of a young woman.

He silently approached her through the crowns of the trees. As the first rays of sun dappled the lawn he saw that she was lovely—her waist slender, her breasts round and full, her skin golden, her hair jet-black. But as he peered through the branches more closely, he saw that her sari was dirty and that she had dark rings under her eyes.

Before Hanuman could speak, the haridans acting as warders started squawking. Ravan himself appeared, the bronze sun and bronze paste smeared over him making him resemble a newly cast statue. He strode across the lawns, with three dozen courtiers and wives in his wake, straight up to Sita. "My morning constitutional, dearest Princess," he said. "Clears the head, after a night's . . ." He laughed and looked behind him. A ripple of obsequious laughter came back. "Sita, I'm still a little drunk, to be honest. Now, there's no need to flutter and pull that bit of rag over your breasts and belly, we're all friends here." (More knowing laughter.)

The Emperor knelt before her. "My God, woman, I can have anyone I want, and still, every time I look at you, I think you're the most beautiful creature I've ever seen—even wasting away and wrapped in that filthy strip of silk, you still affect me, do you know that? Don't worry—I'm not going to force myself on you. Are you still fantasizing about that husband of yours coming to rescue you? Forget it! Come up to the palace, see the silks, the jewellery. The food, the wines—the best in the world! For God's sake, woman, don't you know how to enjoy yourself, have you turned into a nun? Your youth will be gone!"

Sita plucked a blade of grass and, half turning, laid it down between them. Ravan gave a furious growl and stood up. "God damn! The nicer you are to women, the worse they treat you! The trouble is, Sita, I *want* you, and it stops me from giving you what I'd give any other woman who got in my way. Luckily for you!"

Sita turned to him calmly. "I'm surprised such extreme lust doesn't make your ugly yellow eyes fall out of your head and your fat tongue rot, My Lord."

Ravan's yellow eyes dilated with rage. "You have one more month to change your mind, or I'll have you diced and served on a bed of *basmati*!" After a moment he smiled at one of the lovelier women accompanying him—who bore a certain resemblance to Sita herself. "Come on," he said, "back to the palace!"

As the entourage moved away one of Sita's warders, a woman with huge breasts and broken blood vessels all over her face, snarled, "Let's just strangle the bitch! We can tell the King she's died of hunger and I'm sure he'll let us cook her. I ain't touched human flesh for months!"

"You want to watch out, dearie," responded one of the other warders. "If our little princess does decide to give His Majesty access to her precious private parts, the first thing she'll do is ask him to lop your head off for having been so *awfully* unkind to her!"

The women cackled and returned to their fire. Sita began to weep.

Hanuman had been debating how to attract her attention without scaring her to death. He pulled a ball of thread from his pack, looped it through the ring Rama had given him and lowered it until it lay on the grass beside her. Sita gave a sudden gasp, grabbed it, saw the string and cast her eyes up into the branches.

"Shhhh!" hissed Hanuman. "I have a message from your husband!"

Sita's eyes filled with wonder, then suspicion. "This is another of Ravan's tricks—"

"I can describe to you", Hanuman said, "exactly the jewels you dropped when Ravan kidnapped you—because I handed them to your husband. A pearl necklace, two gold bracelets, an emerald on a chain. We found them! That's why Rama gave me his ring to give to you—how could I have faked that? He sent me here! Now, Princess, you have to give me something to prove to him that I saw you! I'll take the word back to him. Believe me, he's as distraught as you are. He is in alliance with my master, King Sugriva, who's promised to commit his troops to rescuing you. It's taken us a long time to find you, My Lady. But you only have to sit tight a little longer, I promise."

Sita leaned against the tree and made Hanuman talk of Rama and Lakshman. As long as he thought it was safe for her, he stayed. Finally, she gave him a jewel to take back to Rama. And Hanuman's adventure in Lanka might have ended there, successfully, if he had not reflected, as he left the garden, how nice it would be to put a frown on Ravan's smug face. He'd seen a temple where Ravan's troops prayed before and after their campaigns. A wide dome was supported by a ring of pillars. In the outhouses nearby, military elephants were tethered. That night, Hanuman couldn't resist waking the *mahouts* and persuading them—at sword-point—to help him. Chains were attached to the farthest pillar and the elephants ordered to pull. After eight pillars went down like dominoes, the roof caved in and Hanuman had the pleasure of seeing a wall of the temple implode as he ran away.

Alas, he hadn't bargained for Ravan's excellent alarm system. Not only Lanka's army, but the entire population, were alerted; Hanuman was cornered by a thousand troops forty miles north of the city of Lanka.

"SRI LANKA GOOD!" my trishaw driver cheerfully told me. "Sri Lankan *man, not* good!" He leaned out of the side of the machine and spat out the *betel* nut he was chewing. A fine red stream issued through his clenched teeth. Nonchalantly, he completed his thought: "This morning, near airport, was bombing."

Above his forehead was a row of three decals the size of playing cards, representing Hindu gods. They'd faded almost to invisibility from being repeatedly rubbed—I realized that, when we passed the *stupa* of a Buddhist temple and he reached up and touched his three talismans in turn, each time returning his fingers to his forehead, then his heart. Sri Lankan popular religion has always been syncretic, the various faiths willing to share their saints and shrines with what some people considered a wonderful spirit of community and others judged a lack of discrimination. Then again, if you were in the business of driving people of all faiths around the city, a certain catholicism made sense.

"Who are they?" I asked his reflection in the rear-view mirror, wondering how he'd describe them.

The first was Sridi Sai Baba, the early twentieth-century hermit and mystic. "He good if you are sick, he help," the driver said. He tapped the next one, Kali, shown with her necklaces and fistfuls of human skulls: "She protect. Bad man come—" He made a slicing motion across his throat to indicate that the bad man would come to a bad end. The third decal was Hanuman, depicted flying along with a chunk of Himalayan mountain like figgy pudding on a platter. "He good, help bring land, buy house." This was the most remarkable misunderstanding of Hanuman I could conceive of.

I asked if he knew the Buddha. He looked briefly anxious and stared at his hand (we'd stopped at a red light). I found that I too was staring at his hand: it was hairless and gently veined and surprisingly soft-looking—auto drivers customarily have coarse, oily hands. His eyes were vague. "He is good man, very good . . . What doing I know not." The lights changed and he vigorously changed the subject. "You are from Japan?"

"Er, no."

"Sir—." He made a gesture to draw me in. I leaned forward. "Every morning," he murmured confidentially, "I, my wife and *baba*, we are praying. 'Lord, protect trishaw. Bring money. *Om Shree Ram, Jai Jai Ram, Jai Jai Ram.*' Twenty-one times repeating—'*Om Shree Ram, Jai Jai Ram, Jai Jai Ram*'."

"Ram, the God?"

He gave a big slow confidential rock of his head from side to side.

"His wife is Sita?"

Again, the affirmation.

"So, you're a Hindu? You speak Tamil?"

He gave an indulgent laugh. "No, no, not Tamil—*Sinhala* speaking."

I did not understand.

ॐ

I HAD WANTED to arrive at Professor Karthigesu Sivathamby's house with a token of some kind. I asked the driver to pull over at a Tamilian sweet shop and told the salesgirl to fill a box with *burfee* and *ladhoos*. It took us a long time to find the block of flats, in a suburb a couple of miles south of Galle Road. A doorman slumped on a stool pointed the way. I was admitted into a small apartment where Professor Sivathamby sat on a sofa. He did not rise to greet me; indeed, I don't know if he was able to rise unaided. On the phone he had told me, "I'm very much at home. In fact, I'm almost immobile." I understood that comment now. He was the vastest man I had ever met in person. He sat, with only a red chequered *lunghi* tucked round his loins, in reach of a side table with a phone and some books. He gestured to me to sit beside him, on an L-shaped sofa. As I did so, I had the unmistakable impression of sitting beside Samuel Johnson, who was similarly immense in old age. I mean the comparison appreciatively, too: Professor Sivathamby is an *intellectual* giant, a masterful interpreter of Tamil political and literary life.

As I arranged myself and my notebook I bemusedly mentioned my taxi driver who prayed to Rama but spoke no Tamil. My lightness of tone was exactly wrong. Sivathamby was appalled. "This is the tragedy of Sri Lanka—the man doesn't *know* he's a Hindu. That's the chasm into which we Tamils have fallen." He gave a troubled sigh.

I moved hastily on. I had come hoping to achieve some clarity about Lord Rama in south Indian life. On the one hand, intense devotion; on the other, denounced as an Aryan invader . . .

"Well, in the pre-modern period, Rama represented no problem—he was a God, like any other. The whole question of tracing the *Ramayana* to an Aryan invasion was inspired during British times. But today the idea of the Aryan invasion is a cornerstone of Dravidian political ideology.

"You know, our entire culture is dominated by these two great narratives, the *Ramayana* and the *Mahabharata*. They're sort of quasi-historical, because virtually every caste group in India traces its relationship to some episode in one of them, in order to be related to a hero or heroine—or to account for their lowliness because their ancestors made a bad choice in an encounter with a hero! But these things hang very heavily on us.

"In the *Mahabharata*, Krishna's a sort of suave diplomat, more Machiavellian than divine. You may be surprised to know his deity was reified only during the British period. As with everything else, the British had political, strategic reasons: they wanted India to be *one*—easier to administer. It's British orientalists who are responsible for making the *Bhagavad Gita* 'the Indian Sermon on the Mount'— it helped unite Indian tradition.

"Now, unlike Krishna, Rama was already an important deity— though he'd undergone a similar evolution. He wasn't a God to start with, but as the *Ramayana* was retold, his divinity was consolidated. Then comes the great Hindu revival from about the seventh century onwards. Shiva became the dominant India-wide deity that he is today; but for the Vaishnavites—the Vishnu worshippers—the presiding deity was Rama. Remember, Rama is considered an incarnation of Vishnu. So his people got busy constructing major, important temples. And in the twelfth century Kambar took up the tradition."

Kambar, perhaps the greatest Tamil poet, is best known for his reworking of the *Ramayana*, the *Ramavataram*. To Tamil-speaking Hindus it has the force and centrality that Tulsidas's version has to the Hindi-speaking north.

"Have you read the *Ramavataram*?" Sivathamby asked sternly.

"I've just read the new Penguin translation."

"He's an outstanding poet, but his *Ramayana* is lyric, not epic, like Valmiki's. Kambar's characterization is utterly supreme—and very different. His Rama is the ultimate human figure, a man of quite beautiful character. But it's Ravan who's crucially different. To Valmiki he's a kind of monster, but Kambar's Ravan is a *man*, full of conflicts and contradictions. A very great man, in fact—so his failure is *profoundly* tragic. This leads us down all kinds of strange and contradictory paths."

Sivathamby grinned and twisted his immense bulk to reach for a two-litre bottle of Coca-Cola. "Kambar reinvented Ravan as a tragic hero. He's so much loved by Tamils that there's a great tradition to sing his praises—and claim descent from him. The joke doesn't end there. Along comes Dravidian political ideology and claims Ravan as its father. Meanwhile, Sinhala tradition—Buddhist—is trying to claim Ravan for its own, as the great Lankan king! So you have this bizarre duality—Sinhala and Tamils, Buddhists and Hindus, all claiming Ravan as their origin! And did you know that another element of Sinhalese nationalism traced its descent and lineage to a great *Aryan* tradition? Even today, you can see restaurants calling themselves *Arya-Sinhala Hotel*. But paradoxically, *they too* want to see Ravan as their king! So Ravan is the black-skinned Dravidian king *and* the pale-skinned nemesis of the Dravidians! Here in Sri Lanka we're knotted up in these paradoxes!"

The Professor drained his glass of Coke. "The idea of an Aryan-

Sinhalaness has been articulated since the 1920s and 1930s. It's caused many people to hate Tamils. The Sinhalese psyche, very much sustained by this country's national press, views Tamils with a sense of separation—even disdain. Even Sinhalese intellectuals—and I speak Sinhalese fairly well—they can be friendly, but in reality their *Weltanshauung* can't admit a multicultural Sri Lanka. So we Sri Lankan Tamils are very conscious of being not simply Sri Lankan— we are Sri Lankan *and* Tamil." He reached out a substantial forefinger and tapped me on the knee. "*This* paradox, Mr Buckley, sums up the Tamil."

"What about history and the *Ramayana*?" I asked. "Can we find any genuine history connecting Sri Lanka and its Hindu population with the story?"

"Oh, the evidence is fragmentary, inconclusive. It's not a historical document per se. There *was* a kingdom of Ayodhya. There is evidence of contacts with the south. A tradition was encountered that was so different, so new, that people were taken to be monkeys. As for connections with Sri Lanka . . . Well, even today in Andhra Pradesh people have the word *Lankasunderam*, the beautiful one from Lanka. And the name Lakshman exists in southern Sri Lanka, where the worship of Rama took place . . . But the greater likelihood is that these correspondences come from *after* the *Ramayana* had achieved its universal popularity. One can go on and on with similarities and correspondences, but they're tiny pieces of a puzzle of which too many pieces are missing . . ."

"And the racial debate? Are Aryans and Dravidians separate races?"

"That's largely a British idea, like the invasion theory—the notion of the indigenous Dravida with his flat nose and dark skin, versus the pale-skinned Aryan invader, made sense to the Victorians. What do we *know*? That northern India is cold, the south is tropical; that people here are very dark, those in the north are very fair. As to who, if anyone, was truly indigenous and who was not . . . With all humility, we have to say we just don't know. But at the same time . . ."

I craned forward. Was the Professor about to break with the consensus and tell me the *Ramayana did* describe historic events? "At the same time?"

"One thing that remains somewhat open is a *cultural* question. The

Indus Valley civilization was not 'Aryan'—but nor could we have described it as 'Dravidian'. Then, last month, something remarkable happened—an object with the distinctive script of the Indus Valley was discovered in Tamil Nadu! It's a profoundly important discovery, the first firm archæological evidence of a connection, possibly indicating an India-wide civilization that stretched from modern-day Pakistan to the south of India—*preceding* the alleged Aryan invasion. It would mean that this Aryan–Dravidian argument is dead."

Before leaving the Professor, I asked him if he knew of any authoritative study of the sites in Sri Lanka connected with the *Ramayana*.

"Hmm . . . The book you need was privately published . . . I cannot currently lay my hands on my own copy, I have recently moved apartments and my library is in disarray." He picked up his address book and dictated a phone number. "This family has a copy. I'm sure they will allow you to photocopy it."

RAVAN COULD NEVER resist grandstanding. It was the weakness that would ultimately seal his fate. As the captive Hanuman was carried, bound, through Lanka's gates, an angry crowd gathered. Lanka's fighting heroes all stepped forward, offering to kill Hanuman in a duel, to restore the city's honour. They included the generals of Ravan's four armies. Ravan agreed, and revenge was scheduled to take place in the Lankan arena. But Ravan carefully loaded the odds against the massive intruder by sending his generals forth on chariots, with a platoon of gladiators.

Hanuman slaughtered the lot of them.

With Hanuman blood-soaked and exhausted, and the crowd baying for revenge, Ravan's son Aska begged to be allowed to make his name. Ravan checked that Hanuman had no arrows left; then Aska, the very image of his father and himself a fine archer, stepped into the arena. He was armed with two quivers of the finest, forge-hardened arrows. When Hanuman had finished with him he lay in the dust with his head and limbs smashed, sinews, muscles and entrails strewn around him.

In the royal box, Ravan struggled to keep a grip on himself. The crowd screamed, ready to storm the arena. In shock, Ravan ordered in fighting elephants. Hanuman was eventually subdued and chained—but not killed.

"Break him!" Ravan yelled at his torturers. As they hesitated, waiting for more detailed instructions, Ravan said, "He's a monkey—burn his tail."

When and how Hanuman escaped the torture chambers is unclear. Ravan's diplomatic, cooler-headed brother Vibhishana told him that the rules of combat did not justify torturing Hanuman—it would be killing the messenger; furthermore, if Rama and Sugriva were going to join forces, holding Hanuman might be the best way of forcing them to fight on Ravan's terms. But it seems most likely that Vibhishana somehow engineered Hanuman's release.

Our hero's final gesture, he always claimed, was to use his burning tail to start a fire. However he lit it, the fire, fed by a fierce wind, burned a quarter of the city. The same wind carried Hanuman by boat to the mainland, where he was reunited with his men a week later. There followed several nights of drunken, soldierish celebration during which they caused enough damage to justify courts martial. The crime was forgotten, however, when Hanuman stood in Sugriva's palace and showed Rama his wife's jewel, and recounted the extraordinary story of his journey to Lanka.

MY TRISHAW MAN took me north again. We drove through the port, past the machine-gun-bristling army base on Galle Face, past the 5-Stars with their concrete anti-suicide bomb cordons. We passed the docks, with their smell of rotten shrimps. We passed a man lying face down, half-on and half-off the pavement in a pool of blood, apparently dead. On the wall behind him were stencilled the words, "Jesus is the only living God, oh God grant peace to Shri Lanka". We passed shops like St Sebastien Religious Articles and Thinussha Fancy House. And Karuna Mattress and Furnitures—which translates, Buddhistically, as "Wish for all sentient beings to be free from suffering Mattress and Furnitures".

At an orthodox Hindu home a grill was drawn open and I stepped into a well-upholstered reception room. With the formality befitting a Hindu matron meeting a male stranger, a lady in a jade silk sari had one of the servants pass me the book I needed.

I took my photocopy to Galle Face, a promenade with a string of booths selling snacks and a strip of bleached grass where groups of men lobbed and batted cricket balls. Along the prom, men and women in expensive sportswear pompously power-walked. The Indian Ocean rolled in, filling the evening air with salt and ozone. Seagulls screeched. Two schoolgirls passed me, gawky and bulging out of tight white uniform dresses, carrying their breasts before them like strange insignia—which is what, when I was young, teenage girls' breasts seemed to be. It was that time of the evening when families strolled and lovers held hands and cooed, with a demureness that seemed almost parodic. A man of thirty had his face buried in the neck of a girl of twenty, a gesture at once boyishly innocent and at the same time a kind of deep and warm penetration, even a concealment. The copper sun touched the sea. The sky darkened, offering the lovers a welcome blanket of obscurity. I sat at the Famous Restaurant, a Muslim-run booth with a little enclosed area of bright red plastic tables and chairs. Eating ice cream, I watched the waves roll endlessly in. Ahead of me was Africa—to be precise, the war-torn and lawless dog-leg of Somalia.

SUCCESS WAS BITTER-SWEET. Rama knew that to invade Lanka was a virtual impossibility. Almost certainly, he would never see his wife again.

But King Sugriva recognized that after Hanuman's foray into Lanka—a virtual declaration of war—conflict with Ravan was inevitable. Their only hope was to seize the initiative. If the army *could* reach Lanka, anything was possible. But how?

The idea of the spring tide was Hanuman's. Astronomers were secretly consulted. Already, every man or boy above the age of fourteen was required by law to undertake military training. There was potentially a vast army. Thousands of woodmen were put to work felling trees. When the time was right, a flood of men spilled out of the western *ghats* into the southern plains. At their head strode Hanuman carrying Rama on his shoulders, to the cheers of 200,000 soldiers. They overwhelmed the *rakashasas* they met, by surprise and sheer weight of numbers. Hundreds of elephants dragged wood to the seashore. When the sun's and moon's combined gravity made the waters fall, Ravan's defenders found themselves high and dry, confined to isolated forts as an army surged past them, sappers flinging down pontoons and lashing together boats to form a highway over broad sandbanks and the narrow stretches of open water that remained.

When news of the invasion reached Ravan, he was profoundly shaken. He assembled his counsellors, who advised an immediate counter-attack. His brother, Vibhishana, was alone in advising restraint. He argued that Rama's vast army had already proved itself resourceful beyond their wildest nightmares. It could no doubt be defeated, but only at great cost. Surely the time had come to return Sita and avoid the danger of losing Lanka altogether?

Ravan leapt to his feet in a rage. "If anyone else had spoken to me like that, he'd be on his way to the scaffold!"

Vibhishana yelled back, "Listening to you is like watching a house burn! Well, I can't put out the flames. Say goodbye to the only man who has the courage to tell you the truth." And he stormed out of the counsel chamber.

Four days later Vibhishana reached the enemy army. It was obvious to Rama that he was hoping to gain the kingship of Lanka for himself. But Vibhishana quickly proved his worth, helping to weed out spies sent by Ravan to assess the enemy army. In truth, though, spies couldn't help Ravan now—Sugriva and Rama had secured the archipelago.

Ravan reflected belatedly on his brother's advice and stood firm in his capital, with its stores and ramparts and access to the sea. His grandfather, Malyavan, tried to talk some sense to him. "My boy, I think we should make peace with Rama. This Sita has become an obsession with you! Frankly, we've had a good run. We've broken a few treaties along the way and the result is an empire. But with Rama it's personal; now, we've managed to provoke him into an alliance with Sugriva. Rama is close to controlling two-thirds of India!"

"*Rama*! He was thrown off his throne by his father's fifteenth wife . . ."

"That's beneath you, my boy. He'll reclaim that crown when the time is right. If they don't give it back to him, he'll simply take it back. Then he'll have united India, he'll be unstoppable; and you'll be written into the history books as a monster. That'll be your reward for twenty years of hard-won victories! Meanwhile, they're already talking about Rama as a god, an incarnation of Vishnu."

"A *god*! He's a . . . a *vagabond*!"

They used to say in India that the victorious commander was the one who kept his calm. By that assessment, Ravan had already lost the war.

I HAD ARRANGED to have lunch with an artist a friend in London had suggested I should meet. I'll call him Anil, not his real name; he was Sinhalese, a Buddhist. And, according to my friend, a "pacifist".

We met at the Barefoot, a chic outpost on the Galle Road with a line in elegant, vaguely ethnic clothes, a good bookshop and a pleasant courtyard café. Anil was a compact but perfectly formed man, with thick, silver-streaked hair and delicate hands. Over jeans he wore an expensive-looking peasant shirt in bright yellow that might well have been bought in the shop above us.

A week earlier, he had lost a friend in a random bombing. He was still in shock. "I remember meeting him in 2002, after the peace accord was signed. You can't imagine how joyful and reaching out everyone was at the start of the peace process. Now . . . The killing of the Foreign Minister, the attack on the army chief . . ." He lowered his voice and leaned forward slightly. "The rumour is that there'll be a big hit in Colombo soon."

"How are people taking it?"

"They're *afraid*, of course—Tamil or Sinhalese, we *live* with fear. I live in Colombo 7, I'm a member of the élite—real fear is in the countryside, among the peasants who'll be slaughtered when the war starts up again. But even in the city we're frightened. We pretend to be brave, because what we don't want to talk about is our pain. People were coming out of my last exhibition sobbing and wanting to hold me. Because we all suppress emotion, as Asian society tells us to do. And I tell you, every person I know wants to get out of here. What's the point of staying? Where's the hope?"

"Are you saying the peace process has had it? The country is condemned to eternal war?"

"But condemned by whom? By *ourselves*! No one is prepared to make the necessary steps towards conciliation, the concessions required of *both* sides. We all play the blame game—we see it as everyone else's fault. You know, it was Indira Gandhi who said she couldn't shake hands with a clenched fist. But there are clenched fists on all sides, currently, a very intransigent atmosphere—and everybody's more hawkish than they were a year ago."

His mobile phone, lying on the table between us, began to ring. He answered it, then said, "Put her on." He looked at me. "Just a minute, I have to instruct my maid." He spoke tartly in Sinhala for half a minute, then gave an amazed shake of his head at how dense people can be.

"Why do you feel there are these entrenched positions?" I asked. "I mean, the war exhausted people, it brought the country to a halt. Why aren't people ready for peace?"

"Listen, Prabhakaran has said he won't accept a peace without recognition of a Tamil state. The government will never accept that. But the Tigers don't want peace—it isn't in their *interest* to have peace. Their leaders need to be bellicose, or they lose their grip, their influence, on the populace. Meanwhile, the national government is playing tough. Now we have ceasefire violations all the time. I give it a year before we're back in a full-scale war.

"But I'll tell you one thing: we Sri Lankans are shit at negotiation. Teaching is done by rote, you're not taught to negotiate, to debate, to *disagree*. In the West, if you don't agree with someone, you *say* so. Here, it's *rude* to do that. People are terrified of losing face—and they don't want to humiliate anyone else, to cause *them* to lose face. As a result, we literally *can't* debate."

"Twenty-five years of national catastrophe because Sri Lankans need to *talk*?"

"You have a better theory?"

I grinned. "I'm just asking questions."

"Well, that's so much easier, isn't it?" he said acidly. "At one level, *yes*—the problem is a kind of inability to talk. The political classes are full of such intransigence. So are the journalistic classes. As for the Tigers, they *won't* talk. And I will say this: considering what the Tigers have done throughout, I'm amazed at how much the government has held back from a full-scale conflict. I've personally lost

284

several close friends, *dear* friends, thanks to the Tigers. But when the foreign minister was killed, I expected the government to relaunch all-out war."

"But why did Tamils take up weapons in the first place? Because they *were* being listened to? Because they *did* have a voice in this country?"

"You sound like you favour the other side! You know, I had a friend *blown to bits* last week—they didn't even find his head, he was *vaporized*. We used to sign our emails to each other, *Karuna, Karuna*. He was a lover of peace! *Karuna*—you know what it means, *Karuna*?"

Karuna Mattress and Furnitures. The wish for all sentient beings to be free from suffering—the quintessential Jain and Buddhist expression of compassion. And the last words of Aldous Huxley's melancholy novel *Island*, about the undoing of an earthly paradise.

"Yes," I said.

We finished our lunch and said a frosty goodbye. I had failed a test—I "favoured the other side". But the remark did seem to blow Anil's even-handed pacifist credentials. When the chips were down, he sided with his own clan—the Buddhists.

I ordered tea and sat for a while in thought. Sri Lankan Hindus *had* been persecuted since Independence. Did their persecution justify the outrages of the Tigers? Clearly not. But the Tamils were a minority caught between the brutality of the Tiger cadres and a government that was intransigent, nationalistic and *aggressively* Buddhist. They had nowhere to turn.

CHAPTER 19

Red-faced Monkeys and Black Sea Tigers

WE CREPT—MY driver was a cautious type—through the nocturnal streets of Colombo. Buddhas sat in their glass cases, illuminated by flickering candle flames. We reached Ratmalana, Colombo's small domestic airport, far too early. When the guards addressed my driver he replied in hushed tones, as though discussing something intimate, or a death. Appropriate gravity in a country too used to cunning suicide bombers.

With guns trained in our direction, the car was meticulously searched, its undersides were scrutinized by magnifying mirrors and torches on long sticks, a sniffer dog gave it the once-over. There was an atmosphere of intense concentration—yet the whole bunch of guards, clad in rather fetching camouflage of taupe squiggles on an indigo background, were almost painfully young, their faces open and kind, their eyes full of innocent warmth. A girl with cotton gloves over slender fingers searched my bags. She wore a skirt over sticklike legs that ended in white socks and black patent shoes. The body search was amateurish—the boy doing it tweaked my penis, symbolizing thoroughness, perhaps, but by the standards of, say, Heathrow Airport, it was superficial.

We climbed back into the Hyundai and crawled forward to a second checkpoint, then a third. "Very tight security!" my driver told me, in an astonished whisper. He was a man in his early sixties, with the excellent staccato English of a certain type of old-school civil servant. "In my earlier career I was in government service, in stores—we provided government officers everything, from a Morris Minor down to the smallest pin." I liked him. He was punctilious and, I was sure, honest. I decided to contact him again when I returned from the north.

Ratmalana's terminal was a squat, cosy art deco building with charming wrought-iron friezes of biplanes set into unglazed windows. It had been built, according to a stone plaque, in 1939. Young Englishmen in baggy khaki would have flown their Spitfires and Typhoons out of here. Now, at dawn, it was almost deserted. A baggage handler pointed me to the staff tea hut, where young Sri Lankans in gabardines with patches of wings or propellers on their shoulders were dipping sweet rolls into cups of tea. The busy chatter dropped when I entered. An old woman in a sarong padded barefoot to my table, setting down a cup of tea with the kind of radiant smile she might have used for a grandson. It was in stark contrast to the forced smiles of the lipsticked, over-made-up ticketing clerks who represented normality, and who were now climbing out of a mini-bus. A politician arrived in a black BMW 4x4, flanked by motorcycle outriders and soldiers with sub-machine guns. There were more body searches. A delay was announced—we couldn't take off until the road from Jaffna airport to the town had been swept for mines.

The plane was an ageing Hawker Siddeley 748, one of two aircraft owned by Aero Lanka, whose *raison d'être* was this daily Jaffna shuttle. Someone had put a movie soundtrack on the sound system—a thriller. As we filed aboard the little plane with its aged seat coverings and yellowed plastic mouldings, the loudspeakers emitted the tense, ominous bass beats that in movies tells you to be afraid—something bad is about to happen. The music stopped abruptly, to be replaced by Vivaldi. A stewardess regarded us gloomily. Hers wasn't a plum job.

The Captain announced that we'd be flying at 13,000 feet for an hour and ten minutes. The engines fired up, a painful turbo whine, the powerful overture to the briefer drama of take-off. The plane climbed over railway goods yards with derelict rolling stock—a reminder that the train line no longer reached Jaffna. The peninsula at the top tip of the country was held by government troops, but a big knuckle of northern Sri Lanka was in rebel hands, run by the Tigers as a de facto state-within-a-state. The railway line did not enter Eelam. Since the peace process had begun, travellers had been crossing by road, but that was a slow and uncertain route. The surest way to Jaffna was by plane.

I had another reason for wanting to fly: to see Adam's Bridge, or

Rama Setu. I had deliberately asked for a seat on the left-hand side of the plane. And the view turned out to be far more spectacular than I had hoped: India was startlingly close. The shoals sat on the surface of the sea like a neat row of beads, closer to each other than I'd expected. The depth of water between the islands is rarely more than thirty feet and is often much shallower. Skeins of golden sand fanned out to disappear gauzily into the turquoise sea. Looking down, it seemed starkly obvious that India and Sri Lanka had been—*still were*—one. But that matter is debated by experts in geology, coral formation, seismic activity and several other sciences. Those Hindus who want to insist that the entire structure is man-made point to evidence that its layers of limestone rest on sand. People who've viewed the limestone blocks up close say the *appearance* of artificiality is certainly remarkable. I find the natural explanations more plausible. As the waters fell after the last Ice Age, 5,000 years ago, various combinations of bridges, causeways and ferry hops came into play. Until a cyclone in 1540 (according to records that are supposed to be at the Rameshwaram Temple), you could still wade across. And yet ultimately it wasn't nature, or a failure of technology, that kept Sri Lanka and India apart—it was politics.

As a precaution against ground-to-air missiles, the plane looped out over the sea before starting its descent. I spotted ground-attack helicopters, the classic anti-insurgency weapon. Transport planes were also parked across the apron, their aft cargo-doors dropped, with streams of men toting weighty packs deplaning and assembling under trees. A major troop build-up was going on.

We waded across hot sand and waited forty-five scorching minutes in a tin-roofed hut, before taking a bus to the edge of the airport security zone. There we transferred to a second, unmarked bus. Apparently the road ahead was being swept for mines, again. We baked. No one liked the fact that there was nothing to distinguish our bus with its black-glass windows from one that carried troops.

At last we began to move. The man next to me was a Dr Mycura from London, making a spiritual pilgrimage to the town of his birth. He peered at the blasted landscape. "This is where the vegetable gardens of Jaffna were. Now . . . nothing."

Jungle had reclaimed the fields, but military bulldozers were at work maintaining a corridor free of vegetation on either side of the road, to eliminate cover. It was a stark illustration of the costs to government of maintaining an anti-insurgency campaign, and the parallel disruption to economic life.

The buildings we passed were buckled and burned-out. Crowns had been blasted off palm trees. Large, once wealthy homes, scarred and starred by the impacts of shells, were deserted, or had been converted into sand-bagged pillboxes. It was a scene of intense urban warfare, every inch of land brutally fought over.

The devastation intruded deep into Jaffna, but still more shocking was the town's ghostly atmosphere. I remembered a proud second city, the location of the country's best university, a place bursting with colleges, schools, cramming institutes, every wall and lamp post plastered with bright-coloured adverts for tuition. This had been the intellectual heart of the Tamils, the secret of their success. Now, young soldiers substituted the students, every junction was heavily defended with uneasy-looking troops.

I'd been told the place to stay in Jaffna was one of the colonial homes that had been turned into a guest house. I'd booked before leaving Colombo. The room next to mine was occupied by an upper-crust young Englishman working for the UNHCR, the United Nations High Commission for Refugees. I introduced myself to him when he emerged briefly from his room. His natural cool turned to ice when he heard what I did for a living. But he did offer some advice.

"It's pretty dangerous around here at the moment," he said. "Caritas have had two deaths, and the brother of a colleague of mine was shot. Basically, it's a lot safer to travel in a vehicle than a trishaw or on foot. NGO vehicles are all white and have big flags on them and blue flashing lights. So try to find a taxi that looks like an NGO vehicle. Be sure you let the army see who you are—keep an arm out the window and so on. You want to avoid 'accidental fire'."

"Thanks for the advice," I said.

"And—Claymores are being let off, once or twice a day. Typically, they strap them to the side of a bike. They're usually targeting government troops—that's what's making the troops jumpy. The Claymores have a range of a hundred metres, so if you see a convoy coming—army or police—get out of the way. Because, if anything *does* happen, these young troops have a tendency to start shooting in all directions. It can get very messy."

There'd been a number of what were ambiguously known as "incidents", several of them major ones. Attacks on government troops on the one hand, arrests, tortures, rapes and murders on the other. Innocent groups of peasants butchered by both sides. Grenades flung into churches.

I found a nice white minivan taxi and asked the driver to take me to the old fort. I was wondering what the museum looked like now. My driver was bemused. He drove me to a patch of ugly scrub close to the sea, and pointed at a mound overgrown with creepers and vines. "No, no," I said, "the old *fort*, the *Portuguese* fort, the one shaped like a—" I tried to sketch the star-shaped fortifications with my fingers.

I told him to pull up at an army checkpoint. He didn't like the idea, and the soldiers didn't like it either. Diplomatically, the driver brought the van to a halt beyond blast range. Two soldiers with semi-automatic rifles and scowls approached us, then relaxed when they saw the foreign face. A tubby sergeant emerged from the sand-bagged bunker with a teacup in his hand. He gave me a friendly look and asked, in American-accented English, what I wanted.

"I'm looking for the fort," I said.

He pointed. "Right there."

I followed his finger to the overgrown mound. The driver had been right—of course. "Destroyed? In the fighting?"

"Destroyed deliberately. The Tigers couldn't hold it. So to prevent us from using it—*poom!*"

There'd been several waves of desperate fighting for Jaffna during the civil war. The Tigers had held swaths of the northern peninsula at different times; the army had wrested back control of Jaffna district after a battle costing thousands of lives.

Later, I read an interesting post-rationalization on a pro-Tiger website: the fort had symbolized more than three hundred years of Tamil enslavement to foreign powers. It had deserved to die.

BACK AT THE guest house, I took one of the easy chairs in the courtyard and ordered a beer. There were two or three other people there, all NGO types. As we chatted, the gate to the street flew open and a man in his early thirties walked in heavily. His face was red and he was covered in sweat. "Two in one fucking week!" he announced, to no one in particular. "God, I need a beer."

I raised an eyebrow at the woman sitting opposite me. "Runs a demining outfit," she said.

The man walked to the fridge behind the bar, helped himself to a beer, threw himself into a chair and took a swig. "Two fucking accidents three days apart. Christ, I can't *believe* it. Months go by without anything happening. Then . . ."

"Demining?" I asked.

He looked up to see who had asked the stupid question. "*Yeah,*" he said sarcastically.

"What happened?"

"The first guy took his visor off. Got complacent, broke the rules. He was off the mine line, thought he was OK, shifted a stone or something. It went up in his face. That was a bad one—he lost an eye. Today, the guy got a signal—you're supposed to go back twenty centimetres or so and dig under. He didn't, he put on pressure. Luckily he had his kit on. Minor injuries to his hand."

"What's the mine line?" I said.

"The military carefully map where they lay mines. There's a line, it's pretty reliable. The Tigers are more random . . ."

"WE *ARE* THE monkey army!" yelled Rama. "Every man will go into battle with his face daubed red, like a monkey!"

When the army reached the gates of Lanka, Rama decided to lay siege at once. He sent a provocative message to Ravan, telling him to have a last look round his city for old times' sake and organize his last rites. Ravan furiously responded by ordering the gates to be opened— and his troops flooded out.

The slaughter that began was indescribable. By nightfall, soldiers were fighting each other ankle-deep in a mire of bloody mud. It went on into the night, senseless butchery where men attacked the man in front of them with no idea if he was friend or foe. "We have to stop this—pull back!" Rama told Hanuman. But there was no way they could.

During the chaos, a party led by Ravan's second son Indrajit—like his dead brother, a skilled archer—managed to get within shooting range of Rama and Lakshman. He let off a volley of arrows before slipping into the darkness.

Dawn revealed a plain stained a deep red. Vultures wheeled overhead. And Sugriva's troops formed a thick figure of eight around the forms of Rama and Lakshman. The *rakashasas* had pulled back behind their ramparts, their commanders ready to admit that, battle-hardened as their troops were, Rama and Sugriva had the advantage of sheer force of numbers. What astonishing fortune, then, that Indrajit had managed to bring down Rama and Lakshman!

It was too soon to write the brothers' obituaries. Both were young and strong enough to recover from their wounds. But Ravan, uncertain how to proceed, held back his troops for four days. Then came another clash. The invaders sustained massive losses, but still they advanced. In dismay, Ravan's troops pulled back to their citadel.

WE'D BEEN STOPPED at a number of checkpoints and had plenty of guns trained on us that morning. But this time the gun was pointed straight at me. Surreally, however, it was a *speed* gun. In a ditch to the side of the road, men in body armour were clearing a minefield. But a police officer, crisply uniformed (white shirt, blue trousers), was officiously writing a ticket—for immediate payment. We'd exceeded the limit on the rutted road from Jaffna to Kilinochchi by six kilometres an hour. For my driver the fine was a day's wages. I reached wearily into my pocket.

Welcome, I thought, to Tamil Eelam. If Eelam's traffic cops thought it was life as normal, they were the only people in Sri Lanka who did.

I wanted to reach Mannar Island, the Sri Lankan end of the archipelago across the Palk Strait from Rameshwaram. To get there I had to drive through Eelam. The driver had told me it was do-able. So we'd set out at first light and driven south, leaving the army-held

Jaffna Peninsula and crossing Elephant Pass, the causeway that traverses the immense bleached flats that used to be salt fields. It had been the scene of desperate fighting several times during the civil war, and shattered buildings were all around, as were red skull-and-crossbones signs warning of uncleared minefields. Leaving the peninsula was easier than I expected: several checkpoints, then—the final glimpse of official Sri Lanka—a soldier whose face was a fabric of burnt skin stretched around a smile.

Entering Eelam was rather harder. All traffic was obliged to halt at a large "customs" compound. The day grew hot, but the atmosphere among those queuing was patient and accepting. Most were used to the delays—and anyway, they had no choice. An ice cream van did a brisk trade.

The walls of the grass-roofed customs building were plastered with garish posters of the Tiger leader Prabhakaran, usually superimposed on a map of Eelam, an inverted "V" comprising all of northern Sri Lanka, the north-west coast and the entire east coast—a far bigger territory than the LTTE actually held. There were rows of curtained booths for body searches. The staff were young and extraordinarily smart. (I was beginning to find Sri Lanka's combination of youth, uniforms and unending civil war obscene.) The women, in blue waistcoats and big-collared blouses, looked less like customs officers than stewardesses of Eelam Airlines—if you could imagine such an entity. They were pedantically inept. Worried that my phone might contain a digital camera (it didn't), they turned it over and over in their hands—ignoring my digital camera, which they left unopened in its case on the table in front of them. My driver's CDs were taken into a special video booth and lengthily inspected in case they were DVDs with pornographic or propagandistic content.

At length, I was given a "55 Division" pass and told to continue on my way.

We bowled along until we met the speed gun, cynically placed to trap travellers who'd been held up for hours by the Tigers' own procedures. By the time we reached the first town, Kilinochchi, the administrative headquarters of the rebel-held territories, it was 11.30 and my driver was looking gloomy.

"Do you want a tea?" I said.

He pulled up at a place he knew, the Pandyan Restaurant, and looked at the map. Mannar Island was just outside Tiger territory. We'd have to go through the palaver of leaving Eelam, re-enter a few hours later and finally leave again where we'd just come in. The driver said that with the day pass we'd been given and the questions he'd be bombarded with by both sides, to carry on wasn't an option—there was no way we could get to Mannar today and back to Jaffna tonight. I felt irritated, but could hardly blame him for misjudging a day trip through surreal Eelam.

I changed my plans. For several days I'd been trying to set up an interview with the press spokesmen of the LTTE, S. P. Tamilselvan. He was based in Kilinochchi and he had agreed to meet me, but was busy frying bigger fish—he was leading the team that was theoretically negotiating peace with the government. Tamilselvan regularly gave interviews to the world's press; he was, in fact, the face of the LTTE (Prabhakaran almost never gave interviews). It was an attractive, smiling face, too—not, you'd think, the face of the Tigers' second-in-command, as he was reputed to be, a man said to have the blood of many people on his hands.

I decided to drive to his office. We passed institutions such as the District Court of Tamil Eelam—claiming to apply the Indian legal code, it was one of many assertions of nationhood. But Eelam had given its inhabitants freedom from Sri Lankan state oppression by imposing a very hard-line regime of its own. Its human rights record was very poor, with a constant trickle of extrajudicial punishments, disappearances and the like. It was no Utopia.

The sign said: "Head Office of the Political Section of the Liberation Tigers of Tamil Eelam". It was a large, cool, suburban house, with comfy sofas and tables spread with reading material. But no Tamilselvan. After ninety minutes I was advised that he would come to the office only "after lunch".

"Come on," I said to my driver, "back to the restaurant."

As we ate, a group of young people entered the Pandyan. They sat soberly in formal attire, the young women wearing purple and turquoise saris, with long strings of flowers in their hair and columns of bangles on their wrists—glass on one, gold on the other. It was a little tableau of the determination of humans to live their lives, to celebrate the milestones in their existences, wherever they found themselves—even in the paranoid quasi-state of Tamil Eelam.

Back at the office, there was still no sign of Mr Tamilselvan, who was now in an "urgent meeting". I waited. His staff were polite and apologetic. At four o'clock, I decided to drive back to Jaffna—my driver was desperate to get past the trigger-happy army checkpoints on the outskirts of Jaffna before nightfall.

The following year, two ground attack aircraft of the Sri Lanka Air Force would drop "bunker-buster" bombs on an LTTE command bunker south-east of Kilinochchi, in retaliation against a Tiger raid on a government airfield (the ceasefire was still supposedly in place). Six officers would be killed, including "Brigadier" S. P. Tamilselvan. Conspiracy theories abounded. Tamilselvan had been bumped off by the Tiger leadership, people theorized—there had allegedly been tensions between Tamilselvan, who was pushing for peace, and Prabhakaran, who supposedly remained intransigent. But for the Sri Lankan government, the death of the senior Tiger strategist and diplomat was a major victory—some compensation, perhaps, for the Tiger assassinations of an Indian Prime Minister and a Sri Lankan President, two Foreign Ministers, three Ministers and a Leader of the Opposition.

RAVAN REALIZED IT was now time for him to enter the fray. If he couldn't lead his army to victory, he would face a humiliating defeat by attrition. The next morning he came through the gates of Lanka to the cheers of its population, his golden chariot gleaming, his old guard— the crack troops that had helped him win and hold on to an empire— flanking him with their gleaming weapons held high. As the two armies met, Sugriva's men were mown down like summer corn before the scythe. Hanuman raced to the front, accompanied by a bandaged and braced Lakshman, to stiffen the line. Rama joined them, sending perfectly aimed arrows deep into the *rakashasa* lines. Men roared, hacked, screamed. Then: an iron-tipped arrow from Rama's bow split Ravan's gold-crowned helmet; he fell. Time seemed to slow down for both armies as men waited to see if the *rakashasa* king was dead. Dazed, helmetless, Ravan staggered to his feet. Bare-headed, he was a sitting target for another of Rama's arrows. But Rama didn't fire. And Ravan left the field, humiliated.

The next day, in a final attempt to rally his troops, Ravan sent his brother Kumbhakarna into battle. It nearly worked. Kumbhakarna, a giant of a man, was a kind of army mascot, who celebrated every victory by feasting for three days and sleeping for a week. But on the front line he was a killing machine. Kumbhakarna waded into the lines of the enemy with their red-painted faces and, like water surging through a breached dam, Ravan's troops flooded after him. Hanuman fought his way to Kumbhakarna, only to receive an appalling blow from the giant's mace. He fell to his knees and vomited blood. But Kumbhakarna didn't press home the attack—he'd realized he was in reach of Sugriva's chariot. Drawing the flood of *rakashasas* behind him, he dragged the King bodily from his chariot and made his way back towards the citadel. Sugriva's soldiers, insane with anxiety, surged after him. Flailing men were climbing upon men and Kumbhakarna resembled a fighting stag with twenty hounds clinging to its flanks. Through the joints in his armour, blood gushed. Still, he roared and laughed. From close quarters, Rama drove heavy arrows into him. Down he went. And with him went Ravan's last hopes of victory.

The *rakashasa* King now became morose and fatalistic. His remaining sons and nephews begged to be allowed into battle. Ravan loaded them with jewels and gold and gifts of land, and wept. He gave them his blessings, but he would not look their parents in the eye. The eager young men rubbed themselves with protective herbs, kissed sacred charms and embraced their mothers, then went out to be butchered.

A FEW MILES east of Jaffna was a well where, according to tradition, Hanuman had drawn water by shooting an arrow into the ground. The next morning we wound our way through narrow lanes until we found it, a pool of water standing on a patch of open ground, covered with the droppings of grazing animals and surrounded by palm trees. It was a typical fresh-water "tank", or source of drinking water, a stone rectangle about the size of a domestic swimming pool. There was little about it to suggest any particular ancientness, a history, or a tradition of pilgrimage. Nearby there was a small Hindu temple. An old man was coming out, bending to put on his sandals. When he saw me, he told me in perfect English that the Hanuman tradition did indeed exist. "In happier times it was better cared-for." He smiled sadly. "Do you think anyone has time for such matters now?"

We walked back to the tank together. "This Sri Lanka of ours is covered with holy spots connected with *Ramayana*, did you know that?" he asked.

"So I believe," I said.

"Hindus and Buddhists have worshipped in tandem here, for centuries. Of course, Hinduism was established here long before Buddhism. You had been to Kataragama?"

He was referring to an important shrine in south-eastern Sri Lanka. "Not yet," I said.

"Do not leave Sri Lanka without going there, it is a very ancient and remarkable place. It pre-dates Buddhism. You had been to Nainativu Island, north of here?"

"As a matter of fact, I was thinking of going today."

"Yes, why not? It is a lovely drive. It was a regular day trip for us, before this war. The festival there used to attract so many pilgrims! Also on the island, five minutes only from the temple, there is a Buddhist *stupa*—according to the Buddhists, it is the spot where the Buddha stepped ashore on his first visit to Sri Lanka. Naturally, he chose to step ashore close to an important Hindu *mandir*! The two holy buildings competed, but later they coexisted. Now they compete again. The ancestors of those who now kill Hindus were themselves Hindus. Now they are Buddhists and they kill Tamils. That is Sri Lanka."

WELCOME to Panni Causeway. Sri Lanka Navy Welcomes You.

The fifteen-foot-wide strip of rutted tarmac crossed swamp and sandy lagoon, passing wading birds and a few high-prowed, beached fishing boats. Bunkers and lookout posts had been constructed every few hundred yards.

We are With You Today for your better Tomorrow.
Thank you. Come again.

Keyt's Island (the name is Dutch) was typical of the islands off the coast of India: low and flat, with palm trees and fishing nets and patches of tilled land. The difference was the soldiers, stationed every half-kilometre—after counting two hundred of them, I stopped.

In other times it would be a serene place to spend time. Tourism would have colonized it—upmarket resorts hidden among the palm groves would make exclusive use of the white-sand beaches. A local tradition has it that one of the three magi who bore gifts to the infant Jesus came from this island—again, like many Indian islands, it was colonized early and has a long-standing Christian tradition. There is also a different, unexpected spiritual connection: the conch shells that play an indispensable role in Hindu *aarthis* have been harvested here for centuries, and are said to be the whitest and most perfectly formed in any of the waters off the Indian coast. Arabs vessels came here to trade, too, and numbers of Arabs who worked as divers ended up marrying local women and settling down here. It is one of the lesser-known acts of the Tamil Tigers that they have expelled virtually every Muslim from the areas they control.

From Keyt's we rolled onto another long causeway, to Punguduthivu Island. Beyond it, the deep water started. A ferry rocked at a jetty. The price I was quoted was cheerfully outrageous. "We have no business," the ferrymen protested, "this war—no pilgrims are coming. We are losing money!" They pointed to the bay, where dozens of boats swung at anchor, unused. I weakened and coughed up.

The ferry was a hefty vessel of about forty feet, loaded with bananas and passengers' mopeds. Men sat on the superstructure, women down in the belly of the hull. We began the twenty-minute chug. Under any circumstances this was a remote spot, but would it seem quite so end-of-the-earth if a civil war hadn't shut it all away from the world for a quarter-century. In 1985 the notorious *Kumundini* Boat Massacre took place here, when more than twenty people travelling in the launch *Kumundini* were hacked to death by members of the Sri Lankan Navy. The dead included children and a one-year-old baby. I'd seen the photographs of that incident and I had it in my mind as I looked around at today's passengers. A handful of teenaged boys sitting alongside me asked all the usual questions—where was I from, did I know such-and-such a cricketer—then lost interest and turned to squint across the hazy water. They leaned absently on each other, stroking each other's hands or hair the way you might absently stroke a cat or a lover. It was a tenderness between friends that is rarely seen in the West. How strange that it should exist in the midst of this unending conflict.

As the boat approached Nainativu I could see the red-and-white-striped walls of the *mandir*. The jetty led straight to the gates of a temple with a modest-sized spire, not formal and whitewashed like those of Rameshwaram, but swarming with gaily painted statuary. A bamboo framework had been erected around the spire and painters were busy slapping on jade and salmon and sky-blue paint. Since the 2002 ceasefire, a few pilgrims had been trickling back to Nainativu. As I approached the porch in front of the temple, a group of *Brahmans* looked up with displeasure. One of them gestured that if I wanted to go any further, I'd have to remove my shirt. I complied, then stuffed a generous couple of banknotes into a giant contribution box. The *Brahmans* became noticeably warmer and my visit became unusually thorough. Most interesting for me was to encounter, in the shed where they kept the floats paraded during festival time, a sphinx. In Khajuraho I'd bought that antique bronze ink well in the shape of a cat with a human face. Several Hindus I'd shown it to had laughed, telling me that no such creature existed in Hindu mythology—it was a hoax, I had been conned. In fact, it was a sphinx. A sphinx features in the *Mahabharata*, where it has a race with Bhima. And here one was—a *purushamriga*, or human-beast—alive and well, as it were, part of a living spiritual tradition.

It took me all of five minutes to walk along the coast to Nagadipa Vihara, where a white *stupa* commemorates where the Buddha stayed during a visit to this island. Buddhist pilgrims were supposed to have been travelling here for over 2,000 years. I felt tired and hungry now, and in no mood to consider the two religions' competing claims to have been the first to colonize this half-kilometre strip of shore.

Back at the jetty, the ferry was waiting for passengers. I sat in the shade of a wooden cabin, then realized that it had two Sri Lankan army soldiers sitting morosely inside it. For the time it took to smoke a cigarette, we exchanged a few words about Liverpool Football Club and George Bush, whom they believed to be the leader of "N Gland"; many people would no doubt have agreed with them.

The ferry master told me he was leaving. One of the passengers was a man selling ice creams from a metal icebox carried on a strap round his neck. The master, feeling sheepish about our cross words over the ticket price, bought us both an ice cream. We sat and contentedly licked the pistachio-green ice.

"Do you think there will be again war?" he asked.

I looked at him. He was short, with the layer of fat of the contented married man. The chubbiness made him look younger than he was; now I noticed the fine lines round his eyes and the white tufts starting at his temples. "I don't *think* so," I said. "I *hope* not."

"War is coming again," he said firmly.

"But nobody wants another war, do they? After twenty-five years of it?"

"Look at this place," he said. "Everyone has left—there's no business. Look: so many boats, no work for them. I have been working in Dubai. Construction. I save money. 2002, they say it is peace. I come home, bring money I have saved, I buy this boat. I think I will have a new life in my home, here, close to my family. Now I think I have to sell the boat—and who will buy? I will not get a good price. But here, war is coming again. You don't think?"

"You really think they'll abandon the peace process?"

"They are fighting!" he said scornfully. "They are not ready to make peace."

When we reached the jetty he asked, with a sort of shy hesitancy, if I could give him a lift to Keyt's Island.

"Of course," I said.

As we sped across the first island my passenger told me about the life of an immigrant construction worker in Dubai, where a desert Manhattan is rising beside the bath-warm waters of the Gulf. Hard work, he said, but the fellowship was good, the money was good. He'd felt overjoyed to come home; now, he was preparing to say goodbye to his children again and return to Dubai.

We crossed the causeway onto Keyt's. At the last checkpoint an official who'd inspected the vehicle earlier now greeted me effusively. He insisted on shaking my hand, then did a kind of theatrical double-take when he saw my passenger. He made me repeat who I was and why I was here, embellishing his questions with supplementaries as to how I'd found the boat ride and how long it had taken and what had I seen on the island. I realized he was probing to see if I was telling the truth.

With a sort of false slowness he now turned his attention to my passenger. "And why are you carrying this man?"

The show of bonhomie had evaporated. He took two steps and flung open the sliding door. The tension inside the bus was palpable now, a physical reality, heavy and visceral. The officer switched into Tamil and battered the boatman with a succession of rapid questions. The driver kept his eyes fixed ahead.

The official ordered my passenger out of the bus and over to the sand-bagged hut of the checkpoint.

My driver kept his eyes forward, a relaxed smile fixed on his lips and both hands at twelve o'clock on the steering wheel, where they could be seen. "This a bad place," he said quietly.

I darted a look at him, but he didn't meet my eyes. "Which place?"

"This checkpoint. Two weeks ago a girl disappear here. Probably they rape. Murder. The people here very much angry. Very much afraid of these policeman."

"*Police*? They're not army?"

"No—police. Mostly army they are young mans, they do not want to be here, they want to go home. They are boys. Army is no problem! But police is very dangerous."

The interrogation went on. For a force fighting a counter-insurgency, a boatman could be suspicious—the Tigers used boats to mount attacks on the Sri Lankan Navy. They were fighting an invisible enemy. But we all knew that if these cops were suspicious, or in a bad mood that day, or just didn't like the look of his face, the boatman might be detained. There'd be every chance of torture, then probably murder. There were psychopathic sadists on both sides, now, an entrenched culture of brutality.

The boatman was dismissed. He turned and walked heavily towards us. He looked nauseous. He climbed in and slid the side door shut, and the driver took us forward at a walking pace, past the police post, whose occupants looked up from the card game they'd resumed to give me a cheery wave.

THAT EVENING AT at the guest house was the regular Friday night get-together. Talking to a female member of a Christian aid organization, I learned that the Indian government planned to cut a hole in Rama's Bridge. The idea was to construct a deep-water channel between India and Sri Lanka. For deep-draught cargo ships it would knock several hundred kilometres off the sea passage round Sri Lanka. For the Indian government, it would allow its cruisers and aircraft carriers to do the same thing, "enhancing national security". The plan, which involved the destruction of a significant chunk of the sand-and-limestone "bridge", had just been given the go-ahead. (Initially, any notions that the bridge had significance as a religious symbol, and might deserve the status of a National Monument, were dismissed. Alternative routes for the canal—there are at least five—were brushed aside. Frustrated that canal construction should be slowed down because of religious sensibilities, the Chief Minister of Tamil Nadu, M Karunanidhi—an avowed atheist and supporter of the Periyar movement—described Rama as a "drunkard . . . (without) engineering expertise". In 2007 the Archæological Survey of India filed an affadavit to the Supreme Court containing the provocative, yet naïve and magnificently irrelevant assertion that Lord Rama couldn't be proven to have been a real person. The result of these statements was a vast, nationwide wave of protest. The Sethusamudram Ship Canal undoubtedly has the potential to become a new Ayodhya—if governments are unwise enough to drive the project ahead with the lofty disdain for Hindu sentiment that they are currently demonstrating.)

Several members of the Sri Lanka Monitoring Mission, the Nordic countries' peace brokers, turned up at the party. They included Lars Bleymann, a man who'd recently had a front-seat view of an unusual Tiger action. It was the most serious breach of the ceasefire, and had just helped prompt an EU decision to brand the LTTE a terrorist organization.

He had experienced the Tigers' infamous suicide squads in action.

Many of us have seen antique newsreel of kamikaze attacks on warships during WWII. But Lars knew how it felt. He'd been with a Sri Lankan navy patrol when it was attacked by Tiger rebels.

"I saw the line of boats close to the shore," he told me, "and as soon as they started to move, I thought, 'Oh God, they're coming for us.' I knew an attack was inevitable."

Guerrillas can't compete with a national navy, but the so-called Sea Tigers have developed a hit-and-run technique using road-trailered, high-speed launches, driven by four high-powered outboard motors. They pack serious firepower. They're accompanied by much smaller, sharp-ended, two-man speedboats, packed with high explosive. These are the so-called Black Sea Tigers—the suicide teams.

The preferred tactic is for two of the larger launches to engage the target, pouring lead at it. Meanwhile, the speedboat tries to ram it and detonate itself.

Lars knew that by attacking, the Tigers would commit a major breach of the ceasefire. But that was now rather academic. A Norwegian national, he was married to "a Scottish lass", he told me. They live in Edinburgh, where they've raised two children. As he watched the Tiger launches with their blue-and-crimson pennants speed across the water, it went through his mind that he might not see them again.

The four naval vessels were attacked by a swarm of fifteen or sixteen Tiger "small ships". The Tigers had powerful high-calibre weapons. With bullets crashing into the boat, Lars saw one of the navy gunners wounded. "He was hit in the ankle," Lars told me, "but in minutes the wound was bandaged and he had jumped right back to his gun." The sailor's cool and sharpness under fire made a powerful impression on Lars. As well it might have. He survived. But one of the suicide boats did get through: and one of the navy vessels went down.

I couldn't resist; I asked the stupid journalist's question: "How did you feel when it was over?"

Lars had a droll delivery and had not lost his sing-song Norwegian accent. "Wull, I woss nott ver-y hap-py! But I have never hugged so many men in my life!"

THE MERCURIAL INDRAJIT, the son of Ravan who'd slipped through the lines that first night and wounded both Ayodhyan princes, had an idea. He brought the concubine who bore a certain resemblance to Sita to the front gates of the city. He let her scream, "Rama! Hanuman!" once or twice, then sliced her in half with his sword. The illusion was effective. Hanuman, who was just fifty feet away, called a general retreat. For the thousands of soldiers who'd seen half of their friends killed to bring back the wife of a foreign prince, it was too much. Something close to mutiny possessed them.

And when the news reached Rama, he was stricken.

It was Vibhishana who saved the day. He tore into Rama's tent and panted, "This tale is as likely as the sun going out. I can tell you one thing about Ravan—he's obsessed by your wife, he'd *never* have her killed. Even now, he probably has some deranged fantasy about saving the situation and winning her love. There was a woman in his entourage who had something of a resemblance to your wife, Prince. She provided Ravan with . . . compensation. I'd be prepared to swear that she died this morning."

Vibhishana then proved his worth once and for all: he told Lakshman where he'd be able to find Indrajit—at a shrine outside the city walls, at dawn, praying to the Gods for victory. Lakshman duly trapped Indrajit. He gave him every chance; but in combat, Lakshman had the edge.

Ravan's last remaining son was dead.

But neither Rama nor Lakshman was well. Forced into battle before they'd fully recovered from their earlier wounds, both now suffered relapses so severe that doctors feared for their lives. Medicines were running low, too. And so came about another of the episodes that later entered legend. Hanuman was chosen to lead a party to the groves on Mount Meeru, where medicinal plants grew wild. But when he arrived there, Hanuman found himself completely unable to be sure he was bringing back the right plants. He decided to take back the entire mountain. His return, leading a convoy of carts with several acres of turf covered in healthily growing wild plants, produced helpless laughter throughout the camp.

CHAPTER 20

Treading the Flowers

A YOGHURT SMELL of human sweat hung in the air. In stifling heat, we shuffled forward. The body searches were being carried out this time by someone who knew what he was doing, a grim-faced, middle-aged soldier. But two paunchy Catholic priests in soutanes he ignored. "The guard respects the cloth," one of them told me, rather too smugly. If Tigers could pose as pregnant women, I thought, then why not as padres?

The little Hawker-Siddely rumbled into the sky. Peering out of the window, I got ready to take a picture of Rama's Bridge, until a stewardess leaned over me and said sternly, "No photographs, sir—security!" A few minutes later I said goodbye to the chain of golden sand bars, wondering if the next time I saw this view it would be a shipping Autobahn like the Suez Canal.

Back in Colombo I tracked down the driver who'd taken me to the airport a week earlier. I proposed a trip around the island and he agreed eagerly—as long as I didn't want him to take me into any Tiger lairs.

We headed south. At noon the next day, my journey in the footsteps of King Rama brought me to the former hippie hang-out of Unawatuna, where Birgitte, my short-lived German Sita of all those years ago, had forged the New World Order with her comrades. Unawatuna's hippie days seemed to have passed. We drove along a dirt road behind a strip of restaurants and hotels that had grown up along the beach. They were low-rise and relaxed, catering to independent travellers, not package tourists, but still they were banal. We went into a restaurant for lunch. After the rigour of the north, the staff seemed slovenly and overfamiliar. It was Sri Lanka, but it was another country.

Standing above Unawatuna is the promontory of Rumassala. It is said to be a chunk of the mountain Hanuman brought back when he'd been unable to select the medicinal herbs Rama needed. (In my version he brings carts of turf, but he's often depicted, as he was on that Colombo rickshaw driver's decal, flying through the air with a mountaintop in his arms.) It's a charming legend: on an otherwise flat coastline, it must have been easy to believe that this leafy crag had fallen from the sky. The hill is still renowned for its flora. And somewhere on it there was a shrine dedicated to Hanuman.

I asked the staff at the restaurant to direct me to the path that led up from the beach to the shrine. Evidently not locals, they had no idea what I was talking about. K. J., my driver (he'd told me he preferred to be known by his first two initials) asked a shopkeeper the same question and received an indifferent shrug. We went back to the main road. There were no signs indicating a way to the shrine, so it seemed to us auspicious, given Rumassala's reputation for herbs, to take advice from a woman running a small roadside nursery. She told us how to wend our way along a dirt track, through the forest, until we reached a point overlooking the ocean.

We nearly didn't find it. But there, on a promontory overlooking the Indian Ocean and the steady passage of ships, was a milk-white *stupa*. It had been recently constructed, its guardian told me, as a signal to the passing vessels—to the world—that Sri Lanka was a Buddhist nation. Setting aside the fact that most of that shipping may soon be passing through a canal at Jaffna, I suspected the *stupa* of having a different, *domestic* purpose: it overshadowed the older and smaller shrine to Hanuman, where the Monkey God stood under a canopy to protect Him from the elements. (Like Rama, Hanuman has slowly evolved into a god.) I wondered if nationalists had wanted to reclaim this spot for their Buddhist, "Aryan" state. Such competition isn't unusual, as at Nainativu Island—or the Mount in Jerusalem, where three religions wrestle for a parcel of holy real estate. But the *stupa* overshadowing Hanuman seemed an unsubtle reminder of who were the bosses around here.

We spent the night in Galle, a fortified Portuguese port town. We passed through its massive ramparts and drove round the quiet, narrow streets searching for a place to stay. I chose the Beatrice Guest

House, a pleasantly rickety colonial joint. Its owner was a Mr Kodikara, a breezy old man with a round face and a tuft of white hair. While his grandchildren sat on the veranda scratching home-work into copybooks with fountain pens, he led me across the road to the great sea wall that girds the old town. The sun was low, seagulls reeled, people took their evening constitutionals.

"I believe this wall saved us," he said, with a melancholy smile.

Galle's new town, built on the flatter land behind the bulge of the ancient port, had been devastated by the 2004 tsunami. Driving south, K. J. and I had passed plenty of evidence, most notably a rusting train. Swept off its tracks, it had cartwheeled four times; a thousand passengers had died.

"Luckily the twenty-sixth of December was a Sunday," said Mr Kodikara, "or more trains would have been running, there would have been four times as many dead . . . The force of the water was incredible, you know. People hung on to buses, but the buses were dragged under. Just recently, a crab fisherman came across another car under the water. Wrecked trucks and buses have been dragged out of the sea, and dozens of motorbikes and bicycles, but they were always unusable.

"Of course, there were miracles. One man was in a bus pushed by the force of the water up against a Buddhist statue. Somehow he climbed out of the bus onto the statue, and thus he escaped!

"But it is a terrible thing we have lived through. For months we were in shock. With my own eyes I saw bodies, heaps of them! They were simply thrown into a pile, a huge pile, all mixed together—no caste or level! We learned a lot from that, you know—not to worry about money, accumulating riches, to live for the moment, not tomorrow. To work together! That conflicts should be settled peaceably, not through fighting and killing each other!"

He paused reflectively, then turned and looked at me with that melancholy smile playing on his lips. "Of course, we're starting to forget again now. The lessons learned—they'll no doubt soon be forgotten too! We will return to our mutual hatreds. That is human nature, no?"

AFTER BREAKFAST, I stuck my head out of the front gate and saw K. J. whistling as he finished cleaning his windscreen. He had stayed in the new town that night, in a place of his own choosing. "I slept *wonderfully!*" he said. "Normally now I am in the traffic of Colombo! Stress, no? Instead—sea breezes!" He had already breakfasted, read his newspaper and cleaned the car. "I am ready to face whatever the day will bring!"

The day brought a gentle drive along the coast. We were heading for Kataragama, the most important pilgrimage site in Sri Lanka, shared between Hindus, Buddhists, Muslims and the jungle-dwelling *Veddhas*, supposedly the oldest inhabitants of the island, who are fond of the God who lives, as they do, in the remote jungle. The archaic rites at Kataragama are said to have come down from the *Veddhas'* prehistoric practices.

As we drove, K. J. wriggled in his seat with childlike enthusiasm. "When I was a boy, we would come on pilgrimage here—my whole family—once a year, *without fail.* We took the bus. It cost nothing in those days. We would leave Colombo and travel directly to Kataragama for the annual festival. But these days . . ."

"What's changed?"

He gave the sort of shrug you'd use to shake something nasty off your shoulder. "Security situation. Killings. During the war, nobody wanted to take such journeys across the country. Anything was possible, anything at all. Since then . . ."

We drove in silence. "So, you're a Hindu?" I asked.

He hesitated before answering. "Yes," he said.

It is a curious thing, this religious ethnicity, that wants to sum you up—whether you're to be liked or trusted, whether you are "one of us", whether you are to live or die—according to the Gods you were brought up to worship. And yet . . . it's one of Sri Lanka's cruellest ironies that its sacred sites have traditionally been *shared* by people of different faiths. Popular Buddhism does not venerate the metaphysical abstractions Westerners believe it to; it isn't even monotheistic. Sri Lankan Buddhists are perfectly happy to co-opt a Hindu god as a *bodhisattva* (a hands-on holy man who spends his time not in self-absorbed meditation, but helping others to achieve enlightenment). They revere the Buddha, but in practice they pray to and petition a variety of spirits and gods, also offering them food and clothing. In so many ways the daily practice of Buddhism has little to distinguish it from Hinduism, evidence that Sri Lanka is a remarkably tolerant land—or so it was believed, until the civil war.

Driving east, we were leaving behind the zones of maximum tourist development and heading into the long strip of eastern Sri Lanka claimed as Eelam. The south-eastern pocket of Tamil influence goes back a long way—perhaps, as the old man in Jaffna had told me, to before the arrival of Buddhism. We stopped at the small coastal town of Kirinda, to peer out to sea to where a slab of black rock that's exposed at low tide is held to be the ruins of Ravan's Castle. In the hazy afternoon light I couldn't see any rocks, or even the needle of lighthouse that marks them. Given Ravan's enduring popularity, I could understand why an outcrop of dark rocks should have retained for centuries its currency in people's imaginations. But I doubted that Ravan's Castle had been accessible from the land only three millennia back . . . The one certainty was that those rocks had ripped the bottom out of many a ship—indeed, a few decades back the late science fiction author Arthur C. Clarke, a Sri Lankan resident, had participated in a diving expedition that found treasure off Ravan's Castle . . .

RAVAN'S GRIEF AT the death of his son Indrajit turned rapidly into all-consuming rage. Lanka was full of the sound of wailing women. The King stumbled his way into the palace courtyard and called for his chariot with its eight horses. His commanders summoned their remaining warriors. The city gates were opened and Ravan's Old Guard stormed forth. The rage in Ravan seemed to infuse his men: they fought with a kind of insanity. It seemed, at last, that Ravan might have the advantage. Seeing a chance, he whipped his horses towards the chariots of Rama and Lakshman. His lance caught Lakshman in the chest. Vibhishana raced forward and managed to bring down one of Ravan's horses. The Lankan King turned in fury to hurl a second lance at his own brother.

For Rama, the darkest moment since his exile from Ayodhya had come. What use this struggle, even if he were to regain Sita, if his own brother was dead? He hesitated, and his men closed protectively round him. Then, word came that Lakshman's heart had not been touched by the lance—he would live. Rama ordered his charioteer to drive straight at Ravan. He killed several of Ravan's remaining horses, then, hurling a discus, managed to catch Ravan in the chest and head. Ravan was rocked back on his heels, and his charioteer swiftly withdrew from the range of Rama's weapons. Delirious with pain and rage, Ravan cursed the man and ordered him back at Rama.

The two men now unleashed arrows at each other from close range. Their horses screamed and fell, their charioteers fell, but the two men battled on. Rama's respect for Ravan grew: but for his own skill with bow and arrow, victory would have been Ravan's by now. And at this close range the advantage was with the Lankan King.

Rama pulled from a quiver the arrow made, according to legend, by Brahma Himself. The secret of its manufacture was lost—no one knew how such a hard metal had been forged. Rama drew his bow to its fullest and released the arrow. It struck Ravan in the chest, piercing his armour and his heart. The King of the *rakashasas*, whose audacity had won him an empire, tumbled from his chariot. At once his men ran for the gates of Lanka, chased by the screaming, whooping victors.

Rama allowed Ravan's body to be claimed, undefiled. Mandodari, Ravan's most beloved wife, watched her husband's bloodstained corpse borne through the gates and asked herself how his lust for another man's wife could have brought about the end of an empire.

Vibhishana was uncertain whether he should, as ritual dictated, perform his brother's last rites, but Rama urged him to do so. Vibhishana was declared King, and the citizens of Lanka brought formal peace offerings to Rama, which he accepted. Then he sent Hanuman to offer his wife greetings, give her news of their victory and bring back any message she might have for him. It was, Hanuman thought, a strangely cool form of greeting . . .

WE TURNED INLAND. It was after nightfall when we reached Kataragama and checked in—at K. J.'s insistence, because he said it was better value—to the Government Guest House. I privately renamed it the Government Filth House, for its clotted hairs, the soiled tiles around the toilet, the general air of surfaces occasionally wiped but never washed. The bedsheet was clean, but I took a look at the mattress and wished I hadn't.

It didn't matter: I spent only four hours in bed. We rose at 4 a.m. and walked to a café where we drank sweet tea. K. J. bustled me along, not wanting us to miss the *aarthi*. We stopped to buy offerings at a stall whose lights blazed alone in a dark street. The stallholder, clad only in a turquoise *lunghi,* set down two woven grass trays before him, clasped his hands and briefly bobbed in front of them, then placed a tiny coconut in the middle of each, rinsed the blade of his knife and rapidly sliced and arranged some watermelon, orange, plantains and mango. He completed our offerings with camphor and incense laid on *betel* leaves, and topped them off with garlands—red in colour, as garlands for Kataragama always are. They were made of plastic.

I caught K. J.'s eye and he gave an apologetic shrug. "Flowers are very difficult to find this side," he mumbled, meaning on the drier south-east coast of the island.

The popularity of Kataragama masks the fact that it ties together many strands of ancient belief and practice. It is a "mystery religion", an esoteric cult that hides its revelations from all but a core of initiates. Yet the annual festival is an all-out carnival, with tens of thousands of ordinary people coming to witness every kind of extreme mortification—devotees suspend themselves by hooks driven through their flesh while others run barefoot across red-hot coals—"treading the flowers", they call it. In sensational terms, Kataragama eclipses even Kandy's festival of elephants.

But the presiding deity of Kataragama remains enigmatic. Modestly, He takes his name from the town; in paintings He's an ever-youthful, familiar-seeming combination of Shiva, Krishna and Rama, merging into the key Hindu God of southern India, Murugan or Skanda. He is said to manifest, as the occasion demands, as a god of war, or wisdom, or love, or as the holy infant Muruga. But that is religion for the masses; more esoterically, Kataragama is worshipped without icons or idols of any kind. His house is a simple place, without monumental architecture—indeed, until recent times it was a collection of huts without even a metalled road to it—yet the reputation of the jungle shrine is almost unparalleled. Brahma, the originator of the universe, is rarely worshipped in contemporary Hinduism and has few temples dedicated to Him. He is too abstract, too hard to imagine, and popular devotion has favoured more readily graspable manifestations of the godhead—notably Shiva. But here at Kataragama, underneath all the razzmatazz, the Creator God mysteriously *is*—a kind of present absence. His most committed devotees see Him as the ultimate formless abstraction that can be worshipped only via symbols, such as the *yantra* of a hexagram with two intersecting triangles.

As we entered the temple the sky was starting to glow. Above our heads a planet blazed. About fifty people were queuing for a *darshan* that morning, in the usual separate lines of men and women. The temple's tiled roof was supported by rows of carved black pillars adorned with long, gold-framed paintings of the God (the sponsors' names prominently displayed). There were ten six-foot brass lamps with trays of lamps, surmounted by peacocks (the vehicle of the God). A drummer with sleepy eyes banged; we worshippers rang the bells suspended above us. I heard the hawk and spit of two struck matches, incense billowed from two large urns and we edged forward with our offerings. Priests deposited ash into our left hands and delicate-scented rosewater into our right. We were handed handfuls of *prasad* as we filed out into the dawn. In the sky a thousand bulbous clouds seemed to be ascending, like a fleet of spaceships. The *prasad*, rice with cashews and fruit, was exquisite. I felt soothed and calm. Whatever it is that ritual *does*—if you allow it to—my state had been transformed by the process of sharing with a group of other people a "sacred" space. Organized light, noise and scent had worked upon us. We had focused our common energy on an idol, symbolic of something mysterious, benign, greater than ourselves. I looked at K. J.: he felt it, too. He had a faint contented smile on his lips. He was happy to be where he was. Here; now.

We wandered through the other shrines, one of them devoted to the less abstract, less intellectually challenging, universally adored elephant-headed God, Ganesh. A further gallery was packed with the images of many Gods, including Rama and Sita. I had read that Kataragama had a notional connection with the *Ramayana*—that Rama and Sita finally left Sri Lanka from there to return to India. It seemed implausible. When devotion to Rama had been at its historic peak, there'd no doubt been competition among holy places to claim a slice of the tourist action. But Kataragama had never needed additional pilgrim traffic: it was held to be one of the nodes of absolute spiritual power in the whole of the Indian subcontinent.

We walked past souvenir and flower vendors, through the extensive landscaped grounds with their regular rows of trees. At the boundary of the compound I was astonished to come upon a statue of Ravan, and more astonished to see a plaque proclaiming him a Sinhalese king. It was another gesture by the nationalists. For all its eclecticism, Kataragama is fundamentally Hindu; but since independence it has been politicized, has undergone "Buddhization". The control of the temple precincts, the use of landscaping, the demolition of old buildings and the construction of new ones have permitted politicians to dilute Kataragama's Hindu character. The construction of a vastly expensive train link with Colombo and rapid urbanization have been decreed by the politicians—against the wishes of the temple's management committee. Controlling this ancient source of mystery has mattered to politicians. They understand the power of symbolism.

SITA WAS APPALLED to find that she would be reunited with Rama in front of a vast crowd, with her husband's allies and generals all around him. When she stood before him at last, she stared at the ground in discomfort. Then, Rama gave vent to an extraordinary public outburst. A king, he announced, cannot take back a wife who has lived in the house of another man. "I cannot believe Ravan kept you here so long without touching you, Sita!" When Sita failed to respond, staring mutely down, Rama seemed to become even more infuriated. "I suggest you go to Lakshman, or Sugriva, or Vibhishana. Because I can no longer accept you as a wife!"

Sita's shoulders shook with sobs. Turning up her face to him at last, she said, "You should know me better than to judge me as though I were a woman of the streets, My Lord. And when you sent Hanuman to find me, why didn't you tell him to give me this news? I could simply have killed myself and saved the lives of thousands of soldiers on both sides. Did you cause their deaths, only to tell me this now?"

The logic of her argument brought a stunned silence to the crowd. Sita turned to Lakshman. "Build a fire, let me walk into the flames. If I was ever disloyal to Rama, let my skin be burned from me!" Lakshman turned to Rama, who grimly nodded.

As thousands watched, logs were brought and a fire was built. Into its flames, across its coals, Sita strode. And emerged unburned. Rama ran forward and took her in his arms.

Lakshman turned to Vibhishana. "Do you see?—He had to test her. She had to be vindicated in public, or people would have said that Rama was blinded by love, that he'd taken back a woman who was no better than a concubine."

NORTH OF KATARAGAMA the country is little frequented by tourists. We saw forests being felled and land coming under cultivation, villages being urbanized, the sense of a population expanding and a landscape being tamed. Sri Lanka has more wild elephants than any place on earth. For how much longer, I wondered.

As we approached the central highlands, the road steepened and twisted, and the jungle reasserted itself. It was mid-afternoon when we reached Sita Falls, where a small road bridge crossed the river and a thousand feet above a waterfall tumbled. A handful of boys stood around with postcards and chunks of quartzite, hopefully accosting the passengers of the vehicles that pulled up every few minutes. One or two people got down to stretch their legs and take in the view, but few took the trouble to climb to the falls.

I scrambled up the rocks. I'd been here with Birgitte a quarter-century earlier. As then, a Hindu family were taking their dip. The menfolk acknowledged me cheerfully, but I kept back until they'd wrapped themselves up and made their way down the path. I slipped alone into the rock pool where Sita bathed and Ravan, husband of three hundred desirable women schooled in the erotic arts, nevertheless crouched in the shrubbery in the form of a small mammal and voyeuristically watched and wished.

We drove on, searching for Sita's Cave. After several false starts, we found ourselves at the end of a lane beside a tiny Buddhist temple. Some boys appeared and I asked them for directions. The cave was in the cliff face above the village, they said. No, visitors never came; it was one of *their* places—the local lads'. It was a steep, fifteen-minute climb, through a grove of trees, through bushes and brambles, and past a final curtain of glossy leaves, where moisture produced an abrupt eruption of dense greenery. The cave was equipped with running water! In fact, it dripped off the ceiling, and I put my chin under it with a feeling of relief. After the hot climb, it was good to be at rest in the dense cool. I scrambled deeper into the cave where Sita had been held prisoner. The three boys scampered ahead of me, holding up their hands to touch the moist ceiling. The cave that began as an imposing stone arch two storeys high narrowed steadily to a scalloped hollow no bigger than a double bed. We squatted there, with the wet and the smell of bat droppings, the boys flicking my torch over sparks of mica and a huge spider that had its long striped legs splayed out radially, like an ancient engraving of the sun. The cave's open mouth was a black oval frame for a pale view of hills.

I do not believe literally that 3,000 years ago a kidnapped princess from Ayodhya squatted fearfully in these shadows, dreaming of her home in northern India, fearful that she might never be rescued, or that the outcome of an unsuccessful campaign by her husband would mean death for him and worse for her. Surely these elements of myth were superimposed by Hindus on the landscape around them— perhaps during the great wave of devotional worship of Rama, of *bhakti*, that swept southern India a thousand years ago? In a sense, it doesn't matter; tradition has given these sites significance. I remember Uluru in the Australian desert and Cuzco in the Peruvian desert, where the human imagination has imposed on the landscapes patterns of symbolic meaning. In the case of the *Ramayana*, a drama that fuses art and religion in a way that has all but vanished from the Western world, perhaps only geography can give adequate expression to the titanic drama of Rama and Sita, Lakshman, Hanuman and Ravan.

THE NEXT DAY we continued upcountry to Hakgala Gardens, where I came with Birgitte all those years ago. Unlike Ooty, which had seemed oddly shrunken, this landscape seemed larger, more epic, than in my memory, overshadowed by the great flat-topped mountain of Hakgala. I walked through the gardens laid out in the 1880s, with their very British flower beds and bridges over ornamental streams. In glasshouses men knelt, meticulously potting seedlings. Hakgala is the second-largest botanic garden in Sri Lanka, first established in the mid-nineteenth century to experiment into the cultivation of tea. It was a Mr William Nock, appointed curator in 1884, who oversaw its transformation into a kind of Kew Gardens, planting sub-tropical and temperate plants and trees from all over Sri Lanka, as well as from California, Japan and England.

As I walked along the park's upper boundary, past massive trees and miniature waterfall features, I met a man wandering, notebook in hand, allowing the fingers of his other hand to caress the twigs and fronds of the flora. He was the Director of Hakgala, who inhabited the perfect little cottage, surrounded by crisp lawns and foaming flower beds, that stands in the heart of the gardens. "I haven't been here very long," he confided, "I am still getting to know what we have. The labelling, as you can see, is far from complete—the same goes for the written records. When I get a few minutes to myself, I like just to wander around. There are many surprises here. Some puzzles, also."

"Was it Ravan's pleasure garden," I asked, "where Sita was held?"

He winced. "Are you asking me if this was an enclosed, artificial garden thousands of years before the British made it a botanical garden? How can I say? There are many legends to the effect that the ancient kings of Sri Lanka had pleasure gardens in these hills. I *will* say this: the conditions are perfect—the mildness of the climate, protection from the elements, the soil, the wide variety of different plants endemic here. It is nature's garden—it would be a natural place for any ruler to want to make into a pleasure garden!"

Fifteen hundred feet over our heads was the flat-topped massif of Hakgala, with its scored, scarred vertical flanks where the spears and flying discuses of Rama and Ravan struck during their ultimate duel. There were giants in those days.

A mile from Hakgala is a small *mandir* beside a stream, the Sita Amman Kovil. Here (the temple literature states unequivocally) Sita bathed during her captivity (until Ravan secreted her in that cave).

The little temple was being expanded, the chocolate-brown earth was being eviscerated for foundations, metal rods destined to reinforce concrete pillars were everywhere. To build a Hindu temple was a kind of miracle, you might say, in the context of Sri Lanka's ethnic war. And yet, another of Sri Lanka's ironies: here, nationalists and environmentalists had united to prevent construction, but were overruled by a decree from the Tourism Ministry.

In the stone stream bed under the temple walls were Hanuman's footprints. Holes had been hollowed, perfect concavities, one in particular appearing to be a complete footprint, a heel and sole: Hanuman left this mark as he leapt. This temple stood at the location of the grove beyond Ravan's castle where Hanuman found Sita; the dark earth, so distinct from the brilliant orange soil elsewhere in Sri Lanka, had been scorched by the fire started by Hanuman's burning tail.

I made an offering; a stall across the road from the temple sold me fruits—this time, however, there was no plastic garland; the shop-keeper scattered a fistful of lightly-held petals, which expanded as they were released, and I had an impression of a man liberating butterflies. A priest offered the food to the lips of the Gods, intoned in Sanskrit and finally painted a brilliant crimson *tikka* on my fore-head. He made it plain, pushing the offerings plate in my direction, that I should now *give*. Unbegrudgingly, I gave.

The temple was conventional enough, its spire decorated with gaily painted cast-concrete figures. The small, hygienically tiled shrines were inhabited by the popular gods, mass-produced statues got up in gilt-fringed crimson nylon satin. But over to one side was something more remarkable: four statues, of Rama, Sita, Hanuman and Lakshman, recovered from the earth nearby a century ago. I say "statues", but they were barely more than humanoid forms, daubed black, with bright orange bird's eyes painted on and, in the case of Sita, a tiny smile. They were pocked and melted as though by the action of wind and rain, but it was equally likely that they had been eroded by constant human touch. To see these blobs of stone elevated to the highest human meaning, painstakingly draped with silk and gilt and necklaces of fresh flower blossoms and anointed with precious ghee and perfumes—and *worshipped*—was to see the ability of human beings to invest their emotions in symbols beyond themselves. In Catholic churches I have seen in glass cases perfect replicas of the dead Christ, His wounds carefully swollen and blood-seeping—and I find myself less moved by these gloomy naturalistic masterpieces than by the primitive-seeming, devotion-eroded idols of Hinduism. If these worn objects can absorb and reflect such intensities of affection and devotion, then why not a cave, a mountain, a chain of sandbanks? To surrender to a symbol and be transported by it is not, I believe, any more diminishing than to be transported by Wordsworth or Whitman, Wagner or Van Morrison; it may even be exalting. But that's a hard sell in our materialistic age. I am not an anti-rationalist, I don't claim that opinions or mystic convictions are superior to evidence and fact. But is religion *necessarily*, as the Richard Dawkinses of the world keep telling us, empty and pernicious? Colour cannot be explained to the blind and religion cannot be explained to the rationalist—nor should it be. The blind cannot open their eyes and see, but religious experiences—however you explain them, and this book is not the place to try to do that— religious experiences sometimes strike the believer and non-believer from the blue. Thereafter it's impossible to imagine a life without that metaphysical tint.

IF SITA'S TEMPLE was managing slowly to grow, then something very different had happened on a hillside halfway between Nuwara Eliya and Kandy. Rising in the tea hills there's a bold new temple containing a massive statue of Hanuman—forty feet high, complete with a staircase to allow the resident *Brahmans* to drop into place hefty floral garlands. It is located opposite a famous view, a distant row of hills that resemble a figure asleep on his back. This is Hanuman in the "giant" form in which he accomplished his famous leaps, en route to Lanka.

The place stirs the faithful, it seems, and if it didn't stir me, it did leave me with the sense that Sri Lanka has just now received its most monumental icon in the continuing veneration of the *Ramayana*. Henceforth, this shrine will be an unmissable stop for Hindu pilgrims. But it's religion as Big Gesture, a Hollywood notion of divinity. Such monumental statuary is commonplace in India and Sri

Lanka—indeed, there's a contemporary trend towards creating more of it. Asia's highest statue is of Hanuman, at Rourkela, in India. Hanuman, Hinduism's superhero, lends himself to such gestures more than any other character. This is, perhaps, one way that Hinduism will survive. The West has had to create its cast of comic-book superheroes to replace the etiolated Christ that was the legacy of milksop Victorian Protestantism. Hinduism merely modernizes the cult of Hanuman—the monkey God has already evolved into the hero of a comic-book series and several other very modern media. As it always has, Hinduism absorbs what it finds around it—and moves on.

Among the cluster of sites in the Sri Lankan highlands that claim connections with the *Ramayana*, it was finally another shrine devoted to Sita that moved me most. The little *mandir*, off the main road, wasn't easy to find. The civil war had killed the pilgrim trade and the two temple attendants who came out blinking to meet me had touching expressions of surprise on their faces. "No," they said, "hardly anybody comes here any more."

The older of them pointed at a broad swath of green just beyond the temple wall. Up in these hills, such a stretch of flat land was an unusual sight. According to tradition, he told me, that was the location of Ravan's palace. At any rate, large and evidently ancient carved stones had been found there—and he showed me where some of them were propped up against a wall. It was also from that plain, he said, that the *Pushpaka* had taken off and landed.

Inside a low building, painted murals illustrated the climax of the *Ramayana*. Out in the courtyard was a shrine. Here it was, they said, that Sita entered the fire. That scene is, in many ways, the darkest in the *Ramayana*. At the climax of the tale, after a great victory over Evil, the human heart with its suspicions and conventions threatens to destroy everything. Sita's remarkable gesture—her "treading the flowers"—is an utterly key moment in Hindu literature. Fire: that purifying, alchemical force, with its special claim to distinguish the true from the false. With what we know about the practice that later became known as *suttee* or *sati*—the compulsion of widows to burn on their husbands' funeral pyres—this scene takes on a particularly sinister quality. Yet for many Hindu women it is a joyful moment, when the purity of this archetypally noble Hindu wife was proven beyond any doubt. I found the white-painted shrine decked with little triangular flags extraordinarily moving. That site, it seemed to me, was at the heart of any *Ramayanan* pilgrimage to Sri Lanka. Surely, when peace returns to Sri Lanka, the pilgrims also will return.

PART VII

CHAPTER 21

Hanuman Over Bangalore

I HAD BEEN looking for something in modern Indian life that mirrored the *Pushpaka*, the aerial chariot in which Lord Rama, victorious, returned to Ayodhya with Sita at his side. I looked for an Indian-made plane. In Bangalore I found one—by the name of Hanuman.

The southern city of Bangalore is India's computing capital, as well as the centre of its nationalized aviation industry. The company Rajhamsa is one of the success stories of Indian aircraft manufacture, although (or probably because) it has nothing to do with the government. Its founder, Joel Koechler, was born in France.

It wasn't easy to organize a meeting, and when I reached Koechler's office he subjected me to an initial string of caustic parries and thrusts. I sensed that he was the kind of man who did what he wanted to do, and if you got in his way, or he just didn't like you— *adieu*.

On the wall of his office was a framed portrait of J. R. D. Tata. I pointed at it and asked if he knew the great man. A flash of emotion warmed his eyes. "J. R. D. founded Air India, you knew that? Back in the forties, long before it was a nationalized dinosaur. He loved aviation."

Business India had taught me about India's biggest industrial conglomerate—Tata Steel, Tata Trucks, Tata Tea . . . It now, in a fascinating reversal of the colonial traffic, owns the quintessentially British car marques Range Rover and Jaguar. The Tata family were Parsees, or Persians, the community who'd made themselves indispensable to the British Raj and cannily amassed fortunes—none of them greater than that of Tata. The name had a cosy appeal to a Brit: in East London, where I came from, "ta" meant thanks, while "ta-ta" meant bye-bye. In India those two syllables had a different ring, even perhaps atavistically resonating with the primordial Sanskrit word *tatwa*, which means essence or substance. I know this, because I read it in a translation of the *Ramayana*.

After leaving *Business India* in 1985 I'd joined a Bombay magazine calling itself *Gentleman*, an old-fashioned title for a publication that strove to be up to date, imitating the American magazines like *GQ* and *Esquire* that thumped into the office every month, glossily and offensively overweight with ads for Rolexes and Corvettes, male America's version of the Good Life—everything that wasn't available in Bombay. The boss, Minhaz Merchant, decreed a "souvenir issue" of *Gentleman*: The 100 Greatest Indians of All Time. For me, it was an accelerated course on the history and culture of India. That was how I first encountered the life story of J. R. D. Tata.

Koechler had originally come to India back in the seventies and, like so many other young Westerners, fallen in love with the place. A hang-gliding fanatic, he began to explore India from the air. "Imagine the joys of seeing this country from the sky—drifting silently across a village at dusk, looking down at the temple, the children taking their dip in the tank . . . Well, in 1981 I returned to India with the silly idea that I was going to manufacture hang gliders here. Somehow I thought that J. R. D. Tata might understand what I wanted to do and help me. Up I went, with my brother, Gaiten, straight to the office of J. R. D. We were stopped by his secretary— Mrs Hawgood was her name. I gave her a presentation of my project. 'Come back tomorrow,' she said. And the next day, he saw us.

"Tata asked a lot of questions. What I find really interesting, with hindsight, is the way he looked at me as I was talking—straight in the eyes. He wasn't interested in the details of the project, so much as in *me*—trying to gauge the quality of the man. Will this guy be capable of doing what he says? Finally he looks at me and says: 'I'm going to help you.'"

Koechler leant back in his chair and flicked his eyes to the portrait of J. R. D., then looked through the glass partition at the factory floor, where a score of people were at work assembling airframes. "That's one of the things that makes me sad. I'd love him to have known that finally, here we are, exporting 150 Indian-made planes a year. Because of him."

"Was it really all because of him?"

"The next day he handed me a list. 'This is what I can do to help you.' It was a grant—several *lakhs* of rupees—a lot of money! The Tata company got nothing out of it. But J. R. D. had the satisfaction of knowing that he'd provided the seed capital for an indigenous aircraft manufacturer. He wasn't doing it to help himself, he wanted to help something new to take root in India. It was patriotism, if you like. And it saddens me to think that he died before we had much to show.

"But that morning in his office, he picked up the phone and called Mahindras. A few days later I found myself driving back to Pondicherry in my own jeep! I started making hang gliders in Pondi and they developed into microlights. The latest Rajhamsas are traditional planes—the archetypal Cessna-type, with an overhead wing and a cabin underneath. We sell to flying clubs, the military, but it's also the ideal personal small plane. That's the Hanuman."

Koechler walked me around the factory floor. "Thirty in the workforce, all castes; a couple of Muslims, half a dozen Christians. No one has ever quit. Of course, we're labour-intensive, while the Western competition try to keep down labour costs by investing in expensive robots. As soon as there's a recession they collapse. After the Twin Towers, our US sales fell by a third. I simply reduced my subcontracting, and rode it out. I didn't have to fire a single worker."

The following afternoon we drove out to the airport. I sensed that Koechler wasn't a man who welcomed personal observations, but I risked one. I said it was pretty clear to me how much he loved India. "Of course I do. Why else would I stay, and put up with the bureaucracy and corruption? To be honest, struggling against them has destroyed a lot of the pleasure I used to feel in living here."

"I thought bureaucracy and corruption were supposed to be diminishing?"

"*What?* They've got *worse*! Don't ask me why. I'm sure the corruption flows from the bureaucracy. What's more, every instinct of every government servant conspires to prevent general aviation. 'Security' paranoia. So almost all of my planes go to export.

"But the bureaucracy has its funny side. The rules and regulations governing aircraft are dated 1933. I had a factory inspector threatening to close my factory for not having spittoons. I refused, dammit! Told him there isn't any spitting in my factory—any guy who spits in here gets the sack, *instantly*. Try getting an Indian factory inspector to believe that!"

Joel Koechler struck me as a sceptical, pugnacious, driven, visionary man. He leads the life he wants to. He has given India something no other man has done: a major foothold in an important international market. India does not seem especially grateful. But J. R. D. sits in his frame opposite Koechler's desk. *He* approves.

We reached the airport and wheeled the plane out of the hangar. "We've never had a case of structural failure," Koechler told me. "I don't like hypersensitive machines—a Rajhamsa will never be on the verge of instability, you can fly hands off, it's comfortable in turbulence, the flying qualities are superb."

We fired up the engine, taxied, murmured a few words to the control tower and took off. I have a pilot's licence, and Koechler gave me the controls. It was good to be flying again, and the Rajhamsa felt taut and stable. I lifted my eyes from the controls and from scanning the sky for other planes—pilots avoid collisions by using not instruments, but their eyes—and surveyed the countryside around Bangalore. I saw trees, tanks, the vineyards of India's burgeoning wine industry. New suburbs were sprouting all around. The city was a green smudge behind us now.

Joel took control and I surrendered myself to a contemplation of the view. This was what I had dreamed of, a perspective few have enjoyed—to drift over the landscape of India in a small plane, to see from the air this verdant land, to have its endless human bustle condensed into a single vision of harmony. Thus flew Rama, the God who was human enough to have suffered, who like every human had to struggle to master the contradictory forces within him, and who had taken back a wife many of those around him frankly saw as a harlot. But Rama still had to face perhaps his cruellest task. The God and his consort were to become the victims of small-minded prejudice and conformism. For the time being, however, victory was sweet, as were the scents of the flowers that decked the miraculous *Pushpaka*. Cosmic order was restored, the lovers were reunited and the great clouds piled over the plains of central India glittered silver and gold.

CHAPTER 22

India Tomorrow

IN THE MID-twentieth century Americans were a pious, parsimonious, industrious, conservative people, who emerged from the Second World War to seize the reins of global influence from the British Empire and spent the 1950s growing fat. It was a decade of mass consumption and hubris, big refrigerators and bigger cars, a suburban housing boom, Madison Avenue unbound, the triumph of TV.

India is about to have its 1950s.

I reached New Delhi, en route to Ayodhya, on Budget day. The following morning a copy of the *Times of India* was slid under my door at the YWCA. As I turned its pages I reflected on how much the Indian media had changed since the hidebound eighties. The broadsheet *TOI* is not the stern newspaper of record it used to be. Every page of budget coverage had photomontages with Hollywood and Bollywood references (complete with bikini shots), and cartoon "tax facts" downloaded from some US website, featuring pole dancers and strippers. Supplements oozed gossip and cheesecake. The newspaper felt as though it had been produced for adolescent college boys—and perhaps it was. Those boys will be the salary men of the Economic Miracle, and the *TOI* would no doubt like to win their loyalty now.

I had arranged to meet for lunch an old friend who works for the paper. I asked him, "What the hell is going on at the *Times*?"

"Blame the UK papers, *yaar*," he said. "You know how slavishly we imitate them."

"But a few years ago you were better than most UK broadsheets," I said, "especially in foreign coverage . . ."

A decade earlier, it seemed to me that the Indian press had made a great leap forward from the poorly printed and dull pages I had first encountered. As India squared up to its new potential as a global player, there was an eager curiosity about the greater world. But while economic development gave India new self-confidence, there was also a new fascination with mass media and mass consumption. Growing domestic markets drove an explosion in advertising, and consumer magazines proliferated. Like America, where radio and television were always primarily advertising media (in contrast to the UK's public service model), India experienced the creation of an ad-driven TV landscape. There were TV news shows with presenters chosen principally for their looks, and a diet of shallow domestic politics, sport, soap operas and gossip, with less and less news of the greater world beyond. Many newspapers, outflanked on two fronts, lurched downmarket. India jumped from the sensibility of Jane Austen to Jerry Springer in a single generation.

"Yes," my friend said, "we followed the British papers—then we just kept going. They're terrified of losing out to competition, or TV—so they just keep driving our standards down. More pix, more tits, more trivia."

By "they", he meant his bosses, Samir and Vineet Jain, the *TOI* media barons who could give Rupert Murdoch lessons in how to turn a newspaper into a cash cow. Their *Bombay Times* supplement has allowed advertisers to buy *editorial* space—to write the paper's stories themselves. To anyone raised on the liberal notion that newspapers have a duty to the truth, this is breathtaking.

"And where we go, everybody else follows," my friend went on. "If the market leader fills its pages with cleavages and crap, the other proprietors have to imitate us. These poor old guys are dropping their standards because the *Times* has. Personally, I think the *Indian Express* is a better paper than us now, but we're remorselessly forcing it downmarket. Don't ask me where it will all end . . ."

It will end, in all likelihood, with India imitating the West once more, and a slew of downmarket, rabble-rousing tabloids.

That evening I saw the Finance Minister interviewed on a febrile TV channel that kept interrupting the programme for interminable ad breaks. P. Chidambaram was dressed (as the Indian political classes still tend to be) in open-toed sandals and Gandhian white. He was cool and self-contained, though occasionally his eyebrow arced in wry amusement. He was the very image of a stoic philosopher stooping to engage with Grub Street.

The *Times*'s budget coverage had included a short piece by a journalist called Manu Joseph, entitled "Chidambaram's Mysterious Adviser". The article referred to the Finance Minister's habit of sneaking into his budget speeches references to the great Tamil poet Thiruvalluvar, supposed to have lived about a millennium ago, who produced a collection of aphorisms on ethics, love and the facts of life.

> The FM's fondness for Thiruvalluvar [wrote Joseph] is used by observers to explain his famous austerity, sometimes wrongly and perilously interpreted as simplicity. However, there is a distinction between Chidambaram's austerity and Thiruvalluvar's. The poet was poor . . . Chidambaram's austerity is an endearing parsimony that was till recently common among affluent forward caste Tamilians . . .
>
> Chidambaram's ancestral home . . . [is an ancient mansion] with clean chessboard floors, narrow corridors, sunbathed courtyards and carved wooden pillars . . . [He] has built a new wing for himself where servants are barred from going . . . [It has] the impoverishment of a hostel—pale walls, metal folding chairs and an unremarkable attached toilet that will offend your wife. But Thiruvalluvar would have understood all this. No man has ever attained enlightenment while sitting on glazed marble.

The article made a telling point. How could the Finance Minister who presided over an orgy of consumerism be privately aloof and spiritual? But such an attitude, a fundamentally Hindu sensibility, was common among Indian public figures until recently—in fact, almost de rigueur. Now it makes a weird contrast with the images of conspicuous consumption that ooze from the mainstream Indian media.

Twenty-five years ago the Indian press and advertising could be laughably earnest and literal-minded, and slavishly imitative of the West. Today the imitation is superficially less obvious, as glossier paper and computer graphics have arrived. But the shared language,

English, makes it all too easy for Indian journalists to cut and paste, and foreign material is still lifted wholesale, with no regard for how it will be received in an Indian context. Foreign aesthetic, political and cultural attitudes are also widely taken as read—because it is cheaper to reproduce them than to commission an Indian film critic or correspondent or foreign affairs analyst to write. Delhi's newly launched *Time Out* magazine is so full of borrowed copy that it cannot credibly claim to offer an Indian perspective on the arts. Many other publications lean heavily on Western source material. Publishers save money and writers feel cosmopolitan—but it can make Indians into uncritical mouthpieces of foreign attitudes. India urgently needs to find its own voice; instead, a line dictated from London and the US is heard across the land.

Arguably it's acceptable for raw news to be taken directly from international wire services or English newspapers—but even that argument bears examining. The Middle East has seen the establishment of news channels and websites like Al Jazeerah, because Arabs recognized that news values express underlying *cultural* values. They wanted a voice that was not by default pro-American. Take away the oil, and the Muslim world is economically decades behind India— but it may put up a harder fight to preserve its cultural distinctness than India.

Recently a low-brow tabloid called the *Mail Today* was launched, produced in collaboration with the UK's most successful newspaper, the *Daily Mail*. Given the British paper's xenophobia and former flirtation with fascism, the arrival of such a publication should be a warning shot to the Indian media. The clone *Mail* has been launched by *India Today*, the country's leading news magazine. With its sales threatened by competition from TV, *India Today* has struggled somewhat, and has become a cheerleader for Indian capitalism. In March 2008 it published an issue on India's most influential people, with the unironic title, "High & Mighty". The businessman Aroon Purie, who runs the magazine, began his editorial, "In his classic novel *1984*, George Orwell wrote about 'the intoxication of power, constantly increasing and constantly growing subtler'." The quote from an anti-establishment thinker, the posture of intellectual independence, is typical; the magazine went on to demonstrate its own unsubtle intoxication with power—forty editorial pages venerating the rich, fetishistically photographed with their cuff-links and Rolexes. The *Times of India*'s proprietors, the Jains, were described as "heroes", ". . . because though the lines between news and commerce are blurring in their newspapers, readers don't seem to have realized it."

The most striking thing about the issue—in an Indian context— was the absence from a list filled by industrialists and politicians, actors and cricketers, of a single Hindu figure (with the exception of a yoga teacher who has become a TV star). India has been powerfully influenced by great figures who combined the deepest insights into Hindu civilization with a clear-minded grasp of Western civilization —Vivekananda, Gandhi, Radhakrishnan, Sri Aurobindo. They towered morally over their Western counterparts—indeed, it's hard to think of their equivalents in Western public life. Have such figures disappeared from the Indian scene? Or do they still exist, ignored by the Rolex-worshipping *Nawabs* of the English-language media?

What the last decade or so *has* seen is the rise of the TV guru and a renewed, populist Hinduism—much to the fury of the sociologists who predicted that, under the benign influence of capitalism, religion would have been on its last legs by now. Surveys suggest that religious practice, especially in India's fast-growing cities, is *increasing*. The queues at certain popular shrines are growing longer. Hindu ritual is ostentatiously practised by film stars and millionaires.

Various explanations have been proposed for this improbable upsurge of popular Hinduism. Some attribute it to the insecurity of the growing urban populations—religious practice is generally higher among lower socio-economic groups. Others see it as a reaction against modernity, driven by a fear that the West is undermining India's eternal values. Against those arguments is the fact that India's new urban classes are actually experiencing *less* financial insecurity, and are doing so well by *exploiting* the Western economic model. Some observers offer a third explanation: that the urban masses are ambivalent or even guilty about their new wealth, and are therefore turning to figures who reassure them that it's *all right*. Tele-gurus and *swamis*-to-the-rich assure their followers that "Hindu values" embrace consumerism—as long as it goes *in parallel with religious practices*. So buy that car—but don't forget a fat and grateful donation to the Gods, via your local temple. It's hardly a new phenomenon—

the line that religion and worldly success go hand in hand has been successfully peddled by American televangelists and management gurus for years.

Many secularist writers, for whom religion is a bad thing per se— number three on the hate list, after imperialism and patriarchy—see in this populist Hinduism an aggressive chauvinism that seeks to target India's religious minorities. Certainly, political Hinduism has often shown an ugly nationalist face. Some writers perceive a mass ideology with the potential to go very wrong indeed—like Nazism —and it's not impossible that present trends could lead to some nationwide episode of "ethnic cleansing". Most rational Indians now desire more strongly than ever to keep religious bigots out of power.

My friends in the Indian press, card-carrying secular liberals all, know whom to blame for all this—they often complain about the "fascist" BJP. But I believe it would be wrong to ignore the extent to which a perceived readiness of the Congress Party and India's élites to dismiss the culture of hundreds of millions of Hindus helped stimulate the growth of populist Hinduism. Was the Ayodhya controversy in part anger at an imported Western culture that for several hundred years had undermined indigenous civilization, and whose secularism was seen as favouring Islam? The Western-dominated English-language media are much resented by the huge vernacular-language press across India. But their power is immense. The country's best schools are Anglophone and run by Christians. The Indian constitution, courts and media are all British in form. The rationalist, often Marxist, thinkers who have dominated much of Indian intellectual life have worked hard to undermine Hinduism as a public force. Their belief that they could marginalize Hinduism in a couple of generations strikes me as naive, arrogant and intolerant. In Iran, the Shah's imposed Westernization brought about Khomeini's Islamic Revolution. A similar backlash is occurring in Turkey—a successful capitalist economy—even now. Those secularists who wish Hinduism dead may be encouraging the growth of something rather more sinister.

No sensible person would suggest that India should abandon democratic statehood for theocracy or ecclesiocracy, along the lines of a Saudi Arabia or Iran. But many Indians desire a way forward that does not reject their country's Hindu traditions. In some ways a land with a history of civilization that would be the envy of most European countries, is expanding economically, but contracting spiritually and intellectually. Much of the English-speaking élite is implacably opposed to the country's ancient culture, which is largely represented by demagogic politicians. For the battle lines to be drawn between intransigent anti-religionists and aggressive Hindu chauvinists can only be bad news for India.

In *The Foundations of Indian Culture* (1950), Sri Aurobindo asked, "Will the spiritual motive which India represents prevail on Europe and create there new forms congenial to the West, or will European rationalism and commercialism put an end for ever to the Indian type of culture?" The question is still unanswered. In one sense those Protestant commercial travellers of the British Empire have won the day—headlong capitalism goes hand in hand with a kind of US-style Hindu evangelicalism. But will the lofty ideals of Hindu spirituality, that so recently inspired great political leaders, exert any influence over the India of the twenty-first century?

CHAPTER 23

Ras

HOWRAH RAILWAY STATION, Old Delhi. The man opposite me in the compartment, a rep with a pharmaceutical firm, was leaning Nero-like along the bench. When a third man came in and went to sit beside him, he folded himself with a slight frown of displeasure. I was surprised: where was his respect for the cloth? The newcomer, bald and bespectacled, wore the orange robe of the *sanyassin*, the renunciate. He looked as though he might be in his mid or late sixties. He settled himself with a smile on the seat opposite mine, his back straight, palms on his knees. There was about his eyes and mouth a kind of spaniel softness, as though they'd spent so many years smiling that the muscles had forgotten how to frown. Large glasses magnified his eyes, increasing the open, unblinking effect. Politely, he asked us each where we were going. I replied "Ayodhya" and he asked, in a schoolmasterish tone that belied his apparent mildness, "Why?"

I was on the spot. So I told him: I was at the end of an exploration of the *Ramayana*, but I felt I still had to discover something of the living spirit of the tale. So—I was headed back to Ayodhya.

Several collections of scholarly writing on the *Ramayana* have been published in recent years. In one, the American scholar Philip Lutgendorf wrote of the esoteric Ayodhyan tradition of *rasik*, the pursuit of divine bliss. The *rasik* tradition is more generally associated with the worship of Krishna, but in Rama-centric Ayodhya it has also survived for hundreds of years. The practice can involve devotees of Lord Rama spending their days and nights in a state of ecstasy, envisioning themselves as courtiers of Rama and Sita, ministering to their every need, playing a role in the holy couple's intimate lives. It might involve a total surrender to Rama, and an outpouring of love towards a figure who has been transformed from Valmiki's *dharmic* warrior into an incarnation of the Supreme Being. Direct comparisons with other traditions are impossible, but one could recall those mediæval Christian cults that adored the Virgin, or the nuns who so passionately surrendered themselves to Christ.

Researching this book, I had been in contact with Lutgendorf, and found him a relaxed and generous man. But on this matter he was unable to help. His research had been done many years earlier, he said, and those who had assisted him were dead. He wished me luck.

"This *rasik* devotion interests you?" the *sanyassin* asked sharply.

"Yes."

"Why should it?"

In truth, I was attracted to the ecstatic surrender to Rama, fed by the adoring verse of Tulsidas—although at the same time I knew I could never share it. A product of a rational, literalistic culture, I could only envy them their surrender, their spiritual bliss.

Measuring my words, I said, "I want to understand—this intense love the devotees have for Rama."

The pharmaceutical rep looked profoundly unimpressed by the turn the conversation had taken. The *swami* was regarding me severely. He said, "You think you *can* understand?"

"I believe so."

"You feel this love?"

"I can't claim to be a devotee . . ."

He frowned thoughtfully.

"*Is* the tradition still alive?" I asked him. "Do you know such people?"

"I do," he replied.

I hesitated. "Do you think I might be able to meet any of them?"

The conductor interrupted us. Glancing at our tickets, he sternly told the *swami* that he was in the wrong carriage—his ticket was second class, *non*-AC, *non*-sleeper. The *swami*'s face became serene. Couldn't the conductor do something—?

No, was the reply—and he'd better move fast, because the train was leaving in five minutes and he'd be lucky even to find a seat. A look of alarm crossed the *swami*'s face. He took up his little orange bag and bustled out of the door.

"These *swami* types," sneered the rep, "they try . . . where are you going?"

"To help him find a seat," I said.

I looked up and down the platform, but couldn't see the orange robe of the *sanyassin*. A gaggle of people without reservations were petitioning the conductor for last-minute cancellations. I tried to attract his attention, but failed. Whistles blew and I clambered back aboard. The rep gave me a vindicated smirk.

IT WAS THE first time I'd travelled to Ayodhya by train. I didn't see the *swami* again; our air-conditioned compartments were hermetically sealed off from the lower orders, and the train spent the night ploughing its way east across the Gangetic Plain and the morning crawling through the sun-baked fields of Uttar Pradesh, west of Ayodhya. We finally reached the town at 11 a.m., four hours late. As the train pulled into the station, I had my backpack on, ready to go. I dropped onto the platform before the train stopped moving and scanned up and down for a flash of saffron—in vain. People detrained, coolies and boarding passengers surged forward, and anyway, most of the long train was invisible behind obstructing pillars and tea stalls. I made my way as rapidly as I could down the platform, jostled by the crowds, then fought my way back towards my compartment. The train began to move off.

So that was that. My chance of an entrée into the esoteric world of Rama *bhakti*, in the company of an articulate English-speaking guide, was gone. I sighed. I'd have to search elsewhere.

The last carriage rumbled by. Exactly opposite me, sitting impassively on a bench by the Platform 1 exit, I spotted an orange robe and bald head. The *swami* raised the flat of a palm in greeting.

I ran across the footbridge and gabbled my thanks. "You waited for me!"

"Of course. We need to take a cycle."

We emerged into the small square in front of the station, where the *swami* began to negotiate with a cycle-rickshaw *wallah* (there are no autorickshaws or taxis in hard-up Ayodhya). The emaciated driver applied his weight to the pedals, his calves bulged; the heavy machine trundled forward over broken tarmac.

"How was your journey?" I asked the *swami*.

"So-so. It is difficult to sleep, no? On a wooden seat. I have no complaints. The ticket was a gift. I have no money, I cannot buy tickets, I accept what I am given. So: what is your good name?"

His own name, he told me, was Ajasranand. "It means Perpetual Bliss. Because I am free!" He gave a warm, complacent smile. "I practise self-acquired poverty! No encumbrances! No obstacles! That is bliss!"

Reaching the old town, our rickshaw *wallah* halted before a large gateway, one of Ayodhya's scores of temple complexes. We removed our shoes and followed gloomy, cool corridors, to the room of the Head Priest, where we squatted on the carpet and waited. After a few minutes he arrived, a man in his late fifties with a round face and a long white beard. Ajasranand explained my presence and the Head Priest beamed cherubically. I was welcome to stay as long as I wished, he said.

An acolyte of the ashram appeared to lead us to our room. He wore a long *kurta* over a neatly folded *dhoti* and walked, barefoot, with a natural, fluid elegance. We passed a hall containing a shrine to Rama and Sita, a vast communal kitchen where enticing smells rose from the largest steel vats I'd ever seen, and thirty or forty pilgrims' rooms. At last, at the rear of the building, overlooking the River Sarayu, a mosquito screen was opened and a double door unpadlocked. The room had not been inhabited for some time and was full of dust. A boy was summoned to clean it—not a cleaner as such, but another acolyte, a boy of about sixteen, who showed little enthusiasm for the task. His name was Sukharam Das. The *swami* stood over him sternly, giving instructions to move beds and dust shelves. I helped. Many buckets of water were thrown down and much swabbing and ineffectual sweeping of the tiled floors with a grass switch went on. At last the boy withdrew and we took showers in the little adjoining bathroom, then sank back onto our respective beds.

The double doors banged open again and several more boys of Sukharam's age rushed in, laughing delightedly, and piled all over the *swami*. Affectionately he ruffled their hair or grabbed them as though to give them a thump.

He turned to me happily. "I give them tuitions in Sanskrit."

"Judging from the reception, I'd say your classes must be the high point of the year."

The heat was stifling now and if I was starting to feel tired then so must the *swami*—he had spent the night upright on a wooden bench. I dropped off, to the sounds of the boys' voices. When I woke they were still talking, the boys with their eager, sweet faces sitting at Ajasranand's feet. Then the doors flew open again and Sukharam Das arrived, bearing food.

Ajasranand dismissed his audience and pulled a small wooden bowl from his saffron bundle. He filled it with a little rice, *dahl* and curry. "I will eat what fills this pot only!" he said. Our cleaner-turned-waiter offered lemon chutney. "I will not—but *you* must!" he ordered me. My food was served in a steel tray. Dessert was plain curd (yoghurt), which tasted satisfyingly earthy from the unfired clay pots it was made and served in.

The heat was torpid and there was no electricity, therefore no fan. We washed our hands, sank back onto our beds and slipped gratefully into sleep.

IT WAS TIME for the evening *aarthi*. The hall housing the shrine was a simple space, the pillars plainly tiled in white and pink and blue. There were ranks of *sadhus*, grizzled characters with roughened feet and missing teeth who had spent their lives wandering between holy sites and ashrams—lives of poverty. Other saffron-clad figures were, I gathered, permanent residents of this establishment, ranging from the Head Priest to young adherents in their teens. Towards the middle of the hall there were twenty or thirty visitors, including several families, whose evident prosperity set them apart from the forty or fifty locals who filled the last third of the hall.

The ceremony was conventional, much as at *Kanak Bhavan*. As the devotees faced the Gods and chanted, Ajasranand leaned towards me and spoke under his breath. "We understand that a living personality of the deity is in the stone, you understand that?"

"I believe so."

"So we offer Him these garlands, sweets . . . Rama is alive, so naturally he will be given a bath in the early hours, then fresh clothes. In morning he gives *darshan* to his devotees. Then, breakfast—we offer some fruits, milk, butter . . . After taking more food at twelve, He will rest . . . So, the day proceeds. At this time, evening *darshan*. Then, He will eat again . . ."

It is ironic that this veneration of the God as a *King*, splendidly attired, installed on a throne, giving his subjects an audience (*darshan*), derives much of its imagery from the court etiquette of the Mughal emperors. A question occurred to me. "Do the clothes vary from season to season?"

"Naturally—He will be given wool in winter, our emotion is that in cold weather he must be warm! And at night, when he sleeps, he will be covered with a blanket."

"I see."

"This is not an idol! This is the Lord! And Sita is *shakti*, the source of all energy. In fact, the deity here is Sita-Ram—'Sitaram'. This is important to understand. Rama cannot live without Sita, Sita could never be without Rama. They are two in one, a single identity."

Following the *aarthi*, most of the worshippers made three circumnavigations of the Gods, via the corridor that ran behind and to the sides of the shrine. As they passed a mural painting of Rama, they touched the space where His feet had once been, but where decades of veneration had resulted in a bare patch of wall. After we returned to our room, Ajasranand continued his explanation. "Why do we worship idols? For their beauty. This is a *spiritual* beauty, of course. It is like this: Rama, after seeing, after touching, after hearing the words of Sita, feels great joy. This is the *ras*, the sweetness, that the *rasik* pursues. It is the same sweetness that you or I feel when we see some lovely child, the innocence, the simplicity—there is something deeply moving in this, no? It stirs one in a profound way, it is a very pure emotion. We feel the same type of pleasure when we read certain words, or we see these Gods or a disciple of God, a truly pious person, like the *guru-ji* of this temple. It's a special sensation that can't be verbalized—it is *beyond words*. And when you are in this condition beyond speech, sometimes something else will be felt . . . Tears will come. Sometimes a tingling will be felt at the base of the spine. In the heart, a sort of surge, a sensation of expansion . . .

"This is the *science* of Hinduism. What do I mean by that? For millennia we have intensely studied these phenomena. They have been analysed, classified, tested, validated by generations of *sadhus*. They have taught us the worthlessness of simple animal existence and the vanity of so much intellectual activity. They have taught us that human beings are selfish and cruel! They had understood the mysteries of human types, of the mind, of the *psyche*, long before the Western world invented 'psychology'. Will a man with no moral education be kind to his fellow, or care about the life of the creature that gave him the milk in his tea or the leather of his shoe? Will sex or the possession of ten houses prepare us for death? Hindus are taught these things: to live ethically, with respect for life; and when the time comes to set aside the cares of life and enter this path that has been prepared for us. To meet the infinity that lies beyond this world of physical phenomena . . ."

He paused, and made a gesture with his hand that indicated that he'd completed what it was he wanted to say and wanted no more questions. But then he turned to me with a final thought. He held up an index finger and pointed at his chest.

"To the extent that you go *deep*, to get to that infinite thing which cannot be defined by categories and words . . . You go not outside into the world, but deeper and deeper inside yourself . . . To the extent that you are able to do that, you will experience that infinity."

An hour later Ajasranand led me into a different room on the first floor, where more than a hundred people were seated on mats. I left my sandals at the door and joined the back row, while he went forward and sat beside the Head Priest and the guru—the founder and *raison d'être* of the ashram. I could not see him very well. Evidently he was a man in his eighties, very frail, dressed only in a simple white cloth. But when he smiled, it was like the appearance of the sun from behind a cloud. An overwhelming force of energy and love seemed to emanate from him.

There was rhythmic chanting and singing, the repetition of *Sitaram, Sitaram, Sitaram—Jai Sitaram* . . .[6] The phrase was sung by a solo singer, then picked up by the whole assembly. Each time it was

---

[6] *Jai*: "Praise be to", or, literally, "Victory to".

repeated there were subtle melodic variations. The effect was—if you surrendered to it—hypnotic.

After forty minutes or so, several visitors to the ashram walked forward and prostrated themselves before the guru. Questions were muttered, blessings were given, a donation to temple funds was made—collected by the Head Priest, who sat at the guru's right hand. And the *darshan* was over.

THE FOLLOWING MORNING Ajasranand woke me soon after dawn. (His technique—a rough shove and the words, "Get up!"—left something to be desired.) It was time for us to take our bath in the Sarayu. Accompanied by Sukharam Das, we walked towards the river bank, pausing when I begged Ajasranand to allow me to have a cup of tea at one of the bus station tea stalls. We heard drums behind us. "Somebody has expired, they are going to see off," said Ajasranand. Six men passed us, dressed only in *dhotis* and turbans. They carried on their shoulders a body wrapped in a saffron cloth, bearing it towards the "burning *ghats*" downriver.

In the presence of death, Ayodhya was, like me, slowly coming to life. The river was opaline in the early light. Sukharam Das grinned. "Ram-*ji* also took his bath in this river!" He strutted jauntily into the shallows, bending to fill a bottle with holy water. With his thin legs and the white wool shawl round his shoulders he resembled a heron.

The *swami* and I sat on the still cool stone of the ghats. As the sun rose rose-pink, he told me the story of his life. He had been a high court lawyer in Ahmedabad, in Gujarat. He was the father of four boys. When his wife had died twenty-four years earlier, he had devoted himself to raising his sons. But when he retired, he lost no time in pursuing this dream: to leave it all behind him, to take *sanyass*—to become a renunciate. He grinned. "And now I am free, to follow the spiritual path! No hindrances, no speed bumps! Perpetual bliss! My children have all done well. They are established, they have successful careers, families—I have six grandsons and two granddaughters. And now my commitment to them is over."

"Don't you miss them?"

He frowned, giving the impression that family life with its million mundane decisions meant nothing to him. "I have fulfilled my responsibilities. Now I have committed myself to something more important."

"But they must miss *you*."

"Oh yes. My children wept when I left. *You made so many sacrifices for us, now, we're grown-up, we want to serve you—and you're going away!*"

I was startled by his readiness to slough off family life. I asked the obvious sentimental question. "You must miss your grandchildren?"

"They can see me from time to time."

Ajasranand now divided up his year. Half of it he spent at an ashram in deepest Gujurat. "It's a one hundred per cent remote place, there is no road, only a track, forest. So many times I have faced lion, bears, but we know the tricks. We are good at climbing trees! Or with a bear, you light a match and it will run! But that is a place of absolute peace. There, I meditate, I study."

But for half the year he came back into the world ("if people invite me; they have to send me a ticket—I have no money of my own"). He saw his family, then spent several months in the homes of other families where his role was that of a guru, a living exemplar of the principles of Hinduism (it's common for Hindu families to have such a figure in their lives). He also visited this ashram once a year, because of his regard for the guru. "He is a very holy person."

THE ROUTINE OF the ashram was, for a place of retreat, unremitting—but after all, *idle hands make work for the Devil*. Ajasranand began to be impatient with Sukharam Das. "Always sleeping! He is lazy, he is supposed to be looking after us, but what does he do? He never sweeps, never tidies, the pans are unwashed, and all he does is *sleep*! He should *work*!" Sukharam Das would pout and give a rueful smile. Privately, I wondered if this slender, pretty, rather dreamy boy was suited for a life of devotion. Was *anyone*, at his age? I'd noticed that his mobile phone seemed to attract him as much as his Sanskrit copybooks—hardly unnatural in a boy of his age. Another of the acolytes was a more rugged young man by the name of Deepnarayan Mishra. He affected no false respect towards me and was challenging, even cheeky, in a way none of the ashram elders would have let him get away with. All the younger monks shared a spontaneity, an absolute absence of cynicism, that would be almost unimaginable in the West. The ashram appeared to be a place of much innocence and goodness. It practised a regime of rigid vegetarianism and utter respect for all forms of life—the guru had famously chastised a monk for killing a snake that had entered the ashram in winter for warmth. They had their own farm, where thirty or so fat, happy cows were spoiled like pets (and, it goes without saying, not slaughtered at three years, like Western cattle, when their milk yield diminished—these cows would die of old age). But the two boys I saw in their Sanskrit classes daily were at stages in their lives when it's natural to look out into the world. Was it enough—as Ajasranand had said of one of the young monks—that his impoverished parents, unable to afford to raise him themselves, had offered him "to the lotus feet of the guru"? On the other hand, for any young Alyosha or Blake—the spiritual seeker, the mystic oddball—here was a place, one of thousands in India, to plunge into the transcendental realm.

Ajasranand had taken me under his wing. My welcome and freedom of access were due entirely to him. I was grateful and I understood that he had to be responsible for my behaviour. I received several abrupt admonishments when I failed to acknowledge a senior with sufficient reverence, or forgot to remove my shoes. I told him that I planned to visit my friend, the translator Ajai Kumar, and was bemused when he announced that he would accompany me. I needed no chaperone; but I had sung Ajai Kumar's praises, so it was perhaps natural that Ajasranand should want to meet him. The guru tradition, so deeply entrenched in the Hindu psyche, would insist that the disciple should do nothing without asking the guru's opinion and permission. I had put myself into Ajasranand's hands in Ayodhya, and I should accept his judgements.

The only practical time for a visit was late morning, and it was hot when we climbed up to *Kanak Bhavan*. Seeing Ajai Kumar again was a pleasure—and he had extraordinary news. In the eighteen months since I last saw him he had forged a deal with an Indian publisher. His earlier two books, plus a third, were already in print. He showed us the hard-bound volumes. Three more were in preparation. With daily, meticulous devotion, Ajai Kumar was bringing into English landmarks of the long history of the Rama tradition in India. It was a remarkable achievement. And Ajai saw his work as, literally, devotion: "I realize now that My Lord has set me this task as a way to glorify Him. Previously I devoted myself so assiduously to caring for His garments. Then I realized that anyone can fulfil such a task! But in this age of the dominance of English—even among young Indians—there is a need for these holy books to be translated. How many people have the skills, the time, the motivation, to bring the gospels of Rama into English?"

We stayed in Ajai Kumar's office for only forty-five minutes. Ajasranand dominated the conversation, then insisted that we start back for lunch. As we left, he complained to me that Ajai Kumar had offered him water, then forgotten to bring it. "He was too caught up in the flow of his publishing!"

I smiled. "Oh, but he was excited, and I hadn't seen him for eighteen months!"

"Your friend has a publishing compulsion!" Ajasranand insisted. "I have also gone through this phase a few years ago. You know, when a person of intellect is isolated . . . the spiritual urge can be channelled, diverted, into other activities. Then it is possible to become so consumed that the original spiritual thirst is forgotten."

I had to accept that he was, to some extent, right about that— indeed, Ajai had admitted as much to me. On the other hand, Ajai Kumar's achievement seemed to me heroic, even saintly.

I HAVE BEEN putting off recounting the end of Valmiki's *Ramayana*. Tulsidas found it so upsetting that he dropped it altogether. If the *Ramayana* had been written by Shakespeare, it would be known as "The Tragedy of King Rama".

Rama and Sita returned to Ayodhya, and were received in pomp and with genuine joy by faithful Bharat and the people of the city. Rama was crowned and, for a while, they lived happily as King and Queen. But the populace began to gossip. Sita became the victim of a steady stream of innuendo, like a modern celebrity trapped by the tabloids' endless appetite for sensation. It is believed that this last chapter is not part of the original epic; once upon a time it ended happily. But perhaps the story's first audiences were unable to believe that Sita had remained faithful, chaste; some academics have asserted that the story's final contortions were the result, as it slowly evolved into a *religious* text, of the *Brahmans'* deep discomfort with fundamental aspects of the story. (How would the Church have explained away a Biblical subplot about Mary's kidnapping by a notorious sensualist and rapist?) In any event a last chapter came to be written, dealing with—imposing a metaphysical framework upon—the aftermath of Sita's abduction. As Ayodhyans began to believe that she must have lived willingly with Ravan as a concubine, her position as Queen became untenable. With infinite reluctance Rama called Hanuman and instructed him to take Sita to live at the ashram of Valmiki. Finally, however, shattered by the whispering and malice that had made her life impossible, Sita called for the earth to open up and receive her. We have to remember that her name means "furrow", and that she had been found by her father as he ploughed the earth. In the end, Sita returned to the earth out of which she was born.

Near Allahabad I had visited in the company of Dhirendra a shrine (one of several) where this event is believed to have occurred. It was one of the most picturesque pilgrimage sites I had visited, a white marble temple built on a bend in a river, surrounded by mudflats with a few beached rowing skiffs, weeping willows and, beyond them, pasture land. Inside the temple there was a statue of Sita. On a bas-relief in the background Hanuman was shown, in an agony of doubt, obeying Rama's orders not to intervene. Yet Rama himself was raising his hand, as though to try to stop Sita. But this time it was too late.

Rama lived on for many years, ruling ably and irreproachably over the kingdom whose people had subjected him and his wife, after the long trauma of their separation and warfare, to a life of misery. He did not complain. He believed that the *dharma* of a king condemned him to the service of his people. When it came to the moment that he decided was the end of his life, he waded into the holy River Sarayu at Ayodhya and was never seen by human eyes again.

IN SO FAR AS RAMA was worshipped in the ashram, Sita was equally the centre of devotion. I couldn't have chosen a better time to visit: it was Her birthday, a red-letter day in the calendar of the ashram. The cooks had been at work preparing special dishes, the hall was decked with streamers like a Western home at Christmas, the Gods were utterly resplendent in the finest jewellery and silks. That evening there was to be a special event, a play put on by and for those who worshipped at the ashram.

A dais had been set up to one side of the prayer hall. A small boy dressed as Sita appeared with her parents and sisters—all were played by boys and men. They were opulently attired in silks, crowns and jewellery, with rings in their noses and their foreheads gleaming orange with sandal paste. The play was a kind of humorous parable about transitions from childhood to adulthood. Sita was told by her mother that her favourite doll was now mature and must be married off. Sita whispered to her doll, "You're my *favourite*—don't worry, darling, I'll *never* let you go." After parental pressure, she finally agreed to allow her doll to be married—but not to leave home. There was a marriage procession, during which Sita's mother danced wildly and even provocatively. Priests performed the wedding rituals, the dolls went through a miniature Hindu wedding ceremony and we, the audience, were the wedding guests.

The cast was well rehearsed, the props were lavish and the witty script drew belly laughs from the audience. I was seated just four or five people away from where the old guru leant sideways on a cushion and I had a chance to observe him. He was very slight and frail. I saw him laughing spontaneously, and at another moment wiping tears from his eyes. During a short interval he spoke to no one, but simply stared blissfully at the idols in the shrine opposite him.

In Act II, after the wedding, Sita's refusal to allow her married doll to move to the home of her in-laws provoked a new incident. Friends and family pleaded, but Sita reminded them of her precondition. At last, for the sake of honour, she agreed to let her doll leave—but only after three more years. The compromise satisfied everyone, honour and peace were preserved.

After the final curtain the festivities began. The *guru-ji* was brought great bowls of coins, sweets, dried dates and *betel*, which with the help of his nimbler assistants were thrown all over the room, devotees diving wildly to catch them. Clouds of perfume were dispensed from an antique chromium-plated syringe. Then people began, as the spirit moved them, to leap to their feet and dance. Immediately next to me a grizzled old man with a white beard jumped up. He wore a gold-flecked chiffon scarf round his head and a woman's bells on his ankles, and danced with abandon, imagining himself—I supposed—to be Sita. He was not the only man in female attire in the audience. Exuberant faces called me to my feet. More to be polite than anything, I jumped up—and found that I had a mysterious spring in my step. I danced as wildly as anyone.

THE FOLLOWING AFTERNOON, I managed to spend a couple of hours with Ajai Kumar. He was sitting in his office at *Kanak Bhavan*, reading the *Times of India*. He looked at me ruefully. "I am not a sincere hermit—I cannot forgo my daily ritual of a newspaper and a cup of tea. It keeps me in touch with the world, too. Sadly, this is the only English-language newspaper available in this little town of ours."

"What about the daily ritual of a meal or two?" I asked. He had become worryingly thin—above the collar of his singlet, his chest bone was a sculpted line against his skin. And he had lost a tooth since I saw him last.

He laughed. "As long as I am doing God's work, He will protect me."

"That is glib, Ajai! You can't do God's work if you don't eat!"

"My dear friend, do not worry about me, I eat enough!"

I told him about the previous evening's festivities. "When we first met, you told me you didn't approve of the *rasiks*," I said.

"Well, even *Kanak Bhavan* is *rasik* in tone—we aren't monks, but the prayers and so on come from the point of view of devotion, of *love*. *Ras* means juice, or something succulent, it describes a kind of blissful state. What I don't personally agree with the *rasiks* about is personification—I don't want to *make Rama into someone*. The *Vedas* don't deal with Sita and this idea of the two complementary halves of the deity, Sita-Ram—but the devotees *do*, and like the tradition of Radha and Krishna, it is long-established. I am more *Vedantic*; I survive spiritually without needing the help of the female aspect of creation."

"How exactly *do* the *rasiks* view Rama?"

"A lady will treat Rama as a lover, and the male too."

"I don't understand."

"A female devotee will worship Rama as a lover and will envision herself being loved by him. Of course, Hindu society does not sanction a woman being loved by any man other than her husband. So, many accommodations have evolved. Males will treat Rama as a wife, almost, or a male devotee may perhaps envision himself as a female attendant of Rama . . . The idea of a male devotee envisioning union with Rama is, of course, unacceptable. Therefore, the reasoning goes, let the male devotee become a female! But to dance dressed in a sari, imagining yourself to be a lover of Rama, seems very absurd to me. It is controversial, of course—and it is discreet. Naturally, many people protest that the deity should be a Lord, not a *lover*. Some have said that it is sanctifying homosexuality, giving it a religious authority. Others say that ecstasy is of course *sublimated*, making questions of any kind of sex irrelevant."

"But you do consider the *rasik* practices a legitimate form of spirituality?"

"Well, without especial enthusiasm, yes, of course, I would acknowledge that."

I grinned at him. "Damned by faint praise?"

"My dear sir, I am a worshipper, not a theologian."

"A worshipper who has immersed himself in Ayodhya for eighteen years."

"Who has kept himself aloof from the thousands of cults and saints and sinners in this city, and immersed himself only in *Rama* for eighteen years!"

"I stand corrected."

After a moment or two, he ventured, "But your *guru-ji* . . ."

"The guru where I am staying?"

"Yes. I have heard good reports of him."

"He seems to me a deeply spiritual person," I said. "Tell me, why would he wear white, not saffron . . .?"

"White means widow or widower. It means that the material, gross world is dead to the devotee. *I am married only to you, Rama, or Sita.*"

I CANNOT REMEMBER exactly when it was that, during *aarthi*, I suddenly caught sight of the God's face and was struck by its childlike beauty—and I felt a welling of affection in my heart. The same thing had happened during my first visit to *Kanak Bhavan*. Was I too falling under the spell of Rama?

IN THE LATE AFTERNOON on the banks of the River Tamasa two men were walking, the poet-priest Valmiki and a disciple. They had nowhere particular to go; they were simply enjoying the play of light on the leaves and the birdsong. Somewhere in the branches above their heads two cranes were mating and Valmiki stopped to listen to their song. He was a priest, but married, a father, a man who knew life's sensual pleasures. It seemed to him that those pleasures were gloriously expressed in the fluid, ecstatic calling of those two graceful birds.

Out of nowhere an arrow struck the male crane. The bird crashed through the branches. Then came the female's scream, the terrible scream of coitus interrupted by death.

The male bird fell to earth. Valmiki knelt and rested two fingers on the crane's warm chest. It had already stopped breathing. Valmiki struggled to control himself—it was as if he had witnessed a human death. He was trembling, nauseous—in fact, he noticed with a shock, he was crying. He looked up and saw one of the Nishada tribesmen stepping forward to retrieve the arrow.

"Why did you do that?" Valmiki yelled angrily.

The man looked at him blankly.

"They were *mating!*" Valmiki spat. "Why at *that* moment . . .?"

The female crane was still screeching. The Nishada shrugged and gripped his arrow just below the head. With a sharp jerk it was free. He ran a piece of rag along the bloody shaft.

"You'll live to regret this day, I promise you that!" Valmiki cried.

The fowler was looking away. Priests, everyone knew, had the evil eye—they could curse you. And this one looked like the big chief of the ashram, who people said was even friendly with the King.

Valmiki was the head of an ashram—wise, holy—he wasn't supposed to lose control. And he had just done so in front of a disciple. He walked away in silence.

As a poet, a bard, Valmiki sometimes found himself thinking aloud in verse. And some lines now came into his head.

> Excessive grief expressed as words,
> A perverse act provokes a verse . . .

As he waded into the sacred river, the soft, warm, rust-brown water felt like silk. He bathed, then returned to the ashram. It grew dark. The ordinary rhythm of life was restored.

That night Valmiki sat to meditate. He found himself drawn deeper, deeper. He realized he could see . . . God! Brahma was here. In the room!

Valmiki scrambled up, joined his palms in greeting and hurried to fetch water for the guest to wash His hands and feet.

God seemed relaxed. He settled Himself comfortably and motioned for Valmiki to do the same. Valmiki obeyed, awestruck, yet at the same time bizarrely absent-minded. Incarnate in front of him was Brahma, God of Gods, self-born in the first moment of creation, and all he could think about was that bird! He murmured the lines that had come to him, ". . . provokes a verse . . ."

Brahma smiled tolerantly. "They augur well, those lines of yours! No need to brood, holy man. The death of that creature has thrown open your heart. I put those verses on your lips. It's time for you to write, Valmiki—a story about the struggle of life to defeat death. Death is part of life, after all, and it's the death of the heart that we have to fear. Don't you agree?"

Awed, Valmiki merely stared back.

"The story you have to write is the life of your King, Rama, his wife Sita, and the demons they had to fight. So unleash the sacred song of Rama! You'll be inspired, Valmiki—I'm going to inspire you myself. It's an eternal story. As long as there are people, as long they question existence, then in many languages and in many forms, the story will live."

No one today could question Brahma's promise. Nearly three millennia after Valmiki had that vision, the story does indeed live on, in many languages and many forms. It would be hard to put the case for the *Ramayana* more absolutely than Tulsidas did at the climax to his *Ramcharitmanas*, the rapturously titled Lake of the Deeds of Rama:

> I have now finished the all-holy history. Merely hearing it will loosen the bonds of existence. All sins engendered of thought, word and deed are absolved in those who attend to this legend . . . Holy pilgrimages, meditation, self-control, wisdom, devotional practices, fasting, almsgiving, temperance, prayer, tenderheartedness to all living creatures—in short, all forms of discipline which the *Vedas* have recommended, have but one aim: devotion to Rama. Whoever wishes to worship at the feet of the Lord, or to attain to final deliverance, should fill the pitchers of his ears from the Lake of the Deeds of Rama.
>
> Is there any creature who has worshipped Rama, the purifier of the fallen, and not found salvation? Did he not redeem Valmiki, who in his early life had been a hunter, responsible for the deaths of hundreds of innocent creatures? Be assured that outcasts and sinners, that non-Hindus and foreigners—all are purified if they but once repeat His name. Rama.

The *Ramayana is* a great work of literature—certainly it stands comparison with Homer's *Odyssey*. But its true wonder lies in its continuity. Long after the spiritual spark left the *Odyssey* and it was relegated to being *merely* literature, the *Ramayana* was still being reinvented, and today it lives on in the hearts of hundreds of millions.

Reading the two other great Indian *Ramayanas*, by Kambar and Tulsidas, I saw how they had transformed Valmiki's poem. The *Ramayana* had begun as the work of wandering bards. As it came to be written down, its hero slowly acquired the aura of a deity. He was a well-established God by the time—more than a millennium later—Kambar and Tulsidas would venerate him as the ultimate object of devotion, and create their soaring verses of religious love. In the West, we might look to Pre-Raphaelite art or a Bach Mass in search of a parallel, but we would have to admit that such devotion is now the preserve of very few indeed. In India the picture is different: the devotional tradition of Rama lives. The *swami* Sri Ramakrishna once said that if, when hearing the name of Rama, you shed tears and your hair stood on end, the word "Rama" merged into the word *Om:* ॐ. The specificities of devotion dissolve into a direct apprehension of God. Rama is the personal God, familiar to the Christians, *and* the gateway to the direct apprehension of a formless God, the architect of the universe, the energy that pervades everything.

As I draw this narrative to a close, I am reminded of two experiences a decade or more apart. I once visited a rather grubby-looking mediæval temple in north-east India. It was still a place of active worship, but the Head Priest told me that because it was an Ancient Monument, the Archæological Survey of India had forbidden him to repaint its glorious statue-encrusted exterior. Every previous generation had painted it, maintaining the worshippers' pride in their temple. But the authorities had ordained that the building should henceforth be preserved, frozen, as a cultural artefact. History and empiricism had officially been recognized as more important than an unbroken tradition of living faith. It was an example of how secular intolerance can destroy spirituality—the future relationship, it would appear, of the Indian state and Hinduism.

My second experience was hearing, just as I was completing this book, a BBC radio interview with a Christian nun. It was one of those few programmes about religion that continue to be broadcast in the UK, more in a spirit of irritable duty than genuine sympathy. The programme had the quality of a freak show—but it wasn't the fault of the presenter, her questions were the usual prosaic probings. The thing that shocked me about the interview was the nun's creepiness. She had spent so many years working out how to communicate the mysteries of her faith in a way that sounded reasonable, likeable and unweird to the average incurious secular sceptic, that she sounded absolutely false—a mass of twitching complexes. I listened with a kind of horror. This was what the Church had done to itself in the Western world—immolated itself willingly on the pyre of others' scepticism.

In the end, you have to stop explaining. You cannot explain; you should not claim to be able to explain. The Dawkins mob's shallow demolitions of doctrinal religions, to which the doctrinal religions have responded with equal shallowness, are so much vanity, *vanity and wind* . . . The spiritual impulse is not to be confused with tribal enmities, with the cruel doctrines of Islam that saw Hindus murdered in their hundreds of thousands, or the Christian doctrines that in mediæval times saw mystics condemned as heretics, and tortured and broken on the wheel.

Why has the Western tradition of spirituality committed suicide? In Europe in the sixteenth century the Church was anxious about the power of mystics and the dangerous absence of a doctrinal God at the core of their beliefs. So it closed down their monasteries and scattered the monks. It sought deliberately to replace mystical abstraction—which was, like Buddhist and Hindu notions, close to being a sort of high-spiritual atheism—with the sentimental love of a personal God, of Christ, His Mother, His bleeding feet . . . As a result, Christian spiritual traditions in direct descent from the mystic traditions of the Middle East and India were all but extinguished. The birth of Protestantism, a materialistic religion, was one result. Rationalism's comprehensive defeat of religion was another. Western spirituality suffered a blow from which it is only now trying to recover. (Although the tradition did struggle on in the Orthodox, Eastern Church.)

Western societies have taken a pragmatic decision: stick to what can be easily explained, and you can have hygienic, heartless, demystified, quasi-rational societies whose citizens enjoy high levels of consumption and physical comfort, and real inequalities are masked by the universal suffrage of the supermarket checkout. Anything that threatens the bland consensus is mocked and condemned, or simply isolated. Ministers of the Church who intervene in ethical debates are told it is a secular society and they should mind their own business. Politicians who claim to have spiritual interests are sneered at. Those, including schoolchildren, who stray outside society's narrow definition of mental stability are drugged to the eyeballs. Empathy becomes an irrelevancy—our human interactions are governed exclusively by respect for each other's Rights. The imaginative lives of billions are dominated by soaps and computer games, and Broadband Internet. Those of the young who do strive towards a form of the ecstatic are obliged to find it in the half-witted dissipations of rock music and street drugs.

And what of India, the land whose literature, when it first became known to the Western world during the eighteenth and nineteenth centuries, struck many of our greatest minds as possessing a staggering degree of moral and spiritual refinement?

That question was going through my mind during those last days in Ayodhya. I knew that for most Westerners the place I was living in would be exotic to the point of deep irrationality. The spiritual passions and compassions that animated it, long since banished from the European world view, would be seen as delusions, close relatives of madness, meaningless and dangerous.

But as I sat in the guru's *darshans*, I found my mind transported to a place of stillness. Here in Ayodhya I was witnessing a tradition where, somehow, personal devotion to God as personified in Rama was blended into the metaphysical abstractions of Hindu mysticism. God was—and was *not*. Rama-*Om*. It was too much for me, more than I could understand, and the work of understanding it lay ahead of me.

The guru, now aged almost ninety, had spent almost his entire life practising an ancient tradition of *bhakti*, of loving devotion. He had trained his soul to love his fellow creatures, human and animal. I could see now that he began every *darshan* with a private *aarthi*, where he scattered petals on a personal shrine, a tiny silver box that he held in one trembling hand. As he did so, murmuring prayers with his eyes fixed on the holy image, tears would fill his eyes.

Eventually he called me forward, and I spent several *darshans* sitting close to him. When his eyes fell on you and you saw his extra-ordinarily smile, a loving, compassionate smile, you felt a surge of spiritual energy that seemed to enter directly into your own heart. You felt yourself almost transfigured. In his company, chanting *Sita-Ram* with his acolytes, I found it easy to meditate—to slip into utter stillness, without thought, the aftermath of which was a deep calm, and an affection for the people and the world around me.

On my last morning at the ashram the guru touched me lightly on the head, and I wept brokenly. I was crying, I think, because I knew that I was going back to my conventional interior world. Because I had lived for a few days with the higher possibilities in myself. I had known something of Rama *bhakti*, of *ras*.

This book began life as a cultural journey, a literary adventure. By the end of the journey I thought I understood what it had meant to a hundred generations of devout Hindus to sit at the feet of the God Rama.

I am back in England now. But if I close my eyes and think of the *Ramayana*, I no longer see a book, or a dusty Ayodhyan hilltop, or headlines about religious clashes, or fragments of a journey from Ayodhya to Sri Lanka. I don't really *see* anything. I seem to hear— indeed, to *sense*—an ancient alchemy: *Sita Rama, Sita-Ram, Sitaram, Sitaram,*

    Sitaram, Sitaram, Sitaram—
    Jai Sitaram.

Acknowledgements

Almost everyone in *An Indian Odyssey* is real, with the principal exception of "Anil", the Sri Lankan artist, who is based on three separate individuals, who might have been at risk if I had named them. A number of people who assisted me cannot be named for reasons of discretion, or (in Sri Lanka's contested zones) to ensure their safety; I offer them my sincere gratitude and best wishes. I won't name here all those others who helped in the course of researching and writing this book and who are named in the text— but I offer them my heart-felt thanks. Without them, the book could not have existed . . .

My thanks go to Tess Callaway, Sue Carpenter and Judith Watson, and in particular to Fiona Dunlop.

My deepest thanks go to my wife Penny, whose unselfish support during the long gestation of this book has been constant, and without whom my *Indian Odyssey* could not have been undertaken—or completed.